C0-BEF-107

CRITICAL SURVEY
OF
SHORT FICTION

Fourth Edition

CRITICAL SURVEY
OF
SHORT FICTION
Fourth Edition

Cumulative Indexes

Editor, Fourth Edition
Charles E. May
California State University, Long Beach

SALEM PRESS
Ipswich, Massachusetts   Hackensack, New Jersey

Some of the essays in this work, which have been updated, originally appeared in the following Salem Press publications, *Critical Survey of Short Fiction* (1981), *Critical Survey of Short Fiction, Supplement* (1987), *Critical Survey of Short Fiction, Revised Edition*, (1993; preceding volumes edited by Frank N. Magill), *Critical Survey of Short Fiction, Second Revised Edition* (2001; edited by Charles E. May).

The paper used in these volumes conforms to the American National Standard for Permanence of Paper for Printed Library Materials, X39.48-1992 (R1997).

LIBRARY OF CONGRESS CATALOGING-IN-PUBLICATION DATA

Critical survey of short fiction / editor, Charles E. May. -- 4th ed.
     p. cm.

Includes bibliographical references and index.
ISBN 978-1-58765-789-4 (set : alk. paper) -- ISBN 978-1-58765-790-0 (set, american : alk. paper) --
ISBN 978-1-58765-791-7 (vol. 1, american : alk. paper) -- ISBN 978-1-58765-792-4 (vol. 2, american : alk. paper) --
ISBN 978-1-58765-793-1 (vol. 3, american : alk. paper) -- ISBN 978-1-58765-794-8 (vol. 4, american : alk. paper) --
ISBN 978-1-58765-795-5 (set, british : alk. paper) -- ISBN 978-1-58765-796-2 (vol. 1, british : alk. paper) --
ISBN 978-1-58765-797-9 (vol. 2, british : alk. paper) -- ISBN 978-1-58765-798-6 (european : alk. paper) --
ISBN 978-1-58765-799-3 (world : alk. paper) -- ISBN 978-1-58765-800-6 (topical essays : alk. paper) --
ISBN 978-1-58765-803-7 (cumulative index : alk. paper)

1. Short story. 2. Short story--Bio-bibliography. I. May, Charles E. (Charles Edward), 1941-
PN3321.C7 2011
809.3'1--dc23

2011026000

First Printing

Printed in the United States of America

CONTENTS

PUBLISHER'S NOTE

Cumulative Indexes is part of Salem Press's greatly expanded and redesigned Critical Survey of Short Fiction Series. The *Critical Survey of Short Fiction, Fourth Edition*, presents profiles of major short-story writers, with sections on other literary forms, achievements, biography, general analysis, and analysis of the writer's most important stories or collections. Although the profiled authors may have written in other genres as well, sometimes to great acclaim, the focus of this set is on their most important works of short fiction.

The *Critical Survey of Short Fiction* was originally published in 1981, with a supplement in 1987, a revised edition in 1993, and a second revised edition in 2001. The *Fourth Edition* includes all writers from the previous edition and adds 145 new ones, covering 625 writers in total. The writers covered in this set represent 44 countries and their short fiction dates from antiquity to the present. The set also offers 53 informative overviews; 24 of these essays were added for this edition. In addition, six resources are provided, one of them new. More than 500 photographs and portraits of writers have been included.

For the first time, the material in the *Critical Survey of Short Fiction* has been organized into five subsets by essay type: a four-volume subset on *American Writers*, a two-volume subset on *British, Irish, and Commonwealth Writers*, a single-volume subset on *European Writers*, a single-volume subset on *World Writers*, and a single volume subset of *Topical Essays*. Each writer appears in only one subset. *Topical Essays* is organized under the categories "Theories, Themes, and Types," "History of Short Fiction," and "Short Fiction Around the World." *Cumulative Indexes* covers all five subsets is free with purchase of more than one subset.

CUMULATIVE INDEXES

Cumulative Indexes functions as both a compilation of materials from the five subsets that make up *Critical Survey of Short Fiction* and a reference guide that simplifies finding material in the five subsets. It begins with a list of contents for the subset and a complete list of contents, which reproduces the tables of contents of the five subsets. The "Resources" section contains comprehensive versions of the bibliography, guide to online resources, time line, major awards, and chronological list of writers found in the first four subsets of *Critical Survey of Writers*.

Bibliography identifies general reference works and other secondary sources that pertain to all subsets.

Guide to Online Resources, new to this edition, provides Web sites pertaining to short fiction and its writers.

Time Line, also new to this edition, lists major milestones and events in short fiction and literature in the order in which they occurred.

Major Awards lists the recipients of major short fiction-specific awards and general awards where applicable to writers or short fiction, from inception of the award to the present day.

Chronological List of Writers lists all 625 writers covered in the *Critical Survey of Short Fiction* by birth, in chronological order.

All writer profiles and topical essays appear in the "Geographical Index of Writers and Essays" and the "Categorized Index of Writers and Essays." The geographical index groups all profiles and essays by country or areas, and the categorized index groups them by culture or group identities, literary movement, historical periods, and forms and themes. The subject index is a comprehensive index, combining all subject indexes in the subsets of the *Critical Survey of Short Fiction*.

ONLINE ACCESS

Salem Press provides access to its award-winning content both in traditional, printed form and online. Any school or library that purchases any of the subsets of the *Critical Survey of Short Fiction* is entitled to free, complimentary access to Salem's fully supported online version of that content. Features include a simple intuitive interface, user profile areas for students and patrons, sophisticated search functionality, and complete context, including appendixes. Access is available through a code printed on the inside cover of the first volume of a subset, and that access is unlimited and immediate. Our online customer service representatives, at (800) 221-1592, are happy to help with any questions. E-books are also available.

ACKNOWLEDGMENTS

Salem Press is grateful for the efforts of the original contributors of these essays and those of the outstanding academicians who took on the task of updating or writing new material for this set. Their names and affiliations are listed in the complete "Contributors" section for all subsets that follows. Finally, we are indebted to our editor, Professor Charles E. May of California State University, Long Beach, for his development of the table of contents for the *Critical Survey of Short Fiction, Fourth Edition* and his advice on updating the original articles to make this comprehensive and thorough revised edition an indispensable tool for students, teachers, and general readers alike.

CONTRIBUTORS

Randy L. Abbott
University of Evansville

Michael Adams
CUNY Graduate Center

Patrick Adcock
Henderson State University

Thomas P. Adler
Purdue University

Karley K. Adney
ITT Technical Institute

A. Owen Aldridge
University of Illinois

Charmaine Allmon-Mosby
Western Kentucky University

Emily Alward
College of Southern Nevada

Nicole Anae
Charles Sturt University

Andrew J. Angyal
Elon University

Jacob M. Appel
The Mount Sinai Medical School

Gerald S. Argetsinger
Rochester Institute of Technology

Karen L. Arnold
Columbia, Maryland

Marilyn Arnold
Brigham Young University

Robert W. Artinian
Original Contributor

Leonard R. N. Ashley
Brooklyn College, City University of New York

Stanley S. Atherton
Original Contributor

Bryan Aubrey
Fairfield, Iowa

Stephen Aubrey
Brooklyn College

Edmund August
McKendree College

L. Michelle Baker
The Catholic University of America

Jane L. Ball
Wilberforce University

Thomas Banks
Ohio Northern University

Carol M. Barnum
Southern Polytechnic State University

Mary Baron
Original Contributor

David Barratt
Montreat College

Melissa E. Barth
Appalachian State University

Angela Bates
Xenia, Ohio

Martha Bayless
University of Oregon

Ben Befu
University of California, Los Angeles

Bert Bender
Original Contributor

Alvin K. Benson
Utah Valley University

Richard P. Benton
Trinity College

Stephen Benz
Barry University

Dorothy M. Betz
Georgetown University

Cynthia A. Bily
Macomb Community College

Margaret Boe Birns
New York University

Nicholas Birns
Eugene Lang College, The New School

Carol Bishop
Indiana University, Southeast

Elizabeth Blakesley
Washington State University Libraries

Richard Bleiler
University of Connecticut

Lynn Z. Bloom
University of Connecticut

Julia B. Boken
Indiana University, Southeast

Jo-Ellen Lipman Boon
Buena Park, California

Thomas Du Bose
Louisiana State University-Shreveport

William Boyle
University of Mississippi

Virginia Brackett
Park University

Jerry Bradley
New Albany, Indiana

Harold Branam
Savannah State University

Gerhard Brand
California State University, Los Angeles

Laurence A. Breiner
Original Contributor

Peter Brigg
University of Guelph

J. R. Brink
Henry E. Huntington Library

Keith H. Brower
Salisbury State University

Alan Brown
Livingston University

Mary Hanford Bruce
Monmouth College

Carl Brucker
Arkansas Tech University

Mitzi M. Brunsdale
Mayville State College

John C. Buchanan
Original Contributor

Stefan Buchenberger
Kanagawa University

Louis J. Budd
Original Contributor

Jeffrey L. Buller
Georgia Southern University

Rebecca R. Butler
Dalton College

Susan Butterworth
Salem State College

Edmund J. Campion
University of Tennessee, Knoxville

Byron Cannon
University of Utah

Larry A. Carlson
Original Contributor

Amee Carmines
Hampton University

John Carpenter
University of Michigan

Thomas Gregory Carpenter
Lipscomb University

John Carr
Original Contributor

Warren J. Carson
University of South Carolina, Spartanburg

Mary LeDonne Cassidy
South Carolina State University

Thomas J. Cassidy
South Carolina State University

Laurie Champion
San Diego State University

Hal Charles
Eastern Kentucky University

Balance Chow
San Jose State University

C. L. Chua
California State University, Fresno

David W. Cole
University of Wisconsin Colleges

Laurie Coleman
Original Contributor

Julian W. Connolly
University of Virginia

Richard Hauer Costa
Texas A&M University

Natalia Costa-Zalessow
San Francisco State University

Ailsa Cox
Edge Hill University

Lisa-Anne Culp
Nuclear Regulatory Commission

Heidi K. Czerwiec
Univeristy of North Dakota

Richard H. Dammers
Normal, Illinois

Dolores A. D'Angelo
American University

Anita Price Davis
Converse College

Mary Virginia Davis
University of California, Davis

Kwame Dawes
University of South Carolina

Frank Day
Clemson University

Danielle A. DeFoe
Sierra College

Bill Delaney
San Diego, California

Joan DelFattore
University of Delaware

Kathryn Zabelle Derounian
University of Arkansas-Little Rock

John F. Desmond
Original Contributor

James E. Devlin
SUNY College at Oneonta

Joseph Dewey
University of Pittsburgh

M. Casey Diana
Arizona State University

Marcia B. Dinneen
Bridgewater State University

Stefan Dziemianowicz
Bloomfield, New Jersey

Wilton Eckley
Colorado School of Mines

Grace Eckley
Drake University

K Edgington
Towson University

Robert P. Ellis
Northborough Historical Society

Sonia Erlich
Lesley University

Thomas L. Erskine
Salisbury University

Christopher Estep
Original Contributor

Walter Evans
Augusta College

Jack Ewing
Boise, Idaho

Kevin Eyster
Madonna University

Nettie Farris
University of Louisville

Howard Faulkner
Original Contributor

James Feast
Baruch College

Thomas R. Feller
Nashville, Tennessee

Christine Ferrari
Monash University

John W. Fiero
University of Louisiana at Lafayette

Edward Fiorelli
St. John's University

Earl E. Fitz
Penn State University

Mary Fitzgerald-Hoyt
Siena College

Rebecca Hendrick Flannagan
Rrancis Marion University

James K. Folsom
Original Contributor

Ben Forkner
Original Contributor

Lydia Forssander-Song
Trinity Western University

David W. Foster
Arizona State University

Joseph Francavilla
Columbus State University

Dean Franco
Wake Forest University

Carol Franks
Portland State University

Timothy C. Frazer
Western Illinois University

Kathy Ruth Frazier
Original Contributor

Tom Frazier
Cumberland College

Rachel E. Frier
Rockville, Maryland

Terri Frongia
Santa Rosa Junior College

Miriam Fuchs
University of Hawaii-Manoa

Jean C. Fulton
Landmark College

Kenneth Funsten
Original Contributor

James Gaash
Humboldt State University

Michelle Gadpaille
Univerza v Mariboru

Louis Gallo
Radford University

Ann Davison Garbett
Averett University

Janet E. Gardner
Falmouth, Massachusetts

James W. Garvey
Original Contributor

Trevor Le Gassick
University of Michigan

Marshall Bruce Gentry
Georgia College & State University

Jill B. Gidmark
University of Minnesota

Sheldon Goldfarb
University of British Colulmiba

M. Carmen Gomez-Galisteo
Esne-Universidad Camilo Jose Cela

Theodore W. Goossen
York University

Linda S. Gordon
Worcester State College

Peter W. Graham
Virginia Polytechnic Institute and State University

Julian Grajewski
Tuscon, Arizona

Charles A. Gramlich
Xavier University of Louisiana

James L. Green
Arizona State University

Glenda I. Griffin
Sam Houston State University

John L. Grigsby
Appalachian Research & Defense Fund of Kentucky, Inc.

William E. Grim
Ohio University

Elsie Galbreath Haley
Metropolitan State College of Denver

David Mike Hamilton
Original Contributor

Marcus Hammond
Longview Community College

Katherine Hanley
St. Bernard's School of Theology and Ministry

Todd C. Hanlin
University of Arkansas

Michele Hardy
Prince George's Community College

Betsy Harfst
Kishwaukee College

Mark Harman
Franklin & Marshall College

Natalie Harper
Simon's Rock College of Bard

David V. Harrington
St. Peter, Minnesota

Stephen M. Hart
University College London

Alan C. Haslam
Sierra College

CJ Hauser
Brooklyn College

Peter B. Heller
Manhattan College

Terry Heller
Coe College

Diane Andrews Henningfeld
Adrian College

DeWitt Henry
Emerson College

Cheryl Herr
Original Contributor

Allen Hibbard
Middle Tennessee State University

Cynthia Packard Hill
University of Massachusetts at Amherst

Jane Hill
Original Contributor

Joseph W. Hinton
Portland, Oregon

Wendy Ho
University of California, Davis

Nika Hoffman
Crossroads School for Arts & Sciences

William Hoffman
Fort Myers, Florida

Hal Holladay
Simon's Rock College of Bard

Kimberley M. Holloway
King College

Gregory D. Horn
Southwest Virginia Commmunity College

Naana Banyiwa Horne
Indiana University-Kokomo

Sylvia Huete
Original Contributor

Edward Huffstetler
Bridgewater College

Theodore C. Humphrey
California State Polytechnic University, Pomona

Mary Hurd
East Tennessee State University

Farhad B. Idris
Frostburg State University

Earl G. Ingersoll
SUNY College at Brockport

Archibald E. Irwin
Indiana University, Southeast

Robert Jacobs
Central Washington University

Kimberley L. Jacobs
Miami University-Ohio

Shakuntala Jayaswal
University of New Haven

Clarence O. Johnson
Joplin, Missouri

Ronald L. Johnson
Northern Michigan University

Sheila Golburgh Johnson
Santa Barbara, California

Eunice Pedersen Johnston
North Dakota State University

Ralph R. Joly
Asbury College

Jane Anderson Jones
Manatee Community College

Paul Kane
Vassar College

Theresa Kanoza
Lincoln Land Community College

William P. Keen
Washington & Jefferson College

Fiona Kelleghan
South Miami, Florida

Karen A. Kildahl
South Dakota State University

Sue L. Kimball
Methodist College

Cassandra Kircher
Elon College

Grove Koger
Boise Public Library

Paula Kopacz
Eastern Kentucky University

Elitza Kotzeva
Appalachian State University

Margaret Wade Krausse
Linfield College

Uma Kukathas
Seattle, Washingtom

Rebecca Kuzins
Pasadena, California

Marvin Lachman
Santa Fe, New Mexico

Thomas D. Lane
Original Contributor

John Lang
Emory & Henry College

Carlota Larrea
Pennsylvania State University

Eugene S. Larson
Los Angeles Pierce College

Donald F. Larsson
Mankato State University

William Laskowski
Jamestown College

Norman Lavers
Arkansas State University

Harry Lawton
University of California, Santa Barbara

David Layton
University of California, Santa Barbara

Allen Learst
Oklahoma State University

Linda Ledford-Miller
University of Scranton

James Ward Lee
University of North Texas

Katy L. Leedy
Marquette University

Leon Lewis
Appalachian State University

Victor Lindsey
East Central University

Elizabeth Johnston Lipscomb
Randolph-Macon Women's College

Douglas Long
Pasadena, California

Michael Loudon
Eastern Illinois University

Robert M. Luscher
University of Nebraska at Kearney

Carol J. Luther
Pellissippi State Community College

R. C. Lutz
CII Group

Laurie Lykken
Century College

Joanne McCarthy
Tacoma Washington

Andrew F. Macdonald
Loyola University

Gina Macdonald
Loyola University

James MacDonald
Humber College

Richard D. McGhee
Arkansas State University

S. Thomas Mack
University of South Carolina-Aiken

Hugh McLean
University of California, Berkeley

Victoria E. McLure
Texas Tech University

Robert J. McNutt
University of Tennessee at Chattanooga

Bryant Mangum
Original Contributor

Barry Mann
Alliance Theatre

Mary E. Markland
Argosy University

Patricia Marks
Valdosta State College

Wythe Marschall
Brooklyn College

Karen M. Cleveland Marwick
Hemel Hempstead, Hertfordshire, England

Paul Marx
University of New Haven

J. Greg Matthews
Washington State University Libraries

Robert N. Matuozzi
Washington State University

Charles E. May
California State University, Long Beach

Laurence W. Mazzeno
Alvernia College

Kenneth W. Meadwell
University of Winnipeg

Patrick Meanor
SUNY College at Oneonta

Martha Meek
Original Contributor

Helen Menke
Original Contributor

Ann A. Merrill
Emory University

Julia M. Meyers

Duquesne University

Walter E. Meyers

North Carolina State University

Jennifer Michaels

Grinnell College

Vasa D. Mihailovich

University of North Carolina, Chapel Hill

Dodie Marie Miller

Fort Wayne, Indiana

Paula M. Miller

Biola University

Robert W. Millett

Original Contributor

Christian H. Moe

Southern Illinois University at Carbondale

Melissa Molloy

Rhode Island College

Robert A. Morace

Daemen College

Sherry Morton-Mollo

California State University, Fullerton

Christina Murphy

Original Contributor

Earl Paulus Murphy

Harris-Stowe State College

Brian Murray

Youngstown State University

John M. Muste

Ohio State University

Susan Nagel

New York, New York

Donna B. Nalley

South University

Keith Neilson

California State University, Fullerton

William Nelles

University of Massachusetts-Dartmouth

Christopher R. Nelson

Seattle, Washington

Lisa Nevárez

Siena College

Evelyn Newlyn

Virginia Polytechnic Institute and State University

John Nizalowski

Mesa State College

Martha Nochimson

Mercy College

Emma Coburn Norris

Troy State University

George O'Brien

Georgetown University

Bruce Olsen

Austin Peay State University

Brian L. Olson

Kalamazoo Valley Community College

James Norman O'Neill

Bryant College

Katherine Orr

University of Chichester

Robert M. Otten

Marymount University

Keri L. Overall

University of South Carolina

Cóilín Owens

George Mason University

Janet Taylor Palmer

Caldwell Community College & Technical Institute

Sally B. Palmer

South Dakota School of Mines & Technology

Robert J. Paradowski

Rochester Institute of Technology

David J. Parent

Original Contributor

David B. Parsell

Furman University

David Partenheimer
Truman State University

Susie Paul
Auburn University, Montgomery

Leslie A. Pearl
San Diego, California

David Peck
Laguna Beach, California

William Peden
University of Missouri-Columbia

William E. Pemberton
University of Wisconsin-La Crosse

Susana Perea-Fox
Oklahoma State University

Chapel Louise Petty
Blackwell, Oklahoma

R. Craig Philips
Michigan State University

Allene Phy-Olsen
Austin Peay State University

Susan L. Piepke
Bridgewater College

Constance Pierce
Original Contributor

Valerie A. Murrenus Pilmaier
University of Wisconsin-Sheboygan

Adrienne Pilon
*University of North Carolina
School of the Arts*

Rosaria Pipia
New York University

Mary Ellen Pitts
Rhodes College

Scott Vander Ploeg
Madisonville Community College

Victoria Price
Lamar University

Karen Priest
Lamar State College, Orange

Norman Prinsky
Augusta State University

Charles Pullen
Queens University

Jere Real
Lynchburg, Virginia

Peter J. Reed
University of Minnesota

Rosemary M. Canfield Reisman
Sonoma, California

Martha E. Rhynes
Oklahoma East Central University

Richard Rice
*University of Tennessee at
Chattanooga*

Dorothy Dodge Robbins
Louisiana Tech University

James Curry Robison
Original Contributor

Mary Rohrberger
New Orleans, Louisiana

Douglas Rollins
Dawson College

Jill Rollins
Trafalgar College

Carl Rollyson
Baruch College, CUNY

Paul Rosefeldt
Delgado Community College

Ruth Rosenberg
Brooklyn, New York

Joseph Rosenblum
*University of North Carolina,
Greensboro*

Stella P. Rosenfeld
Cleveland State University

Harry L. Rosser
Newton Center, Massachusetts

Gabrielle Rowe
McKendree College

Irene Struthers Rush
Boise, Idaho

Amelia A. Rutledge
Original Contributor

Murray Sachs
Brandeis University

David Sadkin
Hamburg, New York

Chaman L. Sahni
Boise State University

Selina Samuels
University of New South Wales

David N. Samuelson
California State University, Long Beach

Victor A. Santi
University of New Orleans

Elizabeth D. Schafer
Loachapoka, Alabama

Barry Scherr
Dartmouth College

Reinhold Schlieper
Embry-Riddle Aeronautical University

Marilyn Schultz
California State University, Fullerton

Barbara Kitt Seidman
Linfield College

D. Dean Shackelford
Concord College

M. K. Shaddix
Dublin University

Chenliang Sheng
Northern Kentucky University

Allen Shepherd
Original Contributor

Nancy E. Sherrod
Georgia Southern University

Thelma J. Shinn
Arizona State University

R. Baird Shuman
University of Illinois at Urbana-Champaign

Paul Siegrist
Fort Hays State University

Karin A. Silet
University of Wisconsin-Madison

Charles L. P. Silet
Iowa State University

Maria Eugenia Silva
Universidad Finis Terrae, Chile

Amy Sisson
Houston Community College

Jan Sjåvik
University of Washington, Seattle

Genevieve Slomski
New Britain, Connecticut

Clyde Curry Smith
University of Wisconsin-River Falls

Roger Smith
Portland, Oregon

Will Smith
University of Nottingham

Ira Smolensky
Monmouth College

Katherine Snipes
Spokane, Washington

Jean M. Snook
Memorial University of Newfoundland

George Soule
Carleton College

Madison V. Sowell
Brigham Young University

Sandra Whipple Spanier
Original Contributor

Sharon Spencer
Original Contributor

Brian Stableford
Reading, United Kingdom

John Stark
Original Contributor

Joshua Stein
Los Medanos College

Karen F. Stein

University of Rhode Island

Judith L. Steininger

Milwaukee School of Engineering

Ingo R. Stoehr

Kilgore College

Louise M. Stone

Bloomsburg University

William B. Stone

Chicago, Illinois

Theresa L. Stowell

Adrian College

Gerald H. Strauss

Bloomsburg University

Ryan D. Stryffeler

Western Nevada College

W. J. Stuckey

Purdue University

Mary J. Sturm

St. Paul, Minnesota

Alvin Sullivan

Alton, Illinois

Eileen A. Sullivan

Tallahassee, Florida

James Sullivan

California State University, Los Angeles

Catherine Swanson

Austin, Texas

Roy Arthur Swanson

University of Wisconsin-Milwaukee

Susan J. Sylvia

Acushnet, Massachusetts

Philip A. Tapley

Louisiana College

James D. Tedder

George Mason University

Christopher J. Thaiss

George Mason University

Terry Theodore

University of North Carolina at Wilmington

Maxine S. Theodoulou

The Union Institute

David J. Thieneman

Original Contributor

Lou Thompson

Texas Woman's University

Rosemary Barton Tobin

Cambridge, Massachusetts

Evelyn Toft

Fort Hays State University

Christine D. Tomei

Columbia University

Michael Trussler

University of Regina

Richard Tuerk

Texas A&M University-Commerce

Dennis Vannatta

University of Arkansas at Little Rock

Jon S. Vincent

University of Kansas

Gary F. Waller

Wilfrid Launer University

Jaquelyn W. Walsh

McNeese State University

Shawncey Webb

Taylor University

Mark A. Weinstein

Original Contributor

James Michael Welsh

Salisbury State University

James Whitlark

Texas Tech University

Barbara Wiedemann

Auburn University at Montgomery

Albert Wilhelm

Tennessee Technological University

Thomas Willard

University of Arizona

Donna Glee Williams
North Carolina Center for the Advancement of Teaching

Patricia A. R. Williams
Original Contributor

Judith Barton Williamson
Sauk Valley Community College

Michael Witkoski
University of South Carolina

Anna M. Wittman
University of Alberta

Qingyun Wu
California State University, Los Angeles

Jennifer L. Wyatt
Civic Memorial High School

Scott D. Yarbrough
Charleston Southern University

Robert B. Youngblood
Washington & Lee University

Mary F. Yudin
State College, Pennsylvania

Hasan Zia
Original Contributor

Gay Pitman Zieger
Santa Fe College

COMPLETE LIST OF CONTENTS

American Volume 1

American Volume 2

American Volume 3

American Volume 4

British Volume 1

British Volume 2

European Volume

World Volume

Topical Essays Volume

KEY TO PRONUNCIATION

To help users of the *Critical Survey of Short Fiction* pronounce unfamiliar names of profiled writers correctly, phonetic spellings using the character symbols listed below appear in parentheses immediately after the first mention of the writer's name in the narrative text. Stressed syllables are indicated in capital letters, and syllables are separated by hyphens.

VOWEL SOUNDS
Symbol: Spelled (Pronounced)

a:	answer (AN-suhr), laugh (laf), sample (SAM-puhl), that (that)
ah:	father (FAH-thur), hospital (HAHS-pih-tuhl)
aw:	awful (AW-fuhl), caught (kawt)
ay:	blaze (blayz), fade (fayd), waiter (WAYT-ur), weigh (way)
eh:	bed (behd), head (hehd), said (sehd)
ee:	believe (bee-LEEV), cedar (SEE-dur), leader (LEED-ur), liter (LEE-tur)
ew:	boot (bewt), lose (lewz)
i:	buy (bi), height (hit), lie (li), surprise (sur-PRIZ)
ih:	bitter (BIH-tur), pill (pihl)
o:	cotton (KO-tuhn), hot (hot)
oh:	below (bee-LOH), coat (koht), note (noht), wholesome (HOHL-suhm)
oo:	good (good), look (look)
ow:	couch (kowch), how (how)
oy:	boy (boy), coin (koyn)
uh:	about (uh-BOWT), butter (BUH-tuhr), enough (ee-NUHF), other (UH-thur)

CONSONANT SOUNDS
Symbol: Spelled (Pronounced)

ch:	beach (beech), chimp (chihmp)
g:	beg (behg), disguise (dihs-GIZ), get (geht)
j:	digit (DIH-juht), edge (ehj), jet (jeht)
k:	cat (kat), kitten (KIH-tuhn), hex (hehks)
s:	cellar (SEHL-ur), save (sayv), scent (sehnt)
sh:	champagne (sham-PAYN), issue (IH-shew), shop (shop)
ur:	birth (burth), disturb (dihs-TURB), earth (urth), letter (LEH-tur)
y:	useful (YEWS-fuhl), young (yuhng)
z:	business (BIHZ-nehs), zest (zehst)
zh:	vision (VIH-zhuhn)

CRITICAL SURVEY
OF
SHORT FICTION

Fourth Edition

RESOURCES

TERMS AND TECHNIQUES

Aestheticism: The European literary movement, with its roots in France, that was predominant in the 1890's. Aestheticism denied that art needed to have any utilitarian purpose and focused on the slogan "art for art's sake." The doctrines of aestheticism were introduced to England by Walter Pater and can be found in the plays of Oscar Wilde and the short stories of Arthur Symons. In American literature, the ideas underlying the aesthetic movement can be found in the short fiction of Edgar Allan Poe.

Allegory: A literary mode in which characters in a narrative personify abstract ideas or qualities and so give a second level of meaning to the work, in addition to the surface narrative. Two famous examples of allegory are Edmund Spenser's *The Faerie Queene* (1590, 1596) and John Bunyan's *The Pilgrim's Progress from This World to That Which Is to Come*, Part I (1678). Modern examples may be found in Nathaniel Hawthorne's story "The Artist of the Beautiful" and the stories and novels of Franz Kafka.

Allusion: A reference to a person or event, either historical or from a literary work, which gives another literary work a wider frame of reference and adds depth to its meaning. For example, Sylvia Townsend Warner's story "Winter in the Air" gains greater suggestiveness from the frequent allusions to William Shakespeare's play *The Winter's Tale* (pr. c. 1610-1611, pb. 1623), and her story "Swans on an Autumn River" is enriched by a number of allusions to the poetry of William Butler Yeats.

Ambiguity: Refers to the capacity of language to suggest two or more levels of meaning within a single expression, thus conveying a rich, concentrated effect. Ambiguity has been defined by William Empson in *Seven Types of Ambiguity* (1930) as "any verbal nuance, however, slight, which gives room for alternative reactions to the same piece of language." It has been suggested that because of the short story's highly compressed form, ambiguity may play a more important role in this genre than it does in the novel.

Anachronism: An event, person, or thing placed outside--usually earlier than--its proper historical era. William Shakespeare uses anachronism in *King John* (pr. c. 1596-1597, pb. 1623), *Antony and Cleopatra* (pr. c. 1606-1607, pb. 1723), and *Julius Caesar* (pr. c. 1599-1600, pb. 1623). Mark Twain employed anachronism to comic effect in *A Connecticut Yankee in King Arthur's Court* (1889).

Anecdote: The short narration of a single interesting incident or event. An anecdote differs from a short story in that it does not have a plot, relates a single episode, and does not range over different times and places.

Antagonist: A character in fiction who stands in opposition, or rivalry, to the protagonist. In William Shakespeare's *Hamlet, Prince of Denmark* (pr. c. 1600-1601, pb. 1603), for example, King Claudius is the antagonist of Hamlet.

Anthology: A collection of prose or poetry, usually by various writers. Often serves to introduce the work of little-known authors to a wider audience.

Aphorism: A short, concise statement that states an opinion, precept, or general truth, such as Alexander Pope's "Hope springs eternal in the human breast."

Aporia: An interpretative point in a story that basically cannot be decided, usually as the result of some gap or absence.

Apostrophe: A direct address to a person (usually absent), inanimate entity, or abstract quality. Examples are the first line of William Wordsworth's sonnet "London, 1802," "Milton! Thou should'st be living at this hour," and King Lear's speech in William Shakespeare's *King Lear* (pr. c. 1605-1606, pb. 1698), "Blow, winds, and crack your cheeks! rage! blow!"

Appropriation: The act of taking over part of a literary theory or approach for one's own ends, for example, male critics appropriating the approach of feminists.

Archetypal theme: Recurring thematic patterns in literature. Common archetypal themes include death and rebirth (Samuel Taylor Coleridge's *The Rime of the Ancient Mariner*, 1798), paradise-Hades (Coleridge's "Kubla Khan," 1816), the fatal woman (Guy de Maupassant's "Doubtful Happiness"), the earth goddess ("Yanda" by Isaac Bashevis Singer), the scapegoat (D. H. Lawrence's "The Woman Who Rode Away," 1925), and the return to the womb (Flannery O'Connor's "The River," 1953).

Archetype: This term was used by psychologist Carl Jung to describe what he called "primordial images," which exist in the "collective unconscious" of humankind and are manifested in myths, religion, literature, and dreams. Now used broadly in literary criticism to refer to character types, motifs, images, symbols, and plot patterns recurring in many different literary forms and works. The embodiment of archetypes in a work of literature can make a powerful impression on the reader.

Architectonics: A term borrowed from architecture to describe the structural qualities, such as unity and balance, of a work of literature. If the architectonics are successful, the work will give the impression of organic unity and balance, like a solidly constructed building in which the total value is more than the sum of the parts.

Asides: In drama, short passages generally spoken by one dramatic character in an undertone or directed to the audience, so as not to be heard by other characters on stage.

Atmosphere: The mood or tone of a work; it is often associated with setting but can also be established by action or dialogue. The opening paragraphs of Edgar Allan Poe's "The Fall of the House of Usher" (1839) and James Joyce's "Araby" (1914) provide good example of atmosphere created early in the works and which pervades the remainder of the story.

Ballad: Popular ballads are songs or verse that tell dramatic, usually impersonal, tales. Supernatural events, courage, and love are frequent themes, but any experience that appeals to ordinary people is acceptable material. Literary ballads--narrative poems based on popular ballads--have frequently been in vogue in English literature, particularly during the Romantic period. One of the most famous is Samuel Taylor Coleridge's *The Rime of the Ancient Mariner*.

Black humor: A general term of modern origin that refers to a form of "sick humor" that is intended to produce laughter out of the morbid and the taboo. Examples are the works of Joseph Heller, Thomas Pynchon, Günter Grass, and Kurt Vonnegut.

Broadside ballad: A ballad printed on one side of a large, single sheet of paper and sung to a popular tune. Dating from the sixteenth century in England, the subject of the broadside ballad was a topical event or issue.

Burlesque: A work that, by imitating attitudes, styles, institutions, and people, aims to amuse. Burlesque differs from satire in that it aims to ridicule simply for the sake of amusement rather than for political or social change.

Canon: The standard or authoritative list of literary works that are widely accepted as outstanding representatives of their period and genre. In recent literary criticism, however, the established canon has come under fierce assault for its alleged culture and gender bias.

Canonize: The act of adding a literary work to the list of works that form the primary tradition of a genre or literature in general. For example, a number of stories by female and African American writers previously excluded from the canon of the short story, such as Charlotte Perkins Gilman's "The Yellow Wallpaper" (1892) and Charles Waddell Chesnutt's "The Sheriff's Children (1899)," have recently been canonized.

Caricature: A form of writing that focuses on unique qualities of a person and then exaggerates and distorts those qualities in order to ridicule the person and what he or she represents. Contemporary writers, such as Flannery O'Connor, have used caricature for serious and satiric purposes in such stories as "Good Country People" (1955) and "A Good Man Is Hard to Find" (1955).

Character type: The term can refer to the convention of using stock characters, such as the *miles gloriosus* (braggart soldier) of Renaissance and Roman comedy, the figure of vice in medieval morality plays, or the clever servant in Elizabethan comedy. It can also describe "flat" characters (the term was coined by E. M. Forster) in fiction who do not grow or change during the course of the narrative and who can be easily classified.

Chronicle: The precursors of modern histories, chronicles were written accounts of national or world events. One of the best known is the *Anglo-Saxon Chronicle*, begun in the reign of King Alfred in the late ninth century. Many chronicles were written in Elizabethan times, and these were used by William Shakespeare as source documents for his history plays.

Classic/Classicism: A literary stance or value system consciously based on the example of classical Greek and Roman literature. While the term is applied to an enormous diversity of artists in many different periods and in many different national literatures, it generally denotes a cluster of values, including formal discipline, restrained expression, reverence of tradition, and an objective rather than subjective orientation. Often contrasted to Romanticism.

Climax: Similar to crisis, the moment in a work of fiction at which the action reaches a turning point and the plot begins to be resolved. Unlike crisis, this term is also used to refer to the moment in which the reader's emotional involvement with the work reaches its highest point of intensity.

Comic story: Encompasses a wide variety of modes and inflections, such as parody, burlesque, satire, irony, and humor. Frequently, the defining quality of comic characters is that they lack self-awareness; the reader tends not to identify with them but perceives them from a detached point of view, more as objects than persons.

Conceit: A type of metaphor that makes highly intellectualized comparisons between seemingly disparate things. It is associated with the Metaphysical poets and the Elizabethan sonneteers; examples can also be found in the poetry of Emily Dickinson and T. S. Eliot.

Conflict: The struggle that develops as a result of the opposition between the protagonist and another person, the natural world, society, or some force within the self. In short fiction, the conflict is most often between the protagonist and some strong force either within the protagonist or within the given state of the human condition.

Connotation/Denotation: Denotation is the explicit, formal definition of a word, exclusive of its emotional associations. When a word takes on an additional meaning, other than its denotative one, it achieves connotation. For example, the word "mercenary" denotes a soldier who is paid to fight in an army not of his own region, but connotatively a mercenary is an unprincipled scoundrel who kills for money.

Conte: French for tale, a conte was originally a short adventure tale. In the nineteenth century, the term was used to describe a tightly constructed short story. In England, the term is used to describe a work longer than a short story and shorter than a novel.

Crisis: A turning point in the plot, at which the opposing forces reach the point that a resolution must take place.

Criticism: The study and evaluation of works of literature. Theoretical criticism, as for example in Aristotle's *Peri poētikēs* (c. 334-323 B.C.E.; *Poetics*, 1705), sets out general principles for interpretation. Practical criticism (Samuel Taylor Coleridge's lectures on William Shakespeare, for example) offers interpretations of particular works or authors.

Deconstruction: A literary theory, primarily attributed to French critic Jacques Derrida, which has spawned a wide variety of practical applications, the most prominent being the critical tactic of laying bare a text's self-reflexivity, that is, showing how it continually refers to and subverts its own way of meaning.

Defamiliarization: A term coined by the Russian Formalists to indicate a process by which the writer makes the reader perceive the concrete uniqueness of an object, event, or idea that has been generalized by routine and habit.

Dénouement: Literally, "unknotting"; the conclusion of a drama or fiction, when the plot is unraveled and the mystery solved.

Detective story: The "classic" detective story (or "mystery") is a highly formalized and logically structured mode of fiction in which the focus is on a crime solved by a detective through interpretation of evidence and clever reasoning. Many modern practitioners of the genre, however, such as Raymond Chandler, Patricia Highsmith, and Ross Macdonald, have placed less emphasis on the puzzlelike qualities of the detective story and have focused instead on characterization, theme, and other elements of mainstream fiction. The form was first developed in short fiction by Edgar Allan Poe; Jorge Luis Borges has also used the convention in short stories.

Deus ex machina: A Latin term meaning "god out of the machine." In the Greek theater, it referred to the use of a god lowered out of a mechanism onto the stage to untangle the plot or save the hero. The term has come to signify any artificial device for the easy resolution of dramatic difficulties.

Device: Any technique used in literature in order to gain a specific effect. The poet uses the device of figurative language, for example, while the novelist may use the devices of foreshadowing, flashback, and so on, in order to create a desired effect.

Dialogics: The theory that fiction is a dialogic genre in which many different voices are held in suspension without merging into a single authoritative voice. Developed by Russian critic Mikhail Bakhtin.

Didactic literature: Literature that seeks to instruct, give guidance, or teach a lesson. Didactic literature normally has a moral, religious, or philosophical purpose, or it will expound a branch of knowledge (as in Vergil's *Georgics*, c. 37-29 B.C.E.; English translation, 1589). It is distinguished from imaginative works, in which the aesthetic product takes precedence over any moral intent.

Diegesis: Refers to the hypothetical world of a story, as if it actually existed in real space and time. It is the illusory universe of the story created by its linguistic structure.

Doggerel: Strictly speaking, doggerel refers to rough and jerky versification, but the term is more commonly applied to worthless verse that contains monotonous rhyme and rhythm and trivial subject matter.

Doppelgänger: A double or counterpart of a person, sometimes endowed with ghostly qualities. A fictional doppelgänger often reflects a suppressed side of a character's personality, as in Fyodor Dostoevski's novella *Dvoynik* (1846; *The Double*, 1917) and the short stories of E. T. A. Hoffmann. Isaac Bashevis Singer and Jorge Luis Borges, among other modern writers, have also employed the doppelgänger with striking effect.

Dream vision: An allegorical form common in the Middle Ages, in which the narrator or a character falls asleep and dreams a dream that becomes the actual framed story. Subtle variations of the form have been used by Nathaniel Hawthorne in "Young Goodman Brown" (1835) and by Edgar Allan Poe in "The Pit and the Pendulum" (1842).

Dualism: A theory that the universe is explicable in terms of two basic, conflicting entities, such as good and evil, mind and matter, or the physical and the spiritual.

Eclogue: In Greek, the term means literally "selection." It is now used to describe a formal pastoral poem. Classical eclogues are constructed around a variety of conventional themes: the singing match, the rustic dialogue, the lament, the love lay, and the eulogy. During the Renaissance, eclogues were employed as veiled satires.

Écriture Féminine: French feminist Hélène Cixous argues for a unique female kind of writing, which in its fluidity disrupts the binary oppositions of male-dominated cultural structures.

Effect: The total, unified impression, or impact, made upon the reader by a literary work. Every aspect of the work--plot, characterization, style, and so on--is seen to directly contribute to this overall impression.3

Elegy: A long, rhymed, formal poem whose subject is meditation upon death or a lamentable theme; Alfred, Lord Tennyson's *In Memoriam* (1850) is a well-known example. The pastoral elegy, such as Percy Bysshe Shelley's *Adonais: An Elegy on the Death of John Keats* (1821), uses a pastoral scene to express grief at the loss of a friend or important person.

Emotive meaning: The emotion that is commonly associated with a word. In other words, emotive meaning includes the connotations of a word, not merely what it denotes. Emotive meaning is contrasted with cognitive or descriptive meaning, in which neither emotions nor connotations are involved.

Epic: Although this term usually refers to a long narrative poem that presents the exploits of a central figure of high position, the term is also used to designate a long novel that has the style or structure usually associated with an epic. In this sense, for example, Herman Melville's *Moby Dick: Or, The Whale* (1851) and James Joyce's *Ulysses* (1922) may be called epics.

Epiphany: The literary application of this religious term was popularized by James Joyce in his book *Stephen Hero* (1944): "By an epiphany he meant a sudden spiritual manifestation, whether in the vulgarity of speech or of gesture or in a memorable phase of the mind itself." Many short stories since Joyce's collection *Dubliners* (1914) have been analyzed as epiphanic stories in which a character or the reader experiences a sudden revelation of meaning.

Episode: In Greek tragedy, the segment between two choral odes. Episode now refers to an incident presented as a continuous action. In a work of literature, many discrete episodes are woven together to form a more complex work.

Epistolary fiction: A work of fiction in which the narrative is carried forward by means of letters written by the characters. Epistolary novels were a quite popular form in the eighteenth century. Examples include Samuel Richardson's *Pamela: Or, Virtue Rewarded* (1740-1741) and *Clarissa: Or, The History of a Young Lady* (1747-1748). The form has not

been much used in the twentieth century.

Essay: A brief prose work, usually on a single topic, that expresses the personal point of view of the author. The essay is usually addressed to a general audience and attempts to persuade the reader to accept the author's ideas.

Essay-sketch tradition: The first sketches can be traced to the Greek philosopher Theophrastus in 300 B.C.E., whose character sketches influenced seventeenth and eighteenth century writers in England, who developed the form into something close to the idea of character in fiction. The essay has an equally venerable history, and, like the sketch, had an impact on the development of the modern short story.

Euphony: Language that creates a harmonious and pleasing effect; the opposite of cacophony, which is a combination of harsh and discordant sounds.

Exemplum: A brief anecdote or tale introduced to illustrate a moral point in medieval sermons. By the fourteenth century these exempla had expanded into exemplary narratives. Geoffrey Chaucer's "The Nun's Priest's Tale" and "The Pardoner's Tale" from *The Canterbury Tales* (1387-1400) are exempla.

Existentialism: A philosophy and attitude of mind that gained wide currency in religious and artistic thought after the end of World War II. Typical concerns of existential writers are human beings' estrangement from society, their awareness that the world is meaningless, and their recognition that one must turn from external props to the self. The novels of Albert Camus and Franz Kafka provide examples of existentialist beliefs.

Exposition: The part or parts of a work of fiction that provide necessary background information. Exposition not only provides the time and place of the action but also introduces readers to the fictive world of the story, acquainting them with the ground rules of the work. In the short story, exposition is usually elliptical.

Expressionism: Beginning in German theater at the start of the twentieth century, expressionism became the dominant movement in the decade following World War I. It abandoned realism and relied on a conscious distortion of external reality in order to portray the world as it is "viewed emotionally."

The movement spread to fiction and poetry. Expressionism influenced the plays of Eugene O'Neill, Tennessee Williams, and Thornton Wilder and can be found in the novels of Franz Kafka and James Joyce.

Fable: One of the oldest narrative forms. Usually takes the form of an analogy in which animals or inanimate objects speak to illustrate a moral lesson. The most famous examples are the fables of Aesop, who used the form orally in 600 B.C.E.

Fabliau: A short narrative poem, popular in medieval French literature and during the English Middle Ages. Fabliaux were usually realistic in subject matter, bawdy, and made a point of satirizing the weaknesses and foibles of human beings. Perhaps the most famous are Geoffrey Chaucer's "The Miller's Tale" and "The Reeve's Tale" from *The Canterbury Tales* (1387-1400).

Fabulation: A term coined by Robert Scholes and used in contemporary literary criticism to describe novels that are radically experimental in subject matter, style, and form. Like the Magical Realists, fabulators mix realism with fantasy. The works of Thomas Pynchon, John Barth, Donald Barthelme, and William H. Gass provide examples.

Fairy tale: A form of folktale in which supernatural events or characters are prominent. Fairy tales usually depict a realm of reality beyond that of the natural world and in which the laws of the natural world are suspended.

Fantastic: In his study *Introduction à la littérature fantastique* (1970; *The Fantastic: A Structural Approach to a Literary Genre*, 1973), the critic Tzvetan Todorov defines the fantastic as a genre that lies between the uncanny and the marvelous. Whereas the marvelous presents an event that cannot be explained by the laws of the natural world and the uncanny presents an event that is the result of hallucination or illusion, the fantastic exists as long as the reader cannot decide which of these two applies. Henry James's *The Turn of the Screw* (1898) is an example of the fantastic.

Figurative language: Any use of language that departs from the usual or ordinary meaning to gain a poetic or otherwise special effect. Figurative language embodies various figures of speech, such as irony, metaphor, simile, and many others.

Fin de siècle: Literally, "end of the century"; refers to the last decade of the nineteenth century, a transitional period in which artists and writers were aware that they were living at the close of a great age and deliberately cultivated a kind of languor, world weariness, and satiety. Associated with the period of aestheticism and the Decadent movement exemplified in the works of Oscar Wilde.

Flashback: A scene that depicts an earlier event; it can be presented as a reminiscence by a character in a story, or it can simply be inserted into the narrative.

Folktale: A short prose narrative, usually handed down orally, found in all cultures of the world. The term is often used interchangeably with myth, fable, and fairy tale.

Form: The organizing principle in a work of literature; the manner in which its elements are put together in relation to its total effect. The term is sometimes used interchangeably with structure and is often contrasted with content: If form is the building, content is what is in the building and what the building is specifically designed to express.

Frame story: A story that provides a framework for another story (or stories) told within it. The form is ancient and is used by Geoffrey Chaucer in *The Canterbury Tales* (1387-1400). In modern literature, the technique has been used by Henry James in *The Turn of the Screw* (1898), Joseph Conrad in *Heart of Darkness* (1899, serial; 1902, book), and John Barth in *Lost in the Funhouse* (1968).

Framework: When used in connection with a frame story, the framework is the narrative setting, within which other stories are told. The framework may also have a plot of its own. More generally, the framework is similar to structure, referring to the general outline of a work.

Gendered: When a work is approached as thematically or stylistically specific to male or female characteristics or concerns, it is said to be "gendered."

Genre study: The concept of studying literature by classification and definition of types or kinds, such as tragedy, comedy, epic, lyrical, and pastoral. First introduced by Aristotle in *Poetics*, the genre principle has been an essential concomitant of the basic proposition that literature can be studied scientifically.

Gothic genre: A form of fiction developed in the late eighteenth century which focuses on horror and the supernatural. Examples include Matthew Gregory Lewis's *The Monk: A Romance*, 1796 (also published as *Ambrosio: Or, The Monk*), Mary Wollstonecraft Shelley's *Frankenstein* (1818), and the short fiction of Edgar Allan Poe. In modern literature, the gothic genre can be found in the fiction of Truman Capote.

Grotesque: Characterized by a breakup of the everyday world by mysterious forces, the form differs from fantasy in that the reader is not sure whether to react with humor or horror. Examples include the stories of E. T. A. Hoffmann and Franz Kafka.

Gynocriticism: American feminist critic Elaine C. Showalter coined this term for her theory that women read and write differently than men do because of biological and cultural differences.

Hasidic tale: Hasidism was a Jewish mystical sect formed in the eighteenth century. The term "Hasidic tale" is used to describe some American short fiction, much of it written in the 1960's, which reflected the spirit of Hasidism, particularly the belief in the immanence of God in all things. Saul Bellow, Philip Roth, and Norman Mailer have been attracted to the genre, as has the Israeli writer Shmuel Yosef Agnon, who won the Nobel Prize in Literature in 1966.

Hegemony: Italian critic Antonio Gramsci maintains that capitalists create and sustain an ideology to support their dominance or hegemony over the working class. By maintaining economic and cultural power, capitalists receive the support of the working class, who adopt their values and beliefs, and thus control the ideology or social consciousness that in turn controls individual consciousness.

Historical criticism: In contrast to formalist criticism, which treats literary works as self-contained artifacts, historical criticism emphasizes the social and historical context of literature and allows itself to take into consideration the relevant facts and circumstances of the author's life. The method emphasizes the meaning that the work had in its own time

rather than interpreting it for the present.

Hyperbole: The term is Greek for "overshooting" and refers to the use of gross exaggeration for rhetorical effect, based on the assumption that the reader will not be persuaded of the literal truth of the overstatement. Can be used for serious or comic effect.

Imagery: Often defined as the verbal stimulation of sensory perception. Although the word betrays a visual bias, imagery, in fact, calls on all five senses. In its simplest form, imagery re-creates a physical sensation in a clear, literal manner; it becomes more complex when a poet employs metaphor and other figures of speech to re-create experience.

In medias res: Latin phrase used by Horace, meaning literally "into the midst of things." It refers to a literary technique of beginning the narrative when the action has already begun. The term is used particularly in connection with the epic, which traditionally begins *in medias res*.

Initiation story: A story in which protagonists, usually children or young persons, go through an experience, sometimes painful or disconcerting, that carries them from innocence to some new form of knowledge and maturity. William Faulkner's "The Bear" (1942), Nathaniel Hawthorne's "Young Goodman Brown" (1835), Alice Walker's "To Hell with Dying" (1967), and Robert Penn Warren's "Blackberry Winter" (1946) are examples of the form.

Interior monologue: Defined as the speech of a character designed to introduce the reader directly to the character's internal life, the form differs from other monologues in that it attempts to reproduce thought before any logical organization is imposed upon it. An example is Molly Bloom's long interior monologue at the conclusion of James Joyce's *Ulysses* (1922).

Interpretation: An analysis of the meaning of a literary work. Interpretation will attempt to explicate the theme, structure, and other components of the work, often focusing on obscure or ambiguous passages.

Irrealism: A term often used to refer to modern or postmodern fiction that is presented self-consciously as a fiction or fabulation rather than a mimesis of external reality. The best-known practitioners of irrealism are John Barth, Robert Coover, and Donald Barthelme.

Lai/Lay: A song or short narrative poem. The term was first applied to twelfth and thirteenth centuries French poems and to English poems in the fourteenth century that were based on them, including Geoffrey Chaucer's "The Franklin's Tale" (1387-1400). In the nineteenth century, the term was applied to historical ballads, such as Sir Walter Scott's *The Lay of the Last Minstrel* (1805).

Legend: A narrative that is handed down from generation to generation, usually associated with a particular place and a specific event. A legend may often have more historical truth than a myth, and the protagonist is usually a person rather than a supernatural being.

Leitmotif: From the German, meaning "leading motif." Any repetition--of a word, phrase, situation, or idea --that occurs within a single work or group of related works.

Literary short story: A term that was current in American criticism in the 1940's to distinguish the short fiction of Ernest Hemingway, Eudora Welty, Sherwood Anderson, and others from the popular pulp and slick fiction of the day.

Local color: Usually refers to a movement in literature, especially in the United States, in the latter part of the nineteenth century. The focus was on the environment, atmosphere, and milieu of a particular region. For example, Mark Twain wrote about the Mississippi region; Sarah Orne Jewett wrote about New England. The term can also be used to refer to any work that represents the characteristics of a particular region.

Logocentrism: Jacques Derrida argues that all Western thought is based on the quest for a nonexistent "transcendental signifier," a sort of primal origin that makes ultimate meaning possible. The Western assumption of some ultimate center, that it calls God, reason, truth, or essence, is what Derrida calls Logocentrism.

Lyric short story: A form in which the emphasis is on internal changes, moods, and feelings. The lyric story is usually open-ended and depends on the figurative language usually associated with poetry.

Examples of lyric stories are the works of Ivan Turgenev, Anton Chekhov, Katherine Mansfield, Sherwood Anderson, Conrad Aiken, and John Updike.

Lyrical ballad: The term is preeminently associated with William Wordsworth and Samuel Taylor Coleridge, whose *Lyrical Ballads* (1798), which drew on the ballad tradition, was one of the seminal books of the Romantic age. *Lyrical Ballads* was a revolt against eighteenth century poetic diction; it was an attempt to create a new kind of poetry by using simple language and taking as subject the everyday lives of common folk and the strong emotions they experience.

Malaprop/Malapropism: A malapropism occurs when one word is confused with another because the two words have a similar sound. The term is derived from the character Mrs. Malaprop in Richard Brinsley Sheridan's *The Rivals* (1775), who, for example, uses the word "illiterate" when she really means "obliterate" and mistakes "progeny" for "prodigy."

Märchen: German fairy tales, as collected in the works of Wilhelm and Jacob Grimm or in the works of nineteenth century writers, such as Novalis and E. T. A. Hoffmann.

Marginalization: The process by which an individual or a group is deemed secondary to a dominant group in power and thus denied access to the benefits enjoyed by the dominant group; for example, in the past women were marginalized by men and non-whites were marginalized by whites.

Medieval romance: Medieval romances, which originated in twelfth century France, were tales of adventure in which a knight would embark on a perilous quest to win the hand of a lady, perform a service for his king, or seek the Holy Grail. He had to overcome many obstacles, including dragons and other monsters; magic spells and enchantments were prominent, and the romance embodied the chivalric ideals of courage, honor, refined manners, and courtly love. English romances include the anonymous *Sir Gawain and the Green Knight* (fourteenth century) and Sir Thomas Malory's *Le Morte d'Arthur* (1485).

Memoir: Usually written by a person prominent in public life, a memoir is the authors' recollections of famous people they have known and great events they have witnessed. Memoir differs from autobiography in that the emphasis in the latter is on the life of the authors.

Metafiction: Refers to fiction that manifests a reflexive tendency, such as Vladimir Nabokov's *Pale Fire* (1962), and John Fowles's *The French Lieutenant's Woman* (1969). The emphasis is on the loosening of the work's illusion of reality to expose the reality of its illusion. Such terms as "irrealism," "postmodernist fiction," and "antifiction" are also used to refer to this type of fiction.

Metaphor: A figure of speech in which two dissimilar objects are imaginatively identified (rather than merely compared) on the assumption that they share one or more qualities: "She is the rose, the glory of the day" (Edmund Spenser). The term is often used in modern criticism in a wider sense to identify analogies of all kinds in literature, painting, and film.

Metonymy: A figure of speech in which an object that is closely related to a word comes to stand for the word itself, such as when one says "the White House" when meaning the "president."

Minimalist movement: A school of fiction writing that developed in the late 1970's and early 1980's and that Roland Barthes has characterized as the "less is more school." Minimalism attempts to convey much by saying little, to render contemporary reality in precise, pared-down prose that suggests more than it directly states. Leading minimalist writers are Raymond Carver and Ann Beattie. A character in Beattie's short story "Snow" (in *Where You'll Find Me*, 1986) seems to sum up minimalism: "Any life will seem dramatic if you omit mention of most of it."

Mise en abîme: A small story inside a larger narrative that echoes or mirrors the larger narrative, thus containing the larger within the smaller.

Modern short story: The modern short story dates from the nineteenth century and is associated with the names of Edgar Allan Poe (who is often credited with inventing the form) and Nathaniel Hawthorne in the United States, Honoré de Balzac in France,

and E. T. A. Hoffmann in Germany. In his influential critical writings, Poe defined the short story as being limited to "a certain unique or single effect," to which every detail in the story should contribute.

Monologue: Any speech or narrative presented by one person. It can sometimes be used to refer to any lengthy speech, in which one person monopolizes the conversation.

Moral tract: A propaganda pamphlet on a political or religious topic, usually distributed free. The term is often associated with the Oxford Movement in nineteenth century England, which was a movement to reform the Church of England.

Motif: An incident or situation in a story that serves as the basis of its structure, creating by repetition and variation a patterned recurrence and consequently a general theme. Russian Formalist critics distinguish between bound motifs, which cannot be omitted without disturbing the thematic structure of the story, and unbound motifs, which serve merely to create the illusion of external reality. In this sense, motif is the same as leitmotif.

Myth: An anonymous traditional story, often involving supernatural beings or the interaction between gods and human beings and dealing with the basic questions of how the world and human society came to be as they are. Myth is an important term in contemporary literary criticism. Northrop Frye, for example, has said that "the typical forms of myth become the conventions and genres of literature." By this, he means that the genres of comedy, romance, tragedy, and irony (satire) correspond to seasonal myths of spring, summer, autumn, and winter.

Narrative: An account in prose or verse of an event or series of events, whether real or imagined.

Narrative persona: Persona means literally "mask": It is the self created by the author and through whom the narrative is told. The persona is not to be identified with the author, even when the two may seem to resemble each other. The narrative persona in Lord Byron's *Don Juan* (1819-1824), for example, may express many sentiments of which Byron would have approved, but he is nevertheless a fictional creation who is distinct from the author.

Narratology: The theoretical study of narrative structures and ways of meaning. Most all major literary theories have a branch of study known as narratology.

Narrator: The character who recounts the narrative. There are many different types of narrators: The first-person narrator is a character in the story and can be recognized by his or her use of "I"; third-person narrators may be limited or omniscient. In the former, the narrator is confined to knowledge of the minds and emotions of one or, at most, a few characters. In the latter, the narrator knows everything, seeing into the minds of all the characters. Rarely, second-person narration may be used. (An example can be found in Edna O'Brien's *A Pagan Place*, 1973.)

Novel: A fictional prose form, longer than a short story or novelette. The term embraces a wide range of types, but the novel usually includes a more complicated plot and a wider cast of characters than the short story. The focus is often on the development of individual characterization and the presentation of a social world and a detailed environment.

Novella, novelette, Novelle, nouvelle: These terms all refer to the form of fiction that is longer than a short story and shorter than a novel. Novella, the Italian term, is the term usually used to refer to American works in this genre, such as Joseph Conrad's *Heart of Darkness* (1899, serial; 1902, book) and Henry James's *The Turn of the Screw* (1898). *Novelle* is the German term; *nouvelle* the French; "novelette" the British. The term "novel" derived from these terms.

Objective correlative: A key concept in modern formalist criticism, coined by T. S. Eliot in *The Sacred Wood* (1920). An objective correlative is a situation, an event, or an object that, when presented or described in a literary work, expresses a particular emotion and serves as a precise formula by which the same emotion can be evoked in the reader.

Oral tale: A wide-ranging term that can include everything from gossip to myths, legends, folktale, and jokes. Among the terms used by Saith Thompson to classify oral tales (*The Folktale*, 1951) are märchen, fairy tale, household tale, *conte populaire*, novella, hero tale, local tradition, migratory legend, explanatory tale, humorous anecdote, and merry tale.

Oral tradition: Material that is transmitted by word of mouth, often through chants or songs, from generation to generation. Homer's epics, for example, were originally passed down orally and employ formulas to make memorization easier. Often, ballads, folklore, and proverbs are also passed down in this way.

Oriental tale: An eighteenth century form made popular by the translations of *Alf layla wa-layla* (fifteenth century; *The Arabian Nights' Entertainments*, 1706-1708) collected during the period. Oriental tales were usually solemn in tone, contained little characterization, and focused on improbable events and supernatural places.

Other: By a process of psychological or cultural projection, an individual or a dominant group accuses those of a different race or gender of all the negative qualities they themselves possess and then respond to them as if they were "other" than themselves.

Oxymoron: Closely related to paradox, an oxymoron occurs when two words of opposite meaning are placed in juxtaposition, such as "wise fool," "devilish angel," or "loving hate."

Parable: A short, simple, and usually allegorical story that teaches a moral lesson. In the West, the most famous parables are those told in the Gospels by Jesus Christ.

Paradox: A statement that initially seems to be illogical or self-contradictory yet eventually proves to embody a complex truth. In New Criticism, the term is used to embrace any complexity of language that sustains multiple meanings and deviates from the norms of ordinary language use.

Parataxis: The placing of clauses or phrases in a series without the use of coordinating or subordinating terms.

Parody: A literary work that imitates or burlesques another work or author for the purpose of ridicule. Twentieth century parodists include E. B. White and James Thurber.

Periodical essay/sketch: Informal in tone and style and applied to a wide range of topics, the periodical essay originated in the early eighteenth century. It is associated in particular with Joseph

Addison and Sir Richard Steele and their informal periodical, *The Spectator*.

Personification: A figure of speech which ascribes human qualities to abstractions or inanimate objects, as in these lines by W. H. Auden: "There's Wrath who has learnt every trick of guerrilla warfare,/ The shamming dead, the night-raid, the feinted retreat." Richard Crashaw's "Hope, thou bold taster of delight" is another example.

Plot: Plot refers to how authors arrange their material not only to create the sequence of events in a play or story but also to suggest how those events are connected in a cause-and-effect relationship. There are a great variety of plot patterns, each of which is designed to create a particular effect.

Point of view: The perspective from which a story is presented to the reader. In simplest terms, it refers to whether narration is first person (directly addressed to the reader as if told by one involved in the narrative) or third person (usually a more objective, distanced perspective.)

Portmanteau words: The term was coined by Lewis Carroll to describe the creation of a new word by telescoping two existing words. In this way, "furious" and "fuming" can be combined to create "frumious." The works of James Joyce, as well as Carroll's *Through the Looking Glass and What Alice Found There* (1871), provide many examples of portmanteau words.

Postcolonial: A literary approach that focuses on English-language texts from countries and cultures formerly colonized or dominated by America, the British Empire, and other European countries. Postcolonialists focus on the literature of such countries as Australia, New Zealand, Africa, and South America, and such cultural groups as African Americans and Native Americans.

Postmodern: Although this term is so broad it is interpreted differently by many different critics, it basically refers to a trend by which the literary work calls attention to itself as an artifice rather than a mirror held up to external reality.

Prosody: The study of the principles of verse structure. Includes meter, rhyme, and other patterns of sound, such as alliteration, assonance, euphony and onomatopoeia, and stanzaic patterns.

Protagonist: Originally, in the Greek drama, the "first actor," who played the leading role. The term has come to signify the most important character in a drama or story. It is not unusual for a work to contain more than one protagonist.

Pun: A pun occurs when words that have similar pronunciations have entirely different meanings. The result may be a surprise recognition of an unusual or striking connection, or, more often, a humorously accidental connection.

Realism: A literary technique in which the primary convention is to render an illusion of fidelity to external reality. Realism is often identified as the primary method of the novel form; the realist movement in the late nineteenth century coincided with the full development of the novel form.

Reception theory: Theorist Hans Robert Jauss argues that since readers from any historical milieu create their own criteria for judging a text, one should examine how a text was received by readers contemporary with it. Since every period creates its own "horizon of expectation," the meaning of a text changes from one period to another.

Reminiscence: An account, written or spoken, of remembered events.

Rhetorical device: Rhetoric is the art of using words clearly and effectively, in speech or writing, in order to influence or persuade. A rhetorical device is a figure of speech, or a way of using language, employed to this end. It can include such elements as choice of words, rhythms, repetition, apostrophe, invocation, chiasmus, zeugma, antithesis, and the rhetorical question (a question to which no answer is expected).

Rogue literature: From Odysseus to William Shakespeare's Autolocus to Huckleberry Finn, the rogue is a common literary type. He is usually a robust and energetic comic or satirical figure whose roguery can be seen as a necessary undermining of the rigid complacency of conventional society. The picaresque novel (*picaro* is Spanish for "rogue"), in which the picaro lives by his wits, is perhaps the most common form of rogue literature.

Romance: Originally, any work written in Old French. In the Middle Ages, romances were about knights and their adventures. In modern times, the term has also been used to describe a type of prose fiction in which, unlike the novel, realism plays little part. Prose romances often give expression to the quest for transcendent truths. Examples of the form include Nathaniel Hawthorne's *The Scarlet Letter* (1850) and Herman Melville's *Moby Dick* (1851).

Romanticism: A movement of the late eighteenth and nineteenth centuries which exalted individualism over collectivism, revolution over conservatism, innovation over tradition, imagination over reason, and spontaneity over restraint. Romanticism regarded art as self-expression; it strove to heal the cleavage between object and subject and expressed a longing for the infinite in all things. It stressed the innate goodness of human beings and the evils of the institutions that would stultify human creativity.

Saga: Originally applied to medieval Icelandic and other Scandinavian stories of heroic exploits and handed down by oral tradition. The term has come to signify any tale of heroic achievement or great adventure.

Satire: A form of literature that employs the comedic devices of wit, irony, and exaggeration to expose, ridicule, and condemn human folly, vice, and stupidity. Justifying satire, Alexander Pope wrote that "nothing moves strongly but satire, and those who are ashamed of nothing else are so of being ridiculous."

Setting: The circumstances and environment, both temporal and spatial, of a narrative. The term also applies to the physical elements of a theatrical production, such as scenery and properties. Setting is an important element in the creation of atmosphere.

Shishōsetsu: Literally translated as "I novel," *shishōsetsu* is a Japanese genre, a form of autobiographical or confessional writing used in novels and short stories. The protagonist and writer are closely identified. The genre originated in the early part of the twentieth century; a good example is *An'ya Koro* (1921-1928; *A Dark Night's Passing*, 1958) by Shiga Naoya.

Short story: A concise work of fiction, shorter than a novella, that is usually more concerned with mood, effect, or a single event than with plot or extensive characterization.

Signifier/Signified: Linguist Ferdinand de Saussure proposed that all words are signs made up of a "signifier," which is the written mark or the spoken sound of the word, and a "signified," which is the concept for which the mark or sounds stands.

Simile: A type of metaphor in which two things are compared. It can usually be recognized by the use of the words "like," "as," "appears," or "seems": "Float like a butterfly, sting like a bee" (Muhammad Ali); "The holy time is quiet as a nun" (William Wordsworth).

Skaz: A term used in Russian criticism to describe a narrative technique that presents an oral narrative of a lowbrow speaker.

Sketch: A brief narrative form originating in the eighteenth century, derived from the artist's sketch. The focus of a sketch is on a single person, place, or incident; it lacks a developed plot, theme, or characterization.

Story line: The story line of a work of fiction differs from the plot. Story line is merely the events that happen; plot is how those events are arranged by the author to suggest a cause-and-effect relationship.

Stream of consciousness: A narrative technique used in modern fiction by which an author tries to embody the total range of consciousness of a character, without any authorial comment or explanation. Sensations, thoughts, memories, and associations pour out in an uninterrupted, prerational and prelogical flow. Examples are James Joyce's *Ulysses* (1922), Virginia Woolf's *To the Lighthouse* (1927), and William Faulkner's *The Sound and the Fury* (1929).

Structuralism: Structuralism is based on the idea of intrinsic, self-sufficient structures that do not require reference to external elements. A structure is a system of transformations that involves the interplay of laws inherent in the system itself. The structuralist literary critic attempts, by using models derived from modern linguistic theory, to define the structural principles that operate intertextually throughout the whole of literature, as well as principles that operate in genres and in individual works.

Style: Style is the manner of expression, or how the writer tells the story. The most appropriate style is that which is perfectly suited to conveying whatever idea, emotion, or other effect that the author wishes to convey. Elements of style include diction, sentence structure, imagery, rhythm, and coherence.

Subjective/Objective: Terms used in critical theory. Subjective refers to works that express the ideas and emotions, the values and judgments of the authors, such as William Wordsworth's *The Prelude* (1850). Objective works are those that appear to be free of the personal sentiments of authors, who take a detached view of the events they record.

Supplement: A term used by Jacques Derrida to refer to the unstable relationship between the two elements in a set of binary opposites. For example, in the opposition between truth and lies, although Western thought assumes that truth is superior to lies, closer study reveals that so-called lies frequently reveal profound truths.

Symbolism: A literary movement encompassing the work of a group of French writers in the latter half of the nineteenth century, a group that included Charles Baudelaire, Stéphane Mallarmé, and Paul Verlaine. According to Symbolism, a mystical correspondence exists between the natural and spiritual worlds.

Synesthesia: Synesthesia occurs when one kind of sense experience is described in terms of another. Sounds may be described in terms of colors, and so on. For example, these lines from John Keats's poem "Isabella," "O turn thee to the very tale,/ And taste the music of that vision pale," combine the senses of taste, hearing, and sight. Synesthesia was used especially by the nineteenth century French Symbolists.

Tale: A general term for a simple prose or verse narrative. In the context of the short story, a tale is a story in which the emphasis is on the course of the action rather than on the minds of the characters.

Tall tale: A humorous tale popular in the American West; the story usually makes use of realistic detail and common speech, but it tells a tale of impossible events that most often focus on a single legendary, superhuman figure, such as Paul Bunyan or David Crockett.

Technique: Refers both to the method of procedure in creating an artistic work and to the degree of expertise shown in following the procedure.

Thematics: According to Northrop Frye, when a work of fiction is written or interpreted thematically, it becomes an illustrative fable. Murray Krieger defines thematics in *The Tragic Vision* (1960) as "the study of the experiential tensions which, dramatically entangled in the literary work, become an existential reflection of that work's aesthetic complexity."

Theme: Loosely defined as what a literary work means, theme is the underlying idea, the abstract concept, that the author is trying to convey: "the search for love," "the growth of wisdom," or some such formulation. The theme of William Butler Yeats's poem "Sailing to Byzantium" (1928), for example, might be interpreted as the failure of the attempt to isolate oneself within the world of art.

Tone: Strictly defined, tone is the authors' attitude toward their subject, their persona, themselves, their audience, or their society. The tone of a work may be serious, playful, formal, informal, morose, loving, ironic, and so on; it can be thought of as the dominant mood of a work, and it plays a large part in the total effect.

Trope: Literally "turn" or "conversion"; a figure of speech in which a word or phrase is used in a way that deviates from the normal or literal sense.

Vehicle: Used with the term "tenor" to understand the two elements of a metaphor. The tenor is the subject of the metaphor, and the vehicle is the image by which the subject is presented. The terms were coined by I. A. Richards. As an example, in T. S. Eliot's line, "The whole earth is our hospital," the tenor is "whole earth" and the vehicle is the "hospital."

Verisimilitude: When used in literary criticism, verisimilitude refers to the degree to which a literary work gives the appearance of being true or real, even though the events depicted may in fact be far removed from the actual.

Vignette: A sketch, essay, or brief narrative character-
    ized by precision, economy, and grace. The term can
    also be applied to brief short stories, less than five
    hundred words long.

Yarn: An oral tale or a written transcription of what
    purports to be an oral tale. The yarn is usually a
    broadly comic tale, the classic example of which is
Mark Twain's "Jim Baker's Bluejay Yarn" (1879).
The yarn achieves its comic effect by juxtaposing
realistic detail and incredible events; tellers of the
tale protest that they are telling the truth; listeners
know differently.

Bryan Aubrey
Updated by Charles E. May

BIBLIOGRAPHY

THEORETICAL AND CRITICAL DISCUSSIONS OF
SHORT FICTION

Aycock, Wendell M., ed. *The Teller and the Tale: Aspects of the Short Story.* Lubbock: Texas Tech Press, 1982. A collection of papers presented at a scholarly conference focusing on various aspects of short fiction, including its oral roots, the use of silences in the text, and realism versus antirealism.

Bader, A. L. "The Structure of the Modern Short Story." *College English* 7 (1945): 86-92. Counters the charge that the short story lacks narrative structure by contrasting the traditional "plotted" story with the "modern story," which is more suggestive, indirect, and technically patterned.

Baker, Falcon O. "Short Stories for the Millions." *Saturday Review*, December 19, 1953, 7-9, 48-49. Argues that as a result of formalist New Criticism, the short story has begun to ignore entertainment value and the ordinary reader.

Baldeshwiler, Eileen. "The Lyric Short Story: The Sketch of a History." *Studies in Short Fiction* 6 (1969): 443-453. A brief survey of the lyrical (as opposed to the epical) story from Ivan Turgenev to John Updike. The lyric story focuses on internal changes, moods, and feelings, using a variety of structural patterns depending on the "shape of the emotion itself."

Bates, H. E. *The Modern Short Story: A Critical Survey.* Boston: The Writer, 1941, 1972. A history of the major short-story writers and their work since Edgar Allan Poe and Nikolai Gogol. More focus on English and European short-story writers than most histories.

Bayley, John. *The Short Story: Henry James to Elizabeth Bowen.* New York: St. Martin's Press, 1988. A discussion of some of what Bayley calls the "special effects" of the short-story form, particularly its relationship to poetic techniques and devices. Much of the book consists of analyses of significant stories by Henry James, Ernest Hemingway, Rudyard Kipling, Anton Chekhov, D. H. Lawrence, James Joyce, and Elizabeth Bowen.

Benjamin, Walter. "The Storyteller: Reflections on the Words of Nikolai Leskov." Reprinted in *Modern Literary Criticism*: 1900-1970, edited by Lawrence Lipking and A. Walton Litz. New York: Atheneum, 1972. Benjamin claims that the art of storytelling is coming to an end because of the widespread dissemination of information and explanation. The compactness of a story precludes analysis and appeals to readers through the rhythm of the work itself. For the storyteller, the old religious chronicle is secularized into an ambiguous network in which the worldly and the eschatological are interwoven.

Bonheim, Helmut. *The Narrative Modes: Techniques of the Short Story.* Cambridge, England: D. S. Brewer, 1982. A systematic and statistical study of the short-story form, focusing on basic short-story techniques, especially short-story beginnings and endings. Argues that a limited set of techniques is used repeatedly in story endings. Discusses open and closed endings and argues that dynamic modes are more apt to be open, while static ones are more apt to be closed.

Boulanger, Daniel. "On the Short Story." *Michigan Quarterly Review* 26 (Summer, 1987): 510-514. A highly metaphoric and impressionistic study of the form, focusing primarily on the detached nature of the short story. Claims that there is a bit of Pontius Pilate in the short-story writer, for he or she is always removed from the tragic outcome. Points out how there are no class distinctions in the short story and no hierarchy.

Bowen, Elizabeth, ed. *The Faber Book of Modern Short Stories.* London: Faber & Faber, 1936. Bowen suggests that the short story, because it is exempt from the novel's often forced conclusiveness, more often approaches aesthetic and moral truth. She also suggests that the short story, more than the novel, is able to place the individual alone on that "stage which, inwardly, every man is conscious of occupying alone."

Brickell, Herschel. "What Happened to the Short Story?" *The Atlantic Monthly* 188 (September, 1951): 74-76. Argues that many contemporary writers have succeeded in breaking the short story away from its formal frame by drawing it nearer to poetry.

Brown, Suzanne Hunter. "The Chronotope of the Short Story: Time, Character, and Brevity." In *Creative and Critical Approaches to the Short Story*, edited by Noel Harold Kaylor, Jr. Lewiston, N.Y.: Edwin Mellen Press, 1997. A survey and analysis of the frequent critical assumption that short stories deal with characters as eternal essence and that novels deal with characters who change over time. Argues that Mikhail Bakhtin's concept of "chronotrope," a literary work's projection of time and space, will help develop a generic theory of the short story that considers both historical and technical factors.

_____. "Discourse Analysis and the Short Story." In *Short Story Theory at a Crossroads*, edited by Susan Lohafer and Jo Ellyn Clarey. Baton Rouge: Louisiana State University Press, 1989. A helpful analytical survey of the research being conducted by psychologists into the nature of discourse, story-ness, and cognitive response to narrative.

Cortázar, Julio. "Some Aspects of the Short Story." *Arizona Quarterly*, Spring, 1982, 5-17. Cortázar, an Argentine writer and notable practitioner of the short story, discusses the invariable elements that give a good short story its particular atmosphere. He compares the novel and the short story to film and the photograph; the short story's most significant element is its subject, the act of choosing a real or imaginary happening that has the mysterious property of illuminating something beyond itself.

Cox, Alisa, ed. *The Short Story*. Newcastle, England: Cambridge Scholars, 2008. A collection of essays that provides a critical international overview of short fiction. Includes A. L. Kennedy's reflections on writing short stories, a discussion of the contemporary short story sequence, an essay pondering a definition of the short story, and analyses of stories by Italo Calvino, Jorge Luis Borges, Anita Desai, Martin Amis, Ray Bradbury, and others.

Dawson, W. J. "The Modern Short Story." *North American Review* 190 (December, 1909): 799-810. Argues that a short story must be complete in itself and consist of a single incident. The finest writing in a short story, Dawson maintains, is that which takes the reader most quickly to the very heart of the matter at hand.

Eichenbaum, Boris. *O. Henry and the Theory of the Short Story*. Translated by I. R. Titunik. Ann Arbor: University of Michigan, 1968. Originally published in 1925, this essay is a good example of the early Russian Formalist approach to fiction through a consideration of genre. Eichenbaum poses a generic distinction between the novel and the short story. Short stories are constructed on the basis of a contradiction, incongruity, error, or contrast and, like the anecdote, build their weight toward the ending.

Eldred, Janet Carey. "Narratives of Socialization: Literacy in the Short Story." *College English* 53 (October, 1991): 686-700. Based on the critical assumption that all fiction historicizes problems of socialization. Argues that the short story is a narrative of arrested socialization which ends with characters between two cultures who find their own speech inadequate but their new language problematic.

Elliott, George P. "A Defense of Fiction." *Hudson Review* 16 (1963): 9-48. Elliott, himself a short-story writer, discusses the four basic impulses that mingle with the storytelling impulse: to dream, to tell what happened, to explain the sense of things, and make a to likeness.

Ermida, Isabel. *The Language of Comic Narratives: Humor Construction in Short Stories*. New York: Mouton de Gruyter, 2008. Analyzes how humor works in short fiction, examining short stories by Dorothy Parker, Graham Greene, Woody Allen, David Lodge, Evelyn Waugh, and other English and American writers.

Farrell, James T. *The League of Frightened Philistines and Other Papers*. New York: Vanguard Press, 1945. Ridicules the short-story handbooks published in the 1920's and 1930's and claims that in many contemporary short stories the revolutionary point of view appears more tacked on than integral to the story.

Ferguson, Suzanne C. "Defining the Short Story: Impressionism and Form." *Modern Fiction Studies* 28 (Spring, 1982): 13-24. Argues that there is no single characteristic or cluster of characteristics that distinguishes the short story from the novel. Suggests that what is called the modern short story is a manifestation of impressionism rather than a discrete genre.

_____. "The Rise of the Short Story in the Hierarchy of Genres." In *Short Story Theory at a Crossroads*, edited by Susan Lohafer and Jo Ellyn Clarey. Baton Rouge: Louisiana State University Press, 1989. A historical and critical survey of the development of the English short story, showing how social factors influenced the rise and fall of the form's prestige.

FitzGerald, Gregory. "The Satiric Short Story: A Definition." *Studies in Short Fiction* 5 (1968): 349-354. Defines the satiric short story as a subgenre that sustains a reductive attack upon its objects and conveys to its readers a significance different from its apparent surface meaning.

Fonlon, Bernard, "The Philosophy, the Science, and the Art of the Short Story, Part II." *Abbia* 34 (1979): 429-438. A discussion of the basic elements of a story, including character and conflict. Lists elements of intensity, detachment, skill, and unity of effect. Primarily presents a set of rules aimed at inexperienced writers.

Friedman, Norman. "Recent Short Story Theories: Problems in Definition." In *Short Story Theory at a Crossroads*, edited by Susan Lohafer and Jo Ellyn Clarey. Baton Rouge: Louisiana State University Press, 1989. A critical review of major short-story critics, including Mary Rohrberger, Charles May, Susan Lohafer, and John Gerlach. Argues against those critics who support a deductive, single-term, mixed category approach to definition of the form. Urges that what is needed is a more inductive approach that follows the principle of suiting the definition to the facts rather than trying to suit the facts to the definition.

_____. "What Makes a Short Story Short?" *Modern Fiction Studies* 4 (1958): 103-117. Makes use of neo-Aristotelian literary theory to determine the issue of the short story's shortness. To deal with the problem, Friedman argues, one must ask the following questions: What is the size of the action? Is the action composed of a speech, a scene, an episode, or a plot? Does the action involve a change? If so, is the change a major one or a minor one?

Gerlach, John. "The Margins of Narrative: The Very Short Story, the Prose Poem, and the Lyric." In *Short Story Theory at a Crossroads*, edited by Susan Lohafer and Jo Ellyn Clarey. Baton Rouge: Louisiana State University Press, 1989. Explores the basic requirements of a story, focusing particularly on two minimalist stories by Enrique Anderson Imbert and Scott Sanders, as well as a short prose poem by W. S. Merwin. Argues that point, not mere length nor fictionality, is the principal constituent of story.

Gordimer, Nadine. "South Africa." *The Kenyon Review* 30 (1968): 457-461. Gordimer, a Nobel Prize-winning writer, argues that the strongest convention of the novel, its prolonged coherence of tone, is false to the nature of what can be grasped as reality in the modern world. Short-story writers deal with the only thing one can be sure of--the present moment.

Görtschacher, Wolfgang, and Holger Klein, eds. *Tale, Novella, Short Story: Currents in Short Fiction*. Tübingen, Germany: Stauffenburg, 2004. Reprints the papers delivered at the Tenth International Salzburg Conference, which focused on the short fictional forms of the tale, novella, and short story. Among the topics discussed are the influence of English short fiction on historical texts, such as The Arabian Nights' Entertainments; theoretical issues, including the aesthetic principles of compactness and brevity; and analyses of contemporary short fiction from Australia, Africa, the United States, Great Britain, and Ireland.

Gullason, Thomas A. "Revelation and Evolution: A Neglected Dimension of the Short Story." *Studies in Short Fiction* 10 (1973): 347-356. Challenges Mark Schorer's distinction between the short story as an "art of moral revelation" and the novel as an "art of moral evolution." Analyzes D. H. Lawrence's "The Horse Dealer's Daughter" and John Steinbeck's "The Chrysanthemums" to show that the short story embodies both revelation and evolution.

_____. "The Short Story: An Underrated Art." *Studies in Short Fiction* 2 (1964): 13-31. Points out the lack of serious criticism of the short story, suggests some of the reasons for this neglect, and concludes with an analysis of Anton Chekhov's "Gooseberries" and Nadine Gordimer's "The Train from Rhodesia" to disprove the charges that the short story is formulaic and lacks life.

Hanson, Clare, ed. *Introduction to Re-Reading the Short Story*. New York: St. Martin's Press, 1989. Claims that the short story is a vehicle for different kinds of knowledge, knowledge that may be in some way at odds with the "story" of dominant culture. The formal properties of the short story--disjunction, inconclusiveness, and obliquity--connect with its ideological marginality and with the fact that the form may be used to express something suppressed or repressed in mainstream literature.

_____. *Short Stories and Short Fictions*, 1880- 1980. New York: St. Martin's Press, 1985. Argues that during this period, the authority of the teller, usually a first-person "framing" narrator who guaranteed the authenticity of the tale, was questioned by many modernist writers, Argues that the movements from "teller" to indirect free narration, and from "tale" to "text," were part of a more general movement from "discourse" to "image" in the art and literature of the period. Includes chapters on Rudyard Kipling, Saki, W. Somerset Maugham, James Joyce, Virginia Woolf, Katherine Mansfield, Samuel Beckett.

_____. "Things out of Words: Towards a Poetics of Short Fiction." In *Re-Reading the Short Story*, edited by Clare Hanson. New York: St. Martin's Press, 1989. Argues that the short story is a more literary form than the novel. Maintains that short stories are framed, an aesthetic device that gives a sense of completeness which allows gaps and absences to remain in the story; thus readers accept a degree of mystery or elision in the short story that they would not accept in the novel.

Hardy, Sarah. "A Poetics of Immediacy: Oral Narrative and the Short Story." *Style* 27 (Fall, 1993): 352-368. Argues that the oral-epic episode clarifies basic characteristics of the short story: It gives the reader a way to understand the density of meaning in the short story and provides a paradigm of the short-story audience as that of a participating community.

Hedberg, Johannes. "What Is a `Short Story?' and What Is an `Essay'?" *Moderna Sprak* 74 (1980): 113-120. Reminds readers of the distinction between the Chekhovian story (lack of plot) and the Maupassantian story (anecdotal and therefore commercial). Discusses basic characteristics of the essay and the story; maintains they are similar in that they are both a whole picture in miniature, not merely a detail of a larger picture--a complete work, not an extract.

Hendricks, William O. "Methodology of Narrative Structural Analysis." In *Essays in Semiolinguistics and Verbal Art*. The Hague, Netherlands: Mouton, 1973. Structuralists, in the tradition of Vladimir Propp and Claude Levi-Strauss, usually bypass the actual sentences of a narrative and analyze a synopsis. This essay is a fairly detailed discussion of the methodology of synopsizing (using William Faulkner's "A Rose for Emily" as an example), followed by a brief discussion of the methodology of structural analysis of the resultant synopsis.

Hesse, Douglas. "A Boundary Zone: First-Person Short Stories and Narrative Essays." In *Short Story Theory at a Crossroads*, edited by Susan Lohafer and Jo Ellyn Clarey. Baton Rouge: Louisiana State University Press, 1989. Argues that the precise boundary point between essays and short stories does not exist. Analyzes George Orwell's essay "A Hanging" as a short story and William Carlos Williams's short story "Use of Force" as an essay. Discusses essays and stories that fall in a boundary zone between essay and story.

Hicks, Granville. "The Art of the Short Story." *Saturday Review* 41 (December 20, 1958): 16. Maintains that the focus of the contemporary short story is an emotional experience for the reader rather than character or plot.

Holloway, John. "Identity, Inversion, and Density Elements in Narrative: Three Tales by Chekhov, James, and Lawrence." In *Narrative and Structure: Exploratory Essays*. Cambridge, England. Cambridge University Press, 1979. Holloway looks at stories in which almost nothing happens. He says there is a distinctive kind of narrative episode introduced by an item that is then followed by another item in inverse relationship to the first, which cancels it out and brings the reader back to where he or she started.

Howe, Irving. "Tone in the Short Story." *Sewanee Review* 57 (Winter, 1949): 141-152. Maintains that because the short story lacks prolonged characterization and a structured plot, it depends mostly on tone to hold it together.

Ibánéz, José R., José Francisco Fernández, and Carmen M. Bretones, eds. *Contemporary Debates on the Short Story*. New York: Peter Lang, 2007. Collection of critical essays about short fiction, some of which are written from the perspectives of globalization and deconstructionism. Includes a discussion of dissent in the modern Irish short story; an overview of short fiction, including a historical overview of the mystery story; and analyses of short fiction by Wyndham Lewis, Henry James, Salman Rushdie, and Judith Ortiz Cofer.

"International Symposium on the Short Story" in *Kenyon Review*. Contributions from short-story writers from all over the world on the nature of the form, its current economic status, its history, and its significance. Part 1, vol. 30, no. 4 (1969): 443-490 features contributions by Christina Stead (England), Herbert Gold (United States), Erih Koš (Yugoslavia), Nadine Gordimer (South Africa), Benedict Kiely (Ireland), Hugh Hood (Canada), and Henrietta Drake-Brockman (Australia); part 2, vol. 31, no. 1 (1969): 58-94 contains comments by William Saroyan (United States), Jun Eto (Japan), Maurice Shadbolt (New Zealand), Chanakya Sen (India), John Wain (England), and Hans Bender (Germany) and "An Agent's View" by James Oliver Brown; part 3, vol. 31, no. 4 (1969): 450-502 features Ana María Matute (Spain), Torborg Nedreaas (Norway), George Garrett (United States), Elizabeth Taylor (England), Ezekiel Mphahlele (South Africa), Elizabeth Harrower (Australia), Mario Picchi (Italy), Junzo Shono (Japan), and Khushwant Singh (India); part 4, vol. 32, no. 1 (1969): 78-108 includes Jack Cope (South Africa), James T. Farrell (United States), Edward Hyams (England), Luigi Barzini (Italy), David Ballantyne (New Zealand), and H. E. Bates (England).

Jarrell, Randall. "Stories." In *The Anchor Book of Stories*. New York: Doubleday, 1958. Jarrell's introduction to this collection focuses on stories as being closer to dream reality than the waking world of everyday life. He argues that there are basically two kinds of stories: stories in which everything is a happening (in which each event is so charged that the narrative threatens to disintegrate into energy), and stories in which nothing happens (in which even the climax may lose its charge and become one more portion of a lyric continuum).

Jouve, Nicole Ward. "Too Short for a Book." In *Re-Reading the Short Story,* edited by Clare Hanson. New York: St. Martin's Press, 1989. An impressionistic, noncritical essay about story length. Discusses The Arabian Nights' Entertainments as an archetypal model standing behind all stories, collections of stories, and storytelling. Makes a case for collections of stories that stand together as organic wholes rather than single individual stories that stand alone.

Lewis, C. S. "On Stories." In *Essays Presented to Charles Williams*. Grand Rapids, Mich.: Wm. B. Eerdmans, 1966. Although stories are series of events, this series, or what is called plot, is only a necessary means to capture something that has no sequence, something more like a state or quality. Thus, the "means" of a story is always at war with its "end"; this very tension, however, constitutes the story's chief resemblance to life: "We grasp at a state and find only a succession of events in which the state is never quite embodied."

Lohafer, Susan. "A Cognitive Approach to Story-Ness." *Short Story* (Spring, 1990), 60-71. A study of what Lohafer calls "preclosure," those points in a story where it could end but does not. Studies the characters of such preclosure sentences-- where they appear and what they signal--as part of a more general effort to clarify what constitutes story-ness.

_____. *Coming to Terms with the Short Story*. Baton Rouge: Louisiana State University Press, 1983. A highly suggestive theoretical study of the short story that focuses on the sentence unit of the form as a way of showing how it differs from the novel.

_____. "Interdisciplinary Thoughts on Cognitive Science and Short Fiction Studies." In *The Tales We Tell: Perspectives on the Short Story*, edited by Barbara Lounsberry et al. Westport, Conn.: Greenwood Press, 1998. A brief summary of psychological approaches to cognitive strategies for reading short fiction. Makes a number of suggestions about the future of short-story criticism based on the cooperation between narrative theorists and cognitive scientists.

_____. "Preclosure and Story Processing." In *Short Story Theory at a Crossroads*, edited by Susan Lohafer and Jo Ellyn Clarey. Baton Rouge: Louisiana State University Press, 1989. Analyzes responses to a story by Kate Chopin in terms of identifying those sentences that could end the story but do not. This essay is a continuation of Lohafer's study of what she has defined as preclosure in short fiction.

_____. "Preclosure in an 'Open' Story." In *Creative and Critical Approaches to the Short Story*, edited by Noel Harold Kaylor, Jr. Lewiston, N.Y.: Edwin Mellen Press, 1997. Presents the results of an experiment in preclosure studies in which 114 students were asked to read Julio Cortázar's story "Orientation of Cats" and report on their understanding of it. Lohafer asks the students to identify points at which the story might have ended, a preclosure procedure which makes them more aware of reading tactics and their inherent sense of story-ness.

_____. *Reading for Storyness: Preclosure Theory, Empirical Poetics, and Culture in the Short Story*. Baltimore: Johns Hopkins University Press, 2003. Lohafer discusses many of the literary theories presented in her previous articles, arguing that "imminent closure" is the defining trait of the short story. She demonstrates her theories by analyzing stories by Kate Chopin, Katherine Mansfield, Julio Cortázar, Raymond Carver, Bobbie Ann Mason, Ann Beattie, and other writers.

_____. "Why the 'Life of Ma Parker' is Not So Simple: Preclosure in Issue-Bound Stories." *Studies in Short Fiction* 33 (Fall, 1996): 475-486. In this particular experiment with student reaction to preclosure markers in a story by Katherine Mansfield, Lohafer is interested in showing how attention to preclosure encourages readers to temporarily suppress their ready-made concepts and engage their story competence.

McSweeney, Kerry. *The Realist Short Story of the Powerful Glimpse: Chekhov to Carver*. Columbia: University of South Carolina Press, 2007. Focuses on the short fiction of five writers--Anton Chekhov, James Joyce, Ernest Hemingway, Flannery O'Connor, and Raymond Carver--to argue that the realist realist short story is a "glimpse--powerful and tightly focused, into a world that the writer must precisely craft and in which the reader must fully invest."

March-Russell, Paul. *The Short Story: An Introduction*. Edinburgh: Edinburgh University Press, 2009. Historical overview of short fiction, defining its origins, the concept of the well-made story, the short story cycle, and specific types of stories, such as ghost stories and modernist, postmodernist, minimalist, and postcolonial short fiction.

Marcus, Mordecai. "What Is an Initiation Story?" *The Journal of Aesthetics and Art Criticism* 14 (1960): 221-227. Distinguishes three types of initiation stories: those that lead protagonists only to the threshold of maturity, those that take the protagonists across the threshold of maturity but leave them in a struggle for certainty, and decisive initiation stories that carry protagonists firmly into maturity.

Matthews, Brander. *The Philosophy of the Short-Story*. New York: Longmans, Green, 1901. An expansion of an 1882 article in which Matthews sets himself forth as the first critic since Edgar Allan Poe to discuss the "short-story" (Matthews contributed the hyphen) as a genre. By asserting that the short story must have a vigorous compression, must be original, must be ingenious, must have a touch of fantasy, and so on, Matthews set the stage for the subsequent host of textbook writers on the short story.

Maugham, W. Somerset. "The Short Story." In *Points of View: Five Essays*. Garden City, N.Y.: Doubleday, 1958. As might be expected, Maugham's preference is for the well-made story exemplified by Guy de Maupassant's "The Necklace." Most of the essay, however, deals with biographical material about Anton Chekhov and Katherine Mansfield.

May, Charles E. "Artifice and Artificiality in the Short Story." *Story* 1 (Spring, 1990): 72-82. Discusses the artificial and formalized nature of the endings of short stories, arguing that the short story is the most aesthetic narrative form. Discusses the ending of several representative stories.

_____. "Metaphoric Motivation in Short Fiction: 'In the Beginning Was the Story.'" In S*hort Theory at a Crossroads*, edited by Susan Lohafer and Jo Ellyn Clarey. Baton Rouge: Louisiana State University Press, 1989. A discussion of how short fiction moves from the "tale" form to the "short story" form through motivation by metaphor in "The Fall of the House of Usher," "Bartleby the Scrivener," "The Legend of Sleepy Hollow," and "Young Goodman Brown."

_____. "The Nature of Knowledge in Short Fiction." *Studies in Short Fiction* 21 (Fall, 1984): 227-238. A theoretical study of the epistemological bases of short fiction. Argues that the short story originates as a primal mythic mode that develops into a metaphoric mode.

_____. "Obsession and the Short Story." In *Creative and Critical Approaches to the Short Story*, edited by Noel Harold Kaylor, Jr. Lewiston, N.Y.: Edwin Mellen Press, 1997. An examination of the common charge that the short story is unhealthily limited and obsessed. Discusses the origins of the relationship between psychological obsession and aesthetic unity in the stories of Edgar Allan Poe, Nathaniel Hawthorne, and Herman Melville. Attempts to account for this relationship as a generic characteristic of the short story.

_____. "Prolegomenon to a Generic Study of the Short Story." *Studies in Short Fiction* 33 (Fall, 1996): 461-474. Tries to lay the groundwork for a generic theory of the short story in terms of new theories of this genre. Discusses the short story's historical focus on the strange and unexpected and the formal demands made by this thematic focus. Argues for a mixed genre theory of the short story that can account for the form's essential, as well as historically changing, characteristics.

_____. "Reality in the Modern Short Story." *Style* 27 (Fall, 1993): 369-379. Argues that realism in the modern short story from Anton Chekhov to Raymond Carver is not the simple mimesis of the realistic novel but rather the use of highly compressed selective detail configured to metaphorically objectify that which cannot be described directly. The result is a "hyperrealism" in which story is unified by tone and meaning is created by aesthetic pattern.

_____. *The Short Story: The Reality of Artifice*. New York: Routledge, 2002. A historical survey of the short story, tracing its origins in the tales of Geoffrey Chaucer and Giovanni Boccaccio through the nineteenth century and its contemporary renaissance.

_____. *Short Story Theories*. Athens: Ohio University Press, 1976. A collection of twenty previously published essays on the short story as a genre in its own right.

_____. "A Survey of Short Story Criticism in America." *The Minnesota Review*, Spring, 1973, 163-169. An analytical survey of criticism beginning with Edgar Allan Poe and focusing on the short story's underlying vision and characteristic mode of understanding and confronting reality.

_____. "The Unique Effect of the Short Story: A Reconsideration and an Example." *Studies in Short Fiction* 13 (1976): 289-297. An attempt to redefine Edgar Allan Poe's "unique effect" in the short story in terms of mythic perception. Maintains that the short story demands intense compression and focusing because its essential subject is a manifestation of what philosopher Ernst Cassirer calls the "momentary deity." A detailed discussion of Stephen Crane's story "An Episode of War" illustrates the concept.

Menikoff, Barry. "The Problematics of Form: History and the Short Story." *Journal of the Short Story in English*, no. 2 (1984): 129-146. After a brief introduction discussing how the short story has been neglected, Menikoff comments briefly on the importance of Charles E. May's *Short Story Theories* (1976) and then discusses essays on the short story that appeared in *Critical Survey of Short Fiction* (1981) and a special issue of *Modern Fiction Studies* (1982).

Miall, David. "Text and Affect: A Model for Story Understanding." In *Re-Reading the Short Story*, edited by Clare Hanson. New York: St. Martin's Press, 1989. A discussion of what readers are doing in emotional terms when they read, using the defamiliarization model of the Russian Formalists. Focuses on three aspects of emotion: self-reference, domain crossing, and anticipation. Basically determines that whereas literary texts constrain response by means of their shared frames and conventions, their affective responses are highly divergent.

Millhauser, Steven. "The Ambition of the Short Story." *The New York Times Book Review*, October 5, 2008, p. 31. Discussion of the short story's essential characteristics and how the form differs from the novel.

Moffett, James. "Telling Stories: Methods of Abstraction in Fiction." *ETC* 21 (1964): 425-50. Charts a sequence covering an "entire range" of ways in which stories can be told, from the most subjective and personal (interior monologue and dramatic monologue) to the most objective and impersonal (anonymous narration). Includes examples of each type.

Moravia, Alberto. "The Short Story and the Novel." In Man as End: *A Defense of Humanism*. Translated by Bernard Wall. New York: Farrar, Straus & Giroux, 1969. Moravia, who wrote many novels and short stories, maintains that the basic difference between the two is that the novel has a bone structure of ideological themes whereas the short story is made up of intuitions of feelings.

Munson, Gorham. "The Recapture of the Storyable." *University Review* 10 (Autumn, 1943): 37-44. Maintains that the best short-story writers are concerned with only three questions: whether they have found a "storyable" incident, how they should cast their characters, and who would best tell their story.

Oates, Joyce Carol. "Beginnings: The Origin and Art of the Short Story." In *The Tales We Tell: Perspectives on the Short Story*, edited by Barbara Lounsberry et al. Westport, Conn.: Greenwood Press, 1998. Defines the short story as a form that represents an intensification of meaning rather than an expansion of the imagination. Briefly discusses the importance of Edgar Allan Poe's aesthetic and Mark Twain's oral tale to the development of the American short story.

_____. "The Short Story." *Southern Humanities Review* 5 (1971): 213-214. Maintains that the short story is a "dream verbalized," a manifestation of desire; its most interesting aspect is its "mystery."

O'Connor, Frank. *The Lonely Voice: A Study of the Short Story*. 1963. Reprint. Hoboken, N.J.: Melville House, 2004. O'Connor, an accomplished master of the short-story form, presented his observations of the genre in this study. The introductory chapter contains extremely valuable "intuitive" criticism. O'Connor maintains that the basic difference between the novel and the short story is that in the latter readers always find an intense awareness of human loneliness. He believes that the protagonist of the short story is less an individual with whom readers can identify than a "submerged population group," that is, someone outside the social mainstream. The remaining chapters of the book treat this theme in the works of Ivan Turgenev, Anton Chekhov, Guy de Maupassant, Rudyard Kipling, James Joyce, Katherine Mansfield, D. H. Lawrence, A. E. Coppard, Isaac Babel, and Mary Lavin.

O'Faoláin, Seán. *The Short Story*. New York: Devin-Adair, 1951. This book on the technique of the short story claims that technique is the "least part of the business." O'Faoláin illustrates his thesis that personality is the most important element in short fiction by describing the personal struggles of Alphonse Daudet, Anton Chekhov, and Guy de Maupassant. He does his duty to the assigned subject of the book by also discussing the technical problems of convention, subject, construction, and language.

O'Rourke, William. "Morphological Metaphors for the Short Story: Matters of Production, Reproduction, and Consumption." In *Short Story Theory at a Crossroads*, edited by Susan Lohafer and Jo Ellyn

Clarey. Baton Rouge: Louisiana State University Press, 1989. Explores a number of analogies drawn from the social and natural sciences to suggest ways of seeing how the short story is different from the novel: The novel has a structure like a vertebrate, whereas the short story is like an animal with an exoskeleton; the novel is a macro form, whereas the short story is a micro form.

Overstreet, Bonaro. "Little Story, What Now?" *Saturday Review of Literature*, 24 (November 22, 1941): 3-5, 25-26. Overstreet argues that as a result of a loss of faith in the old verities of the nineteenth century, the twentieth century short story is concerned with psychological materials, not with the events in the objective world.

Pain, Barry. *The Short Story*. London: Martin Secker, 1916. Pain claims that the primary difference between the short story and the novel is that the short story, because of its dependence on suggestive devices, demands more of the reader's participation.

Palakeel, Thomas. "Third World Short Story as National Allegory?" *Journal of Modern Literature* 20 (Summer, 1996): 97-102. Argues against Frederic Jameson's claim that Third World fictions are always national allegories. Points out that this claim is even more damaging to the short story than to the novel because the short story is the most energetic literary activity in the Third World. He argues that Jameson's theory cripples any non-Western literature that tries to deal with the psychological or spiritual reality of the individual.

Pasco, Allan H. "The Short Story: The Short of It." *Style* 27 (Fall, 1993): 442-451. Suggests a list of qualities of the short story generated by its brevity, such as the assumptions of considerable background on the part of the readers and that readers will absorb and remember all elements of the work. Claims that the short story shuns amplification in favor of inference, that it is usually single rather than multivalent, that it tends toward the general, and that it remains foreign to loosely motivated detail.

Patrick, Walton R. "Poetic Style in the Contemporary Short Story." *College Composition and Communication* (1957): 77-84. Argues that the poetic style appears more consistently in the short story than

in the novel because metaphorical dilations are essential to the writer who "strives to pack the utmost meaning into his restricted space."

Penn, W. S. "The Tale as Genre in Short Fiction." *Southern Humanities Review* 15 (Summer, 1981): 231-241. Discusses the genre from the perspective of structure. Primarily uses suggestions made by Jonathan Culler in Structuralist Poetics for constructing a poetic persona in the lyric poem, what Culler calls an "enunciative posture," that is, the detectable or intuited moral relation of the implied author to both the world at large and the world he or she creates. Develops two kinds of tales: the radical oral and the exponential oral.

Perry, Bliss. *A Study of Prose Fiction*. Boston: Houghton Mifflin, 1920. Perry claims that the short story differs from the novel by presenting unique and original characters, by focusing on fragments of reality, and by making use of the poetic devices of impressionism and symbolism.

Pickering, Jean. "Time and the Short Story." In *Re-Reading the Short Story*, edited by Clare Hanson. New York: St. Martin's Press, 1989. Discusses the distinction between the short story as an art of revelation and the novel as an art of evolution. General implications that derive from this distinction are that short-story writers do not need to know all the details of their characters' lives and that the short story is doubly symbolic. Structure, theme, characterization, and language are influenced by the short story's particular relation to time as a moment of revelation.

Poe, Edgar Allan. "Review of Twice-Told Tales." *Graham's Magazine*, May, 1842. The first critical discussion of the short story, or the "tale" as Poe terms it, to establish the genre as distinct from the novel. Because of its sense of totality, its single effect, and its patterned design, the short story is second only to the lyric in its demands on high genius and in its aesthetic beauty.

Pratt, Mary Louise. "The Short Story: The Long and the Short of It." *Poetics* 10 (1981): 175-194. A theoretical discussion of the form. Presents eight ways that the short story is better understood if its dependence on the novel is understood.

Prince, Gerald. *A Grammar of Stories: An Introduction.* The Hague, Netherlands: Mouton, 1973. An attempt to establish rules to account for the structure of all the syntactical sets that readers intuitively recognize as stories. The model used is Noam Chomsky's theories of generative grammar.

_____. "The Long and the Short of It." *Style* 27 (Fall, 1993): 327-331. Provides a definition of the short story as "an autonomous, short, fictional story written in prose and offered for display." Admits that such a definition has limited usefulness but argues that this is characteristic of generic definitions; maintains that texts belong not to one but to an indefinitely large number of textual families and use an indefinitely large number of clusters of features.

Pritchett, V. S. "Short Stories." *Harper's Bazaar* 87 (July, 1953): 31, 113. In Pritchett's opinion the short story is a hybrid, owing much to the quickness and objectivity of the cinema, much to the poet and the newspaper reporter, and everything to the "restlessness, the alert nerve, the scientific eye and the short breath of contemporary life." He makes an interesting point about the collapse of standards, conventions, and values which has so bewildered the impersonal novelist but has been the making of the story writer.

Reid, Ian. *The Short Story.* London: Methuen, 1977. A brief study that deals with problems of definition, historical development, and related generic forms. Offers a good introduction to the short story as a genre.

Rohrberger, Mary. "Between Shadow and Act: Where Do We Go from Here?" In *Short Story Theory at a Crossroads*, edited by Susan Lohafer and Jo Ellyn Clarey. Baton Rouge: Louisiana State University Press, 1989. A thought-provoking review of a number of modern short-story critics and theorists, largely by way of responding to, and disagreeing with, the strictly scientific and logical approach to definition of the form suggested by Norman Friedman. Also includes a restatement of the view that Rohrberger enunciated in her earlier book on Nathaniel Hawthorne, in which she argued for the essentially romantic nature of the short-story form.

_____. *Hawthorne and the Modern Short Story: A Study in Genre.* The Hague, Netherlands: Mouton, 1966. Attempts a generic definition of the short story as a form that derives from the Romantic metaphysical view that there is more to the world than can be apprehended through the senses. Nathaniel Hawthorne is the touchstone for Rohrberger's definition, which she then applies to twentieth century stories by Eudora Welty, Ernest Hemingway, Sherwood Anderson, William Faulkner, and others.

Ruthrof, Horst. "Bracketed World and Reader Construction in the Modern Short Story." In *The Reader's Construction of Narrative.* London: Routledge & Kegan Paul, 1981. Discusses the "boundary situation" as the basis for the modern short story. In the pure boundary situation, the reader's act of bracketing transforms the presented crisis into the existential experience of the reading act.

Scott, A. O. "A Good Tale Isn't Hard to Find." *The New York Times*, April 5, 2009, p. WK1. Discussion of the remarkable durability of the short story, suggesting that it may be poised for a resurgence at the end of the first decade of the twenty-first century.

Shaw, Valerie. *The Short Story: A Critical Introduction.* London: Longman, 1983. A discussion of the form that primarily focuses on British writers, with one chapter on the transitional figure Robert Louis Stevenson. The rest of book deals with the patterned form to the artless tale form, with chapters on character, setting, and subject matter. Shaw argues that the short story cannot be defined by unity of effect or by a history of its "favorite devices and eminent practitioners."

Siebert, Hilary. "'Outside History': Lyrical Knowledge in the Discourse of the Short Story." In *Creative and Critical Approaches to the Short Story*, edited by Noel Harold Kaylor, Jr. Lewiston, N.Y.: Edwin Mellen Press, 1997. A discussion of how readers of short stories must often shift from expectations of a revealed, discursive meaning typical of prose to a gradually apprehended suggestive meaning typical of lyric poetry.

Stanzel, Franz K. "Textual Power in (Short) Short Story and Poem." In *Modes of Narrative: Approaches to American, Canadian, and British Fiction*, edited by Reingard M. Vischik and Barbara Korte. Wursburg, Germany: Konigshausen and Neumann, 1990. Argues that the short story and poetry, which at the beginning of the twentieth century were far apart, have come closer together in both form and content. Suggests some of the similarities between the two forms, such as their focusing the reader's attention on beginnings and endings and their insistence on close readings of the structure of each line and sentence.

Stevick, Philip, ed. *Anti-Story: An Anthology of Experimental Fiction*. New York: Free Press, 1971. An influential collection of contemporary short fiction with a helpful introduction that characterizes antistory as against mimesis, reality, event, subject, the middle range of experience, analysis, and meaning.

Stroud, Theodore A. "A Critical Approach to the Short Story." *Journal of General Education* 9 (1956): 91-100. Makes use of American New Criticism to determine the pattern of the short story, that is, why apparently irrelevant episodes are included and why some events are expanded and others excluded.

Suckow, Ruth. "The Short Story." *Saturday Review of Literature* 4 (November 19, 1927): 317-318. Suckow strongly argues that no one can define the short story, for it is an aesthetic method for dealing with diversity and multiplicity.

Sullivan, Walter. "Revelation in the Short Story: A Note of Methodology." In *Vanderbilt Studies in Humanities*, edited by Richard C. Beatty, John Philip Hyatt, and Monroe K. Spears. Vol. 1. Nashville, Tenn.: Vanderbilt University Press, 1951. The fundamental methodological concept of the short story is a change of view from innocence to knowledge. This change can be either "logical" (coming at the end of the story) or "anticipated" (coming near the beginning); it can be either "intraconcatinate" (occurring within the main character) or "extra-concatinate" (occurring within a peripheral character). Thus defined, the short story did not begin until the final years of the nineteenth century.

Summers, Hollis, ed. *Discussions of the Short Story*. Boston: D. C. Heath, 1963. The nine general pieces on the short story include essays by Edgar Allan Poe and A. L. Bader; excerpts of books by Ray B. West, Seán O'Faoláin, and Brander Matthews; a chapter each from Percy Lubbock's Craft of Fiction (1954) and Kenneth Payson Kempton's The Short Story (1947); and Bret Harte's "The Rise of the Short Story." Also includes seven additional essays on specific short-story writers.

Szávai, János. "Towards a Theory of the Short Story." *Acta Litteraria Academiae Scientiarum Hungariae*, Tomus 24 (1982): 203-224. Discusses the Giovanni Boccaccio model as a genre that gives the illusion of reflecting reality directly and spontaneously, whereas it is actually a complex, structured entity that both retains and enriches the basic structure of the story. The enrichment resides, on the one hand, in the careful preparation of the point and its attachment to a key motif and, on the other, in the introduction of a new dimension in addition to the anecdote.

Todorov, Tzvetan. "The Structural Analysis of Literature." In *Structuralism: An Introduction*, edited by David Robey. London: Clarendon Press, 1973. The "figure in the carpet" in Henry James's stories is the quest for an absolute and absent cause. This cause is either a character, an event, or an object; its effect is the story readers are told. Everything in the story owes its existence to this cause, but because it is absent, the reader sets off in quest of it.

Trask, Georgianne, and Charles Burkhart, ed. *Storytellers and Their Art*. New York: Doubleday Anchor, 1963. A valuable collection of comments on the short-story form by practitioners from Anton Chekhov to Truman Capote. Noteworthy in part 1 are "Definitions of the Short Story" and "Short Story vs. Novel."

Trussler, Michael. "The Short Story: Interview with Charles May and Susan Lohafer." *Wascana Review* 33 (Spring, 1998): 14-24. Interview with two well-known theorists of the short story, who discuss reasons for past critical neglect of the form, conditions of the recent renaissance of interest in the form by both critics and general readers, unique generic characteristics of the short story, and current and future trends in the short story and theoretical approaches to it.

_____. "Suspended Narratives: The Short Story and Temporality." *Studies in Short Fiction* 33 (Fall, 1996): 557-577. An analysis of the critical view that the short-story form focuses on atemporality. Synthesizes a number of theories that emphasize short fiction's focus on existential confrontations while refusing to mitigate such experiences with abstraction, context, or continuity.

Wain, John. "Remarks on the Short Story." *Journal of the Short Story in English* 2 (1984): 49-66. Wain, himself a short-story writer, argues that the short story is a form of its own, with its own laws and logic, and that it is a modern form, beginning with Edgar Allan Poe. He observes that the novel is like a painting, whereas the short story is like a drawing, which catches a moment and is satisfying on its own grounds. He says there are perfectly successful short stories and totally unsuccessful ones, and nothing in between.

Welty, Eudora. "The Reading and Writing of Short Stories." *The Atlantic Monthly*, February, 1949, 54-58; March, 1949, 46-49. An impressionistic but suggestive essay in two installments that focuses on the mystery of the story and the fact that one cannot always see the solid outlines of the story because of the atmosphere that it generates.

West, Ray B. "The Modern Short Story and the Highest Forms of Art." *English Journal* 46 (1957): 531-539. Describes how the rise of the short story in the nineteenth century was a result of the shift in narrative view from the "telescopic" (viewing nature and society from the outside) to the "microscopic" (viewing the unseen world of inner motives and impulses).

Wharton, Edith. "Telling a Short Story." In *The Writing of Fiction*. New York: Charles Scribner's Sons, 1925. Wharton maintains that the chief technical difference between the novel and the short story is that the novel focuses on character while the short story focuses on situation, "and it follows that the effect produced by the short story depends almost entirely on its form."

Williams, William Carlos. *A Beginning on the Short Story: Notes*. Yonkers, N.Y.: The Alicat Bookshop Press, 1950. In these notes from a writers' workshop session, Williams makes several interesting, if fragmentary and impressionistic, remarks about the short-story form: The short story, as contrasted with the novel, is a brushstroke instead of a picture. Stressing virtuosity instead of story structure, it is "one single flight of the imagination, complete: up and down." It is best suited to depicting the life of "briefness, brokenness, and heterogeneity."

Winther, Per, Jacob Lothe, and Hans H. Skei, eds. *The Art of Brevity: Excursions in Short Fiction Theory and Analysis*. Columbia: University of South Carolina Press, 2004. Collection of essays, including some written by noted short-story theorists, such as Mary Rohrberger, Charles E. May, Susan Lohafer, and John Gerlach. Some of the essays examine reasons for readers' neglect of short stories. Other essays analyze short fiction by Robert Olen Butler, Chris Offutt, James Joyce, Sarah Orne Jewett, Linda Hogan, Flannery O'Connor, Eudora Welty, William Faulkner, and Herman Melville; Danish short stories from the 1990's; and works by Australian writers.

Wright, Austin. "On Defining the Short Story: The Genre Question." In *Short Story Theory at a Crossroads*, edited by Susan Lohafer and Jo Ellyn Clarey. Baton Rouge: Louisiana State University Press, 1989. Discusses some of the theoretical problems involved in defining the short story as a genre. Argues for the formalist view of a genre definition as a cluster of conventions.

_____. "Recalcitrance in the Short Story." In *Short Story Theory at a Crossroads*, edited by Susan Lohafer and Jo Ellyn Clarey. Baton Rouge: Louisiana State University Press, 1989. A discussion of stories with endings that resist the reader's efforts to assimilate them and to make sense of them as a whole. Such final recalcitrance, Wright claims, is the extreme kind of resistance that the short story has developed to thwart final closure and reduce the complexity of the story to a conceptual understanding.

AMERICAN SHORT FICTION

Adams, Alice. "The American Short Story in the Cybernetic Age." *Journal of the Short Story in English* 17 (Autumn, 1991): 9-22. After summarizing critical condemnation of the short story in the early twentieth century as mechanical and formulaic, Adams argues that the metafictional story of the 1960's and 1970's tries to reclaim the short story from its lowbrow mechanistic state by making formula palpable.

Allen, Walter. *The Short Story in English.* Oxford, England: Clarendon Press, 1981. A historical study of the development of the genre in England and the United States. Primarily a series of biographical discussions of authors and summary discussions of stories. Good for providing a framework for the development of the form.

Bendixen, Alfred, and James Nagel, eds. *A Companion to the American Short Story.* Malden, Mass.: Wiley-Blackwell, 2010. A comprehensive collection of essays surveying the short fiction genre, divided into four parts. Part 1 focuses on the nineteenth century, with discussions of the emergence and development of the American short story, Herman Melville's "Bartleby the Scrivener," and the works of Edgar Allan Poe, Nathaniel Hawthorne, Charles Waddell Chesnutt, Mark Twain, Charlotte Perkins Gilman, Edith Wharton, and the New England local-colorists. Part 2 charts transitional short fiction of the late nineteenth and early twentieth centuries, including essays on the works of Stephen Crane, Kate Chopin, Frank Norris, and Jack London. Part 3 surveys twentieth century short fiction, specifically the works of Ernest Hemingway, William Faulkner, Katherine Anne Porter, Eudora Welty, F. Scott Fitzgerald, Richard Wright, Saul Bellow, John Updike, Raymond Carver, and Denise Chávez. Part 4, "Expansive Considerations," examines American women's short stories; ghost and detective stories; Asian American, Jewish American, and other multiethnic short fiction; and short story cycles.

Bierce, Ambrose. "The Short Story." In *The Collected Works of Ambrose Bierce.* New York: Gordian Press, 1966. Bierce criticizes William Dean Howells and other writers of the realistic school for their prosaic and pedestrian realism, which fails to perceive the mystery of human life.

Boddy, Kasia. *The American Short Story Since 1950.* Edinburgh: Edinburgh University Press, 2010. Analyzes short fiction by Flannery O'Connor, Eudora Welty, J. D. Salinger, John Cheever, Raymond Carver, Lorrie Moore, Grace Paley, and other writers. The introduction provides a history of the American short story up to 1950; the initial chapters discuss major trends in the short fiction of the period, such as minimalism, fabulism, and realism, as well as short-story sequences written between 1950 and 2000.

Bone, Robert, *Down Home: A History of Afro-American Short Fiction from Its Beginnings to the End of the Harlem Renaissance.* New York: Capricorn Books, 1975. Provides a background for the African-American folktale, the Brer Rabbit Tales, and the local-color writers. Devotes a chapter each to Paul Laurence Dunbar, Charles Waddell Chesnutt, Jean Toomer, Langston Hughes, and Arna Bontemps. Also contains a chapter on the Harlem Renaissance, with mention of Zora Neale Hurston and other writers. Shows how the African-American short story is the child of a mixed heritage.

Bostrom, Melissa. *Sex, Race, and Family in Contemporary American Short Stories.* New York: Palgrave Macmillan, 2007. Describes how the market for contemporary short fiction has affected the depiction of sexual power, the relationships of mothers and daughters, and race in many short stories.

Canby, Henry S. *The Short Story in English.* New York: Holt, Rinehart, and Winston, 1909. A classic historical survey of English-language short fiction, from the Middle Ages through the nineteenth century, with discussion of both British and American writers. Canby argues that the Romantic movement gave birth to the modern short story and that Edgar Allan Poe is its first important figure; the rest of the nineteenth century writers applied Poe's theory of single effect to new subjects, primarily the contrasts of civilization in flux

Clarke, John H. "Transition in the American Negro Short Story." *Phylon* 21 (1960): 360-366. A shorter version of this article appears as the introduction to *American Negro Short Stories*, edited by John

Henrik Clarke (1966). A brief historical survey of the African American short story from Paul Laurence Dunbar and Charles Waddell Chesnutt at the beginning of the twentieth century, through the Harlem Renaissance of the 1920's, to the emergence of Richard Wright, who marked the end of the double standard for black writers.

Crow, Charles L., ed. *A Companion to the Regional Literatures of America*. New York: Wiley-Blackwell, 2003. A comprehensive study comprising essays arranged in three sections: an introductory survey of theoretical and historical approaches (eleven essays); a middle section on various regional literatures from New England and the South to the Southwest and Hawaii (fourteen essays); and concluding essays on individual Western regionalist writers, including Bret Harte, Mark Twain, Willa Cather, and Wallace Stegner. Nearly all the pieces discuss their topics in depth and detail.

Curnutt, Kirk. *Wise Economies: Brevity and Storytelling in American Short Stories*. Moscow: University of Idaho Press, 1997. A historical analysis of the short story's development as the structuring of the tension between brevity and storytelling. Shows how stylistic brevity as an evolving aesthetic practice redefined the interpretative demands placed on readers.

Current-Garcia, Eugene. *The American Short Story, Before 1850*. Boston: Twayne, 1985. Focuses on the types of magazine fiction published before 1820. Devotes individual chapters to Washington Irving, Nathaniel Hawthorne, and Edgar Allan Poe. Also includes a chapter on William Gilmore Simms and the frontier humorists, such as George Washington Harris. The shift toward realism described in the last chapter is largely a result of the fiction of Herman Melville.

Current-Garcia, Eugene, and Walter R. Patrick. *Introduction to American Short Stories*. Rev. ed. Chicago: Scott, Foresman, 1964. A historical survey of the American short story through four periods: Romanticism, realism, naturalism, and the modern period of both traditionalists (those who have carried on the tradition of Edgar Allan Poe, Guy de Maupassant, and Henry James) and experimentalists (those

who have focused more on the fragmented inner world of the mind).

_____, eds. *What Is the Short Story?* Rev. ed. New York: Scott, Foresman, 1974. Although this volume is primarily a short-story anthology, it contains a generous selection of mostly American criticism on the short story, arranged in chronological order. Contains a four-page general bibliography on the short story.

Del George, Dana. *The Supernatural in Short Fiction of the Americas: The Other World in the New World*. Westport, Conn.: Greenwood Press, 2001. Describes how cultural encounters between European and indigenous societies and between "scientific materialism" and "premodern supernaturalism" resulted in the creation of new narrative forms, including supernatural short fiction.

Fallon, Erin, et al., eds. *A Reader's Companion to the Short Story in English*. Westport, Conn.: Greenwood Press, 2001. Produced under the auspices of the Society for the Study of the Short Story, this collection of essays, aimed at the general reader, provides brief biographies of numerous writers and analyses of their short fiction. Some of the writers examined are Toni Cade Bambara, John Barth, Donald Barthelme, Anne Beattie, Raymond Carver, Sandra Cisneros, Robert Coover, Louise Erdrich, Richard Ford, Ernest J. Gaines, Maxine Hong Kingston, Bernard Malamud, James Alan McPherson, Lorre Moore, Tim O'Brien, Grace Paley, and Amy Tan.

Firchow, Peter E. "The Americaness of the American Short Story." *Journal of the Short Story in English* 10 (Spring, 1988): 45-66. Examines the common claim that the short story is a particularly American art form. Surveys and critiques a number of critics who have debated the issue. Analyzes generic criteria for determining what is a short story, such as self-consciousness and length; concludes that a short story is simply a story that is short and that the American short story is not unique to America but is merely a story that deals with American cultural contexts.

Fusco, Richard. *Maupassant and the American Short Story: The Influence of Form at the Turn of the Century*. University Park: Pennsylvania State University Press, 1994. Argues that Guy de Maupassant's influence on the twentieth century short story rivals that of Anton Chekhov. Discusses seven different short-story forms in Maupassant's stories: linear, ironic coda, surprise-inversion, loop, descending helical, contrast, and sinusoidal. Describes Maupassant's influence on Ambrose Bierce, O. Henry, Kate Chopin, and Henry James.

Geismar, Maxwell. "The American Short Story Today." *Studies on the Left* 4 (Spring, 1964): 21-27. Criticizes J. D. Salinger, Philip Roth, Bernard Malamud, John Updike, and other writers for ignoring the social realities of the time in their short stories.

Gelfant, Blanche H., ed. *The Columbia Companion to the Twentieth-Century American Short Story*. New York: Columbia University Press, 2000. An excellent introductory overview of the genre. Part 1 contains general, thematic essays, such as discussions of the American short story cycle and of short fiction by African Americans, Asian Americans, Chicanos, Latinos, lesbians and gay men writers, Native Americans, and non-English authors. Part 2 features analyses of the works of about one hundred individual writers, from Alice Adams to Anzia Yezierska.

Gerlach, John. *Toward the End: Closure and Structure in the American Short Story*. Tuscaloosa: University of Alabama Press, 1985. A detailed theoretical study of the American short story, focusing particularly on the importance of closure, or the ending of the form; examines a number of stories in some detail in terms of the concept of closure.

Gerould, Katherine Fullerton. "The American Short Story." *Yale Review*, n.s. 13 (July, 1924): 642-663. Urges that the short story be read as critically as the novel. Argues that the short story must be well-made and must focus on a significant event that is either truly momentous for the individual character or typical of the lives of many people.

Gullason, Thomas A. "The 'Lesser' Renaissance: The American Short Story in the 1920's." In *The American Short Story: 1900-1945*, edited by Philip Stevick. Boston: Twayne, 1984. A historical survey of some of the major American short-story writers of the 1920's. The essay analyzes briefly some of the best-known stories of Sherwood Anderson, F. Scott Fitzgerald, Ring Lardner, Ernest Hemingway, Dorothy Parker, Katherine Anne Porter, and William Faulkner.

Howells, William Dean. "Some Anomalies of the Short Story." *North American Review* 173 (September, 1901): 422-432. Claims that when read in a volume, each story requires so much of the reader's attention that he or she becomes exhausted. Argues that a defect of the short story is that it creates no memorable characters.

Huang, Guiyou, ed. *Asian American Short Story Writers: An A-to-Z Guide*. Westport, Conn.: Greenwood Press, 2003. An encyclopedia containing alphabetically arranged entries about forty-nine Asian American authors living in the United States and Canada, including Frank Chin, Bharti Mukherjee, and Toshio Mori. Each entry provides a biography, a discussion of the writer's major works and themes, and a bibliography. Also contains an introductory overview of Asian American short fiction.

Joselyn, Sister Mary. "Edward Joseph O'Brien and the American Short Story." *Studies in Short Fiction* 3 (1965): 1-15. Attempts a synthesis of O'Brien's philosophic and aesthetic attitudes, which may have determined his choices of "best stories" for his annual anthologies. Discusses O'Brien's contribution to the history, theory, and growth of the American short story.

Karrer, Wolfgang, and Barbara Puschmann-Nalenz, eds. *The African American Short Story, 1970-1990: A Collection of Critical Essays*. Trier, Germany: Wissenschaftlicher Verlag Trier, 1993. These essays provide a historical overview of African American short fiction, as well as analyses of stories by Ann Petry, Toni Cade Barbara, Alice Walker, James Alan McPherson, Ntozake Shange, John Edgar Wideman, and other writers.

Kennedy, J. Gerald. "Short Story and the Short Story Sequence, 1865-1914." In *A Companion to American Fiction*, 1865-1914, edited by Robert Paul Lamb and G. R. Thompson. Malden, Mass.: Blackwell, 2005. An overview of the short story in this period, including discussion of works by Kate Chopin, Charles Waddell Chesnutt, Stephen Crane, Mark Twain, Rebecca Harding Davis, and other writers.

Kimbel, Ellen. "The American Short Story: 1900-1920." In *The American Short Story, 1900-1945*, edited by Philip Stevick. Boston: Twayne, 1984. A historical survey of the development of the short story in the first two decades of the twentieth century. Begins with Henry James and writers, such as Edith Wharton and Willa Cather, who were strongly influenced by James's work. Discusses the innovations of Sherwood Anderson and points out how he differs from earlier writers in developing the modern short story.

Kostelanetz, Richard. "Notes on the American Short Story Today." *The Minnesota Review* 5 (1966): 214-221. Argues that contemporary short-story writers focus on extreme rather than typical experiences and tend to emphasize the medium of language itself more than ever before. In a shift that pulls the genre farther away from narrative and pushes it closer to nonlinear forms of poetry, the contemporary short-story writer attempts to depict the workings of the mad mind, to simulate the feel of madness itself.

Leitch, Thomas M. "The Debunking Rhythm of the American Short Story." In *Short Story Theory at a Crossroads*, edited by Susan Lohafer and Jo Ellyn Clarey. Baton Rouge: Louisiana State University Press, 1989. Argues that a particular kind of closure is typical of the American short story. Uses the phrase "debunking rhythm" to characterize the kind of story in which a character realizes the falseness of one kind of knowledge but achieves no new kind of knowledge to take its place.

_____. "The New Yorker School." In *Creative and Critical Approaches to the Short Story*, edited by Noel Harold Kaylor, Jr. Lewiston, N.Y.: Edwin Mellen Press, 1997. A brief history of the development of the so-called New Yorker story. Charts the rise of the magazine as a powerful force in the development of the modern short story. Argues that, much like the modern short story generally, the New Yorker story has defined itself in terms of its departure from its own norms.

Levy, Andrews. *The Culture and Commerce of the American Short Story*. Cambridge, England: Cambridge University Press, 1993. A historical survey showing how the short story became an image of American values through political movements, editorial policies, and changes in education. Devotes chapters to Edgar Allan Poe's efforts to create a magazine that would accommodate his particular kind of story. Summarizes short-story criticism and theory in the late nineteenth and early twentieth centuries. Provides a brief history of creative writing programs and handbooks.

Marler, Robert F. "From Tale to Short Story: The Emergence of a New Genre in the 1850's." *American Literature: A Journal of Literary History, Criticism, and Bibliography* 46 (1974): 153-169. Using Northrop Frye's distinction between the tale (embodies "stylized figures which expand into psychological archetypes") and the short story (deals with characters who wear their "personae or social masks"), Marler surveys the critical condemnation of the tale form and the increasing emphasis on realism in the 1850's. The broad shift is from Edgar Allan Poe's overt romance to Herman Melville's mimetic portrayals, especially in "Bartleby the Scrivener."

O'Brien, Edward J. *The Advance of the American Short Story*. Rev. ed. New York: Dodd, Mead, 1931. A survey of the development of the American short story from Washington Irving to Sherwood Anderson. The focus is on contributions to the form by various authors: Irving's development of the story from the eighteenth century essay, Nathaniel Hawthorne's discovery of the subjective method for psychological fiction, Edgar Allan Poe's formalizing, Bret Harte's caricaturing, Henry James's development of the "central intelligence," and Anderson's freeing the story from O. Henry's formalism.

_____. *The Dance of the Machines: The American Short Story and the Industrial Age*. New York: Macaulay, 1929. Chapter 4 of this polemic against the machinelike standardization of the industrial age describes thirty characteristics that the short story ("the most typical American form") shares with the machine: For example, it is patterned, impersonal, standardized, speeded-up, and cheap.

Pache, Walter. "Towards the Modern English Short Story." In *Modes of Narrative: Approaches to American, Canadian, and British Fiction*, edited by Reingard M. Vischik and Barbara Korte. Wurzburg, Germany: Konigshausen and Neumann, 1990. A study of the relationship between the short fiction of the 1890's and the modern short story. Surveys changes in periodical publishing during the period, analyzes new directions in short-story theory at the turn of the twentieth century, and suggests some of the basic structural patterns of the end-of-nineteenth-century short story.

Pattee, Fred Lewis. *The Development of the American Short Story*. New York: Harper & Row, 1923. The most detailed and historically complete survey of the American short story from Washington Irving to O. Henry. Charts the changes in taste of the short-story reading public and indicates the major contributions to the form of such classic practitioners as Irving, Nathaniel Hawthorne, Edgar Allan Poe, and Bret Harte. Surveys the effect of the "Annuals," the "Ladies' Books," local color, Brander Matthews's *The Philosophy of the Short-Story* (1901), and the writing handbooks.

Peden, William. *The American Short Story: Continuity and Change, 1940-1975*. 2d ed. Boston: Houghton Mifflin, 1975. Includes chapters on publishing and the short story since 1940; the stories of suburbia by John Cheever, John Updike, and others; stories of physical illness and abnormality by James Purdy, Tennessee Williams, Flannery O'Connor, and Joyce Carol Oates; stories by Jewish writers, such as Bernard Malamud, Saul Bellow, J. D. Salinger, Grace Paley, Philip Roth, and Isaac Bashevis Singer; and stories by African American writers, such as Langston Hughes, Richard Wright, Ann Petry, and Toni Cade Bambera.

_____. "The American Short Story During the Twenties." *Studies in Short Fiction* 10 (1973): 367-371. A highly abbreviated account of the causes of the explosion of short stories during the 1920's. Some of the causes discussed are the new freedom from plotted stories, new emphasis on "now-ness," the

boom of little magazines, and the influence of cinematic techniques.

_____. *The American Short Story: Front Line in the National Defense of Literature*. Boston: Houghton Mifflin, 1964. A discussion of major trends in the American short story since 1940. The center of the book consists of a chapter on those writers who focus on everyday life in contemporary society (John Cheever, John O'Hara, Peter Taylor, John Updike, J. F. Powers, and J. D. Salinger) and a chapter on those who are preoccupied with the grotesque, abnormal, and bizarre (Carson McCullers, Flannery O'Connor, James Purdy, Truman Capote, and Tennessee Williams). An additional chapter surveys other short-story subjects, such as the war, minorities, regions, and science fiction.

Price, Kenneth M., and Susan Belasco Smith, eds. *Periodical Literature in Nineteenth-Century America*. Charlottsville: University Press of Virginia, 1995. A collection of essays by various scholars about how the periodical transformed the American literary marketplace between 1830 and 1890. Critics suggest how the development of the periodical as a market for short fiction had a powerful influence on the development of the form as a unique American genre.

Purcell, William M. *The Rhetorical Short Story: Best American Short Stories on War and the Military, 1915-2006*. Lanham, Md.: University Press of America, 2009. Examines more than ninety stories depicting war from World War I through the twenty-first century conflicts in Iraq and Afghanistan. Argues that during this period the perspective of war short fiction has changed from an insular one, stressing the actions of strong, purposeful individuals, to one in which individuals are uncontrollably caught in an "all-determining stream of events."

Rhode, Robert D. *Setting in the American Short Story of Local Color: 1865-1900*. The Hague, Netherlands: Mouton, 1975. A study of the various functions that setting plays in the local-color story of the late nineteenth century, from setting as merely background to setting in relation to character and setting as personification.

Rohrberger, Mary. "The Question of Regionalism: Limitation and Transcendence." In *The American Short Story, 1900-1945*, edited by Philip Stevick. Boston: Twayne, 1984. Focuses on such writers as Ruth Suckow, Jesse Stuart, Langston Hughes, and Jean Toomer. Calls Toomer's Cane the most significant work produced by the Harlem Renaissance and compares it with Sherwood Anderson's *Winesburg, Ohio*. Also discusses works by Ellen Glasgow, Sinclair Lewis, James T. Farrell, Erskine Caldwell, John O'Hara, and John Steinbeck.

Ross, Danforth. *The American Short Story.* Minneapolis: University of Minnesota Press, 1961. A sketchy survey that measures American stories since Edgar Allan Poe against Aristotelian criteria of action, unity, tension, and irony. Ends with the Beat writers who rebelled against the Poe-Aristotle tradition by using shock tactics.

Scofield, Martin. *The Cambridge Introduction to the American Short Story*. New York: Cambridge University Press, 2006. A concise and chronological overview of the genre, with some of the chapters focusing on Washington Irving, Nathaniel Hawthorne, Edgar Alan Poe, Herman Melville, Bret Harte, Mark Twain, Stephen Crane, Kate Chopin, Willa Cather, Edith Wharton, O. Henry, Jack London, Ernest Hemingway, F. Scott Fitzgerald, Katherine Anne Porter, Flannery O'Connor, Richard Wright, James Baldwin, and Raymond Carver.

Shivani, Anis. "Whatever Happened to the American Short Story?" *Contemporary Review* 291 (Summer, 2009): 216-225. Based on his analysis of the stories in *The O. Henry Prize Stories 2007* and *Best New American Voices 2008*, Shivani argues that the contemporary short story represents categories of victimization, reflecting America's decadence, insularity, and sad masochism.

Siebert, Hilary. "Did We Both Read the Same Story? Interpreting Cultural Contexts from Oral Discourses with the American Short Story." *Short Story* n.s. 6 (Spring, 1998). The history of the short story is one of many different types of discourses, both oral and written, blending together. The result of this textual tension and diversity is that educated readers may not be familiar with the variety of discourse conventions and thus read the stories incorrectly.

Stevick, Philip, ed. *Introduction to The American Short Story: 1900-1945*. Boston: Twayne, 1984. Stevick's extensive introduction to this collection of essays by various critics is a helpful historical overview of the development of the twentieth century short story. A good introduction to many of the features of the modern short story and how they came about at the beginning of the twentieth century.

Voss, Arthur. *The American Short Story: A Critical Survey*. Norman: University of Oklahoma Press, 1973. A comprehensive survey of the major short-story writers in American literature. Valuable for an overview of the stories and criticism.

Watson, James G. "The American Short Story: 1930-1945." In *The American Short Story, 1900-1945*, edited by Philip Stevick. Boston: Twayne, 1984. Claims that the period between 1930 and 1945 produced the most prolific outpouring of short fiction in the history of American literature. Focuses on the importance of the little magazines and discusses the contributions of Ernest Hemingway, William Faulkner, and F. Scott Fitzgerald.

Werlock, Abby H. P., ed. *The Facts On File Companion to the American Short Story*. 2d ed. 2 vols. New York: Facts On File, 2010. Alphabetically arranged entries cover numerous aspects of the American short story from the early nineteenth century to the early twenty-first century. The entries include author biographies and bibliographies, plot synopses, character sketches, and analyses of major short stories.

West, Ray B. "The American Short Story." In *The Writer in the Room*. Detroit: Michigan State University Press, 1968. Originally appeared as West's *Introduction to American Short Stories* (1959). Contrasts the short story's "microscopic" focus on inner motives with the novel's "telescopic" view of human beings from the outside. The novel is concerned with human beings' attempt to control nature through social institutions; the short story presents the individual's confrontation with nature as an indifferent force.

_____. *The Short Story in America: 1900-1950*. Chicago: Henry Regnery, 1952. Probably the most familiar and most often recommended history of the American short story. Chapter 1, "The American

Short Story at Mid-Century," is a short survey of the development of the short story since Washington Irving, Nathaniel Hawthorne, and Edgar Allan Poe. Chapter 4 is devoted completely to Ernest Hemingway and William Faulkner.

Windholz, Anne M. "The American Short Story and Its British Critics: Athenaeum Reviews, 1880- 1900." *Victorian Periodicals Review* 23 (Winter, 1990): 156-166. Argues that between 1880 and 1900, reviews of British and American short stories in the British journal Athenaeum helped establish an aesthetic that dominated critical analysis of the Anglo-American short story. Surveys reviewers' comments on American humor, dialect, and local color, as well as the importance of conciseness and unity of effect in both British and American short stories between 1880 and 1900.

Wright, Austin. *The American Short Story in the Twenties*. Chicago: University of Chicago Press, 1961. Using a canon of 220 stories, one set selected from the 1920's and the other from the period immediately preceding, Wright examines differing themes and techniques to test the usual judgments of what constitutes the "modern short story." The examination concludes by proving that the short story of the 1920's is different from the short story of the earlier period, that of the naturalists.

BRITISH SHORT FICTION

Allen, Walter. *The Short Story in English*. Oxford, England: Clarendon Press, 1981. A historical study of the development of the form in England and the United States. Primarily a series of biographical discussions of authors and summary discussions of stories. Good for providing a framework for the development of the form.

Baldwin, Dean. "The English Short Story in the Fifties." In *The English Short Story, 1945-1980*, edited by Dennis Vanatta. Boston: Twayne, 1985. Argues that after World War II, Great Britain experienced a bureaucratization of everyday life. Focuses on stories of social protest, especially those of Alan Sillitoe; the supernatural stories of Sylvia Townsend Warner and Muriel Spark; the mainstream writers H. E. Bates, V. S. Pritchett, Spark, and Rhys Davies;

and the major writers Doris Lessing, Sillitoe, Roald Dahl, Angus Wilson, William Sansom, and Elizabeth Taylor.

_____. "The Tardy Evolution of the English Short Story." *Studies in Short Fiction* 30 (Winter, 1993): 23-34. Discusses how the business of literary production, as well as various aesthetic issues, retarded the evolution of the short story in England until late in the nineteenth century.

Beachcroft, T. O. *The Modest Art: A Survey of the Short Story in English*. London: Oxford University Press, 1968. A historical survey of the major figures of the English short story from Geoffrey Chaucer to Doris Lessing. The result of the basic difference between antique stories (listening) and modern stories (reading) is that modern short-story writers attempt to portray rather than expound; they remove their own personalities from the stories and present the flashes of insight through poetic needs.

Boyce, Benjamin. "English Short Fiction in the Eighteenth Century: A Preliminary View." *Studies in Short Fiction* 5 (1968): 95-112. Discusses the types of short fiction found in periodicals and inserted in novels: character sketches, Oriental tales, and stories of passion. Usually the purpose of these works was didactic and the mode was either "hovering pathos" or "hovering irony." The most distinctive characteristic is the formal, even elegant language.

Broich, Ulrich. "Muted Postmodernism: The Contemporary British Short Story." *Zeitschrift für Anglistik und Amerikanistik* 41 (1993): 31-39. Analyzes the market conditions of contemporary British short fiction. Argues that in spite of a remarkable number of excellent British short stories, the form is neglected by readers and critics. Surveys three major types of British short stories: the feminist story, the cultural conflict story, and the experimental postmodernist story.

Canby, Henry S. *The Short Story in English*. New York: Holt, Rinehart, and Winston, 1909. A classic historical survey of English-language short fiction from the Middle Ages through the nineteenth century, with discussion of both British and American writers. Canby argues that the Romantic movement gave birth to the modern short story and that Edgar

Allan Poe is its first important figure; the rest of the nineteenth century writers applied Poe's theory of single effect to new subjects, primarily the contrasts of civilization in flux.

Carruthers, Gerard. *Scottish Literature*. Edinburgh: Edinburgh University Press, 2009. A comprehensive history of Scottish literature. Includes debate about Scotland's languages and analyses of writers, such as Sir Walter Scott, Margaret Oliphant, and Alasdair Gray, among many others.

Chan, Winnie. *The Economy of the Short Story in British Periodicals of the 1890's*. New York: Routledge, 2007. Focuses on the commercial pressures of the publishing industry and how they contributed to the types of short stories that were published in three periodicals of the period: *Strand*, *Yellow Book*, and *Black and White*.

Crawford, Robert. *Scotland's Books: A History of Scottish Literature*. Oxford, England: Oxford University Press, 2009. An excellent introduction to Scottish literature, written in accessible and engaging language. Crawford argues that the development of the short-story genre owes much to the literary reviews and journals of eighteenth century Edinburgh.

Duncan, Edgar Hill. "Short Fiction in Medieval English: A Survey." *Studies in Short Fiction* 9 (1972): 1-28. A survey of short pieces in the Old English period, primarily in verse, that have in common the characteristic of "artfully telling a story in a relatively brief compass" and that focus on "singleness of character, of action, and/or impression." The fall of the angels and the fall of man in the "Genesis B", the "St. Guthlac" poems, and "The Dream of the Rood" are analyzed.

_____. "Short Fiction in Medieval English: 2. The Middle English Period." *Studies in Short Fiction* 11 (1974): 227-241. A brief sampling of short fiction elements in the "shorter romance" form, the exemplary narrative, the beast tale, and the fabliau introduced to Middle English by the French. Also noted are paraphrases of biblical stories, saints' lives, the dream visions of "The Pearl", and Geoffrey Chaucer's "The Book of the Duchess" and the "Prologue to the Legend of Good Women."

Dunn, Douglas. *The Oxford Book of Scottish Short Stories*. Oxford, England: Oxford University Press, 1995. A collection of stories, including traditional and oral examples, dating from the eighteenth century through the twentieth century. Dunn notes in his introduction that Scottish short stories largely relate to and are written in the language of common people.

Evans, Walter. "The English Short Story in the Seventies." In *The English Short Story*, 1945-1980, edited by Dennis Vanatta. Boston: Twayne, 1985. Focuses on new writers of the period, such as Susan Hill, Angela Carter, Gabriel Josipovici, and Christine Brooke-Rose. The emphasis here is on different themes in these works, such as personal crises and the individual in conflict with society. Briefly discusses the avant-garde, especially Josipovici and Brooke-Rose. Claims the decade's finest collection of stories is *The Ebony Tower* by John Fowles.

Fallon, Erin, et al., eds. *A Reader's Companion to the Short Story in English*. Westport, Conn.: Greenwood Press, 2001. Produced under the auspices of the Society for the Study of the Short Story, this collection of essays, aimed at the general reader, provides brief biographies of numerous writers and analyses of their short fiction. Some of the writers examined are Chinua Achebe, Margaret Atwood, Morley Callaghan, Angela Carter, Janet Frame, Mavis Gallant, Nadine Gordimer, Elizabeth Jolley, Alice Munro, R. K. Narayan, Jean Rhys, Salman Rushdie, and Olive Senior.

Ferguson, Suzanne. "Local Color and the Function of Setting in the English Short Story." In *Creative and Critical Approaches to the Short Story*, edited by Noel Harold Kaylor, Jr. Lewiston, N.Y.: Edwin Mellen Press, 1997. Ferguson argues that whereas the function of setting in early stories was to establish a degree of verisimilitude, greater emphasis on setting in later stories served to establish the emotional interaction of the characters with elements of the physical environment.

Flora, Joseph M., ed. *The English Short Story, 1880-1945*. Boston: Twayne, 1985. A collection of essays on a number of British short-story writers during the period, including Rudyard Kipling, D.

H. Lawrence, Virginia Woolf, Saki, A. E. Coppard, P. G. Wodehouse, and V. S. Pritchett.

Harris, Wendell V. "Beginnings of and for the True Short Story in England." *English Literature in Transition* 15 (1972): 296-276. Argues that the true short story did not begin in England until Rudyard Kipling discovered the means to control the reader's angle of vision and establish a self-contained world within the story that keeps the reader at a distance. Maintains that the externality of the reader to the story's participants is a basic characteristic of the short story.

_____. "English Short Fiction in the Nineteenth Century." *Studies in Short Fiction* 6 (1968): 1-93. After distinguishing between "short fiction" appearing before 1880 and the "short story" after 1880, Harris surveys examples from both periods. The turning point was the definition posed by Brander Matthews, which first appeared in the *Saturday Review* in 1884.

_____. "Vision and Form: The English Novel and the Emergence of the Short Story." *Victorian Newsletter*, no. 47 (1975): 8-12. The short story did not begin in England until the 1880's because the presentation of isolated individuals, moments, or scenes was not considered a serious intellectual task for fiction to undertake. Only at the end of the century was reality perceived as congeries of fragments; the primary vehicle of this perception is the short story.

Hunter, Adrian. *The Cambridge Introduction to the Short Story in English*. Cambridge, England: Cambridge University Press, 2007. Hunter begins his literary history in the nineteenth century, describing the form and cultural context of short fiction from that time until the late twentieth century. He discusses the works of Charles Dickens, Thomas Hardy, Rudyard Kipling, Joseph Conrad, James Joyce, Virginia Woolf, Katherine Mansfield, Samuel Beckett, Frank O'Connor, Seán O'Faoláin, Elizabeth Bowen, V. S. Pritchett, Angela Carter, Ian McEwan, Chinua Achebe, James Kelman, Alice Munro, and others.

Killick, Tim. *British Short Fiction in the Early Nineteenth Century: The Rise of the Tale*. Burlington, Vt.: Ashgate, 2008. Describes how nineteenth century British writers and publishers sought to publish short fiction in book-length volumes in order to compete with the more prestigious novels. Discusses the publishing conditions of the period that promoted the creation of short fiction, explaining how the popular collections of American writer Washington Irving influenced the British periodical market for short fiction. Analyzes the stories and sketches of Mary Russell Mitford, James Hogg, Hannah More, Maria Edgeworth, and other writers.

Malcolm, Cheryl Alexander, and David Malcolm, eds. *A Companion to the British and Irish Short Story*. Malden, Mass.: Wiley-Blackwell, 2008. Collection of essays focusing on British and Irish short fiction from 1880 to the present day. Includes discussions of detective and crime stories, ghost stories, science-fiction tales, and gay and lesbian short stories, as well as women's writing. Analyzes the work of Rudyard Kipling, Robert Louis Stevenson, Thomas Hardy, Joseph Conrad, Saki, James Joyce, D. H. Lawrence, Virginia Woolf, Katherine Mansfield, Frank O'Connor, Liam O'Flaherty, Elizabeth Bowen, Ben Okri, Salman Rushdie, Hanif Kureishi, Alan Sillitoe, and John McGehern, among others.

Maunder, Andrew, ed. *The Facts On File Companion to the British Short Story*. New York: Facts On File, 2007. Provides more than 450 alphabetically arranged encyclopedia entries about short stories, novellas, short-fiction collections, writers, concepts, terms, themes, and literary movements in literature written from 1790 until the early twenty-first century. Although the entries focus on Great Britain, Ireland, and the Commonwealth, they also include some writers, such as Henry James and Salman Rushdie, who have strong ties to the British short-story tradition.

Mish, Charles C. "English Short Fiction in the Seventeenth Century." *Studies in Short Fiction* 6 (1969): 223-330. Mish divides the period into two parts: 1600-1660, in which short fiction declined into sterile imitation and preciousness, and 1660-1700, in which it was revitalized by the French influence of such works as Madame de la Fayette's "La Princesse de Clèves" (1678; The Princess of Clèves, 1679). The French direction toward interiorization, psychological analysis, and verisimilitude in action and setting, combined with the English style of the self-conscious narrator, moves fiction toward the novel of the eighteenth century.

Orel, Harold. *The Victorian Short Story: Development and Triumph of a Literary Genre*. Cambridge, England: Cambridge University Press, 1986. Contains chapters on Joseph Sheridan Le Fanu, Charles Dickens, Anthony Trollope, Thomas Hardy, Robert Louis Stevenson, Rudyard Kipling, H. G. Wells, and Joseph Conrad. Focuses on the relevant biographical and sociocultural factors and discusses writers' relationships with editors and periodicals. Does not attempt a formal history of the evolution of the genre.

Pache, Walter. "Towards the Modern English Short Story." In *Modes of Narrative: Approaches to American, Canadian, and British Fiction*, edited by Reingard M. Vischik and Barbara Korte. Wurzburg, Germany: Konigshausen and Neumann, 1990. A study of the relationship between the short fiction of the 1890's and the modern short story. Surveys changes in periodical publishing during the period, analyzes new directions in short-story theory at the turn of the twentieth century, and suggests some of the basic structural patterns of the end-of-the-nineteenth-century short story.

Pickering, Jean. "The English Short Story in the Sixties." In *The English Short Story, 1945-1980*, edited by Dennis Vanatta. Boston: Twayne, 1985. Pickering says that few of the cultural developments in England in the 1960's were reflected in the short story and claims that the short story was in decline during this period. Focuses on short-story collections by Roald Dahl, William Sansom, Doris Lessing, V. S. Pritchett, and H. E. Bates.

Schlauch, Margaret. "English Short Fiction in the Fifteenth and Sixteenth Centuries." *Studies in Short Fiction* 3 (1966): 393-434. A survey of types of short fiction from the romantic lai to the exemplum, and from the bawdy fabliau to the novella. Schlauch's conclusions are that modern short-story writers are heirs both in subject matter (for example internal psychological conflict) and in technique (such as the importance of dialogue) to a long tradition that antedates the seventeenth century, a tradition that is still worth studying.

Schoene-Harwood, Berthold, ed. *The Edinburgh Companion to Contemporary Scottish Literature*, Edinburgh: Edinburgh University Press, 2007. International critics discuss Scottish writing in the context of devolution and self-rule, voted by referendum in 1997, in nearly four-dozen essays.

Stevenson, Lionel. "The Short Story in Embryo." *English Literature in Transition* 15 (1972): 261-268. A discussion of the "agglomerative urge" in the English fiction of the eighteenth and nineteenth centuries that contributed to the undervaluing of the short story. Not until 1880, when the fragmentation of the well-integrated view of society began in England, did the short story come into its own in that country.

Stinson, John J. "The English Short Story, 1945-1950." In *The English Short Story*, 1945-1980, edited by Dennis Vanatta. Boston: Twayne, 1985. Discusses some of the reasons why the short story was in decline in England during this period and claims there was no new direction in the form at the time. Discusses W. Somerset Maugham, A. E. Coppard, Graham Greene, Sylvia Townsend Warner, V. S. Pritchett, and Angus Wilson.

Sullivan, C.W. *Welsh Celtic Myth in Modern Fantasy*, Greenwood, 1989. A fascinating study that shows the constant interplay of fantasy elements in otherwise realistic Welsh fiction. Makes the essential connection between the earliest writings in Welsh having a modern-day influence on short fiction and poetry writing by Welsh authors.

Vanatta, Denis, ed. *The English Short Story, 1945-1980*. Boston: Twayne, 1985. Includes survey essays by various critics on the short story in England in the 1950's, 1960's, and 1970's.

Windholz, Anne M. "The American Short Story and Its British Critics: Athenaeum Reviews, 1880-1900." *Victorian Periodicals Review* 23 (Winter, 1990): 156-166. Argues that between 1880 and 1900, reviews of British and American short stories in the British journal Athenaeum helped establish an aesthetic that dominated critical analysis of the Anglo-American short story. Surveys reviewers' comments on American humor, dialect, and local color, as well as the importance of conciseness and unity of effect in both British and American short stories between 1880 and 1900.

IRISH SHORT FICTION

Averill, Deborah. *The Irish Short Story from George Moore to Frank O'Connor*. Washington, D.C.: University Press of America, 1982. An introductory study of the Irish short story intended primarily for teachers and students. Surveys historical conditions in the nineteenth and early twentieth centuries that contributed to the development of the Irish short story and discusses the major stories of George Moore, James Joyce, Seumas O'Kelly, Daniel Corkery, Liam O'Flaherty, Seán O'Faoláin, and Frank O'Connor. Discusses each writer's basic style or concept of form and recurrent themes.

Carens, James F. "In Quest of a New Impulse: George Moore's The Untilled Field and James Joyce's Dubliners." In *The Irish Short Story: A Critical History*, edited by James F. Kilroy. Boston: Twayne, 1984. Carens provides analyses of the major stories in these two most influential collections of Irish short fiction. Discusses the major contributions of the stories of Moore and Joyce that were responsible for creating the modern Anglo-Irish short story. Explains Moore's influence on Joyce, analyzing Joyce's "Counterparts" as a reworking of Moore's "The Clerk's Quest."

Chatman, Seymour. "New Ways of Analyzing Narrative Structure, with an Example from Joyce's Dubliners." *Language and Style* 2 (1969): 3-36. A "test" of the narrative theories of Ronald Barthes and Tzvetan Todorov, with a detailed analysis of James Joyce's "Eveline." The story is considered both in terms of the internal relations of the narrative and the external relations between narrator and reader.

Delargy, J. H. "The Gaelic Story-Teller." *Proceedings of the British Academy* 31 (1945). An important study of the early Irish oral tradition of storytelling.

Dunleavy, Janet Egleson. "Mary Lavin, Elizabeth Bowen, and a New Generation: The Irish Short Story at Mid-Century." In *The Irish Short Story: A Critical History*, edited by James F. Kilroy. Boston: Twayne, 1984. Discusses Lavin's art as economic, disciplined, and compressed; argues that she neither

romanticizes nor trivializes Irish experience. Examines the basic characteristics of the fiction of Bowen, Benedict Kiely, Michael McLaverty, and Bryan MacMahon.

Hogan, Robert. "Old Boys, Young Bucks, and New Women: The Contemporary Irish Short Story." In *The Irish Short Story: A Critical History*, edited by James F. Kilroy. Boston: Twayne, 1984. A general survey of contemporary Irish short-story writers, such as old guards Anthony C. West, James Plunkett, William Trevor, and Patrick Boyle; young-buck writers Eugene McCabe, John Morrow, Bernard Mac Laverty, Desmond Hogan, and Gillman Noonan; and women writers, such as Edna O'Brien, Maeve Kelly, Emma Cooke, Kate Cruise O'Brien, and Juanita Casey.

Ingman, Heather. *A History of the Irish Short Story*. New York: Cambridge University Press, 2009. A historical survey of Irish short fiction from its beginnings in the nineteenth century to the present day. Each chapter concludes with an analysis of major stories from the period discussed, including works by William Carleton, Emily Lawless, William Butler Yeats, George Egerton, James Joyce, Frank O'Connor, Norah Hoult, Mary Lavin, Seán O'Faoláin, William Trevor, Edno O'Brien, John McGahern, and Eilis Ni Dhuibhne.

Kiberd, Declan. *Inventing Ireland: The Literature of the Modern Nation*. Cambridge, Mass.: Harvard University Press, 1996. An important study of the development of Irish literature from Oscar Wilde to the late twentieth century.

Kilroy, James F. *Introduction to The Irish Short Story: A Critical History*. Boston: Twayne, 1984. Collection of five essays surveying the development of the Irish short story in the nineteenth and twentieth centurys. Kilroy's focus is on the relationship between historical and social events in Ireland and the development of fiction in this country, including political conflicts and upheavals and the rise of periodical publication.

_____. "Setting the Standards: Writers of the 1920's and 1930's." In *The Irish Short Story: A Critical History*, edited by Kilroy. Boston: Twayne, 1984. Argues that the major Irish writers who set the standards for short fiction in the 1920's and 1930's were Liam O'Flaherty, Frank O'Connor, and Seán O'Faoláin. Kilroy compares and contrasts the three writers by analyzing some of their best-known stories. The essay also includes brief discussions of writers Daniel Corkery and Seamus O'Kelley.

Malcolm, Cheryl Alexander, and David Malcolm, eds. *A Companion to the British and Irish Short Story.* Malden, Mass.: Wiley-Blackwell, 2008. Collection of essays focusing on British and Irish short fiction from 1880 to the present day. Includes discussions of detective and crime stories, ghost stories, science-fiction tales, and gay and lesbian short stories, as well as women's writing. Analyzes the work of Rudyard Kipling, Robert Louis Stevenson, Thomas Hardy, Joseph Conrad, Saki, James Joyce, D. H. Lawrence, Virginia Woolf, Katherine Mansfield, Frank O'Connor, Liam O'Flaherty, Elizabeth Bowen, Ben Okri, Salman Rushdie, Hanif Kureishi, Alan Sillitoe, and John McGehern, among others.

Martin, Augustine, ed. *The Genius of Irish Prose.* Dublin: Mercier Press, 1985. Includes two relevant essays: "The Short Story: 1900-1945" and "The Short Story After the Second World War."

Mercier, Vivian. "The Irish Short Story and Oral Tradition." In *The Celtic Cross: Studies in Irish Culture and Literature,* edited by Ray B. Browne, William John Roselli, and Richard Loftus. West Lafayette, Ind.: Purdue University Studies, 1964. An influential essay that examines the relationship between the Irish folktale and the contemporary Irish short story.

Orel, Harold. *The Victorian Short Story.* Cambridge, England: Cambridge University Press, 1986. A helpful historical study with important chapters on William Carleton and Joseph Sheridan Le Fanu.

Rafroidi, Patrick, ed. *The Irish Short Story*. Atlantic Highlands, N.J.: Humanities Press, 1979. Collection of essays on general historical-critical issues concerning the Irish short story and on a number of important Irish short-story writers from William Carleton and Joseph Sheridan Le Fanu to Patrick Boyle and John McGahern.

Schirmer, Gregory A. "Tales from Big House and Cabin: The Nineteenth Century." In *The Irish Short Story: A Critical History*, edited by James F. Kilroy. Boston: Twayne, 1984. Surveys the short fiction of Maria Edgeworth, William Carleton, and Joseph Sheridan Le Fanu, among others. Schirmer emphasizes the ironic voice of Edgeworth's Castle Rackrent, the comic realism and the sophisticated use of narrative voice by William Carleton, and the use of the gothic tradition and psychological complexity by Joseph Sheridan Le Fanu.

Storey, Michael L. *Representing the Troubles in Irish Short Fiction.* Washington, D.C.: Catholic University of America Press, 2004. Examines short stories about Ireland's longstanding conflict with England during the period beginning with the 1916 Easter Rising to the 1990's sectarian violence in Northern Ireland, placing these stories in their political and historical contexts. Chronicles how depictions of the "troubles" evolved from expressions of Romantic Irish nationalism to realistic depictions of violence and sectarian strife. Some of the writers whose works are analyzed include Daniel Corkery, Frank O'Connor, Liam O'Flaherty, Seán O'Faoláin, Mary Lavin, Benedict Kiely, William Trevor, Bernard MacLaverty, and Colum McCann.

Thompson, Richard J. *Everlasting Voices: Aspects of the Modern Irish Short Story*. Troy, N.Y.: Whitston, 1989. A study of George Moore's The Untilled Field, James Joyce's Dubliners, and the stories of Frank O'Connor, Seán O'Faoláin, Liam O'Flaherty, and Mary Lavin.

CANADIAN SHORT FICTION

Bennett, Bruce. "Short Fiction and the Canon: Australia and Canada." *Antipodes* 7, no. 2 (1993): 109-114. A useful introductory essay, concentrating particularly on the "new" writing of the 1960's and 1970's.

Dvořák, Marta, and W. H. New, eds. *Tropes and Territories: Short Fiction, Postcolonial Readings, Canadian Writing in Context*. Montreal: McGill-Queen's University Press, 2007. Examines contemporary short fiction written in Canada and the Commonwealth, including works by Native Canadians, Maoris, and writers Katherine Mansfield,

Janet Frame, Alice Munro, Mavis Gallant, R. K. Narayan, and David Malouf, among others. Two of the essays provide general analyses of short fiction from South Asia and Australia, while another discusses Caribbean diasporic writing.

Huang, Guiyou, ed. *Asian American Short Story Writers: An A-to-Z Guide.* Westport, Conn.: Greenwood Press, 2003. An encyclopedia containing alphabetically arranged entries about forty-nine Asian American authors living in the United States and Canada, including Frank Chin, Bharti Mukherjee, and Toshio Mori. Each entry provides a biography, a discussion of the writer's major works and themes, and a bibliography. Also contains an introductory overview of Asian American short fiction.

Kruk, Laurie. *The Voice Is the Story: Conversations with Canadian Writers of Short Fiction.* Oakville, Ont.: Mosaic Press, 2003. Sandra Birdsell, Timothy Findley, Alistair MacLeod, Carol Sheilds, and Guy Vanderhaeghe are among the short-fiction writers who discuss their work.

Lynch, Gerald. *The One and the Many: English-Canadian Short Story Cycles.* Toronto: University of Toronto Press, 2001. A literary-historical survey of the Canadian short-story cycle. Lynch examines Stephen Leacock's "Sunshine Sketches of a Little Town" in order to describe how a short-story cycle conveys meaning and the significant function of its concluding story. He then examines six other cycles, including works by Duncan Campbell Scott, Frederick Philip Grove, and Alice Munro.

New, W. H. *Dreams of Speech and Violence: The Art of the Short Story in Canada and New Zealand.* Toronto: University of Toronto Press, 1987. An excellent analysis of the development of the short story and its relationship to the development of a Canadian national literary identity. The comparison between the short story in New Zealand and in Canada is interesting.

_____, ed. *Encyclopedia of Literature in Canada.* Toronto, Ont.: University of Toronto Press, 2002. A thousand-page reference covering the full panoply of Canada's literary heritage. Includes discussions of literature in English and French, as well as

other languages, First Nation writers, and historical and cultural events that have influenced Canadian literature.

Nischik, Reingard M., ed. *The Canadian Short Story: Interpretations.* Rochester, N.Y.: Camden House, 2007. Collection of essays providing a comprehensive overview of Canadian short fiction. Includes a historical survey of the nation's short fiction and discussions of animal stories, the Canadian writer as an expatriate, Canadian modernism, prairie fiction, and the work of numerous writers, including Stephen Leacock, Frederick Philip Grove, Morley Callaghan, Ethel Wilson, Hugh Garner, Mordecai Richler, Mavis Gallant, Alice Munro, Margaret Laurence, Leon Rooke, and Carol Shields.

AUSTRALIA AND NEW ZEALAND SHORT FICTION

Bennett, Bruce. *Australian Short Fiction: A History.* St. Lucia, Qld..: University of Queensland Press, 2002. Examines short fiction of the nineteenth and twentieth centuries, including works by Henry Lawson and Steele Rudd.

_____. "Short Fiction and the Canon: Australia and Canada." *Antipodes* 7, no. 2 (1993): 109-114. A useful introductory essay, concentrating particularly on the "new" writing of the 1960's and 1970's.

Goldsworthy, Kerryn. "Short Fiction." In *The Penguin New Literary History of Australia*, edited by Laurie Hergenhan. Ringwood, Vic.: Penguin Australia, 1988. One of the few essays that covers the development of the Australian short story from the 1890's to the 1980's in detail, with attention paid to the form and its relationship to the development of a national literary identity.

Goodwin, Ken. *A History of Australian Literature.* Basingstoke, England: Macmillan, 1986. A useful general text that covers the development of the short story from the 1890's to the 1980's, with particular attention paid to the Social Realist writers of the 1940's and 1950's and the "new" writing of the 1960's and 1970's.

Hadgraft, Cecil, ed. *The Australian Short Story Before Lawson.* Melbourne, Vic.: Oxford University Press, 1986. A collection of early short stories with a comprehensive and entertaining introduction not only covering the early writing but also touching on the short story of the 1890's.

New, W. H. *Dreams of Speech and Violence: The Art of the Short Story in Canada and New Zealand.* Toronto: University of Toronto Press, 1987. An excellent analysis of the development of the short story and its relationship to the development of a New Zealand national literary identity. New provides an interesting general discussion of particular writers and close readings of stories by Katherine Mansfield and others. The comparison between the short story in New Zealand and in Canada is interesting.

Pierce, Peter, ed. *The Cambridge History of Australian Literature.* New York: Cambridge University Press, 2009. This overview of Australian literature contains two essays focusing on short fiction: "Short Story, 1890's to 1950," by Bruce Bennett, and "Short Story Since 1950," by Stephen Torre.

Wevers, Lydia. "The Short Story." In *The Oxford History of New Zealand Literature*, edited by Terry Sturm. Auckland, New Zealand: Oxford University Press, 1991. An excellent account of the development of the short story in New Zealand. Contains detailed discussions not only of the development of the form but also of individual writers and particular literary movements.

FRENCH SHORT FICTION

Bryant, David. *Short Fiction and the Press in France, 1829-1841: Followed by a Selection of Short Fiction from the Periodical and Daily Press.* Lewiston, N.Y.: Edwin Mellen Press, 1995. In the 1830's, changes in the form and distribution of French magazines and newspapers promoted the publication of short fiction, enabling editors and readers to shape the direction of French literature. Bryant examines this development, focusing his analysis on the short fiction published in two major reviews, *La Revue de Paris* and *La Revue des Deux Mondes*, and two leading newspapers, *La Presse* and *Le Siecle.*

Cogman, Peter. *Narration in Nineteenth Century French Short Fiction: Prosper Mérimée to Marcel Schwob.* Durham, England: University of Durham, 2002. Good examination of the technical aspects of narration and its development and different uses by French writers.

Engstrom, Alfred G. "The Formal Short Story in France and Its Development Before 1850." *Studies in Philology* 42 (1945): 627-639. After making distinctions between the nouvelle and the conte (a complex line of action versus a compressed one), Engstrom points out the lack of any significant examples of conte until Prosper Mérimée's "Mateo Falcone" (1829), the first formal short story in French literature. The only other significant contributors to the form before 1850 are Honoré de Balzac and Théophile Gautier.

Flower, John T., ed. *Short French Fiction: Essays on the Short Story in France in the Twentieth Century.* Exeter, England: University of Exeter Press, 1998. Essays discuss the contributions of the short story to French literature and culture. Defines the short story as a genre and charts its evolution in the twentieth century.

Smith, Horatio E. "The Development of Brief Narrative in Modern French Literature: A Statement of the Problem." *PMLA* 32 (1917): 583-597. Surveys the confusion between the conte and nouvelle and calls for a critical investigation of the practice and theory of the French forms similar to those published on the American short story and the German Nouvelle.

GERMAN-LANGUAGE SHORT FICTION

Decker, Craig, ed. *Austrian Identities: Twentieth-Century Short Fiction.* Riverside, Calif.: Ariadne Press, 2004. An anthology of short stories which depict Austrian characters whose lives and identities have been shaped by the historical events of the twentieth century. An inroductory essay, "Austrian Identities in a Twentieth-Century Landscape of Historical Change," provides an overview of the stories, which include works by Robert Musil, Ingeborg Bachman, Thomas Bernhard, and Hugo von Hofmannstahl.

Hutchinson, Peter, ed. *Landmarks in German Short Prose.* New York: Peter Lang, 2003. Collection of twelve essays analyzing *Novellen* and other forms of German-language short fiction published between 1810 and 1978. Includes analyses of works by Johann Wolfgang von Goethe, Heinrich von Kleist, Heinrich Heine, Thomas Mann, Franz Kafka, and Robert Walser,

Plouffe, Bruce. *The Post-War Novella in German Language Literature: An Analysis.* New York: AMS Press, 1998. Examines Novellen written after World World II, particularly works by Robert Walser, Rolf Hochhuth, and Friedrich Dürrenmatt. Compares the German-language Novella to its Anglo-Saxon counterparts--the short story and novella.

Remak, Henry H. H. *Structural Elements of the German Novella from Goethe to Thomas Mann.* New York: Peter Lang, 2001. Comprehensive analysis of the German Novelle, examining how this genre of short fiction evolved from the classicism of authors like Johann Wolfgang von Goethe to works of Romanticism by such writers as Heinrich von Kleist and E. T. A. Hoffmann to the naturalism of Gerhart Hauptmann and to twentieth century Novellen by Thomas Mann, Robert Musil, Franz Kafka, and Günter Grass, among others.

Steirle, Karl-Heinz. "Story as Exemplum--Exemplum as Story: On the Pragmatics and Poetics of Narrative Texts." In *New Perspectives in German Literary Criticism*, edited by Richard E. Amacher and Victor Lange. Translated by David Wilson et al. Princeton, N.J.: Princeton University Press, 1979. A generic discussion of how readers move from exemplum, which is definite, to story, which is relativistic. Argues that if one wants to find the link between the short story and the exemplum, the answer must be found in Immanuel Kant's theory of discernment, that is, the ability to realize the particular as contained in the general.

Weing, Siegfried. *The German Novella: Two Centuries of Criticism.* Columbia, S.C.: Camden House, 1994. Surveys literary criticism and conflicting theories about the form and function of the German Novella from the genre's origins until 1991.

ITALIAN SHORT FICTION

Hainswoth, Peter, and David Robey, eds. The Oxford Companion to Italian Literature. Oxford, England: Oxford University Press, 2002. A comprehensive treatment of the subject in English.

Pacifici, Sergio. A Guide to Contemporary Italian Literature. New York: World, 1962. Though dated, this book is recommended for its outstanding coverage of post-World War II Italian writers.

Panizza, Letizia, and Sharon Wood, eds. *A History of Women's Writing in Italy*. New York: Cambridge University Press, 2000. Helpful essays by a variety of scholars outlining the importance of women in Italian belles-lettres.

Riva, Massimo, ed. *Italian Tales: An Anthology of Contemporary Italian Fiction.* New Haven, Conn.: Yale University Press, 2004. In addition to the stories, this anthology features an introduction providing an informative overview of contemporary Italian short fiction.

ROMANIAN SHORT FICTION

Orlich, Ileana Alexandra. *Silent Bodies: (Re)discovering the Women of Romanian Short Fiction.* Boulder, Colo.: East European Monographs, 2002. Examines how Romanian short fiction depicts gender issues, including the social organization of sex, obligatory heterosexuality, and constraints on female sexuality. Examines four representative short stories by Romanian writers Ioan Slavici, Ioan Luca Caragiale, Mikhail Sadoveanu, and Liviu Rebreanu.

SCANDINAVIAN SHORT FICTION

Naess, Harald S., ed. *A History of Norwegian Literature.* Lincoln: University of Nebraska Press in cooperation with the American-Scandinavian Foundation, 1993.

Neijmann, Daisy, ed. *A History of Icelandic Literature.* Lincoln: University of Nebraska Press in cooperation with the American-Scandinavian Foundation, 2006.

Rossel, Sven H., ed. *A History of Danish Literature.* Lincoln: University of Nebraska Press in cooperation with the American-Scandinavian Foundation, 1992.

Schoolfield, George C., ed. *A History of Finland's Literature.* Lincoln: University of Nebraska Press in cooperation with the American-Scandinavian Foundation, 1998.

Warme, Lars G., ed. *A History of Swedish Literature.* Lincoln: University of Nebraska Press in cooperation with the American-Scandinavian Foundation, 1996. This series of books provides comprehensive historical overviews of the literature from their respective countries. Although they do not contain individual chapters about short fiction, references to short fiction are listed in their indexes.

AFRICAN SHORT FICTION

Balogun, F. Odun. *Tradition and Modernity in the African Short Story: An Introduction to a Literature in Search of Critics*. New York: Greenwood Press, 1991. In part 1 of this study, Balogun conducts a general survey of African short fiction, discussing its themes, structure of irony, linguistic characteristics, and other components. Part 2 provides a close reading of short stories by two African writers-- Chinua Achebe and Taban lo Liyong.

Gaylard, Gerald. *After Colonialism: African Postmodernism and Magical Realism*. Johannesburg: Wits University, 2006. Gaylard describes how two genres of fiction--postmodernism and Magical Realism--provide reflections on and responses to colonialism in Africa. He argues that genres such as Magical Realism, which allow writers freedom and release, provide African writers a sense of liberty in an era of colonization and assimilation.

MacKenzie, Craig. *The Oral-Style South African Short Story in English: A. W. Drayson to H. C. Bosman*. Atlanta, Ga.: Rodopi, 1999. Examines a particular type of South African short story known as the fireside tale, the skaz narrative, or the oral-style story, which has its origin in nineteenth century hunting and camp-fire tales. Focuses on the stories of A. W. Drayson and Herman Charles Bosman but also discusses works by other South African writers.

AFRICAN, INDIAN, AND CARIBBEAN SHORT FICTION IN ENGLISH

Fallon, Erin, et al., eds. *A Reader's Companion to the Short Story in English*. Westport, Conn.: Greenwood Press, 2001. Produced under the auspices of the Society for the Study of the Short Story, this collection of essays, aimed at the general reader, provides brief biographies of numerous writers and analyses of their short fiction. Some of the writers examined are Chinua Achebe, Margaret Atwood, Morley Callaghan, Angela Carter, Janet Frame, Mavis Gallant, Nadine Gordimer, Elizabeth Jolley,

Alice Munro, R. K. Narayan, Jean Rhys, Salman Rushdie, and Olive Senior.

Hunter, Adrian. *The Cambridge Introduction to the Short Story in English*. Cambridge, England: Cambridge University Press, 2007. Hunter begins his literary history in the nineteenth century, describing the form and cultural context of short fiction from that time until the late twentieth century. He discusses the works of Charles Dickens, Thomas Hardy, Rudyard Kipling, Joseph Conrad, James Joyce, Virginia Woolf, Katherine Mansfield, Samuel Beckett, Frank O'Connor, Seán O'Faoláin, Elizabeth Bowen, V. S. Pritchett, Angela Carter, Ian McEwan, Chinua Achebe, James Kelman, Alice Munro, and others.

Malcolm, Cheryl Alexander, and David Malcolm, eds. *A Companion to the British and Irish Short Story*. Malden, Mass.: Wiley-Blackwell, 2008. Collection of essays focusing on British and Irish short fiction from 1880 to the present day. Includes discussions of detective and crime stories, ghost stories, science-fiction tales, and gay and lesbian short stories, as well as women's writing. Analyzes the work of Rudyard Kipling, Robert Louis Stevenson, Thomas Hardy, Joseph Conrad, Saki, James Joyce, D. H. Lawrence, Virginia Woolf, Katherine Mansfield, Frank O'Connor, Liam O'Flaherty, Elizabeth Bowen, Ben Okri, Salman Rushdie, Hanif Kureishi, Alan Sillitoe, and John McGehern, among others.

ARABIC SHORT FICTION

Akers, Deborah S., and Abubaker A. Bagader, eds. and trans. *Oranges in the Sun: Short Stories from the Arabian Gulf*. Boulder, Colo.: Lynne Rienner, 2008. Following Akers's introduction, in which she discusses the origins and development of the short story in the Arabian Gulf region, this volume contains a selection of short stories that have been translated into English. These stories are written by authors from Saudi Arabia, Yemen, Oman, the United Arab Emirates, Bahrain, Qatar, and Kuwait.

Chorin, Ethan, comp. and trans. *Translating Libya: The Modern Libyan Short Story*. London: Saqi, in association with London Middle East Institute, School of Oriental and African Studies, 2008. Curious about the lack of "place" in Libya's contemporary short fiction, Chorin compiled and translated this collection of stories that mention Libyan cities and landmarks. He interprets the stories to describe their common characteristics and their depiction of the Libyan psyche, economy, and the status of women, minorities, and immigrants.

Hafez, Sabry. *The Quest for Identities: The Development of the Modern Arabic Short Story.* San Francisco: Saqi, 2007. Analyzes work by Yusuf Idris, Abd al-Rahman al-Sharqawi, Edwar al-Kharrat, and other contemporary authors to determine if the short story genre provides readers with a wider understanding of Arabic culture. Examines how writers in one Arabic-speaking country have influenced writers in another.

Shaheen, Mohammad. *The Modern Arabic Short Story: Shahrazad Returns.* 2d ed., rev. and expanded. New York: Palgrave Macmillan, 2002. The first part of this study provides an extensive analysis of contemporary Arabic short fiction, comparing it to classic Arabic storytelling and discussing the shared use of myth and folklore in Arabic short stories and poems. Part 2 features a selection of short stories that have been translated into English,

Yazici, Hüseyin. *The Short Story in Modern Arabic Literature.* Cairo: G. B. O., 2004. A literary historical survey of Arabic short fiction written in the nineteenth and twentieth centuries.

BRAZILIAN SHORT FICTION

Balderston, Daniel, ed. *The Latin American Short Story: An Annotated Guide to Anthologies and Criticism.* Westport, Conn.: Greenwood Press, 1992. Organizes the enormous body of short-story anthologies from the nineteen countries of Spanish America and Brazil for systematic study. The main section comprises annotated listings of 1,302 short-story anthologies; a second section comprises annotated bibliographies of criticism of the short story. Includes bibliographical references and an index.

Echevarría, Roberto González, and Enrique Pupo-Walker, eds. *The Cambridge History of Latin American Literature.* 3 vols. New York: Cambridge University Press, 1996. Volume 3 covers Brazilian literature. Includes bibliographical references and an index.

Foster, David William, ed. *Handbook of Latin American Literature.* New York: Garland, 1992. Offers separate essays on the literature of all Latin American countries, including French and Creole Haiti and Portuguese Brazil, written by scholars who focus on dominant issues and major movements, figures, and works, with emphasis on sociocultural and interpretive assessments. Includes bibliographical references and an index.

Jackson, K. David, ed. *Oxford Anthology of the Brazilian Short Story.* New York: Oxford University Press, 2006. Contains a selection of short stories published from the 1880's through the late twentieth century, including works by Joaquim Maria Machado de Assis, Jorge Amado, Clarice Lispector, and João Guimarães Rosa. A lengthy introductory essay, "World World Vast World of the Brazilian Short Story," provides background information about the history and development of this genre in Brazil .

Lopes, M. Angélica, ed. *The Brazilian Short Story in the Late Twentieth Century: A Selection from Nineteen Authors.* Lewiston, N.Y.: Edwin Mellen Press, 2009. An introductory essay to this anthology provides an overview of Brazilian fiction and of sociopolitical developments in this nation from the late nineteenth through the twentieth century. In addition, each story is accompanied by a brief biography of the author and a bibliography of his or her works.

CARIBBEAN SHORT FICTION

Arnold, A. James, Julio Rodríguez-Luis, and J. Michael Dash, eds. *A History of Literature in the Caribbean.* Philadelphia: J. Benjamins, 1994. A historical and critical look at literature from this region. Includes bibliographical references and an index.

Bloom, Harold, ed. *Caribbean Women Writers.* Philadelphia: Chelsea House, 1997. A thorough examination of contemporary, female Caribbean authors who write in English, including Jean Rhys, Jamaica Kincaid, Beryl Gilroy, and Edwidge Danticat. Includes bibliographical references and an index.

Dvořák, Marta, and W. H. New, eds. *Tropes and Territories: Short Fiction, Postcolonial Readings, Canadian Writing in Context.* Montreal: McGill-Queen's University Press, 2007. Examines contemporary short fiction written in Canada and the Commonwealth, including works by Native Canadians, Maoris, and writers Katherine Mansfield, Janet Frame, Alice Munro, Mavis Gallant, R. K. Narayan, and David Malouf, among others. Two of the essays provide general analyses of short fiction from South Asia and Australia, while another discusses Caribbean diasporic writing.

Evans, Lucy, Mark McWatt, and Emma Smith, eds. *The Caribbean Short Story: Critical Perspectives.* Leeds, England: Peepal Tree Press, 2011. Collection of twenty-five original essays that examine the significance of short fiction to Caribbean culture of the twentieth and twenty-first centures. Some of the essays discuss the publishing histories of island-specific literary cultures; genre, narrative, and orality in Caribbean short fiction; and the sociopolitical contexts of short stories from this region.

Foster, David William, ed. *Handbook of Latin American Literature.* New York: Garland, 1992. Offers separate essays on the literature of all Latin American countries, including French and Creole Haiti and Portuguese Brazil, written by scholars who focus on dominant issues and major movements, figures, and works, with emphasis on sociocultural and interpretive assessments. Includes bibliographical references and an index.

CHINESE SHORT FICTION

Chiang, Sing-chen Lydia. *Collecting the Self: Body and Identity in Strange Tale Collections of Late Imperial China.* Boston: Brill, 2005. A Freudian interpretation of short-story collections by Pu Songling and two of his contemporaries. Examines how the era's "strange tales" about ghosts, animal spirits, gods, monsters, and other supernatural phenomena were a means of writing about suppressed cultural anxieties, gender issues, and the authors' self-identity.

Huters, Theodore, ed. *Reading the Modern Chinese Short Story.* Armonk, N.Y.: M. E. Sharpe, 1990. Collection of essays analyzing six contemporary short stories, including works by Mao Dun, Lao She, Xiao Jun, and Sui Tuo.

CUBAN SHORT FICTION

Alvarez, José B IV. *Contestatory Cuban Short Story of the Revolution.* Lanham, Md.: University Press of America, 2002. Examines counter-cultural narratives written by Cuban writers after that nation's revolution. Alvarez provides a historical and cultural context for these stories and a history of the short story in Cuba. He also discusses homoeroticism in Cuban short fiction and the works of the novísimos, writers born after the revolution whose works began to appear in the late 1980's.

Whitfield, Esther. "Covering for Banknotes: Books, Money, and the Cuban Short Story." In *Cuban Currency: The Dollar and "Special Period" Fiction.* Minneapolis: University of Minnesota Press, 2008. After the collapse of the Soviet Union in the 1990's, Cuba instated the U.S. dollar as domestic currency, the country was opened to foreign markets, and the nation's culture boomed. Whitfield examines the impact of these developments upon Cuban literature, devoting a chapter to short fiction's depiction of money and cross-cultural economic relations.

INDIAN SHORT FICTION

Bande, Usha, and Atma Ram. *Woman in Indian Short Stories: Feminist Perspective.* Jaipur, India: Rawat, 2003. Examines women writers' depiction of the "new woman" in Marathi, Hindi, Punjab, and Indian-English short stories published from the mid-1940's through the late 1990's.

Daiya, Krishna. *Post-Independence Women Short Story Writers in Indian English.* New Delhi, India: Sarup and Sons, 2006. Provides an overview of the works of women short-story writers, analyzing the themes, characterization, and styles of their stories. Assesses the status of the short fiction genre and describes the contributions of women's short fiction to the genre and to Indian literature. Some of the writers whose works are analyzed are Shashi Deshpande, Anita

Desai, Jhumpa Lahiri, Githa Hariharan, and Ruth Prawer Jhabvala.

Mehta, Kamal, ed. *The Twentieth Century Indian Short Story in English*. New Delhi, India: Creative Books, 2004.Collection of essays analyzing short-fiction by Indian writers, including R. K. Narayan, Raja Rao, Gautam Bhatia, Jhumpa Lahiri, and Salman Rushdie. Includes an introductory essay chronicling the emergence and growth of the Indian short story in English.

Melwani, Murli. *Indian English Stories: From Colonial Beginnings to Post-Modern Times*. Calcutta: Sampark, 2007. Charts the historical development of the Indian short story in English. Includes discussions of short-story writers, including Raja Rao, R. K. Narayan, and Ruth Prawer Jhabvala.

Prasad, Amar Nath, and S. John Peter Joseph, eds. *Indian Short Stories in English: Critical Explorations*. New Delhi, India: Sarup, 2008. Collection of more than twenty critical research papers analyzing the works of short-story writers, including Mulk Raj Anand, R. K. Narayan, Raja Rao, Shashi Deshpande, Rusking Bond, Vishnu Prabhakar, Jhumpa Lahiri, and Sarah Joseph. Also provides a historical overview of the Indian short story in English.

Ramanan, Mohan, and P. Sailaja, eds. *English and the Indian Short Story: Essays in Criticism*. New Delhi, India: Orient Longman, 2000. Collection of essays examining the short-story genre in India and its relationship to the English language and to English-language literature. Some of the essays discuss the impact of colonialism on Indian short fiction, how English has shaped Indian short-story writing, and the Indian diaspora; other essays provide feminist perspectives of short stories by women writers.

JAPANESE SHORT FICTION

Katō, Shūichi. *A History of Japanese Literature*. 3 vols. Tokyo: Kodansha International, 1979. A wide-ranging study that pays special heed to the sociohistorical background of Japan's literary development. A good counterbalance to Donald Keene's literary history.

Keene, Donald. *Seeds in the Heart: Japanese Literature from the Earliest Times to the Late Sixteenth Century*. New York: Henry Holt, 1993.

_____. *World Within Walls: Japanese Literature of the Pre-Modern Era*. New York: Holt, Rinehart and Winston, 1976.

_____. *Dawn to the West: Japanese Literature in the Modern Era*. New York: Columbia University Press, 1984. A three-volume English-language history of Japanese literature up to Yukio Mishima written by a leading scholar.

Tsuruta, Kinya, and Thomas Swann, eds. *Approaches to the Modern Japanese Short Story*. Tokyo: Waseda University Press, 1982. An immensely useful critical study of thirty-four stories by Japanese writers.

LATIN AMERICAN SHORT FICTION

Balderston, Daniel, ed. *The Latin American Short Story: An Annotated Guide to Anthologies and Criticism*. Westport, Conn.: Greenwood Press, 1992. Organizes the enormous body of short-story anthologies from the nineteen countries of Spanish America and Brazil for systematic study. The main section comprises annotated listings of 1,302 short-story anthologies; a second section comprises annotated bibliographies of criticism of the short story. Includes bibliographical references and an index.

Brushwood, John S. "The Spanish American Short Story from Quiroga to Borges." In *The Latin American Short Story: A Critical History*, edited by Margaret Sayers Peden. Boston: Twayne, 1983. Argues that Horacio Quiroga was the first Spanish American writer to pay close attention to how a story is created. Provides a historical survey of Spanish American short fiction, in which the late 1920's and early 1930's were characterized by innovative narration, a movement to regionalism took place in the mid-1930's, and a return to innovation and cosmopolitanism characterized the early 1940's.

Del George, Dana. *The Supernatural in Short Fiction of the Americas: The Other World in the New World*. Westport, Conn.: Greenwood Press, 2001. Describes how cultural encounters between European and indigenous societies and between "scientific materialism" and "premodern supernaturalism" resulted in the creation of new narrative forms, including supernatural short fiction.

Echevarría, Roberto González, and Enrique Pupo-Walker, eds. *The Cambridge History of Latin American Literature*. 3 vols. New York: Cambridge University Press, 1996. Volume 1 covers the period from discovery to modernism, volume 2 covers the twentieth century, and volume 3 covers Brazilian literature. Includes bibliographical references and an index.

Erro-Peralta, Nora, and Caridad Silva-Núñez, eds. *Beyond the Border: A New Age in Latin American Women's Fiction*. Pittsburgh, Pa.: Cleis Press, 1991. Covers works by Latin American female writers. Includes bibliographical references.

Foster, David William, ed. *Handbook of Latin American Literature*. New York: Garland, 1992. Offers separate essays on the literature of all Latin American countries, including French and Creole Haiti and Portuguese Brazil, written by scholars who focus on dominant issues and major movements, figures, and works, with emphasis on sociocultural and interpretive assessments. Includes bibliographical references and an index.

Lindstrom, Naomi. "The Spanish American Short Story from Echeverria to Quiroga." In *The Latin American Short Story: A Critical History*, edited by Margaret Sayers Peden. Boston: Twayne, 1983. Discusses the first Latin American short story, Estaban Echeverría's 1838 "The Slaughtering Grounds." Chronicles the movement from Romanticism to realism and naturalism and then to modernism. Notes that while Edgar Allan Poe and Guy de Maupassant were not taken so seriously elsewhere, they were taken more seriously in Latin America, where readers see these writers as providing channels to alternate realms of experience.

McMurray, George R. "The Spanish American Short Story from Borges to the Present." In *The Latin American Short Story: A Critical History*, edited by Margaret Sayers Peden. Boston: Twayne, 1983. Discusses Jorge Luis Borges as a writer who ushered in a new literary era in South America and describes the shift to political and social problems during the

1950's. Argues that the most talented Spanish American writer since Borges is Julio Cortázar from Argentina. Also examines works by José Donoso and Carlos Fuentes.

Ocasio, Rafael. *Literature of Latin America*. Wesport, CT: Greenwood Press, 2004. Examines Latin American literary production from colonial times to the twenty-first century.

Partnoy, Alicia, ed. *You Can't Drown the Fire: Latin American Women Writing in Exile*. Pittsburgh, Pa.: Cleis Press, 1988. Covers twentieth century female writers whose works have been translated into English. Includes bibliographical references.

Plimpton, George, ed. *Latin American Writers at Work*. New York: Modern Library, 2003. A compilation of conversations and anecdotes with contemporary Latin American authors that provides a glimpse into their literary ideas.

Smith, Verity, ed. *Encyclopedia of Latin American Literature*. Chicago: Fitzroy Dearborn, 1997. Contains entries on writers, works, and topics relating to the literature of Latin America, including survey articles on all the continent's countries. Includes bibliographical references and an index.

Swanson, Philip. "Culture Wars: Ways of Reading Latin American Fiction." In *Latin American Fiction: A Short Introduction*. Malden, Mass.: Blackwell, 2005. Offers relevant information to better understand contemporary Latin American fiction.

RUSSIAN SHORT FICTION

Connolly, Julian. "The Russian Short Story, 1880-1917." In *The Russian Short Story: A Critical History*, edited by Charles A. Moser. Boston: Twayne, 1986. Most of this essay focuses on Nikolai Leskov, Anton Chekhov, Maxim Gorky, Ivan Bunin, and Leonid Andreyev. Connolly briefly discusses the Symbolist movement's influence on Russian literature at the end of the nineteenth century.

Cornwell, Neil, ed. *The Society Tale in Russian Literature: From Odoevskii to Tolstoi*. Atlanta, Ga.: Rodopi, 1998. Collection of essays about the Russian "society tale," a genre of nineteenth century short fiction that examined the individual in relation to his or her society. Focuses on the development of this genre from around 1820 until later in the century, when the genre was subsumed by the realist novel. Some of the writers whose works are examined are Alexander Pushkin, Leo Tolstoy, Vladimir Odoevskii, and Maria Zhukhova.

Kagan-Kans, Eva. "The Russian Short Story, 1850-1880." In *The Russian Short Story: A Critical History*, edited by Charles A. Moser. Boston: Twayne, 1986. Focuses primarily on Ivan Turgenev, Leo Tolstoy, Fyodor Dostoevski, and the radical, populist, and feminist writers of the period. Representative stories of the writers are discussed and analyzed in terms of their contributions to the form and their relationship to, or reflection of, Russian social life at the time.

May, Charles E. "Chekhov and the Modern Short Story." In *A Chekhov Companion*, edited by Toby Clyman. Westport, Conn.: Greenwood Press, 1985. A detailed analysis of Anton Chekhov's influence on the development of the modern short story. Isolates Chekhov's most important innovations in the form and then shows how these elements have been further used and developed by such modern writers as Katherine Mansfield, Ernest Hemingway, Bernard Malamud, Raymond Carver, and others.

Moser, Charles A. ed. *The Russian Short Story: A Critical History*. Boston: Twayne, 1986. Surveys the development of the Russian short story from 1830 to 1980. Analyzes the works of short-story writers, including Alexander Pushkin. Argues that the short story might have developed as a genre that combined prose and verse.

Neuhauser, Rudolf. "The Russian Short Story, 1917-1980." In *The Russian Short Story: A Critical History*, edited by Charles A. Moser. Boston: Twayne, 1986. Discussion of postrevolution writers in Russia, such as Yevgeny Zamyatin, as well as the influence of Russian Formalist critics and writers, such as Viktor Shklovsky and Boris Eikhenbaum. A brief discussion of Isaac Babel is included here, although his influence on the short story as a form should probably receive more attention than this. Separate sections are devoted to Russian literature and World War II, the thaw after the death of Joseph Stalin, the woman question, and science prose and village prose.

O'Toole, L. Michael. *Structure, Style, and Interpretation in the Russian Short Story*. New Haven, Conn.: Yale University Press, 1982. An analysis of a few major stories by Nikolai Leskov, Nikolai Gogol, Alexander Pushkin, Maxim Gorky, Ivan Turgenev, and Anton Chekhov in terms of the Russian Formalist theories of Viktor Shklovsky, Boris Eikhenbaum, Boris Tomashevsky, Mikhail Bakhtin, and Vladimir Propp and the structuralist theories of Roland Barthes and Tzvetan Todorov. The introduction provides a general methodological introduction to interpretation through structural analysis.

Parts, Lyudmila, ed. *The Russian Twentieth-Century Short Story: A Critical Companion*. Brighton, Mass.: Academic Studies Press, 2010. Collection of essays analyzing short stories by Anton Chekhov, Ivan Bunin, Isaac Babel, Vladimir Nabokov, Varlam Shalamov, and other writers. Parts's introduction discusses the short story as "the genre of cultural transition."

Terras, Victor. "The Russian Short Story: 1830-1850." In *The Russian Short Story: A Critical History*, edited by Charles A. Moser. Boston: Twayne, 1986. Points out that 1830 was a watershed in the history of Russian literature in that it marked the end of the golden age of poetry and the shift to prose fiction, particularly short fiction. Discusses the Romantic origins of short fiction in Russia with Alexander Pushkin, the transition to psychological realism with Mikhail Lermontov, the significant contributions of the stories of Nikolai Gogol, the transition to the so-called natural school, and the early works of Fyodor Dostoevski and Ivan Turgenev.

SHORT FICTION IN TAMIL

Gros, François. *Deep Rivers: Selected Writings on Tamil Literature*. Translated by M.P. Boseman, edited by Kannan M. and Jennifer Clare. Berkeley: Tamil Chair, Department of South and Southeast Asian Studies, University of California, 2009. Includes an essay entitled "Tamil Short Stories: An Introduction."

SHORT FICTION IN URDU

Suhrawardy, Shaista Akhtar Bano. *A Critical Survey of the Development of the Urdu Novel and Short Story*. Karachi, Pakistan: Oxford University Press, 2006. Part 3 focuses on the Urdu short story. After a brief history of the short story in European literature, Suhrawardy chronicles the development of Urdu short fiction from the 1870's through the present day, including discussions of women short-story writers, modern short fiction, and the future of the Urdu novel and short story.

SOUTHEAST ASIAN SHORT FICTION

Chee, Tham Seong, ed. *Essays on Literature and Society in Southeast Asia*. Singapore: Singapore University Press, 1981. Many of the essays cover the development, impact, and relevance of the short story in select Southeast Asian nations.

Davidson, Jeremy, and Helen Cordell, eds. *The Short Story in South East Asia: Aspects of a Genre*. London: School of Oriental and African Studies, University of London, 1982. One of the first sustained literary studies of the short story in Southeast Asia. Provides a good historical introduction to the topic, with bibliography and notes for each essay.

Patke, Rajeev S., and Philip Holden, eds. *The Routledge Concise History of Southeast Asian Writing in English*. New York: Routledge, 2010. Discusses short stories written in English from the Philippines, Malaysia, and Singapore. A subchapter discusses fiction by nonnative writers that is set in Southeast Asia.

Smyth, David. *The Canon in Southeast Asian Literatures*. Richmond, England: Curzon Press, 2000. Collection of essays which discuss the importance of short stories for the literary canon of select Southeast Asian countries and their relevance in that nation's literary tradition and culture.

Yamada, Teri Shaffer, ed. *Modern Short Fiction of Southeast Asia: A Literary History*. Ann Arbor, Michigan: Association for Asian Studies, 2009. Excellent collection of eleven outstanding essays that cover the development of the short story in almost every Southeast Asian nation and discuss key authors and exemplary texts. Very informative, with a concise introduction by the editor.

_____. *Virtual Lotus: Modern Fiction of Southeast Asia*. Ann Arbor: University of Michigan Press, 2002. The best introduction to the topic. Gives both a concise, critical overview of the development of the short story and a well-chosen sample of stories for every Southeast Asian country but Timor-Leste.

SOUTH KOREAN SHORT FICTION

Holstein, John, trans. *A Moment's Grace: Stories from Korea in Transition*. Ithaca, N.Y.: Cornell University East Asia Program, 2009. The stories, published from 1936 through 1999, depict how South Koreans were affected by the country's modernization, including its liberation from Japan in 1945 and the Seoul Olympics of 1988. Includes a chapter that provides background about the political and social context of these stories.

TYPES OF SHORT FICTION

MODERNIST SHORT FICTION

Childs, Peter. *Modernism*. 2d ed. New York: Routledge, 2008. Chronicles the origins of the modernist movement and describes its impact on late nineteenth and early twentieth century literature. Devotes a chapter to the short story.

Goldberg, Michael E. "The Synchronic Series as the Origin of the Modernist Short Story." *Studies in Short Fiction* 33 (Fall, 1996): 515-527. Goldberg suggests that the cumulative power of modernist collections of stories, such as James Joyce's *Dubliners* (1914) and Ernest Hemingway's *In Our Time* (1924, 1925), is modeled after a synchronic series of stories innovated by Sir Arthur Conan Doyle.

Head, Dominic. *The Modernist Short Story*. Cambridge: Cambridge University Press, 1992. An examination of the short story's formal characteristics from a theoretical framework derived from Louis Althusser and Mikhail Bakhtin. Argues that the short story's emphasis on literary artifice lends itself to modernist experimentalism. Illustrates this thesis with chapters on James Joyce, Tobias Woolf, Katherine Mansfield, and Wyndham Lewis.

POSTMODERN SHORT FICTION

Clark, Miriam Marty. "After Epiphany: American Stories in the Postmodern Age." *Style* 27 (Fall, 1993): 387-394. Argues that contemporary short stories can no longer be read in terms of epiphany. Claims that critics must develop a new reading strategy, shifting from metaphoric ways of meaning to metonymic ones to redefine the short story in its postmodern context.

Ifterkharrudin, Farhat, et al., eds. *Postmodern Approaches to the Short Story*. Westport, Conn.: Praeger, 2003. This volume, created under the auspices of the Society for the Study of the Short Story, analyzes elements of postmodernism in the works of Jorge Luis Borges, Italo Calvino, Katherine Mansfield, Henry James, Janette Turner Hospital, Jean Toomer, Homi K. Bhabba, and other writers.

_____. *The Postmodern Short Story: Forms and Issues*. Westport, Conn.: Praeger, 2003. Created under the auspices of the Society for the Study of the Short Story, this collection of essays demonstrates how postmodernism has altered the styles and themes of short fiction. Includes analyses of the personal essay, the nonfiction short story, Canadian and American postmodern stories, and works of short fiction by Sandra Cisneros, Lelie Marmon Silko, Joyce Carol Oates, Lorrie Moore, Thom Jones, Tom Paine, Denis Johnson, Edmund White, Ernest Hemingway, Richard Ford, Richard Brautigam, and R. R. R. Dhlomo.

MINIMALIST SHORT FICTION

Bell, Madison Smartt. "Less Is Less: The Dwindling American Short Story." *Harpers*, April, 1986, 64-69. Discusses several collections of short stories by minimalist writers and points out weaknesses, such as lack of plot and trivial themes.

Campbell, Ewing. "How Minimal Is Minimalism?" *In The Tales We Tell: Perspectives on the Short Story*, edited by Barbara Lounsberry et al. Westport, Conn.: Greenwood Press, 1998. A brief, suggestive essay which tries to define minimalist short fiction not in terms of length but in terms of the demands it makes on the reader. Argues that minimalist stories arrange significant details in such a way that the brain must supply missing information.

Hallett, Cynthia J. "Minimalism and the Short Story." *Studies in Short Fiction* 33 (Fall, 1996): 487-495. Defines minimalism, summarizes the negative connotations of the label "minimalist writer," and points out that the minimalist short story makes connections through intricate patterns that reveal meaning under the surface. Analyzes Mary Robison's "Yours" and Amy Hempel's "In a Tub" as exemplary of minimalist short stories.

Herzinger, Kim. "Minimalism as Postmodernism: Some Introductory Notes." *New Orleans Review* 16 (1989) 73-81. A survey of techniques used in minimalist fiction. Discusses what critics have said about minimalism and compares this style of writing to postmodernism.

March-Russell, Paul. "Minimalism/Dirty Realism/Hyperrealism." In *The Short Story: An Introduction*. Edinburgh, Edinburgh University Press, 2009. Gives an informative overview of minimalism and shows how the realism used in minimalism is similar to elements found in postmodern writing.

Sodowsky, Roland. "The Minimalist Short Story: Its Definition, Writers, and (Small) Heyday." *Studies in Short Fiction* 33 (Fall, 1996): 529-540. A historical survey of minimalism's dominance of the short-story marketplace in the late 1970's and early 1980's in the United States. Based on an examination of short stories in such magazines as *The New Yorker*, *The Atlantic Monthly*, *Esquire*, and *Harper's* between 1975 and 1990, Sodowsky isolates and summarizes some of the basic characteristics of the minimalist short story.

THE HYPERSTORY

Coover, Robert. "Storying in Hyperspace: `Linkages.'" *In The Tales We Tell: Perspectives on the Short Story*, edited by Barbara Lounsberry et al. Westport, Conn.: Greenwood Press, 1998. A discussion of the future of the short story in computerized hyperspace as a form that is nonsequential, multidirectional, and interactive. Discusses linked short fictional pieces in the past in the Bible, in medieval romances, and by Giovanni Boccaccio, Miguel de Cervantes, and Geoffrey Chaucer.

May, Charles E. "HyperStory: Teaching Short Fiction with Computers." In *The Tales We Tell: Perspectives on the Short Story*, edited by Barbara Lounsberry et al. Westport, Conn.: Greenwood Press, 1998. Describes HyperStory, a computer program developed by the author, which teaches students how to read short fiction more carefully and thoughtfully. Uses Edgar Allan Poe's "The Cask of Amontillado" as an example; attempts to explain, with the help of student comments, the success of the program.

MAGICAL REALISM

Benito, Jesús, Ana Ma Manzanas, and Begoña Simal. *Uncertain Mirrors: Magical Realisms in U.S. Ethnic Literatures*. New York: Rodopi, 2009. Examines Magical Realism in comparison to other literary movements, such as postmodernism and postcolonialism, Studies the use of Magical Realism in works by various authors, discussing how these writers represent themselves and their characters.

Bowers, Maggie Ann. *Magic(al) Realism*. London: Routledge, 2004. Serves as a helpful introduction to the Magical Realism movement. Bowers provides an overview of the genre and a close examination of the genre's connections with postcolonialism.

Faris, Wendy B. *Ordinary Enchantments: Magical Realism and the Remystification of Narrative*. Nashville, Tenn.: Vanderbilt University Press, 2004. Faris discusses key components of Magic Realist fiction and explores the work of authors from around the world. Each chapter focuses on a different aspect of Magical Realism, ranging from studies of narrative structure to the representation of women. Examines the importance of the Magical Realism tradition and its greater cultural implications.

Gaylard, Gerald. *After Colonialism: African Postmodernism and Magical Realism*. Johannesburg: Wits University, 2006. Gaylard describes how two genres of fiction--postmodernism and Magical Realism--provide reflections on and responses to colonialism in Africa. He argues that genres such as Magical Realism, which allow writers freedom and release, provide African writers a sense of liberty in an era of colonization and assimilation.

Hart, Stephen, and Wen-chin Ouyang, eds. *A Companion to Magical Realism*. Rochester, N.Y.: Tamesis, 2006. Collection of essays providing a close examination of the Magical Realism genre. Essayists trace the genre's history, its common symbols, and the politics of representation in close readings of texts, including works by Gabriel García Márquez, Jorge Luis Borges, and Isabel Allende.

Hegerfeldt, Anne C. *Lies That Tell the Truth: Magic Realism Seen Through Contemporary Fiction in Britain*. New York: Rodopi, 2005. Hegerfeldt discusses the debate over the definition of the genre and gives in-depth analyses of literary techniques employed often in Magical Realism.

Schroeder, Shannin. *Rediscovering Magical Realism in the Americas*. Westport, Conn.: Praeger, 2004. Examines works of Magical Realism in North and South America, paying special attention to North American Magical Realists. Schroeder acknowledges that the genre is often associated primarily or only with Latin and Central American writers and confronts this assumption with discussion of often neglected Magical Realist writers.

Takolander, Maria. Catching Butterflies: *Bringing Magical Realism to Ground*. Bern, Switzerland: Peter Lang, 2007. Takolander, like other scholars of Magical Realism, discusses the debate over how the genre should be defined, as well as its inception and its influence around the world. By examining historical context, Takolander attempts to provide answers to questions about the genre's presence, dominance, and influence in the literary world.

Zamora, Lois Parkinson, and Wendy B. Faris, eds. *Magical Realism: Theory, History, Community*. London: Duke University Press, 1995. Collection of essays about developments in the Magical Realism movement in art, literature, and other media.

FOLK TALES AND FAIRY TALES

Ashliman, D. L. *Folk and Fairy Tales: A Handbook*. Westport, Conn.: Greenwood Press, 2004. Ashliman provides readers with a history of fairy tales and folktales, examines the definitions of these genres, and explores some examples of each type of tale.

Bettelheim, Bruno. *The Uses of Enchantment: The Meaning and Importance of Fairy Tales*. New York: Alfred A. Knopf, 1977. This book discusses the tradition of and patterns present in fairy tales, then gives extensive analyses of well-known fairy tales, including "Hansel and Gretel," "Little Red Riding Hood," "Snow White," "Goldilocks and the Three Bears," "The Sleeping Beauty," and "Cinderella."

Bottigheimer, Ruth B. *Grimms' Bad Girls and Bold Boys: The Moral and Social Vision of the Tales*. New Haven, Conn.: Yale University Press, 1987. Bottigheimer discusses the fairy-tale tradition, including specific patterns of the characters' speech, how they endure punishment, their struggle for power, and the value systems implicit in these tales.

Georges, Robert A., and Michael Owen Jones. *Folkloristics: An Introduction*. Bloomington: Indiana University Press, 1995. Defines folklore as a historical tradition, focusing on its role in various cultures, in human psychology, and as a historical science.

Jones, Steven Swann. *The Fairy Tale: The Magic Mirror of the Imagination*. New York: Routledge, 2002. Provides a history of the fairy-tale genre, awarding special attention to the roles of men and women in fairy tales of the past and describing how those figures influenced more contemporary stories.

Leeming, David Adams, ed. *Storytelling Encyclopedia*. Phoenix, Ariz.: Oryx Press, 1997. Provides a general discussion of the storytelling tradition and a look at a number of countries and their specific cultural contributions to the tradition. In addition, there are brief entries regarding the most popular people and theories related to the oral and written traditions.

Propp, Vladimir. *Morphology of the Folktale*. Edited by Svatava Pirkova-Jakovson, translated by Laurence Scott. Bloomington: Indiana University Research Center, 1958. All formalist and structuralist studies of narrative owe a debt to this pioneering early twentieth century study. Using one hundred fairy tales, Propp defines the genre itself by analyzing the stories according to characteristic actions or functions.

_____. *Theory and History of Folklore*. Minneapolis: University of Minnesota Press, 1984. This collection of Propp's essays expands on his theory of the narrative that he presented in *Morphology of the Folktale*.

Tatar, Maria. *Off With Their Heads: Fairy Tales and the Culture of Childhood*. Princeton, N.J.: Princeton University Press, 1992. Tatar examines how important writers in the fairy-tale tradition revised these stories in order to be more didactic for children. She argues that the typical portrayal of children in fairy tales is problematic, especially since the contemporary target audience of fairy tales is children.

Thompson, Stith. *The Folktale*. New York: Dryden Press, 1946. Discusses the nature, theories, and form of the folktale and presents a varied collection of international tales. Selected are tales from many categories, such as the complex and the simple tale.

Warner, Marina. *From the Beast to the Blonde: On Fairy Tales and Their Tellers*. New York: Farrar, Straus and Giroux, 1994. Warner studies the characters whose role is the telling of fairy tales and analyzes gender roles, specifically those of women, including the typical portrayals of daughters, mothers, stepmothers, brides, and runaway girls

Zipes, Jack. *Fairy Tales and the Art of Subversion: The Classical Genre for Children and the Process of Civilization*. New York: Routledge, 1991. Zipes focuses on the didactic function of fairy tales, ranging from the work of the Grimm brothers to later fairy tales. He argues that the primary function of fairy tales is to instill morals and lessons in their child readers.

_____. *Fairy Tale as Myth, Myth as Fairy Tale*. Lexington: University Press of Kentucky, 1994. Examines the history of the fairy tale and its rise as the genre preceding the folktale. Discusses many well-known fairy tales and their role in society.

SCIENCE-FICTION SHORT STORIES

Amis, Kingsley. *New Maps of Hell: A Survey of Science Fiction*. London: Gollancz, 1960. A slightly superficial study by a critic whose relative ignorance of the genre's history is amply compensated by his insights into the distinctive forms and merits of short science fiction.

Ashley, Michael. *The Time Machines: The Story of the Science-Fiction Pulp Magazines from the Beginning to 1950*. Liverpool, England: Liverpool University Press, 2000.

_____. *Transformations: The Story of the Science-Fiction Magazines from 1950 to 1970, the History of the Science-Fiction Magazine*. Liverpool, England: Liverpool University Press, 2005.

_____. *Gateways to Forever: The Story of the Science-Fiction Magazines from 1970 to 1980, the History of the Science-Fiction Magazine*. Liverpool, England: Liverpool University Press, 2007. A three-volume history of the American and English pulp science-fiction magazines and the types of short stories they published.

Carter, Paul A. *The Creation of Tomorrow: Fifty Years of Magazine Science Fiction*. New York: Columbia University Press, 1977. An intelligent and well-informed history of the genre, which pays more careful attention to short fiction than most other books on the subject.

Clute, John, and Peter Nicholls. *The Encyclopedia of Science Fiction*. London: Orbit, 1993. By far the most comprehensive guide to the genre's history, practitioners, and themes.

Monk, Patricia. *Alien Theory: The Alien as Archetype in the Science Fiction Short Story*. Lanham, Md.: Scarecrow Press, 2006. Examines the use of alien characters in science-fiction short stories, including stories published in pulp magazines and contemporary works of the genre. Argues that the creation of the alien contributes to readers' understanding of their present-day lives and the future potential of their universe.

Scholes, Robert. *Structural Fabulation: An Essay on Fiction of the Future*. Notre Dame, Ind.: University of Notre Dame Press, 1975. Scholes argues that fabular futuristic fictions are more pertinent to present concerns in a fast-changing world than any fiction set in the present-day can be.

MYSTERY AND DETECTIVE SHORT FICTION

Haining, Peter. *The Classic Era of American Pulp Magazines*. Chicago: Chicago Review Press, 2001. This American edition of a book originally published in England provides historical, biographical, and literary analyses of pulp stories published in a number of genres. Chapter 3, "The Coming of the Hard-boiled Dicks," focuses on the "crime" pulps which published detective stories.

Herbert, Rosemary, ed. *The Oxford Companion to Crime and Mystery Writing*. New York: Oxford University Press, 1999. Essays and brief entries by hundreds of authorities span every conceivable aspect of the genre, making this an invaluable reference work for the student, casual reader, and scholar.

Kayman, Martin A. "The Short Story from Poe to Chesterton." In *The Cambridge Companion to Crime Fiction*, edited by Martin Priestman. Cambridge, England; Cambridge University Press, 2003. This section will be of particular interest to those looking for information about the development of the genre. The work as a whole is a useful reference tool for all genres, eras, styles, and writers of crime fiction in eighteenth, nineteenth, and twentieth century England and America.

Moore, Lewis D. *Cracking the Hard-Boiled Detective: A Critical History from the 1920's to the Present*. Jefferson, N.C.: McFarland, 2006. Traces the development of the private investigator subgenre from the early days of Raymond Chandler and Dashiell Hammett to current practitioners.

Rzepka, Charles J. *Detective Fiction*. Cambridge, England: Polity, 2005. Rzepka's well-written survey of the genre pays particular attention to the development of scientific investigative methods and cultural issues that shaped the genre. Includes specific essays on Edgar Allan Poe, Sir Arthur Conan Doyle, Dorothy Sayers, and Raymond Chandler.

Symons, Julian. *Bloody Murder*. New York: Mysterious Press, 1993. Written by a leading critic and mystery-fiction writer, this is one of the most thorough, balanced, and readable histories and critical analyses of the genre. Although a bit dated now, it remains indispensable both for the fan and for the student of crime fiction.

THE SHORT-STORY CYCLE

Davis, Rocío G. *Transcultural Reinventions: Asian American and Asian Canadian Short-Story Cycles.*

Toronto: TSAR, 2001. Examines how Asian American and Asian Canadian writers have adopted the short-story cycle as a means of both self-representation and empowerment. Some of the writers whose works are analyzed include Amy Tan, Rohinton Mistry, Sara Suleri, Garrett Hongo, Terry Watada, Sylvia Watanabe, M. G. Vassanji, and Wayson Choy.

Harde, Roxanne, ed. *Narratives of Community: Women's Short Story Sequences*. Newcastle, England: Cambridge Scholars, 2007. Collection of essays analyzing women's roles in domestic, social, and literary communities and how they attain their identities in these communities. Some of the writers whose works are examined include Sandra Cisneros, Margaret Laurence, Salwa Bakr, Mary Caponegro, Gloria Naylor, Elizabeth Gaskell, Virginia Woolf, Alice Munro, and Maxine Hong Kingston.

Ingram, Forrest L. "The Dynamics of Short Story Cycles." *New Orleans Review* 2 (1979): 7-12. A historical and critical survey and analysis of short stories that form a single unit, such as James Joyce's *Dubliners* (1914), Ernest Hemingway's *In Our Time* (1924, 1925), and Sherwood Anderson's *Winesburg, Ohio* (1919). Attempts to define some of the basic devices used in such cycles.

Kennedy, J. Gerald, ed. *Modern American Short Story Sequences: Composite Fictions and Fictive Communities*. Cambridge, England: Cambridge University Press, 1995. An anthology of essays by various critics on short-story sequence collections, such as Jean Toomer's *Cane* (1923), Ernest Hemingway's *In Our Time* (1924, 1925), William Faulkner's *Go Down, Moses* (1942), John Updike's *Olinger Stories: A Selection* (1964), Sherwood Anderson's *Winesburg, Ohio* (1919), and several others. Kennedy's introduction provides a brief survey of the short-story cycle, a definition of the cycle, and a discussion of the implications of the short-story sequence.

Kuttainen, *Victoria. Unsettling Stories: Settler Postcolonialism and the Short Story Composite*. Newcastle upon Tyne, England: Cambridge Scholars, 2010. Examines how the interconnected short-story collection has been used to express issues of postcolonialism in American, Canadian, and Australian literature. Analyzes works by Tim Winton, Margaret Laurence, William Faulkner, Stephen Leacock, Sherwood Anderson, Tim O'Brien, and others to describe how they describe the nature of the colonial settlement experience.

Lynch, Gerald. *The One and the Many: English-Canadian Short Story Cycles*. Toronto: University of Toronto Press, 2001. A literary-historical survey of the Canadian short-story cycle. Lynch examines Stephen Leacock's Sunshine Sketches of a Little Town in order to describe how a short-story cycle conveys meaning and the significant function of its concluding story. He then examines six other cycles, including works by Duncan Campbell Scott, Frederick Philip Grove, and Alice Munro.

Lundén, Rolf. *The United Stories of America: Studies in the Short Story Composite*. Amsterdam: Rodopi, 1999. Analyzes short-story cycles, focusing on the authors' strategies for closing these texts and attaining a sense of unity. Some of the authors who are examined include Eudora Welty, William Faulkner, Ernest Hemingway, and Sherwood Anderson.

Luscher, Robert M. "The Short Story Sequence: An Open Book." In *Short Story Theory at a Crossroads*, edited by Susan Lohafer and Jo Ellyn Clarey. Baton Rouge: Louisiana State University Press, 1989. Discusses the need for readers of story cycles, such as Winesburg, Ohio, to extend their drive to find a pattern to cover a number of individual sequences. Compares story cycles with mere aggregates of stories, as well as with novelistic sequences.

Nagel, James. *The Contemporary American Short-Story Cycle: The Ethnic Resonance of Genre*. Baton Rouge: Louisiana State University Press, 2001. Argues that the concentric plot of the short-story cycle lends itself particularly well to issues of ethnic assimilation. Demonstrates this argument by analyzing short-story cycles by eight authors: Louise Erdrich, Jamaica Kincaid, Susan Minot, Sandra Cisneros, Tim O'Brien, Julia Alvarez, Amy Tan, and Robert Olen Butler.

Pacht, Michelle. *The Subversive Storyteller: The Short Story Cycle and the Politics of Identity in America*. Newcastle upon Tyne, England: Cambridge Scholars, 2009. Analyzes the works of nineteenth and twentieth century American authors to demonstrate how they adapted the short-story cycle in order to convey controversial ideas without alienating readers and publishers. Focuses on short stories by Washington Irving, Nathaniel Hawthorne, Sarah Orne Jewett, Charles Waddell Chesnutt, Willa Cather, Henry James, Ernest Hemingway, William Faulkner, Flannery O'Connor, Raymond Carver, Maxine Hong Kingston, and Louise Erdrich.

SHORT FICTION AND WOMEN

Bande, Usha, and Atma Ram. *Woman in Indian Short Stories: Feminist Perspective*. Jaipur, India: Rawat, 2003. Examines women writers' depiction of the "new woman" in Marathi, Hindi, Punjab, and Indian-English short stories published from the mid-1940's through the late 1990's.

Bloom, Harold, ed. *Caribbean Women Writers*. Philadelphia: Chelsea House, 1997. A thorough examination of contemporary, female Caribbean authors who write in English, including Jean Rhys, Jamaica Kincaid, Beryl Gilroy, and Edwidge Danticat. Includes bibliographical references and an index.

Brown, Julie, ed. *American Women Short Story Writers: A Collection of Critical Essays*. New York: Garland, 2000. Collection of essays that analyze short fiction by nineteenth and twentieth century women writers, ranging from serious works of literature to popular tales about "sob sisters." Some of the writers whose works are examined are Lydia Maria Child, Elizabeth Stoddard, Louisa May Alcott, Ellen Glasgow, Edith Wharton, Eudora Welty, Dorothy Parker, Joyce Carol Oates, and Denise Chávez.

Burgin, Mary. "The 'Feminine' Short Story: Recuperating the Moment." *Style* 27 (Fall, 1993): 380-386. Argues that there is a connection between so-called feminine writing that focuses on isolated moments and the concerns of women who have chosen the short story as a form. Claims that the twentieth century epiphanic short story is a manifestation of women's tradition of temporal writing as opposed to the spatial writing of men.

Daiya, Krishna. *Post-Independence Women Short Story Writers in Indian English*. New Delhi, India: Sarup and Sons, 2006. Provides an overview of the works of women short-story writers, analyzing the themes, characterization, and styles of their stories. Assesses the status of the short-fiction genre and describes the contributions of women's short fiction to the genre and to Indian literature. Some of the writers whose works are analyzed are Shashi Deshpande, Anita Desai, Jhumpa Lahiri, Githa Hariharan, and Ruth Prawer Jhabvala.

Erro-Peralta, Nora, and Caridad Silva-Núñez, eds. *Beyond the Border: A New Age in Latin American Women's Fiction*. Pittsburgh, Pa.: Cleis Press, 1991. Covers works by Latin American female writers. Includes bibliographical references.

Hanson, Clare. "The Lifted Veil: Women and Short Fiction in the 1880's and 1890's." *The Yearbook of English Studies* 26 (1996): 135-142. Argues that British women writers in the early modernist period chose the short story to challenge the existing dominant order. Shows how this challenge is embodied in such stories as Charlotte Mew's "Mark Stafford's Wife" as an encounter, presented in iconic, painterly terms, between a male protagonist and a woman, who is then unveiled.

Harde, Roxanne, ed. *Narratives of Community: Women's Short Story Sequences*. Newcastle, England: Cambridge Scholars, 2007. Collection of essays analyzing women's roles in domestic, social, and literary communities and how they attain their identities in these communities. Some of the writers whose works are examined are Sandra Cisneros, Margaret Laurence, Salwa Bakr, Mary Caponegro, Gloria Naylor, Elizabeth Gaskell, Virginia Woolf, Alice Munro, and Maxine Hong Kingston.

Harrington, Ellen Burton, ed. *Scribbling Women and the Short Story Form: Approaches by American and British Women Writers*. New York: Peter Lang, 2008. Collection of essays providing feminist analyses of short fiction by British and American women, focusing on how this genre "liberated" women writers in the period from 1850 through the late twentieth century. Some of the women writers whose works are analyzed are Rebecca Harding

Davis, Louise May Alcott, Kate Chopin, Katherine Anne Porter, Flannery O'Connor, Cynthia Ozick, and Lydia Davis.

Palumbo-DeSimone, Christine. *Sharing Secrets: Nineteenth-Century Women's Relations in the Short Story.* Madison, N.J.: Fairleigh Dickinson University Press, 2000. Palumbo-DeSimone contradicts the criticism that many short stories by nineteenth century women writers are framed around a "seemingly meaningless incident," arguing that these stories are detailed, meaningful, and intricately designed works of serious fiction.

Partnoy, Alicia, ed. *You Can't Drown the Fire: Latin American Women Writing in Exile.* Pittsburgh, Pa.: Cleis Press, 1988. Covers twentieth century female writers whose works have been translated into English. Includes bibliographical references.

PERSONAL ACCOUNTS BY SHORT-FICTION WRITERS

Allende, Isabel. "The Short Story." *Journal of Modern Literature* 20 (Summer, 1996): 21-28. This personal account of storytelling makes suggestions about the differences between the novel and the short story, the story's demand for believability, the story's focus on change, the story's relationship to dream, and the story as events transformed by poetic truth.

Bailey, Tom, ed. *On Writing Short Stories.* 2d ed. New York: Oxford University Press, 2011. In addition to containing a sampling of some classic short stories, this book also features a section in which short-story writers discuss some basic issues regarding the definition and form of these works. These writers include Francine Prose, who explains what makes a short story, and Andre Dubus, who explores the "habit of writing." Bailey also contributes an essay about character, plot, setting, time, metaphor, and voice in short fiction.

Barth, John. "It's a Short Story." In *Further Fridays: Essays, Lectures, and Other Nonfiction, 1984-1994.* New York: Little, Brown, 1995. A personal account by a "congenital novelist" of his brief love affair with the short story during the writing of Chimera (1972) and the stories in Lost in the Funhouse (1968).

Blythe, Will, ed. *Why I Write: Thoughts on the Craft of Fiction.* Boston: Little, Brown, 1998. A collection of essays by various authors about writing fiction. The essays most relevant to the short story are those by Joy Williams, who says that writers must cherish the mystery of discovery in the process of writing; Thom Jones, who discusses his passionate engagement in the writing of short stories; and Mary Gaitskill, who calls stories the "rich, unseen underlayer of the most ordinary moments."

Burgess, Anthony. "Anthony Burgess on the Short Story." *Journal of the Short Story in English*, no. 2 (1984): 31-47. Burgess admits that he disdains the short story because he cannot write it. He says that the novel presents an epoch, while the short story presents a revelation. Discusses different types of stories, distinguishing between the literary short story, which is patterned, and the commercial form, which is anecdotal.

Charters, Ann, ed. *The Story and Its Writer: An Introduction to Short Fiction.* 6th ed. Boston: Bedford/ St. Martin's, 2003. A collection of classic short stories, with commentaries by their authors and other writers that analyze the works and describe how the stories were written. Includes appendixes chronicling storytelling before the emergence of the short story and the history of the short story.

Gioia, Dana, and R. S. Gwynn, eds. *The Art of the Short Story.* New York: Pearson Longman, 2006. This anthology includes an "author's perspective" from each of its fifty-two authors, in which the writers comment on the aims, context, and workings of their short stories. For example, Sherwood Anderson and Raymond Carver provide advice on the craft of writing; Margaret Atwood discusses Canadian identity; Alice Walker writes about race and gender; and Flannery O'Connor explains the importance of religious grace in her work. Some of the other authors included in the anthology are John Cheever, Albert Camus, F. Scott Fitzgerald, Ernest Hemingway, Anton Chekhov, James Joyce, Jorge Luis Borges, William Faulkner, Chinua Achebe, Ha Jin, Sandra Cisneros, and Gabriel García Márquez.

Iftekharuddin, Farhat, Mary Rohrberger, and Maurice Lee, eds. *Speaking of the Short Story: Interviews with Contemporary Writers*. Jackson: University Press of Mississippi, 1997. Collection of twenty-one interviews with short-story writers, such as Isabel Allende, Rudolfo A. Anaya, Ellen Douglas, Richard Ford, Bharati Mukherjee, and Leslie Marmon Silko, and short story critics, such as Susan Lohafer, Charles E. May, and Mary Rohrberger.

Lee, Maurice A., ed. *Writers on Writing: The Art of the Short Story*. Westport, Conn.: Praeger, 2005. A collection of essays in which short-story writers from around the world discuss their craft and analyze stories and types of short fiction. Some of the contributors include Amiri Baraka, Olive Senior, Jayne Anne Philips, Janette Turner Hospital, Ivan Wolfers, Singapore writer Kirpal Singh, and Ivan Wolfers.

Mandelbaum, Paul, ed. *Twelve Short Stories and Their Making*. New York: Persea Books, 2005. These twelve stories by contemporary writers have been selected to illustrate six elements of the short story: character, plot, point of view, theme, setting, and structure. The book also includes individual interviews with the twelve authors in which they describe their writing processes and the challenges they faced in composing their selected stories. The featured writers include Elizabeth Tallent, Charles Johnson, Allan Gurganus, Ursula K. Le Guin, Jhumpa Lahiri, Sandra Cisneros, and Tobias Wolff.

O'Connor, Flannery. "Writing Short Stories." In *Mystery and Manners*, edited by Sally and Robert Fitzgerald. New York: Farrar, Straus & Giroux, 1969. In this lecture at a southern writers' conference, O'Connor discusses the two qualities necessary for the short story: "sense of manners," which writers get from the texture of their immediate surroundings, and "sense of mystery," which is always the mystery of personality--"showing how some specific folks will do, in spite of everything."

Senior, Olive. "Lessons from the Fruit Stand: Or, Writing for the Listener." *Journal of Modern Literature* 20 (Summer, 1996): 40-44. An account of one writer's development of the short story as a personal engagement between teller and listener. Discusses the relationship between the oral tradition of gossip and folklore and the development of short-story conventions. Claims that the short story is a form based on bits and pieces of human lives for which there is no total picture.

Turchi, Peter, and Andrea Barrett, eds. The *Story Behind the Story: Twenty-six Writers and How They Work*. New York: W. W. Norton, 2004. The stories in this collection were written by faculty members in the writing program at Warren Wilson College, including Antonya Nelson, Margot Livesey, David Shields, C. J. Hribal, Andrea Barrett, Steven Schwartz, and Jim Shepard. Accompanying each story is a brief essay in which the writer describes how his or her story was created.

Wright, Austin. "The Writer Meets the Critic on the Great Novel/Short Story Divide." *Journal of Modern Literature* 20 (Summer, 1996): 13-19. A personal account by a short-story critic and novelist of some of the basic differences between the critical enterprise and the writing of fiction, as well as some of the generic differences between the short story and the novel.

Charles E. May
Updated by Rebecca Kuzins

GUIDE TO ONLINE RESOURCES

Web Sites

The following sites were visited by the editors of Salem Press in 2011. Because URLs frequently change, the accuracy of these addresses cannot be guaranteed; however, long-standing sites, such as those of colleges and universities, national organizations, and government agencies, generally maintain links when sites are moved or updated.

African Literature and Writers on the Internet
http://www-sul.stanford.edu/depts/ssrg/africa/lit.html

This page is included in the Africa South of the Sahara Web site created by Karen Fung of Stanford University. It provides an alphabetical list of links to numerous resources about Chinua Achebe, Ben Okri, Ngugi wa Thiong'o, Chimamanda Ngozi Adichie, and other African writers; online journals and essays; association Web sites; and other materials. It also contains a link to the full text of Joseph Conrad's novella *Heart of Darkness*.

The American Short Story: A Selective Chronology
http://www.iwu.edu/~jplath/sschron.html

This time line has been compiled by James Plath, a professor and chair of the English department at Illinois Western University, and is part of his Web site, Plath Country. The chronology charts the development of the American short story from 1741 until the present day, listing the publication dates of many important works of short fiction. It also features a bibliography of books about the short story.

Australian Literature
http://www.middlemiss.org/lit/lit.html

Perry Middlemiss, a Melbourne-based blogger, created this useful resource about Australian writers and their works. It features an alphabetical list of authors which links to biographies and lists of their works; some of the listed works link to a synopsis and an excerpt. Peter Carey, David Malouf, and Frank Moorhouse are among the writers listed. The site also contains information about Australian literary awards.

Bibliomania: Short Stories
http://www.bibliomania.com/0/5/frameset.html

Among Bibliomania's more than two thousand texts are short stories written by American and foreign writers. The stories can be retrieved via lists of titles and authors.

Books and Writers
http://www.kirjasto.sci.fi/indeksi.htm

A broad, comprehensive, and easy-to-use resource about hundreds of authors throughout the world, extending from 70 B.C.E to the twenty-first century. Books and Writers contains an alphabetical list of authors with links to pages featuring a biography, a list of works, and recommendations for further reading about each author; each writer's page also includes links to related pages in the site. Although brief, the biographical essays provide a solid overview of the authors' careers, their contributions to literature, and their literary influence.

A Celebration of Women Writers
http://digital.library.upenn.edu/women

An extensive compendium of information about the contributions of women writers throughout history. Users can obtain biographical and bibliographical information about American, British, Australian, Canadian, African, Latin American, Russian, and other women writers by using the Browse by Country feature, or they can browse by the writers' names, ethnicities, and centuries in which they lived.

Classic Short Stories

http://www.classicshorts.com

Features the texts of American and British short stories, as well as some stories by Guy de Maupassant, Anton Chekhov, and other European writers. Stories can be accessed via title or author's name.

Contemporary Writers

http://www.contemporarywriters.com

Created by the British Council, this site offers, in its own words, "up-to-date profiles of some of the U.K. [United Kingdom] and Commonwealth, and Republic of Ireland's most important living writers." The available information includes biographies, bibliographies, critical reviews, news about literary prizes, and photographs. Users can search the site by author, genre, nationality, gender, publisher, book title, and prize name and date.

Internet Public Library: Native American Authors

http://www.ipl.org/div/natam

Internet Public Library, a Web-based collection of materials, contains this index to resources about Native American literature. An alphabetical list of authors enables users to link to biographies, lists of works, electronic texts, tribal Web sites, and other online resources. The majority of writers are contemporary Indian authors, but some historical authors are also featured. Users can also retrieve information via lists of titles and tribes. In addition, the site contains a bibliography of print and online materials about Native American literature.

The Latin American Short Story: A Cultural Tradition

http://www.yale.edu/ynhti/curriculum/units/1987/1/87.01.08.x.html#b

This page is included in the Web site for the Yale-New Haven Teachers Institute and contains a lesson plan for teaching students about the Latin American short story. In addition to listing the plan's objectives and strategies, this page provides a historical overview and reading lists for both teachers and students of works by Jorge Luis Borges, Gabriel García Márquez, and other writers.

The Literary Gothic

http://www.litgothic.com/index_html.html

The Literary Gothic describes itself as a guide to "all things concerned with literary Gothicism," including ghost stories, with the majority of its resources related to literary works written and published from 1764 through 1820. The site defines gothic literature in broad terms, including some authors usually not associated with the genre, such as Joseph Addison and Willa Cather. An alphabetical list of authors and of titles provides links to biographies and other Web-based resources, including electronic texts of many works of gothic literature.

LiteraryHistory.com

http://www.literaryhistory.com

An excellent source of Web-based academic, scholarly, and critical literature about eighteenth, nineteenth, and twentieth century American and English writers. This site provides numerous pages about specific eras and literary genres, including individual pages for eighteenth, nineteenth, and twentieth century literature and for African American and postcolonial literature. These pages contain alphabetical lists of authors which link to articles, reviews, overviews, excerpts of works, teaching guides, podcast interviews, and other materials.

Literary Resources on the Net

http://andromeda.rutgers.edu/~jlynch/Lit

Jack Lynch of Rutgers University maintains this extensive collection of links to Internet sites that are useful to academics, including Web sites about a broad range of literary topics. The site is organized chronically, with separate pages for information about classical Greece and Rome, the Middle Ages, the Renaissance, the eighteenth century, Romantic and Victorian eras, and twentieth century British and Irish literature. There are also separate pages providing links to Web sites about American literature and to women's literature and feminism.

Literature: What Makes a Good Short Story
http://www.learner.org/interactives/literature

Annenberg Learner.org, a site providing interactive resources for teachers, contains this section describing the elements of short fiction, including plot construction, point of view, character development, setting, and theme. This section also features the text of "A Jury of Her Peers," a short story by Susan Glaspell, in order to illustrate the components of short fiction.

LitWeb
http://litweb.net

LitWeb provides biographies of more than five hundred world authors throughout history which can be accessed via an alphabetical listing. The pages about each writer contain a list of his or her works, suggestions for further reading, and illustrations. LitWeb also offers information about past and present winners of major literary prizes.

Luminarium: Anthology of English Literature
http://www.luminarium.org/lumina.htm

Luminarium has been a reliable source for more than a decade, providing information about English literature from the Middle Ages through the eighteenth century. Some of the authors it covers are Geoffrey Chaucer, Robert Greene, Sir Thomas Malory, Sir Richard Steele, and Samuel Johnson. Uses can assess a biography, list of quotable remarks, and bibliographies of books about each author, as well as links to electronic texts of the writers' works, essays about the writers, and related Web sites.

The Modern Word: The Libyrinth
http://www.themodernword.com/authors.html

The Modern Word provides a great deal of critical information about postmodern writers and contemporary experimental fiction. The core of the site is "The Libyrinth," which lists authors for which there are links to essays and other resources. There are also sections devoted to Samuel Beckett, Jorge Luis Borges, Gabriel García Márquez, James Joyce, Franz Kafka, and Thomas Pynchon.

Outline of American Literature
http://www.america.gov/publications/books/outline-of-american-literature.html

This page of the America.gov site provides access to *Outline of American Literature*, a historical overview of prose and poetry from colonial times to the present. The ten-chapter book was written by Kathryn Van Spanckeren, professor of English at the University of Tampa, and was published by the Department of State. This site contains abbreviated versions of each chapter, as well as access to the entire publication in pdf format.

The Short Story Library at American Literature
http://www.americanliterature.com/sstitleindex.html

A compilation of more than two thousand short stories which can be accessed via alphabetical lists of story titles and authors. Although the majority of the authors are American, the site also features English translations of stories by Anton Chekhov, Guy de Maupassant, and other writers, as well as works by British authors, such as Charles Dickens, Saki, and Rudyard Kipling. The site provides texts of some of the most well-known works of short fiction, including "The Tell-Tale Heart" by Edgar Allan Poe, "Bartleby the Scrivener" by Herman Melville, and "The Lottery" by Shirley Jackson.

The Victorian Web
http://www.victorianweb.org

One of the finest Web sites about the nineteenth century, providing a wealth of material about Great Britain during the reign of Queen Victoria, including information about the era's literature. The home page links to a section called "Authors," offering an alphabetical listing of more than one hundred nineteenth century writers; the list links to additional pages of information about the individual authors, including biographies, bibliographies, analyses of their work, and, in some cases, excerpts of their writings. "Authors" also links to lists of pre- and post-Victorian writers and to British and other European authors associated with the Aesthetic and Decadent movements. The information about some of the writers, such as Charles Dickens, Thomas Hardy, George Eliot, and William Makepeace Thackeray, is quite extensive, with discussions of the themes, characterization, imagery, narration, and other aspects of their work and essays and other resources placing their writings in social, political, and economic context.

Voice of the Shuttle
http://vos.ucsb.edu

The most complete and authoritative place for online information about literature. Created and maintained by professors and students in the English department at the University of California, Santa Barbara, Voice of the Shuttle is a database with thousands of links to electronic books, academic journals, association Web sites, sites created by university professors, and many, many other resources about the humanities. The "Literature in English" page provides links to separate pages about the literature of the Anglo-Saxon era, Middle Ages, Renaissance and seventeenth century, Restoration and eighteenth century, Romantic age, Victorian age, and modern and contemporary periods in Great Britain and the United States, as well as a page about minority literature. Another page in the site, "Literatures Other than English," offers a gateway to information about the literature of numerous countries and world regions, including Africa, Eastern Europe, Arabic-speaking na-

tions, China, France, and Germany.

Voices from the Gaps
http://voices.cla.umn.edu

This site from the English department at the University of Minnesota is "dedicated to bringing together marginalized resources and knowledge about women artists of color," including women writers. Users can retrieve information by artists' names or by a range of subjects. The "Short Stories" subject page lists writers of short fiction, such as Edwidge Danticat, Maxine Hong Kingston, Ann Petry, Leslie Marmon Silko, and Helena María Viramontes.

Western European Studies Section
http://wess.lib.byu.edu/index.php/Main_Page

The Western European Studies Section of the Association of College and Research Libraries maintains this collection of resources useful to students of Western European history and culture, and it is a good place to find information about non-English literature. The site includes separate pages about the literature and languages of the Netherlands, France, Germany, Iberia, Italy, and Scandinavia where users can find links to electronic texts, association Web sites, journals, and other materials, the majority of which are written in the language of each country.

Western European Studies Section: British Studies Web
http://wess.lib.byu.edu/index.php/Great_
Britain_%28British_Studies%29

The Western European Studies Section of the Association of College and Research Libraries maintains a collection of resources useful to students of Western European history and culture. The site includes the British Studies Web, with links to a separate page of information about the language and literature of England, the Republic of Ireland, Northern Ireland, Scotland, and Wales.

ELECTRONIC DATABASES

Electronic databases usually do not have their own URLs. Instead, public, college, and university libraries subscribe to these databases, provide links to them on their Web sites, and make them available to library card holders or specified patrons. Readers can check library Web sites or ask reference librarians to check on availability.

Bloom's Literary Reference Online

Facts On File publishes this database of thousands of articles by renowned scholar Harold Bloom and other literary critics, examining the lives and works of great writers worldwide. This database also includes information on more than forty-six thousand literary characters, literary topics, themes, movements, and genres, plus video segments about literature. Users can retrieve information by browsing writers' names, titles of works, time periods, genres, or writers' nationalities.

Canadian Literary Centre

Produced by EBSCO, the Canadian Literary Centre database contains full-text content from ECW Press, a Toronto-based publisher, including *Canadian Writers and Their Work*, *George Woodcock's Introduction to Canadian Fiction*, and *Essays on Canadian Writing*. Author biographies, essays and literary criticism, and book reviews are among the database's offerings.

Literary Reference Center

EBSCO's Literary Reference Center (LRC) is a comprehensive full-text database containing information from reference works, books, literary journals, and other materials. The database's contents include more than 34,000 plot summaries, synopses, and overviews of literary works; almost 100,000 essays and articles of literary criticism; about 180,000 author biographies; more than 683,000 book reviews; and more than 6,200 author interviews. It also contains the entire contents of Salem Press's MagillOnLiterature Plus. Users can retrieve information by browsing a list of authors' names or titles of literary works; they can also use an advanced search engine to access information by numerous categories, including an author's name, gender, cultural identity, national identity, and the years in which he or

she lived, or by literary title, character, locale, genre, and publication date.

Literary Resource Center

Published by Gale, this comprehensive literary database contains information on the lives and works of more than 135,000 authors from Gale reference sources in all genres, all time periods, and throughout the world. In addition, the database offers more than 75,000 full-text critical essays and reviews from some of Gale's reference publications, including *Short Story Criticism*; more than 11,000 overviews of frequently studied works; and more than 300,000 full-text short stories, poems, and plays. Literary Resource Center also features a literary-historical time line and an encyclopedia of literature.

MagillOnLiterature Plus

MagillOnLiterature Plus is a comprehensive, integrated literature database produced by Salem Press and available on the EBSCO host platform. The database contains the full-text of Salem's many literature-related reference works, including *Masterplots* (series I and II), *Cyclopedia of World Authors*, *Cyclopedia of Literary Characters*, *Cyclopedia of Literary Places*, and *Critical Surveys of Literature*. Among its contents are critical essays, brief plot summaries, extended character profiles, and detailed setting discussions about works of literature by more than eighty-five hundred short- and long-fiction writers, poets, dramatists, essayists, and philosophers. The database also features biographical essays on more than twenty-five hundred authors, with lists of each author's principal works and current secondary bibliographies.

NoveList

NoveList is a readers' advisory service produced by EBSCO Publishing. The database provides access to 155,000 titles of both adult and juvenile fiction, including collections of short fiction. Users can type the words "short story" into the search engine and retrieve more than fourteen thousand short-story collections; users can also search by author's name to access titles of books, information about the author, and book reviews.

Short Story Index

This index, created by the H. W. Wilson Company, features information on more than 76,500 stories from more than 4,000 collections. Users can retrieve information by author, title, keyword, subject, date, source, literary technique, or a combination of these categories. The subject searches provide information about the stories' themes, locales, narratives techniques, and genres.

Rebecca Kuzins

TIME LINE

c. 2000 B.C.E.	The main portion of the poem *Gilgamesh* (*Gilgamesh Epic*, 1917), is written on cuneiform clay tablets. This epic recounts the exploits of Gilgamesh, the legendary king of Uruk and the first literary hero.
c. 750 B.C.E.	Homer revises and arranges the Greeks' oral stories about the Trojan War to compose the first of his two written epics, *Iliad*. Both this and his subsequent epic *Odyssey* (c. 725 B.C.E.) will continue to influence other writers into the twenty-first century.
c. 620 B.C.E.	Aesop is born in Greece. He will create many stories, the best known of which are his fables, particularly the more than one hundred animal fables that have been attributed to him.
8 C.E.	Ovid creates his fifteen-book epic poem *Metamorphoses* (English translation, 1567). Although written in verse, the epic's telling of continuous stories demonstrates a range of narrative techniques that will influence the history of short fiction.
c. 60 C.E.	Petronius creates *The Satyricon*, a long prose epic interspersed with verse.
c. 430	Liu Yiqing composes *Shi-shuo xinyu* (*A New Account of Tales of the World*), a collection of stories about famous statesmen and military figures and one of the earliest surviving works of Chinese short fiction.
c. 800	The *Hildebrandslied*, a heroic verse-narrative written in Old High German, is composed.
10th century	*The Maginogion*, a collection of Welsh prose tales, both oral and written, begins to take shape. These tales will be collated from medieval manuscripts and published in book form beginning in 1838.
c. 1167	Marie de France's creates her collection of twelve narratives, *Lais*, (*Lays of Marie de France*, 1911; better known as *The Lais of Marie de France*, 1978).
c. 1190	Chrétien de Troyes dies. The medieval French author is the first acknowledged writer of Arthurian romance in the vernacular and the originator of the Arthurian version of the Grail legend.
c. early 13th century	Snorri Sturluson creates the *Prose Edda*, a text on Old Norse poetics which contains the narratives of many Norse myths.
1349-1351	Giovanni Boccaccio composes the collection of one hundred tales that constitute *Decameron: O, Prencipe Galeotto* (*The Decameron*, 1620). These stories, told by a group of people who have fled Florence during the Black Death, or bubonic plague, will influence subsequent generations of short-fiction writers.

1387-1400	Geoffrey Chaucer creates *The Canterbury Tales*, a collection of stories about a group of pilgrims en route to Canterbury. The collection is unprecedented in its use of a wide variety of short-story types, including the Breton lai, fabliau, beast-fable, exemplum, and allegory.
15th century	*Alf layla wa-layla* (*The Arabian Nights' Entertainments* 1706-1708; also known as *A Thousand and One Nights*) is published. This collection of stories from Persia, Arabia, India, and Egypt was handed down orally for hundreds of years before it was compiled and presented in written form.
1485	*Le Morte d'Arthur* is written by Sir Thomas Mallory and is the first text to bring unity and coherence to the mass of material regarding the Arthurian legend.
1559	Marguerite de Navarre composes *L'Heptaméron* (*The Heptameron*, 1597), the most important and influential sixteenth century collection of nouvelles. Modeled on *The Decameron,* Navarre's book is a collection of short stories told by five men and five women.
1592	English Renaissance writer Robert Greene publishes *A Disputation Between a Hee Conny-Catcher and a Shee Conny-Catcher.*
1613	Miguel de Cervantes, best known as the author of one of the first novels, *Don Quijote de la Mancha*, publishes his only collection of short fiction, *Novelas ejemplares* (*Exemplary Novels*, 1846).
1668-1694	French writer Jean de la Fontaine revives interest in the fable genre by publishing twelve books of these tales.
1686	Ihara Saikaku publishes the work considered his masterpiece, *Kōshoku Gonin Onna* (*Five Women Who Loved Love*, 1956), a collection of five scandalous love stories.
1692	Playwright William Congreve publishes his only work of short fiction, *Incognita: Or, Love and Duty Reconcil'd.*
1697	Aphra Behn, better known as a dramatist and novelist, creates one of the most important works of Restoration short fiction, *The Nun: Or, The Perjur'd Beauty*.
1697	French author Charles Perrault publishes *Histoires ou contes du temps passé avec des moralités* (*Stories or Tales of Past Times, with Morals)*, his children's stories about Mother Goose, Cinderella, and other characters that mark the creation of the fairy-tale genre.
1706	Daniel Defoe publishes "A True Relation of the Apparition of One Mrs. Veal," the earliest short narrative in English literature to contribute to the development of the short story.
1711-1712, 1714	Joseph Addison and Sir Richard Steele write their semifictional essays for *The Spectator* newspaper, in which they create the characters of Sir Roger de Coverley and Mr. Spectator.
1759	Samuel Johnson publishes *Rasselas, Prince of Abyssinia.*

1759	Voltaire publishes *Candide: Ou, L'Optimisme* 1759 (*Candide: Or, All for the Best*, 1759).
1760-1761	*The Public Ledger* publishes *The Citizen of the World*, Oliver Goldsmith's version of the "Asian tale," a popular genre of the time.
1766	Chinese writer Pu Songling publishes the work on which his literary reputation rests, *Liaozhai zhiyi* (*Strange Stories from a Chinese Studio*, 1880), a compilation of 431 stories.
1774	Johann Wolfgang von Goethe publishes *Die Leiden des jungen Werthers* (*The Sorrows of Young Werther*, 1779), a novella that forgoes eighteen century conventions of rationality and lays the groundwork for the new genre of Romantic literature.
1789	American magazines begin to publish short fiction.
1808	Heinrich von Kleist publishes his novella *Michael Kohlhaas* (English translation, 1844).
1812	Jacob and Wilhelm Grimm publish the first edition of *Kinder- und Hausmärchen*, a collection of stories that will eventually make their names synonymous with the term "fairy tale."
1819-1820	Washington Irving lays the foundation for the American short story in *The Sketch Book of Geoffrey Crayon,* Gent, a collection that includes the tales "Rip Van Winkle" and "The Legend of Sleepy Hollow."
1819-1821	E. T. A. Hoffmann, a major figure in German Romantic literature, publishes a four-volume short-fiction collection, *Die Serapionsbrüder* (*The Serapion Brethren*, 1886-1892).
1821	*The Saturday Evening Post* debuts. This magazine will publish numerous short stories aimed at the general public.
1827	Sir Walter Scott publishes "The Two Drovers." In his book *The Short Story in English* (1981), Walter Allen begins his survey of the genre with Scott's story, which Allen describes as "the first modern short story in English."
1830-1833	William Carleton publishes his most popular short-story collection, the five-volume *Traits and Stories of the Irish Peasantry*. Carleton was the first Irish writer to provide a realistic depiction of his nation's peasants.
1830-1865	Romantic Period of American short-story writing
1832-1837	Honoré de Balzac publishes *Les Contes drolatiques* (*Droll Stories*, 1874, 1891).
1834	*Pikovaya dama* (*The Queen of Spades*, 1858) by Russian writer Alexander Pushkin, is published. This complex story, one of the most well-known in short fiction, uses an omniscient narrator to present the points of view of six characters.

1835	Hans Christian Andersen publishes the first edition of *Eventyr*. Between 1835 and 1872, he will revise and expand this collection, which includes some of the world's best-known fairy tales.
1835	Augustus Baldwin Longstreet, the foremost writer among the Southwest humorists, publishes *Georgia Scenes, Characters, Incidents, Etc. in the First Half Century of the Republic*, a collection of tall tales told in the vernacular speech of the Georgia frontier.
1837	Nathaniel Hawthorne publishes *Twice-Told Tales*, a short-fiction collection that will be expanded in a second edition five years later.
1840	Edgar Allan Poe's first short-story collection, *Tales of the Grotesque and Arabesque*, is published.
1842	"Shinel" ("The Overcoat," 1923), Nikolai Gogol's tale of a poor and hapless civil servant and his new coat, is published. This story will influence many other writers and will help shape the direction of Russian short fiction.
1843	*A Christmas Carol*, Charles Dickens's best-known holiday story, is published.
1844	Different versions of "The Purloined Letter" by Edgar Allan Poe are published in two magazines. In this and other stories about C. Auguste Dupin, including "The Murders in the Rue Morgue," Poe establishes the conventions of the modern detective story.
1852	Ivan Turgenev publishes *Zapiski okhotnika* (*Russian Life in the Interior*, 1855; better known as *A Sportsman's Sketches*, 1932), considered by some critics to be the greatest book of short stories ever written.
1856	Herman Melville's collection *The Piazza Tales*, which includes "Bartleby the Scrivener" and "Benito Cereno," is published.
1857	*The Atlantic Monthly* begins publishing and will become an important venue for short fiction.
1865-1900	Realistic Period of American short-story writing
1865	Mark Twain's "The Celebrated Jumping Frog of Calaveras County" makes its first appearance in the *New York Saturday Press*.
1868	*The Overland Monthly* publishes Bret Harte's "The Luck of Roaring Camp."
1869	Alphonse Daudet publishes his first short-story collection, *Lettres de mon moulin* (*Letters from My Mill*, 1880).
1870	Brazilian writer Joaquim Maria Machado de Assis publishes his first short-fiction collection, *Contos fluminenses*.
1875-1900	A number of American literary magazines and journals begin publishing, creating a demand for short fiction.

1876	Joel Chandler Harris publishes his first story about an elderly black man. This character, later named Uncle Remus, will be featured in several short-story collections to be published between 1880 and 1905.
1881	Guy de Maupassant publishes his first short-story collection, *La Maison Tellier* (*Madame Tellier's Establishment and Short Stories*, 1910). The unquestioned master of the nineteenth century French short story, Maupassant's short fiction will influence many major writers, including Thomas Mann, Katherine Mansfield, and Luigi Pirandello.
1882	Robert Louis Stevenson publishes his first short-fiction collection, *The New Arabian Nights*. He will follow this up three years later with a sequel, *More New Arabian Nights*.
1886	Leo Tolstoy publishes the novella *Smert' Ivana Il'icha* (*The Death of Ivan Ilyich*, 1887).
1888	Thomas Hardy publishes *Wessex Tales*, a volume of short stories that will prove a popular success.
1890	Welsh writer Arthur Machen publishes *The Great God Pan*, which some critics consider the best horror story ever written.
1891	Hamlin Garland publishes *Main-Travelled Roads: Six Mississippi Valley Stories*. The collection is an example of the "local color" literature of the late nineteenth century--works that focus on the dialects, characters, customs, and other elements of a specific region of the United States. Other local color short-fiction writers include Mary E. Wilkins Freeman and Sarah Orne Jewett of New England; Kate Chopin, George Washington Cable, and Charles W. Chestnutt from the South: and Bret Harte and Mark Twain from the West.
1892	The detective story gains sophistication and popularity with the publication of *The Adventures of Sherlock Holmes* by Sir Arthur Conan Doyle.
1894	At the height of his career, popular Australian writer Henry Lawson publishes a short-fiction collection *While the Billy Boils*.
1894	Kate Chopin's *Bayou Folk*, a collection of stories and sketches, is published.
1894-1914	Sholom Aleichem's collection *Tevye der Milkhiger* (*Tevye's Daughters*, 1949) is published. Writing in Yiddish, Aleichem recounts tales of Jewish life in czarist Russia.
1897	Stephen Crane produces "The Open Boat," which many critics consider his greatest short story.
1897	H. G. Wells, whose "scientific romances" gave shape to the science-fiction genre, publishes *Thirty Strange Stories*.
1899	Joseph Conrad's *Heart of Darkness* is serialized and will be published in book form three years later.
1900-1910	Naturalistic Period of American short-story writing

1900	Naturalist writer Jack London publishes his first short-story collection, *The Son of the Wolf*.
1901	Brander Matthews, a Columbia University professor, publishes *The Philosophy of Short Fiction*, the first full-length study of the short story.
1904	Anton Chekhov dies. Often described as the greatest short-story writer ever, Chekhov created the modern short story with works characterized by almost scientific objectivity, irony, the evocation of a single dominant mood, and relatively insignificant action.
1904	M. R. James, an academic and scholar who wrote ghost stories for his friends, publishes his first collection of these tales, *Ghost Stories of an Antiquary*.
1905	"Paul's Case," a widely anthologized story by Willa Cather, is published in Cather's collection *The Troll Garden*.
1906	*The Four Million*, one of numerous short-story collections by O. Henry, is published. O. Henry's popular stories will influence the development of magazine fiction and the modern narrative.
1907	Rudyard Kipling, an accomplished short-story writer, wins the Nobel Prize in Literature.
1910-1945	Period of Modernism in American short-story writing
1911	Katherine Mansfield publishes her first short-story collection, *In a German Pension*. This New Zealand-born writer will attain a reputation as one of the greatest practitioners of short-fiction writing.
1912	Thomas Mann publishes *Der Tod in Venedig* (*Death in Venice*, 1925), considered to be one of the best novellas in Western literature.
1914	James Joyce publishes *Dubliners*, which shapes the modernist conception of short fiction.
1914	D. H. Lawrence publishes his first short-fiction collection, *The Prussian Officer, and Other Stories*.
1915	*The Best American Short Stories* debuts and will continue to be published annually into the twenty-first century. The anthology features the best short stories published that year in American and Canadian magazines.
1916	Franz Kafka writes one of his best-known short stories, "Ein Landartz" ("A Country Doctor"), which three years later will be published in a collection of the same name.
1919	The O. Henry Awards are established. The award-winning short stories are published each year in a volume entitled *Prize Stories*. In 2009, prize officials will partner with the PEN American Center to present the renamed PEN/O. Henry Award.
1919	*Winesburg, Ohio*, Sherwood Anderson's innovative collection of short stories, is published.

1920	*Flappers and Philosophers*, the first collection of short fiction by F. Scott Fitzgerald, is published.
1921	Anatole France wins the Noble Prize in Literature.
1921	Chinese writer Lu Xun publishes his longest and most important work of short fiction, *Ah Q zheng zhuan* (*The True Story of Ah Q*).
1923	*Cane*, Jean Toomer's collection of prose and poetry, is published.
1924	Agatha Christie publishes her first collection of stories, *Poirot Investigates*, featuring one of her best-known sleuths, Belgian detective Hercule Poirot.
1925	*The New Yorker* magazine debuts and will become an important venue for the works of short-fiction writers.
1927	Ernest Hemingway's *Men Without Women*, a collection of short fiction that includes "The Killers," is published.
1928	H. E. Bates publishes his second collection of short fiction, *Day's End, and Other Stories*.
1931	Miguel de Unamuno y Jugo, Spain's most important modernist writer, publishes his novella *San Manuel Bueno, mártir* (*Saint Manuel Bueno, Martyr*, 1954).
1932	British writer John Galsworthy receives the Nobel Prize in Literature.
1933	Russian writer Ivan Bunin wins the Nobel Prize in Literature.
1934	Luigi Pirandello wins the Nobel Prize in Literature. In addition to his better-known plays, this prolific Italian writer published 233 short stories.
1934	Samuel Beckett, the unchallenged master of absurdist literature, publishes his first short-fiction collection, *More Pricks than Kicks*.
1934	Langston Hughes publishes his first short-fiction collection, *The Ways of White Folks*.
1935	The Akutagawa Prize, a Japanese literary award presented semiannually, is established in honor of Ryūnosuke Akutagawa, whose numerous short stories include "Rashōmon" (1915). The prize is most often awarded to short stories or novellas.
1936	*Bannen*, the first short-fiction collection by Japanese writer Osamu Dazai, is published.
1938	Pearl S. Buck wins the Nobel Prize in Literature. The American author's short stories and other works helped shape Western readers' perceptions of China.
1941	Kimitake Hiraoka begins using the pseudonym Yukio Mishima, under which he will write more than eighty short stories, as well as novels, plays, and other works.

1941	Frederic Dannay and Manfred B. Lee, who collectively write under the pseudonym Ellery Queen, establish *Ellery Queen's Mystery Magazine*, which will rejuvenate the detective short story.
1942	*My World---And Welcome to It!* by James Thurber is published. The collection includes one of his most popular stories, "The Secret Life of Walter Mitty."
1943	Mary Lavin wins the James Tait Black Memorial Prize for *Tales from Bective Bridge*. As of 2011, her collection was the only work of short fiction to receive this prestigious award.
1944	Jorge Luis Borges establishes his reputation as the most important short-fiction writer in Latin American history with the publication of *Ficciones, 1935-1944*. These and other stories by the Argentinean writer eschew realistic depiction of external Latin life in favor of imaginative tales about universal themes appealing to more intelligent readers.
1945	Dashiell Hammett publishes his first collection of detective stories about The Continental Op, a tough San Francisco-based private investigator whose name is never revealed.
1946	Swiss writer Hermann Hesse receives the Nobel Prize in Literature. Although best-known for his novels, such as *Der Steppenwolf*, Hesse also published numerous short stories that address many of the same themes as his longer fiction.
1948	Polish writer Tadeusz Borowski publishes his two collections of short stories that relate the horrors of the Holocaust and the immediate postwar world: *Pożegnanie z Marią* and *Kamienny świat*.
1948	James Michener wins the Pulitzer Prize for *Tales of the South Pacific*.
1948	Shirley Jackson's short story "The Lottery" is published in *The New Yorker*, eliciting the largest reader response in the history of the magazine to date.
1950	"Young prose" and "village prose" emerge as new short-fiction genres in the Soviet Union.
1951	Canadian writer Mavis Gallant publishes her first short story, "Madeline's Birthday," in *The New Yorker*. Gallant will earn a reputation of one of the premiere short-fiction writers of her time, and in 2002 she will receive the Rea Award for the Short Story.
1951	Pär Lagerkvist, the preeminent Swedish literary figure of the mid-twentieth century, wins the Nobel Prize in Literature.
1951	William Faulkner's *Collected Stories* receives the National Book Award.

1951	Carson McCullers publishes *The Ballad of the Sad Café*, a collection of novels and short stories.
1952	Alberto Moravia wins Italy's Strega Prize for *I racconti, 1927-1951*, a collection of his short fiction.
1953	Two collections of short fiction by major American writers are published: *The Enormous Radio* by John Cheever and *Nine Stories* by J. D. Salinger.
1955	Flannery O'Connor, considered to be one of the most important writers of the short story, publishes her first collection of short fiction: *A Good Man Is Hard to Find, and Other Stories*.
1957	Existentialist writer Albert Camus publishes his sole collection of short fiction, *L'Exil et le royaume* (*Exile and the Kingdom*, 1958).
1957	Isaac Bashevis Singer publishes his first short-story collection, *Gimpel the Fool, and Other Stories*. Singer, more than any other twentieth century writer, kept alive the vanishing language of Yiddish and the disappearing Jewish culture of Eastern Europe.
1958	"Babette's Feast" is one of the stories included in *Skæbne-Anekdoter* (*Anecdotes of Destiny*, 1958), one of Danish writer Isak Dinesen's short-story collections.
1959	Grace Paley publishes *The Little Disturbances of Man: Stories of Men and Women in Love*.
1959	*The Magic Barrel* by Bernard Malamud wins the National Book Award.
1960	Philip Roth wins the National Book Award for *Goodbye Columbus, and Five Short Stories*.
1962	Nigerian writer Chinua Achebe publishes *The Sacrificial Egg, and Other Stories*.
1963	Czech writer Milan Kundera publishes his first short-story collection, *Směšné lásky; Tři melancholické anekdoty*.
1963	Irish writer Frank O'Connor publishes *The Lonely Voice*, a study of short fiction focusing on nine writers, including Ernest Hemingway, Guy de Maupassant, and Anton Chekhov.
1963	H. P. Lovecraft publishes his first collection of horror stories, *The Dunwich Horror and Others*.
1963-1980	Confessional Period of American short-story writing
1964	Postmodernist writer Donald Barthelme publishes his first short-fiction collection, *Come Back, Dr. Caligari*.
1964	J. G. Ballard publishes *The Terminal Beach*, an innovative work of short fiction he describes as a "condensed novel."
1965	James Baldwin's short stories are published in *Going to Meet the Man*.

1966	Israeli writer Shmuel Yosef Agnon is one of two writers to receive the Nobel Prize in Literature. Agnon is best known for his more than two hundred short stories.
1966	*The Collected Stories of Katherine Anne Porter* wins both the National Book Award and the Pulitzer Prize.
1967	Heinrich Böll wins the Georg-Büchner-Preis, the most significant literary award in Germany. Böll's oeuvre includes several collections of short stories and novellas.
1967	Guatemalan writer Miguel Ángel Asturias is awarded the Nobel Prize in Literature.
1970	*The Collected Stories of Jean Stafford* receives the Pulitzer Prize.
1970	Ama Ata Aidoo of Ghana publishes *No Sweetness Here, and Other Stories*, a collection of female portraits offering various images of womenhood.
1971	Tomás Rivera's *. . . y no se lo tragó la tierra/ . . . and the earth did not part* is published in Spanish and will later be published in a bilingual English-Spanish edition. A Chicano classic, the book contains fourteen stories about the life of migrant farmworkers.
1973	Pushcart Press is established and will soon begin publishing annual anthologies of the best short fiction to appear in small literary magazines.
1974	*Aiiieeeee! An Anthology of Asian American Writers*, a trailblazing collections for and by Asian Americans, is published.
1974	Angela Carter publishes *The Bloody Chamber, and Other Stories*. Carter's stories combine eroticism with feminist criticism of patriarchal legends and folk tales.
1975	*Todos los cuentos de Gabriel García Márquez*, the collected stories of Colombian writer Gabriel García Márquez, are published and will be translated into English nine years later.
1977	Alejo Carpentier wins the Premio Miguel de Cervantes. The works of this Cuban-born writer include a short-story collection, *Guerra del tiempo* (1958; *War of Time*, 1970).
1978	Ann Beattie's stories from *The New Yorker* are published in *Secrets and Surprises*.
1980	American short-story writing enters its Period of Postmodernism
1981	Raymond Carver, the master of minimalist short fiction, attains critical and popular acclaim with his collection *What We Talk About When We Talk About Love*. Other American minimalist writers of the 1970's and 1980's are Ann Beattie, Tobias Wolff, Mary Robison, Bobbie Ann Mason, and sometimes Richard Ford, Jayne Anne Phillips, and David Leavitt.

1983	The University of Georgia Press presents the first annual Flannery O'Connor Award for Short Fiction to David Walton for *Evening Out* and Leigh Allison Wilson for *From the Bottom Up.*
1984	Ellen Gilchrist receives the National Book Award for *Victory over Japan: A Book of Stories.*
1986	Cynthia Ozick receives the first Rea Award, presented annually to writers who have made a contribution to the short-story form.
1987	Nigerian writer Ben Okri receives the Commonwealth Writer's Prize for the African region for *Incidents at the Shrine* (1986), his first short-fiction collection.
1988	John Updike receives the first annual PEN/Malamud Award for excellence in the "art of the short story."
1989	Susan Hubbard wins the Grace Paley Prize for Short Fiction for *Walking on Ice.*
1991	Frederick Busch and Andre Dubus receive the PEN/Malamud Award.
1991	Janis Galloway publishes her first short-fiction collection, *Blood*, in which she depicts postindustrial Scotland as a bleak and often violent place.
1992	Eudora Welty receives the PEN/Malamud Award.
1994	Tillie Olsen receives the Rea Award.
1995	*The Collected Stories of Peter Carey* is published. Carey, the world's most famous Australian writer, is one of only two authors to twice win the prestigious Man Booker Prize.
1996	Joyce Carol Oates receives the PEN/Malamud Award.
1996	Andrea Barrett receives the National Book Award for *Ship Fever, and Other Stories.*
1996	The publication of *McOndo*, a collection of Latin American short fiction, ushers in a new style of writing that will continue into the twenty-first century. Proponents of *McOndismo* criticize the Latin Boom writers for exploiting Magical Realism, and they are preoccupied with popular culture, fast food, television, films, and the Internet.
1997	Chinese-born writer Ha Jin wins the PEN/Hemingway Award for his first short-story collection *Ocean of Words: Army Stories.* Jin will go on to write other award-winning works of short fiction.
1997	Gina Berriault receives the PEN/Faulkner Award for Fiction for *Women in Their Beds: New and Selected Stories.*
1998	John Edgar Wideman receives the Rea Award.
1999	John Updike edits *The Best American Short Stories of the Century*, featuring one of the stories that appeared in each edition of *The Best American Short Stories* from 1915 through 1999.

2000	Australian writer David Malouf wins the Neustadt International Prize for Literature for his body of work. *The Complete Stories*, a compendium of his short fiction, will appear seven years later.
2000	Aleksandar Hemon publishes his first collection of short fiction, *The Question of Bruno*. Hemon was born in Sarajevo, Yugoslavia (now in Bosnia and Herzegovina) and immigrated to the United States.
2000	The first Caine Prize, which annually recognizes the best work of African short fiction, is presented at the Zimbabwe Book Fair. The winner is Leila Aboulela of Sudan for her story "The Museum."
2001	V. S. Naipaul, a writer born in Trinidad and Tobago who has published several short-story collections, receives the Nobel Prize in Literature.
2002	*Virtual Lotus: Modern Fiction of Southeast Asia,* edited by Teri Shaffer Yamada, is published. This anthology features English translations of short stories from this region.
2003	Barry Hannah and Maile Meloy receive the PEN/Malamud Award.
2003	The four-volume collection *The Complete Stories* of Canadian writer Morley Callaghan is posthumously published.
2004	Lorrie Moore receives the Rea Award.
2004	Edwidge Danticat, a Haitian American writer, receives the first Story Prize for *The Dew Breaker*. The prize is presented annually for a collection of outstanding short fiction that is written in English and initially published in the United States.
2005	Japanese writer Haruki Murakami receives the Frank O'Connor International Short Story Award for his collection *Blind Willow, Sleeping Woman*. The prize, inaugurated in 2005, is named in honor of Irish writer Frank O'Connor.
2005	*Natasha, and Other Stories* by David Bezmozgis receives the Danuta Gleed Literary Awarded, presented annually by the Writers' Union of Canada to a Canadian writer who has written the best first collection of short fiction in English.
2006	Stanisław Lem, considered by many to be the best Continental European science-fiction writer, dies in Kráków, Poland.
2006	Adam Haslett and Tobias Wolff win the PEN/Malamud Award.
2007	*Walk the Blue Fields*, the second short-fiction collection by Claire Keegan, establishes the Irish writer's reputation as one the most significant practitioners of the short-story genre.

2007	Nam Le wins the Pushcart Prize for his story "Cartagena."
2007	Doris Lessing receives the Nobel Prize in Literature.
2008	J. M. G. Le Clézio wins the Nobel Prize in Literature. The French author has published several short-story collections.
2008	*Nachtsaison*, a collection of short stories by German writer Christoph Meckel, is published.
2008	Ezekiel Mphahlele, considered the most significant black South African writer of the twentieth century, dies in Pretoria. His oeuvre includes five short-fiction collections.
2009	Alice Munro, often called the "Canadian Chekhov," receives the Man Booker International Prize.
2009	Daniyal Mueenuddin receives the Story Prize for *In Other Rooms, Other Wonders*.
2010	The Bank of New Zealand (BNZ) Katherine Mansfield Short Story Awards is inaugurated in New Zealand in 1958, is renamed the BNZ Literary Awards, with the Premier Award becoming the BNZ Katherine Mansfield Award. Recipients in the twenty-first century have included Tracey Slaughter for "Wheat" (2004), Susan Wylie for "Lolly" (2005), Charlotte Grimshaw for "Plain Sailing" (2006), and Carl Nixon for "My Beautiful Balloon" (2007).
2010	Sherman Alexie receives the PEN/Faulkner Award for *War Dances*.
2010	Mario Vargas Llosa of Peru receives the Noble Prize in Literature.
2011	California writer Brando Skyhorse wins the PEN/Hemingway Award for *The Madonnas of Echo Park*, a collection of short stories about Mexican Americans living in a neighborhood near downtown Los Angeles.

Rebecca Kuzins

MAJOR AWARDS

AFRICAN AWARDS

CAINE PRIZE FOR AFRICAN WRITING

The Caine Prize is awarded annually for the best original short story by an African writer published in English, and it is given to writers residing in African countries or elsewhere. The prize was first presented in 2000.

2000: Leila Aboulela--"The Museum"--Sudan
2001: Helon Habila--"Love Poems"--Nigeria
2002: Binyavanga Wainaina--"Discovering Home"--Kenya
2003: Yvonne Adhiambo Owuor--"Weight of Whispers"--Kenya
2004: Brian Chikwava--"Seventh Street Alchemy"--Zimbabwe

2005: S. A. Afolabi--"Monday Morning"--Nigeria
2006: Mary Watson--"Jungfrau"--South Africa
2007: Monica Arac de Nyeko--"Jambula Tree"--Uganda
2008: Henrietta Rose-Innes--"Poison"--South Africa
2009: E. C. Osondu--"Waiting"--Nigeria
2010: Olufemi Terry--"Stickfighting Days"--Sierra Leone

THOMAS PRINGLE AWARD

This annual award, administered by the English Academy of South Africa, is presented on a rotating basis for literary works, including short stories. This list includes only those authors who have received this award for short stories.

1969: Nadine Gordimer
1979: J. A. Maimane
1981: Andre Lemmer
1982: Greg Latter
1984: Sheila Roberts
1988: Rose Zwi
1990: Patrick Cullinan
1992: Andries Walter Oliphant

1994: Ivan Vladislavic
1996: Peter Merrington
1998: Lerothodi La Pula
2000: Evan Kaplan
2002: Dan Wylie
2004: Ananda Cersh
2006: Ken Barris
2008: David Medalie

AMERICAN AWARDS

AMERICAN ACADEMY OF ARTS AND LETTERS AWARD OF MERIT

The Award of Merit is presented annually, in rotation, to an outstanding writer in one of the following arts: the short story, the novel, poetry, drama, painting, and drama. This list includes all of the short-story winners.

1983: Elizabeth Spencer
1989: Doris Betts

1995: Larry Woiwode
2001: Frederick Busch
2007: Charles Baxter

THE BEST AMERICAN SHORT STORIES

Published annually since 1915, *The Best American Short Stories* includes the best stories that were published in American or Canadian magazines during the year. Selection for the volume is considered a high honor.

The Best Short Stories of 1915, and the Yearbook of the American Short Story,
edited by **Edward J. O'Brien**

Burt, Maxwell Struthers-- "The Water-Hole"
Byrne, Donn-- "The Wake"
Comfort, Will Levington-- "Chautonville"
Dwiggins, W. A.-- "La Derniere Mobilisation"
Dwyer, James Francis-- "The Citizen"
Gregg, Frances-- "Whose Dog?"
Hecht, Ben-- "Life"
Hurst, Fannie-- "T. B."
Johnson, Arthur-- "Mr. Eberdeen's House"
Jordan, Virgil-- "Vengeance Is Mine"

Lyon, Harris Merton-- "The Weaver Who Clad the Summer"
Muilenburg, Walter J.-- "Heart of Youth"
Noyes, Newbold-- "The End of the Path"
O'Brien, Seumas-- "The Whale and the Grasshopper"
O'Reilly, Mary Boyle-- "In Berlin"
Roof, Katharine Metcalf-- "The Waiting Years"
Rosenblatt, Benjamin-- "Zelig"
Singmaster, Elsie-- "The Survivors"
Steele, Wilbur Daniel-- "The Yellow Cat"
Synon, Mary-- "The Bounty-Jumper"

The Best Short Stories of 1916, and the Yearbook of the American Short Story,
edited by **Edward J. O'Brien**

Atherton, Gertrude-- "The Sacrificial Altar"
Benefield, Barry-- "Miss Willett"
Booth, Frederick-- "Supers"
Burnet, Dana-- "Fog"
Buzzell, Francis-- "Ma's Pretties"
Cobb, Irvin S.-- "The Great Auk"

Dreiser, Theodore-- "The Lost Phoebe"
Gordon, Armistead C.-- "The Silent Infare"
Greene, Frederick Stuart-- "The Cat of the Cane-Brake"
Hallet, Richard Matthews-- "Making Port"
Hurst, Fannie-- "Ice water, Pl--!"

The Best Short Stories of 1917, and the Yearbook of the American Short Story,
edited by **Edward J. O'Brien**

Babcock, Edwina Stanton-- "Excursion"
Beer, Thomas-- "Onnie"
Burt, Maxwell Struthers-- "Cup of Tea"
Buzzell, Francis-- "Lonely Places"
Cobb, Irvin S.-- "Boys Will Be Boys"
Dobie, Charles Caldwell-- "Laughter"
Dwight, H. G.-- "Emperor of Elam"
Ferber, Edna-- "Gay Old Dog"
Gerould, Katharine Fullerton-- "Knight's Move"
Glaspell, Susan-- "Jury of Her Peers"

Greene, Frederick Stuart-- "Bunker Mouse"
Hallet, Richard Matthews-- "Rainbow Pete"
Hurst, Fannie-- "Get Ready the Wreaths"
Johnson, Fanny Kemble-- "Strange Looking Man"
Kline, Burton-- "Caller in the Night"
O'Sullivan, Vincent-- "Interval"
Perry, Lawrence-- "Certain Rich Man"
Pulver, Mary Brecht-- "Path of Glory"
Steele, Wilbur Daniel-- "Ching, Ching, Chinaman"
Synon, Mary-- "None So Blind"

The Best Short Stories of 1918, and the Yearbook of the American Short Story,
edited by **Edward J. O'Brien**

Abdullah, Achmed-- "A Simple Act of Piety"

Babcock, Edwina Stanton-- "Cruelties"

Brown, Katharine Holland-- "Buster"

Dobie, Charles Caldwell-- "The Open Window"

Dudly, William-- "The Toast to Forty-five"

Freedley, Mary Mitchell-- "Blind Vision"

Gerould, Gordon Hall-- "Imagination"

Gilbert, George-- "In Maulmain Fever-Ward"

Humphrey, G.-- "The Father's Hand"

Johnson, Arthur-- "The Visit of the Master"

Kline, Burton-- "In the Open Code"

Lewis, Sinclair-- "The Willow Walk"

Moseley, Katharine Prescott-- "The Story Vinton Heard at Mallorie"

Rhodes, Harrison-- "Extra Men"

Springer, Fleta Campbell-- "Solitaire"

Steele, Wilbur Daniel-- "The Dark Hour"

Street, Julian-- "The Bird of Serbia"

Venable, Edward C.-- "At Isham's"

Vorse, Mary Heaton-- "De Vilmarte's Luck"

Wood, Frances Gilchrist-- "The White Battalion"

The Best Short Stories of 1919, and the Yearbook of the American Short Story,
edited by **Edward J. O'Brien**

Alsop, G. F.-- "The Kitchen Gods"

Anderson, Sherwood-- "An Awakening"

Babcock, Edwina Stanton-- "Willum's Vanilla"

Barnes, Djuna-- "A Night Among the Horses"

Bartlett, Frederick Orin-- "Long, Long Ago"

Brownell, Agnes Mary-- "Dishes"

Burt, Maxwell Struthers-- "The Blood-Red One"

Cabell, James Branch-- "The Wedding-Jest"

Fish, Horace-- "The Wrists on the Door"

Glaspell, Susan-- "'Government Goat'"

Goodman, Henry-- "The Stone"

Hallet, Richard Matthews-- "To the Bitter End"

Hergesheimer, Joseph-- "The Meeker Ritual"

Ingersoll, Will E.-- "The Centenarian"

Johnston, Calvin-- "Messengers"

Jones, Howard Mumford-- "Mrs. Drainger's Veil"

La Motte, Ellen N.-- "Under a Wine-Glass"

Lieberman, Elias-- "A Thing of Beauty"

Vorse, Mary Heaton-- "The Other Room"

Yezierska, Anzia-- "'The Fat of the Land'"

The Best Short Stories of 1920, and the Yearbook of the American Short Story,
edited by **Edward J. O'Brien**

Anderson, Sherwood-- "The Other Woman"

Babcock, Edwina Stanton-- "Gargoyle"

Bercovici, Konrad-- "Ghitza"

Bryner, Edna Clare-- "The Life of Five Points"

Camp, Wadsroth-- "The Signal Tower"

Crew, Helen Oale-- "The Parting Genius"

Gerould, Katharine Fullerton-- "Habakkuk"

Hartman, Lee Foster-- "The Judgment of Vulcan"

Hughes, Rupert-- "The Stick-in-the-Muds"

Mason, Grace Sartwell-- "His Job"

Oppenheim, James-- "The Rending"

Roche, Arthur Somers-- "The Dummy-Chucker"

Sidney, Rose-- "Butterflies"

Springer, Fleta Campbel-- "The Rotter"

Steele, Wilbur Daniel-- "Out of Exile"

Storm, Ethel-- "The Three Telegrams"

Wheelwright, John T.-- "The Roman Bath"

Whitman, Stephen French-- "Amazement"

Williams, Ben Ames-- "Sheener"

Wood, Frances Gilchrist-- "Turkey Red"

The Best Short Stories of 1921, and the Yearbook of the American Short Story,
edited by **Edward J. O'Brien**

Anderson, Sherwood-- "Brothers"

Bercovici, Konrad-- "Fanutza"

Burt, Maxwell Struthers-- "Experiment"

Cobb, Irvin S.-- "Darkness"

Colcord, Lincoln-- "An Instrument of the Gods"

Finger, Charles J.-- "The Lizard God"

Frank, Waldo-- "Under the Dome"

Gerould, Katherine Fullerton-- "French Eva"

Glasgow, Ellen-- "The Past"

Glaspell, Susan-- "His Smile"

Hallet, Richard Matthews-- "The Harbor Master"

Hart, Frances Noyes-- "Green Gardens"

Hurst, Fannie-- "She Walks in Beauty"

Komroff, Manuel-- "The Little Master of the Sky"

Mott, Frank Luther-- "The Man with the Good Face"

O'Sullivan, Vincent-- "Master of Fallen Years"

Steele, Wilbur Daniel-- "The Shame Dance"

Thayer, Harriet Maxon-- "Kindred"

Towne, Charles Hanson-- "Shelby"

Vorse, Mary Heaton-- "The Wallow of the Sea"

The Best Short Stories of 1922, and the Yearbook of the American Short Story,
edited by **Edward J. O'Brien**

Aiken, Conrad-- "The Dark City"

Anderson, Sherwood-- "I'm a Fool"

Bercovici, Konrad-- "The Death of Murdo"

Boogher, Susan M.-- "An Unknown Warrior"

Booth, Frederick-- "The Helpless Ones"

Bryner, Edna-- "Forest Cover"

Cohen, Rose Gollup-- "Natalka's Portion"

Finger, Charles J.-- "The Shame of Gold"

Fitzgerald, F. Scott-- "Two for a Cent"

Frank, Waldo-- "John the Baptist"

Freedman, David-- "Mendel Marantz: Housewife"

Gerould, Katharine Fullerton-- "Belshazzar's Letter"

Hecht, Ben-- "Winkelburg"

Hergesheimer, Joseph-- "The Token"

Jitro, William-- "The Resurrection and the Life"

Lardner, Ring-- "The Golden Honeymoon"

Oppenheim, James-- "He Laughed at the Gods"

Rosenblatt, Benjamin-- "In the Metropolis"

Steele, Wilbur Daniel-- "From the Other Side of the South"

Wood, Clement-- "The Coffin"

The Best Short Stories of 1923, and the Yearbook of the American Short Story,
edited by **Edward J. O'Brien**

Adams, Bill-- "Way for a Sailor"

Anderson, Sherwood-- "The Man's Story"

Babcock, Edwina Stanton-- "Mr. Cardeezer"

Bercovici, Konrad-- "Seed"

Burnet, Dana-- "Beyond the Cross"

Clark, Valma-- "Ignition"

Cobb, Irvin S.-- "The Chocolate Hyena"

Cournos, John-- "The Samovar"

Dreiser, Theodore-- "Reina"

Ferber, Edna-- "Home Girl"

Goodman, Henry-- "The Button"

Hemingway, Ernest-- "My Old Man"

Hurst, Fannie-- "Seven Candle"

Montague, Margaret Prescott-- "The Today Tomorrow"

Stewart, Solon K.-- "The Contract of Corporal Twing"

Stimson, F. J.-- "By Due Process of Law"

Sukow, Ruth-- "Renters"

Toomer, Jean-- "Blood-Burning Moon"

Vorse, Mary Heaton-- "The Promise"

Wilson, Harry Leon-- "Flora and Fauna"

The Best Short Stories of 1924, and the Yearbook of the American Short Story,
edited by Edward J. O'Brien

Burke, Morgan-- "Champlin"
Cram, Mildred-- "Billy"
Dell, Floyd-- "Phantom Adventure"
Dobie, Charles Caldwell-- "The Cracked Teapot"
Drake, Carlos-- "The Last Dive"
Finger, Charles J.-- "Adventures of Andrew Lang"
Gale, Zona-- "The Biography of Blade"
Greenwald, Tupper-- "Corputt"
Hervey, Harry-- "The Young Men Go Down"
Hess, Leonard L.-- "The Lesser Gift"
Hughes, Rupert-- "Grudges"

Morris, Gouverneur-- "A Postscript to Divorce"
Reese, Lizette Woodworth-- "Forgiveness"
Sergel, Roger-- "Nocturne: A Red Shawl"
Shiffrin, A. B.-- "The Black Laugh"
Suckow, Ruth-- "Four Generations"
Van den Bark, Melvin-- "Two Women and Hog-Back Ridge"
Van Dine, Warren L.-- "The Poet"
Wescott, Glenway-- "In a Thicket"
Wood, Frances Gilchrist-- "Shoes"

The Best Short Stories of 1925, and the Yearbook of the American Short Story,
edited by Edward J. O'Brien

Alexander, Sandra-- "The Gift"
Anderson, Sherwood-- "The Return"
Asch, Nathan-- "Gertude Donovan"
Benefield, Barry-- "Guard of Honor"
Bercovici, Konrad-- "The Beggar of Alcazar"
Cohen, Bella-- "The Laugh"
Dobie, Charles Caldwell-- "The Hands of the Enemy"
Fisher, Rudolph-- "The City of Refuge"
Gerould, Katherine Fullerton-- "An Army with Banners"
Gilkyson, Walter-- "Coward's Castle"

Komroff, Manuel-- "How Does It Feel to Be Free?"
Lardner, Ring-- "Haircut"
Robinson, Robert-- "The Ill Wind"
Scott, Evelyn-- "The Old Lady"
Stanley, May-- "Old Man Ledge"
Steele, Wilber Daniel-- "Six Dollars"
Waldman, Milton-- "The Home Town"
Wescott, Glenway-- "Fire and Water"
Willoughby, Barrett-- "The Devil Drum"
Wylie, Elinor-- "Gideon's Revenge"

The Best Short Stories of 1926, and the Yearbook of the American Short Story,
edited by Edward J. O'Brien

Benefield, Barry-- "Carrie Snyder"
Carver, Ada Jack-- "Maudie"
Corley, Donald-- "The Glass Eye of Throgmorton"
Crowell, Chester T.-- "Take the Stand, Please"
Dingle, A. E.-- "Bound for Rio Grande"
Dudley, Henry Walbridge-- "Query"
Fauset, Arthur Huff-- "Symphonesque"
Gale, Zona-- "Evening"
Greenwald, Tupper-- "Wheels"
Hemingway, Ernest-- "The Undefeated"

Komroff, Manuel-- "The Christian Bite"
Krunich, Milutin-- "Then Christs Fought Hard"
Lardner, Ring-- "Travelogue"
Mason, Grace Sartwell-- "The First Stone"
Meriwether, Susan-- "Grimaldi"
Morris, Ira V.-- "A Tale from the Grave"
Sherwood, Robert E.-- "'Extra! Extra!'"
Steele, Wilbur Daniel-- "Out of the Wind"
Strater, Edward L.-- "The Other Road"
Tracy, Virginia-- "The Giant's Thunder"

The Best Short Stories of 1927, and the Yearbook of the American Short Story,
edited by Edward J. O'Brien

Anderson, Sherwood-- "Another Wife"
Bradford, Roark-- "Child of God"
Brecht, Harold W.-- "Vienna Roast"
Burman, Ben Lucien-- "Minstrels of the Mist"
Finley-Thomas, Elisabeth-- "Mademoiselle"
Hare, Amory-- "Three Lumps of Sugar"
Hemingway, Ernest-- "The Killers"
Hergesheimer, Joseph-- "Trial by Armes"
Heyward, DuBose-- "The Half Pint Flask"
Hopper, James-- "When It Happens"

La Farge, Oliver-- "North Is Black" Lane, Rose Wilder-- "Yarbwoman"
Le Sueur, Meridel-- "Persephone"
Marquand, J. P.-- "Good Morning, Major"
Saxon, Lyle-- "Cane River"
Sexton, John S.-- "The Pawnshop"
Shay, Frank-- "Little Dombey"
Sullivan, Alan-- "In Portofino"
Weeks, Raymond-- "The Hound-Tuner of Callaway"
Wister, Owen-- "The Right Honorable, the Strawberries"

The Best Short Stories of 1928, and the Yearbook of the American Short Story,
edited by Edward J. O'Brien

Brennan, Frederick Hazlitt-- "The Guardeen Angel"
Bromfield, Louis-- "The Cat That Lived at the Ritz"
Brush, Katharine-- "Seven Blocks Apart"
Callaghan, Morley-- "A Country Passion"
Canfield, Dorothy-- "At the Sign of the Three Daughters"
Chambers, Maria Cristina-- "John of God, the Water Carrier"
Cobb, Irvin S.-- "No Dam' Yankee"
Connolly, Myles-- "The First of Mr. Blue"
Edmonds, Walter D.-- "The Swamper"

Harris, Eleanor E.-- "Home to Mother's" Hughes, Llewellyn-- "Lady Wipers of Ypres"
Hurst, Fannie-- "Give This Little Girl a Hand"
McKenna, Edward L.-- "Battered Armor"
Parker, Dorothy-- "A Telephone Call"
Paul, L.-- "Fences"
Roberts, Elizabeth Madox-- "On the Mountain-Side"
Seaver, Edwin-- "The Jew"
Stevens, James-- "The Romantic Sailor"
Suckow, Ruth-- "Midwestern Primitive"
Ware, Edmund-- "So-Long, Oldtimer"

The Best Short Stories of 1929, and the Yearbook of the American Short Story,
edited by Edward J. O'Brien

Addington, Sarah-- "'Hound of Heaven'"
Anderson, Sherwood-- "The Lost Novel"
Beede, Ivan-- "The Country Doctor"
Bercovici, Konrad-- "'There's Money in Poetry'"
Callaghan, Morley-- "Soldier Harmon"
Cather, Willa-- "Double Birthday"
Coates, Grace Stone-- "Wild Plums"
Edmonds, Walter D.-- "Death of Red Peril"
Glover, James Webber-- "First Oboe"
Hall, James Norman-- "Fame for Mr. Beatty"

Herald, Leon Srabian-- "Power of Horizon"
Jenkins, MacGregor-- "Alcantara"
Leech, Margaret-- "Manicure"
McAlmon, Robert-- "Potato Picking"
McCarty, Wilson-- "His Friend the Pig"
McKenna, Edward L.-- "I Have Letters for Marjorie"
Mullen, Robert-- "Light Without Heat"
Patterson, Pernet-- "'Cunjur'"
Wescott, Glenway-- "A Guilty Woman"
Williams, William Carlos-- "The Venus"

The Best Short Stories of 1930, and the Yearbook of the American Short Story,
edited by Edward J. O'Brien

Bishop, Ellen-- "Along a Sandy Road"

Bragdon, Clifford-- "Suffer Little Children"

Burnett, Whit-- "Two Men Free"

Callaghan, Morley-- "The Faithful Wife"

Coates, Grace Stone-- "The Way of the Transgressor"

Draper, Edythe Squier-- "The Voice of the Turtle"

Furniss, Ruth Pine-- "Answer"

Gilkyson, Walter-- "Blue Sky"

Gordon, Caroline-- "Summer Dust"

Hahn, Emily-- "Adventure"

Hartwick, Harry-- "Happiness Up the River"

Kittredge, Eleanor Hayden-- "September Sailing"

Komroff, Manuel-- "A Red Coat for Night"

Lewis, Janet-- "At the Swamp"

March, William-- "The Little Wife"

Parker, Dorothy-- "The Cradle of Civilization"

Paulding, Gouverneur-- "The White Pidgeon"

Polk, William-- "The Patriot"

Porter, Katherine Anne-- "Theft"

Upson, William Hazlett-- "The Vineyard at Schloss Ramsburg"

The Best Short Stories of 1931, and the Yearbook of the American Short Story,
edited by Edward J. O'Brien

Adamic, Louis-- "The Enigma"

Barber, Solon R.-- "The Sound That Frost Makes"

Bessie, Alvah C.-- "Only We Are Barren"

Boyle, Kay-- "Rest Cure"

Bromfield, Louis-- "Tabloid News"

Burnett, Whit-- "A Day in the Country"

Caldwell, Erskine-- "Dorothy"

Callaghan, Morley-- "The Yound Priest"

Edmonds, Walter D.-- "Water Never Hurt a Man"

Faulkner, William-- "That Evening Sun Go Down"

Fitzgerald, F. Scott-- "Babylon Revisited"

Foley, Martha-- "One with Shakespeare"

Gilpatric, Guy-- "The Flaming Chariot"

Gowen, Emmett-- "Fiddlers of Moon Mountain"

Herbst, Josephine-- "I Hear You, Mr. and Mrs. Brown"

Horgan, Paul-- "The Other Side of the Street"

March, William-- "Fifteen from Company K"

Marquis, Don-- "The Other Room"

Milburn, George-- "A Pretty Cute Little Stunt"

Parker, Dorothy-- "Here We Are"

Read, Allen-- "Rhodes Scholar"

Stevens, James-- "The Great Hunter of the Woods"

Upson, William Hazlett-- "The Model House"

Ward, Leo L.-- "The Threshing Ring"

Wilson, Anne Elizabeth-- "The Miracle"

Wimberly, Lowry Charles-- "White Man's Town"

The Best Short Stories of 1932, and the Yearbook of the American Short Story,
edited by Edward J. O'Brien

Adams, Bill-- "The Foreigner"

Bessie, Alvah C.-- "Horizon"

Bragdon, Clifford-- "Love's So Many Things"

Brennan, Louis-- "Poisoner in Motley"

Burnett, Wanda-- "Sand"

Burnett, Whit-- "Sherrel"

Caldwell, Erskine-- "Warm River"

Callaghan, Morley-- "The Red Hat"

Caperton, Helena Lefroy-- "The Honest Wine Merchant"

Cournos, John-- "The Story of the Stranger"

DeJong, David Cornel-- "So Tall the Corn"

Diefenthaler, Andra-- "Hansel"

Faulkner, William-- "Smoke"

Komroff, Manuel-- "Napoleon's Hat under Glass"

Le Sueur, Meridel-- "Spring Story"

Lockwood, Scammon-- "An Arrival at Carthage"

March, William-- "Mist on the Meadow"

Milburn, George-- "Heel, Toe, and a 1, 2, 3, 4"

Morris, Ira V.-- "The Kimono"

Neagoe, Peter-- "Shepherd of the Lord"

Schnabel, Dudley-- "Load"

Stallings, Laurence-- "Gentlemen in Blue"

Tuting, Bernhard Johann-- "The Family Chronicle"

Villa, José García-- "Untitled Story"

Ward, Leo L.-- "The Quarrel"

The Best Short Stories of 1933, and the Yearbook of the American Short Story,
edited by **Edward J. O'Brien**

Albee, George-- "Fame Takes the J Car"

Bessie, Alvah C.-- "A Little Walk"

Bishop, John Peale-- "Toadstools Are Poison"

Boyd, Albert Truman-- "Elmer"

Burnett, Whit-- "Serenade"

Caldwell, Erskine-- "The First Autumn"

Callaghan, Morley-- "A Sick Call"

Cantwell, Robert-- "The Land of Plenty"

Dobie, Charles Caldwell-- "The Honey Pot"

Edmonds, Walter D.-- "Black Wolf"

Farrell, James T.-- "Helen, I Love You!"

Fitzgerald, F. Scott-- "Crazy Sunday"

Flandrau, Grace-- "What Was Truly Mine"

Foley, Martha-- "Martyr"

Gowen, Emmett-- "Fisherman's Luck"

Hale, Nancy-- "Simple Aveu"

Halper, Albert-- "Going to Market"

Joffe, Eugene-- "In the Park"

Lambertson, Louise-- "Sleet Storm"

Leenhouts, Grant-- "The Facts in the Case"

Milburn, George-- "The Apostate"

Morris, Ira V.-- "The Sampler"

Morris, Lloyd-- "Footnote to a Life"

Porter, Katherine Anne-- "The Cracked Looking-Glass"

Reed, Louis-- "Episode at the Pawpaws"

Shumway, Naomi-- "Ike and Us Moons"

Steele, Wilbur Daniel-- "How Beautiful with Shoes"

Thomas, Dorothy-- "The Joybell"

Villa, José García-- "The Fence"

The Best Short Stories of 1934, and the Yearbook of the American Short Story,
edited by **Edward J. O'Brien**

Appel, Benjamin-- "Winter Meeting"

Bessie, Alvah C.-- "No Final Word"

Burnett, Whit-- "The Cats Which Cried"

Caldwell, Erskine-- "Horse Thief"

Callaghan, Morley-- "Mr. and Mrs. Fairbanks"

Childs, Marquis W.-- "The Woman on the Shore"

Corle, Edwin-- "Amethyst"

Corning, Howard McKinley-- "Crossroads Woman"

Faulkner, William-- "Beyond"

Fisher, Rudolph-- "Miss Cynthie"

Foley, Martha-- "She Walks in Beauty"

Godin, Alexander-- "My Dead Brother Comes to America"

Gordon, Caroline-- "Tom Rivers"

Goryan, Sirak-- "The Broken Wheel"

Hall, James Norman-- "Lord of Marutea"

Hughes, Langston-- "Cora Unashamed"

Joffe, Eugene-- "Siege of Love"

Komroff, Manuel-- "Hamlet's Daughter"

Lineaweaver, John-- "Mother Tanner"

McCleary, Dorothy-- "Winter"

Mamet, Louis-- "The Pension"

March, William-- "This Heavy Load"

Marshall, Alan-- "Death and Transfiguration"

Ryan, Paul-- "The Sacred Thing"

Sabsay, Nahum-- "In a Park"

Sheean, Vincent-- "The Hemlock Tree"

Sherman, Richard-- "Now There Is Peace"

Tate, Allen-- "The Immortal Woman"

Terrell, Upton-- "Money at Home"

Zugsmith, Leane-- "Home Is Where You Hang Your Childhood"

The Best Short Stories of 1935, and the Yearbook of the American Short Story,
edited by **Edward J. O'Brien**

Appel, Benjamin-- "Outside Yuma"

Benson, Sally-- "The Overcoat"

Brace, Ernest-- "The Party Next Door"

Brown, Carlton-- "Suns That Our Hearts Harden"

Burnett, Whit-- "Division"

Caldwell, Erskine-- "The Cold Winter"

Callaghan, Morley-- "Father and Son"

Cole, Madelene-- "Bus to Biarritz"

Cooke, Charles-- "Triple Jumps"

DeJong, David Cornel-- "Home-Coming"

Faulkner, William-- "Lo!"
Godchaux, Elma-- "Wild Nigger"
Haardt, Sara-- "Little White Girl"
Haines, William Wister-- "Remarks: None"
Hale, Nancy-- "The Double House"
Horgan, Paul-- "A Distant Harbour"
McCleary, Dorothy-- "Sunday Morning"
McHugh, Vincent-- "Parish of Cockroaches"
Mamet, Louis-- "Episode from Life"

Morang, Alfred-- "Frozen Stillness"
Morris, Edita-- "Mrs. Lancaster-Jones"
Saroyan, William-- "Resurrection of a Life"
Seager, Allan-- "This Town and Salamanca"
Sylvester, Harry-- "A Boxer: Old"
Thielen, Benedict-- "Souvenir of Arizona"
White, Max-- "A Pair of Shoes"
Wolfe, Thomas-- "The Sun and the Rain"

The Best Short Stories of 1936, and the Yearbook of the American Short Story, edited by Edward J. O'Brien

Burlingame, Roger-- "In the Cage"
Callaghan, Morley-- "The Blue Kimono"
Canfield, Dorothy-- "The Murder on Jefferson Street"
Carr, A. H. Z.-- "The Hunch"
Cooke, Charles-- "Catafalque"
Coombes, Evan-- "The North Wind Doth Blow"
Faulkner, William-- "That Will Be Fine"
Fessier, Michael-- "That's What Happened to Me"
Field, S. S.-- "Torrent of Darkness"
Flannagan, Roy-- "The Doorstop"
Foley, Martha-- "Her Own Sweet Simplicity"
Gilkyson, Walter-- "Enemy Country"
Hall, Elizabeth-- "Two Words Are a Story"
Kelly, Frank K.-- "With Some Gaiety and Laughter"
Kelm, Karlton-- "Tinkle and Family Take a Ride"

Komroff, Manuel-- "That Blowzy Goddess Fame"
Larsen, Erling-- "A Kind of a Sunset"
Le Sueur, Meridel-- "Annuciation"
McCleary, Dorothy-- "The Shroud"
Maltz, Albert-- "Man on a Road"
Porter, Katherine Anne-- "The Grave"
Richmond, Roaldus-- "Thanks for Nothing"
Seager, Allan-- "Fugue for Harmonica"
Slesinger, Tess-- "A Life in the Day of a Writer"
Thomas, Elisabeth Wilkins-- "Traveling Salesman"
Vines, Howell-- "The Mustydines Was Ripe"
Whitehand, Robert-- "American Nocturne"
Williams, Calvin-- "On the Sidewalk"
Wilson, William E.-- "The Lone Pioneer"
Wolfe, Thomas-- "Only the Dead Know Brooklyn"

The Best Short Stories of 1937, and the Yearbook of the American Short Story, edited by Edward J. O'Brien

Buckner, Robert-- "The Man Who Won the War"
Burlingame, Roger-- "The Last Equation"
Callaghan, Morley-- "The Voyage Out"
Cooke, Charles-- "Enter Daisy; to Her, Alexandra"
Faulkner, William-- "Fool About a Horse"
Field, S. S.-- "Goodbye to Cap'n John"
Foley, Martha-- "Glory, Glory, Hallelujah!"
Godchaux, Elma-- "Chains"
Halper, Albert-- "The Poet"
Hemingway, Ernest-- "The Snows of Kilimanjaro"
Heth, Edward Harris-- "Homecoming"
Horgan, Paul-- "The Surgeon and the Nun"
Komroff, Manuel-- "The Girl with the Flaxen Hair"
Krantz, David E.-- "Awakening and the Destination"
Kroll, Harry Harrison-- "Second Wife"

Linn, R. H.-- "The Intrigue of Mr. S. Yamamoto"
MacDougall, Ursula-- "Titty's Dead and Tatty Weeps"
McGinnis, Allen-- "Let Nothing You Dismay"
March, William-- "Maybe the Sun Will Shine"
Morris, Edita-- "A Blade of Grass"
Morris, Ira V.-- "Marching Orders"
Porter, Katharine Anne-- "The Old Order"
St. Joseph, Ellis-- "A Passenger to Bali"
Saroyan, William-- "The Crusader"
Stuart, Jesse-- "Hair"
Thielen, Benedict-- "Lieutenant Pearson"
Thompson, Lovell-- "The Iron City"
Wright, Wilson-- "Arrival on a Holiday"
Zugsmith, Leane-- "Room in the World"

The Best Short Stories of 1938, and the Yearbook of the American Short Story,
edited by Edward J. O'Brien

Ayre, Robert-- "Mr. Sycamore"

Benedict, Libby-- "Blind Man's Buff"

Benét, Stephen Vincent-- "A Tooth for Paul Revere"

Bond, Nelson S.-- "Mr. Mergenthwirkers Lobblies"

Callaghan, Morley-- "The Cheat's Remorse"

Cheever, John-- "The Brothers"

Cherkasski, Vladimir-- "What Hurts Is That I Was in a Hurry"

Cook, Whitfield-- "Dear Mr. Flessheimer"

Creyke, Richard Paulett-- "Niggers Are Such Liars"

Di Donato, Pietro-- "Christ in Concrete"

Fessier, Michael-- "Black Wind and Lightning"

Hannum, Alberta Pierson-- "Turkey Hunt"

Komroff, Manuel-- "The Whole World Is Outside"

Le Sueur, Meridel-- "The Girl"

Ludlow, Don-- "She Always Wanted Shoes"

McCleary, Dorothy-- "Little Bride"

March, William-- "The Last Meeting"

Moll, Elick-- "To Those Who Wait"

Pereda, Prudencio de-- "The Spaniard"

Prokosch, Frederic-- "A Russian Idyll"

Rayner, George Thorp-- "A Real American Fellow"

Roberts, Elizabeth Madox-- "The Haunted Palace"

Schorer, Mark-- "Boy in the Summer Sun"

Seager, Allan-- "Pro Arte"

Steinbeck, John-- "The Chrysanthemums"

Stuart, Jesse-- "Huey, the Engineer"

Swados, Harvey-- "The Amateurs"

Warren, Robert Penn-- "Christmas Gift"

Welty, Eudora-- "Lily Daw and the Three Ladies"

Wolfert, Ira-- "Off the Highway"

The Best Short Stories of 1939, and the Yearbook of the American Short Story,
edited by Edward J. O'Brien

Beck, Warren-- "The Blue Sash"

Caldwell, Ronald-- "Vision in the Sea"

Callaghan, Morley-- "It Had to Be Done"

Cheever, John-- "Frère Jacques"

Clark, Gean-- "Indian on the Road"

Coates, Robert M.-- "Passing Through"

Cohn, David L.-- "Black Troubadour"

Danielson, Richard Ely-- "Corporal Hardy"

Ellson, Hal-- "The Rat Is a Mouse"

Halper, Albert-- "Prelude"

Horgan, Paul-- "To the Mountains"

Jenison, Madge-- "True Believer"

Komroff, Manuel-- "What Is a Miracle?"

Le Sueur, Meridel-- "Salutation to Spring"

MacDonald, Alan-- "An Arm Upraised"

Maltz, Albert-- "The Happiest Man on Earth"

St. Joseph, Ellis-- "Leviathan"

Saroyan, William-- "Piano"

Schoenstedt, Walter-- "The Girl from the River Barge"

Seager, Allan-- "Berkshire Comedy"

Seide, Michael-- "Bad Boy from Brooklyn"

Stuart, Jesse-- "Eustacia"

Sylvester, Harry-- "The Crazy Guy"

Thielen, Benedict-- "The Thunderstorm"

Warren, Robert Penn-- "How Willie Proudfit Came Home"

Welty, Eudora-- "A Curtain of Green"

Werner, Heinz-- "Black Tobias and the Empire"

Wolfert, Ira-- "The Way the Luck Runs"

Wright, Eugene-- "The White Camel"

Wright, Richard-- "Bright and Morning Star"

The Best Short Stories of 1940, and the Yearbook of the American Short Story,
edited by Edward J. O'Brien

Boyle, Kay-- "Anschluss"

Caldwell, Erskine-- "The People vs. Abe Lathan, Colored"

Callaghan, Morley-- "Getting on in the World"

Eisenberg, Frances-- "Roof Sitter"

Farrell, James T.-- "The Fall of Machine Gun McGurk"

Faulkner, William-- "Hand upon the Waters"
Fitzgerald, F. Scott-- "Design in Plaster"
Gordon, Caroline-- "Frankie and Thomas and Bud Asbury"
Hemingway, Ernest-- "Under the Ridge"
King, Mary-- "The Honey House"
Komroff, Manuel-- "Death of an Outcast"
Lull, Roderick-- "That Fine Place We Had Last Year"
Lussu, Emilio-- "Your General Does Not Sleep"
McCleary, Dorothy-- "Something Jolly"
Morris, Edita-- "Kullan"
Morris, Ira V.-- "The Beautiful Fire"
Pasinetti, P. M.-- "Family History"
Pereda, Prudencio de-- "The Way Death Comes"
Pooler, James-- "Herself"

Porter, Katherine Anne-- "The Downward Path to Wisdom"
Saroyan, William-- "The Presbyterian Choir Singers"
Seide, Michael-- "Words Without Music"
Shaw, Irwin-- "Main Currents of American Thought"
Slocombe, George-- "The Seven Men of Rouen"
Stern, Morton-- "Four Worms Turning"
Storm, Hans Otto-- "The Two Deaths of Kaspar Rausch"
Stuart, Jesse-- "Rich Men"
Sylvester, Harry-- "Beautifully and Bravely"
Thielen, Benedict-- "Night and the Lost Armies"
Welty, Eudora-- "The Hitch-Hikers"
Zara, Louis-- "Resurgam"

The Best Short Stories of 1941, and the Yearbook of the American Short Story, *edited by* **Martha Foley**

Ashton, E. B.-- "Shadow of a Girl"
Benét, Stephen Vincent-- "All Around the Town"
Caldwell, Erskine-- "Handy"
Callaghan, Morley-- "Big Jules"
Coates, Robert M.-- "The Net"
DeJong, David Cornel-- "Mamma Is a Lady"
Exall, Henry-- "To the Least . . ."
Fante, John-- "A Nun No More"
Faulkner, William-- "Gold Is Not Always"
Garfinkel, Harold-- "'Color Trouble'"
Gizycka, Felicia-- "The Magic Wire"
Herman, Justin-- "Smile for the Man, Dear"
Kees, Weldon-- "The Life of the Mind"
King, Mary-- "The White Bull"
Kober, Arthur-- "Some People Are Just Plumb Crazy"

La Farge, Christopher-- "Scorn and Comfort"
Levin, Meyer-- "The System Was Doomed"
Lull, Roderick-- "Don't Get Me Wrong"
Maltz, Albert-- "Sunday Morning on Twentieth Street"
Neagoe, Peter-- "Ill-Winds from the Wide World"
Saroyan, William-- "The Three Swimmers and the Educated Grocer"
Shaw, Irwin-- "Triumph of Justice"
Shore, Wilma-- "The Butcher"
Stegner, Wallace-- "Goin' to Town"
Stuart, Jesse-- "Love"
Thielen, Benedict-- "The Psychologist"
Weidman, Jerome-- "Houdini"
Weller, George-- "Strip-Tease"
Wright, Richard-- "Almos' a Man"

The Best American Short Stories, 1942, and the Yearbook of the American Short Story, *edited by* **Martha Foley**

Algren, Nelson-- "Biceps"
Bemelmans, Ludwig-- "The Valet of the Splendide"
Benson, Sally-- "Fifty-one Thirty-five Kensington: August, 1903"
Boyle, Kay-- "Nothing Ever Breaks Except the Heart"
Bryan, Jack Y.-- "For Each of Us"

Clark, Walter Van Tilburg-- "The Portable Phonograph"
DeJong, David Cornel-- "That Frozen Hour"
Eakin, Boyce-- "Prairies"
Fineman, Morton-- "Tell Him I Waited"
Gibbons, Robert-- "A Loaf of Bread"
Hale, Nancy-- "Those Are as Brothers"

Kantor, MacKinlay--"That Greek Dog"

Knight, Eric--"Sam Small's Better Half"

Lavin, Mary--"At Sallygap"

Medearis, Mary--"Death of a Country Doctor"

Morris, Edita--"Caput Mortuum"

O'Hara, Mary--"My Friend Flicka"

Peattie, Margaret Rhodes--"The Green Village"

Saroyan, William--"The Hummingbird That Lived Through Winter"

Schulberg, Budd Wilson--"The Real Viennese Schmalz"

Seide, Michael--"Sacrifice of Isaac"

Shaw, Irwin--"Search Through the Streets of the City"

Stegner, Wallace--"In the Twilight"

Steinbeck, John--"How Edith McGillcuddy Met R. L. Stevenson"

Stuart, Jesse--"The Storm"

Taylor, Peter--"The Fancy Woman"

Thomas, Dorothy--"My Pigeon Pair"

Thurber, James--"You Could Look It Up"

Vatsek, Joan--"The Bees"

Worthington, Marjorie--"Hunger"

The Best American Short Stories, 1943, and the Yearbook of the American Short Story, *edited by* **Martha Foley**

Baum, Vicki--"The Healthy Life"

Beck, Warren--"Boundary Line"

Boyle, Kay--"Frenchman's Ship"

Cheever, John--"The Pleasures of Solitude"

D'Agostino, Guido--"The Dream of Angelo Zara"

Dyer, Murray--"Samuel Blane"

Faulkner, William--"The Bear"

Field, Rachel--"Beginning of Wisdom"

Fisher, Vardis--"A Partnership with Death"

Flandrau, Grace--"What Do You See, Dear Enid?"

Gibbons, Robert--"Time's End"

Gray, Peter--"Threnody for Stelios"

Hale, Nancy--"Who Lived and Died Believing"

Horgan, Paul--"The Peach Stone"

Knight, Laurette MacDuffie--"The Enchanted"

Laidlaw, Clara--"The Little Black Boys"

Lavin, Mary--"Love Is for Lovers"

Morris, Edita--"Young Man in an Astrakhan Cap"

Saroyan, William--"Knife-like, Flower-like, Like Nothing at All in the World"

Schwartz, Delmore--"An Argument in 1934"

Shaw, Irwin--"Preach on the Dusty Roads"

Shedd, Margaret--"My Public"

Stegner, Wallace--"Chip off the Old Block"

Stuart, Alison--"Death and My Uncle Felix"

Stuart, Jesse--"Dawn of Remembered Spring"

Sullivan, Richard--"The Women"

Thurber, James--"The Catbird Seat"

Treichler, Jessie--"Homecoming"

Weidman, Jerome--"Philadelphia Express"

Welty, Eudora--"Asphodel"

The Best American Short Stories, 1944, and the Yearbook of the American Short Story, *edited by* **Martha Foley**

Alexander, Sidney--"The White Boat"

Barrett, William E.--"Señor Payroll"

Bellow, Saul--"Notes of a Dangling Man"

Canfield, Dorothy--"The Knot Hole"

De Lanux, Eyre--"The S.S. Libertad"

Eastman, Elizabeth--"Like a Field Mouse over the Heart"

Eustis, Helen--"The Good Days and the Bad"

Fifield, William--"The Fishermen of Patzcuaro"

Fleming, Berry--"Strike up a Stirring Music"

Hawthorne, Hazel--"More Like a Coffin"

Houston, Noel--"A Local Skirmish"

Jackson, Shirley--"Come Dance with Me in Ireland"

Johnson, Josephine W.--"The Rented Room"

Kaplan, H. J.--"The Mohammedans"

McCullers, Carson--"The Ballad of the Sad Café"

March, William--"The Female of the Fruit Fly'"

Meighan, Astrid--"Shoe the Horse and Shoe the Mare"

Mian, Mary-- "Exiles from the Creuse"

Morris, Edita-- "Heart of Marzipan"

Nabokov, Vladimir-- "'That in Aleppo Once . . . '"

Portugal, Ruth-- "Neither Here Nor There"

Powers, J. F.-- "Lions, Harts, Leaping Does"

Schmitt, Gladys-- "All Souls'"

Shaw, Irwin-- "The Veterans Reflect"

Stiles, George-- "A Return"

Surmelian, Leon Z.-- "My Russian Cap"

Trilling, Lionel-- "Of This Time, of That Place"

Warner, Elizabeth-- "An Afternoon"

West, Jessamyn-- "The Illumination"

Winters, Emmanuel-- "God's Agents Have Beards"

The Best American Short Stories, 1945, and the Yearbook of the American Short Story,
edited by **Martha Foley**

Algren, Nelson-- "How the Devil Came Down Division Street"

Beck, Warren-- "The First Fish"

Bromfield, Louis-- "Crime Passionnel"

Bulosan, Carlos-- "My Brother Osong's Career in Politics"

Deasy, Mary-- "Harvest"

Fenton, Edward-- "Burial in the Desert"

Fineman, Morton-- "The Light of Morning"

Gerry, Bill-- "Understand What I Mean?"

Gill, Brendan-- "The Test"

Hagopian, Richard-- "'Be Heavy'"

Hahn, Emily-- "It Never Happened"

Hardy, W. G.-- "The Czech Dog"

Johnson, Josephine W.-- "Fever Flower"

McLaughlin, Robert-- "Poor Everybody"

McNulty, John-- "Don't Scrub off These Names"

Miller, Warren-- "The Animal's Fair"

Panetta, George-- "Papa, Mama, and Economics"

Pennell, Joseph Stanley-- "On the Way to Somewhere Else"

Portugal, Ruth-- "Call a Solemn Assembly"

Pratt, Theodore-- "The Owl That Kept Winking"

Rosenfeld, Isaac-- "The Hand That Fed Me"

Rowell, Donna-- "A War Marriage"

Schmitt, Gladys-- "The Mourners"

Shaw, Irwin-- "Gunners' Passage"

Stafford, Jean-- "The Wedding: Beacon Hill"

Tartt, Ruby Pickens-- "Alabama Sketches"

Taylor, Peter-- "Rain in the Heart"

Warren, Robert Penn-- "Cass Mastern's Wedding Ring"

West, Jessamyn-- "First Day Finish"

Zugsmith, Leane-- "This Is a Love Story"

Zukerman, William-- "A Ship to Tarshish"

The Best American Short Stories, 1946, and the Yearbook of the American Short Story,
edited by **Martha Foley**

Angoff, Charles-- "Jerry"

Beck, Warren-- "Out of Line"

Berryman, John-- "The Lovers"

Bradbury, Ray-- "The Big Black and White Game"

Breuer, Bessie-- "Bury Your Own Dead"

Brown, T. K., III-- "The Valley of the Shadow"

Burnett, W. R.-- "The Ivory Tower"

Clark, Walter Van Tilburg-- "The Wind and the Snow of Winter"

Critchell, Laurence-- "Flesh and Blood"

Deasy, Mary-- "A Sense of Danger"

Elkin, Samuel-- "In a Military Manner"

Gottlieb, Elaine-- "The Norm"

Hardwick, Elizabeth-- "The Mysteries of Eleusis"

Johnson, Josephine W.-- "Story Without End"

Lampman, Ben Hur-- "Old Bill Bent to Drink"

Liben, Meyer-- "The Caller"

Liebling, A. J.-- "Run, Run, Run, Run"

Mitchell, W. O.-- "The Owl and the Bens"

Nabokov, Vladimir-- "Time and Ebb"

Petry, Ann-- "Like a Winding Sheet"

Ruml, Wentzle, III-- "For a Beautiful Relationship"

Schmitt, Gladys-- "The King's Daughter"

Stark, Irwin-- "The Bridge"

Stern, James-- "The Woman Who Was Loved"

Still, James-- "Mrs. Razor"

Taylor, Peter-- "The Scout Master"

Trilling, Lionel-- "The Other Margaret"

Weigel, Henrietta-- "Love Affair"

West, Jessamyn-- "The Singing Lesson"

Woods, Glennyth-- "Death in a Cathedral"

The Best American Short Stories, 1947, and the Yearbook of the American Short Story,
edited by **Martha Foley**

Broderick, Francis L.-- "Return by Faith"

Canfield, Dorothy-- "Sex Education"

Capote, Truman-- "The Headless Hawk"

Fontaine, Robert-- "Day of Gold and Darkness"

Gerstley, Adelaide-- "The Man in the Mirror"

Goodwin, John B. L.-- "The Cocoon"

Goss, John Mayo-- "Bird Song"

Griffith, Paul-- "The Horse like September"

Guérard, Albert J.-- "Turista"

Hardwick, Elizabeth-- "The Golden Stallion"

Harris, Ruth McCoy-- "Up the Road a Piece"

Heggen, Thomas-- "Night Watch"

Heth, Edward Harris-- "Under the Ginkgo Trees"

Humphreys, John Richard-- "Michael Finney and the Little Men"

Lincoln, Victoria-- "Down in the Reeds by the River"

Lowry, Robert-- "Little Baseball World"

Martenet, May Davies-- "Father Delacroix"

Mayhall, Jane-- "The Darkness"

Powers, J. F.-- "Prince of Darkness"

Raphaelson, Samson-- "The Greatest Idea in the World"

Schorer, Mark-- "What We Don't Know Hurts Us"

Seager, Allan-- "Game Chickens"

Shaw, Irwin-- "Act of Faith"

Shirley, Sylvia-- "The Red Dress"

Stafford, Jean-- "The Interior Castle"

Stark, Irwin-- "Shock Treatment"

Stegner, Wallace-- "The Women on the Wall"

Tucci, Niccolò-- "The Seige"

Weaver, John D.-- "Bread and Games"

Williams, Lawrence-- "The Hidden Room"

The Best American Short Stories, 1948, and the Yearbook of the American Short Story,
edited by **Martha Foley**

Alexander, Sidney-- "Part of the Act"

Bowles, Paul-- "A Distant Episode"

Bradbury, Ray-- "I See You Never"

Canfield, Dorothy-- "The Apprentice"

Cheever, John-- "The Enormous Radio"

Clay, George R.-- "That's My Johnny-Boy"

Clayton, John Bell-- "Visitor from Philadelphia"

Cousins, Margaret-- "A Letter to Mr. Priest"

Fisher, M. F. K.-- "The Hollow Heart"

Garrigan, Philip-- "'Fly, Fly, Little Dove'"

Gellhorn, Martha-- "Miami-New York"

Grennard, Elliott-- "Sparrow's Last Jump"

Gustafson, Ralph-- "The Human Fly"

Hersey, John-- "Why Were You Sent out Here?"

Jeffers, Lance-- "The Dawn Swings In"

Lincoln, Victoria-- "Morning, a Week Before the Crime"

Lowry, Robert-- "The Terror in the Streets"

Lynch, John A.-- "The Burden"

McHugh, Vincent-- "The Search"

Morse, Robert-- "The Professor and the Puli"

Portugal, Ruth-- "The Stupendous Fortune"

Post, Mary Brinker-- "That's the Man"

Root, Waverley-- "Carmencita"

Sharp, Dolph-- "The Tragedy in Jancie Brierman's Life"

Stegner, Wallace-- "Beyond the Glass Mountain"

Sulkin, Sidney-- "The Plan"

Welty, Eudora-- "The Whole World Knows"

White, E. B.-- "The Second Tree from the Corner"

The Best American Short Stories, 1949, and the Yearbook of the American Short Story,
edited by **Martha Foley**

Albee, George-- "Mighty, Mighty Pretty"

Biddle, Livingston, Jr.-- "The Vacation"

Bishop, Elizabeth-- "The Farmer's Children"

Bowles, Paul-- "Under the Sky"

Brookhouser, Frank-- "My Father and the Circus"

Deal, Borden-- "Exodus"

Dolokhov, Adele-- "Small Miracle"

Dorrance, Ward-- "The White Hound"

Felsen, Henry Gregor-- "Li Chang's Million"

Gibbons, Robert-- "Departure of Hubbard"

Griffith, Beatrice-- "In the Flow of Time"

Hardwick, Elizabeth-- "Evenings at Home"

Heller, Joseph-- "Castle of Snow"

Herschberger, Ruth-- "A Sound in the Night"

Hunter, Laura-- "Jerry"

Kjelgaard, Jim-- "Of the River and Uncle Pidcock"

Lull, Roderick-- "Footnote to American History"

Mabry, Thomas-- "The Vault"

Macdonald, Agnes-- "Vacia"

Mayhall, Jane-- "The Men"

Morgan, Patrick-- "The Heifer"

Pfeffer, Irving-- "All Prisoners Here"

Rogers, John-- "Episode of a House Remembered"

Salinger, J. D.-- "A Girl I Knew"

Segre, Alfredo-- "Justice Has No Number"

Shapiro, Madelon-- "An Island for My Friends"

Stafford, Jean-- "Children Are Bored on Sunday"

West, Jessamyn-- "Road to the Isles"

The Best American Short Stories, 1950, and the Yearbook of the American Short Story,
edited by **Martha Foley**

Angoff, Charles-- "Where Did Yesterday Go?"

Aswell, James-- "Shadow of Evil"

Babb, Sanora-- "The Wild Flower"

Beck, Warren-- "Edge of Doom"

Bellow, Saul-- "A Sermon by Doctor Pep"

Bennett, Peggy-- "Death Under the Hawthornes"

Bowles, Paul-- "Pastor Dowe at Tacaté"

Christopher, Robert-- "Jishin"

Elliott, George P.-- "The NRACP"

Fiedler, Leslie A.-- "The Fear of Innocence"

Gustafson, Ralph-- "The Pigeon"

Hauser, Marianne-- "The Mouse"

Johnson, Josephine W.-- "The Author"

Kaplan, Ralph-- "The Artist"

Karchmer, Sylvan— "Hail Brother and Farewell"

Lamkin, Speed-- "Comes a Day"

Lincoln, Victoria-- "The Glass Wall"

McCoy, Esther-- "The Cape"

Maier, Howard-- "The World Outside"

Newhouse, Edward-- "My Brother's Second Funeral"

Norris, Hoke-- "Take Her Up Tenderly"

Parker, Glidden-- "Bright and Morning"

Putman, Clay-- "The Old Acrobat and the Ruined City"

Rothberg, Abraham-- "Not with Our Fathers"

Stewart, Ramona-- "The Promise"

Still, James-- "A Master Time"

Strong, Joan-- "The Hired Man"

Taylor, Peter-- "A Wife of Nashville"

The Best American Short Stories, 1951, and the Yearbook of the American Short Story,
edited by **Martha Foley, assisted by Joyce F. Hartman**

Angell, Roger-- "Flight Through the Dark"

Asch, Nathan-- "Inland, Western Sea"

Bennett, Peggy-- "A Fugitive from the Mind"

Bolté, Mary-- "The End of the Depression"

Calisher, Hortense-- "In Greenwich There Are Many Gravelled Walks"

Casper, Leonard-- "Sense of Direction"

Cassill, R. V.-- "Larchmoor Is Not the World"

Cheever, John-- "The Season of Divorce"

Downey, Harris-- "The Hunters"

Enright, Elizabeth-- "The Temperate Zone"

Gardon, Ethel Edison-- "The Value of the Dollar"

Goodman, J. Carol-- "The Kingdom of Gordon"

Goyen, William-- "Her Breath upon the Windowpane"

Jackson, Shirley-- "The Summer People"

Johnson, Josephine W.-- "The Mother's Story"

Karmel, Ilona-- "Fru Holm"

La Farge, Oliver-- "Old Century's River"

Lanning, George-- "Old Turkey Neck"

Lewis, Ethel G.-- "Portrait"

Livesay, Dorothy-- "The Glass House"

Macauley, Robie-- "The Wishbone"

Malamud, Bernard-- "The Prison"

Patt, Esther-- "The Butcherbirds"

Powers, J. F.-- "Death of a Favorite"

Rader, Paul-- "The Tabby Cat"

Stafford, Jean-- "The Nemesis"

West, Ray B., Jr.-- "The Last of the Grizzly Bears"

Williams, Tennessee-- "The Resemblance Between a Violin Case and a Coffin"

The Best American Short Stories, 1952, and the Yearbook of the American Short Story, *edited by* **Martha Foley, assisted by Joyce F. Hartman**

Berge, Bill-- "That Lovely Green Boat"

Bethel, Laurence-- "The Call"

Bowen, Robert O.-- "The Other River"

Boyle, Kay-- "The Lost"

Bradbury, Ray-- "The Other Foot"

Calisher, Hortense-- "A Wreath for Miss Totten"

Cardozo, Nancy-- "The Unborn Ghosts"

Chaikin, Nancy G.-- "The Climate of the Family"

Chidester, Ann-- "Wood Smoke"

Eaton, Charles Edward-- "The Motion of Forgetfulness Is Slow"

Elliott, George P.-- "Children of Ruth"

Enright, Elizabeth-- "The First Face"

Garner, Hugh-- "The Conversion of Willie Heaps"

Gellhorn, Martha-- "Weekend at Grimsby"

Glen, Emilie-- "Always Good for a Belly Laugh"

Hale, Nancy-- "Brahmin Beachhead"

Horton, Philip-- "What's in a Corner"

Kuehn, Susan-- "The Searchers"

Rooney, Frank-- "Cyclists' Raid"

Saroyan, William-- "Palo"

Schulberg, Stuart-- "I'm Really Fine"

Stafford, Jean-- "The Healthiest Girl in Town"

Stegner, Wallace-- "The Traveler"

Still, James-- "A Ride on the Short Dog"

Swados, Harvey-- "The Letters"

Van Doren, Mark-- "Nobody Say a Word"

Waldron, Daniel-- "Evensong"

Weston, Christine-- "Loud Sing Cuckoo"

Yamamoto, Hisaye-- "Yoneko's Earthquake"

The Best American Short Stories, 1953, and the Yearbook of the American Short Story, *edited by* **Martha Foley, assisted by Joyce F. Hartman**

Agee, James-- "A Mother's Tale"

Ballard, James-- "A Mountain Summer"

Becker, Stephen-- "The Town Mouse"

Carroll, Joseph-- "At Mrs. Farrelly's"

Cassill, R. V.-- "The Life of the Sleeping Beauty"

Coates, Robert M.-- "The Need"

Deasy, Mary-- "Morning Sun"

Downey, Harris-- "Crispin's Way"

Duke, Osborn-- "Struttin' with Some Barbecue"

Elliott, George P.-- "Faq'"

Froscher, Wingate-- "A Death in the Family"

Gregory, Vahan Krikorian-- "Athens, Greece, 1942"

Hall, James B.-- "A Spot in History"

Jackson, Charles Tenney-- "The Bullalo Wallow"

Jackson, Roberts-- "Fly away Home"

Jones, Madison P., Jr.-- "Dog Days"

Marsh, Willard-- "Beachhead in Bohemia"

Marshall, Elizabeth-- "The Hill People"

Noland, Felix-- "The Whipping"

Pendergast, Constance-- "The Picnic"

Purdy, Ken-- "Change of Plan"

Putman, Clay-- "Our Vegetable Love"

Shattuck, Roger-- "Workout on the River"

Shultz, Henry-- "Oreste"

Sultan, Stanley-- "The Fugue of the Fig Tree"
Van Doren, Mark-- "Still, Still So"
Wesely, Donald-- "A Week of Roses"

Weston, Christine-- "The Forest of the Night"
Williams, Tennessee-- "Three Players of a Summer Game"
Wincelberg, Simon-- "The Conqueror"

The Best American Short Stories, 1954, and the Yearbook of the American Short Story"

Bush, Geoffrey-- "A Great Reckoning in a Little Room"
Clay, Richard-- "A Beautiful Night for Orion"
DeMott, Benjamin-- "The Sense That in the Scene Delights"
Dorrance, Ward-- "A Stop on the Way to Texas"
Doughty, LeGarde S.-- "The Firebird"
Enright, Elizabeth-- "Apple Seed and Apple Thorn"
Frazee, Steve-- "My Brother Down There"
Gold, Ivan-- "A Change of Air"
Heath, Priscilla-- "Farewell, Sweet Love"
Hebert, Anne-- "The House on the Esplanade"
Holwerda, Frank-- "Char on Raven's Bench"

Jarrell, Randall-- "Gertrude and Sidney"
Jenks, Almet-- "No Way Down"
Loveridge, George-- "The Latter End"
Patton, Frances Gray-- "The Game"
Payne, Robert-- "The Red Mountain"
Robinson, Rosanne Smith-- "The Mango Tree"
Shaw, Irwin-- "In the French Style"
Stafford, Jean-- "The Shorn Lamb"
Taylor, Kressmann-- "The Pale Green Fishes"
Traven, B.-- "The Third Guest"
Weston, Christine-- "The Man in Gray"
Wolfert, Ira-- "The Indomitable Blue"
Yentzen, Vurell-- "The Rock"

The Best American Short Stories, 1955, and the Yearbook of the American Short Story,
edited by **Martha Foley**

Bowen, Robert O.-- "A Matter of Price"
Cardozo, Nancy-- "The Excursionists"
Chaikin, Nancy G.-- "Bachelor of Arts"
Cheever, John-- "The Country Husband"
Connell, Evan S., Jr.-- "The Fisherman from Chihuahua"
Coogan, Joe-- "The Decline and Fall of Augie Sheean"
Curley, Daniel-- "The Day of the Equinox"
Eastlake, William-- "Little Joe"
Elliott, George P.-- "Brother Quintillian and Dick the Chemist"
Hyman, Mac-- "The Hundredth Centennial"
La Farge, Oliver-- "The Resting Place"
Malumud, Bernard-- "The Magic Barrel"

Merril, Judith-- "Dead Center"
Middleton, Elizabeth H.-- "Portrait of My Son as a Young Man"
Mudrick, Marvin-- "The Professor and the Poet"
Nemerov, Howard-- "Yore"
O'Connor, Flannery-- "A Circle in the Fire"
Shaw, Irwin-- "Tip on a Dead Jockey"
Stegner, Wallace-- "Maiden in a Tower"
Stuart, David-- "Bird Man"
Swados, Harvey-- "Herman's Day"
Van Doren, Mark-- "I Got a Friend"
Vukelich, George-- "The Scale Room"
Welty, Eudora-- "Going to Naples"

The Best American Short Stories, 1956, and the Yearbook of the American Short Story,
edited by **Martha Foley**

Angell, Roger-- "In an Early Winter"
Brown, Morris-- "The Snow Owl"
Clay, George R.-- "We're All Guests"
Coates, Robert M.-- "In a Foreign City"

Davis, Wesley Ford-- "The Undertow"
Dorrance, Ward-- "The Devil on a Hot Afternoon"
Downey, Harris-- "The Hobo"
Eastlake, William-- "The Quiet Chimneys"

Elliott, George P.-- "Is He Dead?"

Granit, Arthur-- "Free the Canaries from Their Cages!"

Housepian, Marjorie-- "How Levon Dai Was Surrendered to the Edemuses"

Jackson, Shirley-- "One Ordinary Day, with Peanuts"

Kerouac, Jack-- "The Mexican Girl"

LaMar, Nathaniel-- "Creole Love Song"

Lyons, Augusta Wallace-- "The First Flower"

Molloy, Ruth Branning-- "Twenty Below, at the End of a Lane"

O'Connor, Flannery-- "The Artificial Nigger"

Roth, Philip-- "The Contest for Aaron Gold"

Shepley, John-- "The Machine"

Weston, Christine-- "Four Annas"

Yellen, Samuel-- "Reginald Pomfret Skelton"

The Best American Short Stories, 1957, and the Yearbook of the American Short Story, *edited by* **Martha Foley**

Algren, Nelson-- "Beasts of the Wild"

Berriault, Gina-- "Around the Dear Ruin"

Betts, Doris-- "The Proud and Virtuous"

Blassingame, Wyatt-- "Man's Courage"

Butler, Frank-- "To the Wilderness I Wander"

Clemons, Walter-- "The Dark Roots of the Rose"

Connell, Evan S., Jr.-- "Arcturus"

Downey, Harris-- "The Song"

Eastlake, William-- "The Unhappy Hunting Grounds"

Hale, Nancy-- "A Summer's Long Dream"

Langdon, John-- "The Blue Serge Suit"

Mabry, Thomas-- "Lula Borrow"

McClintic, Winona-- "A Heart of Furious Fancies"

O'Connor, Flannery-- "Greenleaf"

Olsen, Tillie-- "I Stand Here Ironing"

Robinson, Anthony-- "The Farlow Express"

Robinson, Rosanne Smith-- "The Impossible He"

Smith, John Campbell-- "Run, Run away, Brother"

Weigel, Henrietta-- "Saturday Is a Poor Man's Port"

Woodward, Gordon-- "Escape to the City"

The Best American Short Stories, 1958, and the Yearbook of the American Short Story, *edited by* **Martha Foley and David Burnett**

Agee, James-- "The Waiting"

Baldwin, James-- "Sonny's Blues"

Bowles, Paul-- "The Frozen Fields"

Bradbury, Ray-- "The Day It Rained Forever"

Bradshaw, George-- "'The Picture Wouldn't Fit in the Stove'"

Chester, Alfred-- "As I Was Going up the Stair"

Grau, Shirley Ann-- "Hunter's Home"

Hill, Pati-- "Ben"

Macauley, Robie-- "Legend of Two Swimmers"

McCord, Jean-- "Somewhere out of Nowhere"

Nemerov, Howard-- "A Delayed Hearing"

O'Connor, Flannery-- "A View of the Woods"

Ostroff, Anthony-- "La Bataille des Fleurs"

Parker, Dorothy-- "The Banquet of Crow"

Robin, Ralph-- "Mr. Pruitt"

Scoyk, Bob Ban-- "Home from Camp"

Stafford, Jean-- "A Reasonable Facsimile"

Swados, Harvey-- "Joe, the Vanishing American"

Thurman, Richard-- "Not Another Word"

White, Robin-- "House of Many Rooms"

Wright, Richard-- "Big, Black, Good Man"

The Best American Short Stories, 1959, and the Yearbook of the American Short Story, *edited by* **Martha Foley and David Burnett**

Berry, John-- "Jawaharlal and the Three Cadavers"

Bingham, Sallie-- "Winter Term"

Butler, Frank-- "Amid a Place of Stone"

Cheever, John-- "The Bella Lingua"

Coates, Robert M.-- "Getaway"

Finney, Charles G.-- "The Iowan's Curse"

Gass, William H.-- "Mrs. Mean"

Geeslin, Hugh, Jr.-- "A Day in the Life of the Boss"

Gold, Herbert-- "Love and Like"

Holwerda, Frank-- "In a Tropical Minor Key"

Malamud, Bernard-- "The Last Mohican"

Nemerov, Howard-- "A Secret Society"

Rosten, Leo-- "The Guy in Ward Four"

Roth, Philip-- "The Conversion of the Jews"

Sayre, Anne-- "A Birthday Present"

Swados, Harvey-- "The Man in the Toolhouse"

Taylor, Peter-- "Venus, Cupid, Folly, and Time"

Updike, John-- "A Gift from the City"

Williams, Thomas-- "The Buck in Trotevale's"

Wilson, Ethel-- "The Window"

The Best American Short Stories, 1960, and the Yearbook of the American Short Story, *edited by* **Martha Foley and David Burnett**

Babb, Sanora-- "The Santa Ana"

Ellin, Stanley-- "The Day of the Bullet"

Elliott, George P.-- "Words Words Words"

Fast, Howard-- "The Man Who Looked like Jesus"

Gallant, Mavis-- "August"

Garrett, George-- "An Evening Performance"

Graves, John-- "The Last Running"

Hall, Lawrence Sargent-- "The Ledge"

Hardwick, Elizabeth-- "The Purchase"

MacDonald, Lachlan-- "The Hunter"

Malamud, Bernard-- "The Maid's Shoes"

Miller, Arthur-- "I Don't Need You Any More"

Nemerov, Howard-- "Unbelievable Characters"

Roberts, Phyllis-- "Hero"

Roth, Philip-- "Defender of the Faith"

Sturgeon, Theodore-- "The Man Who Lost the Sea"

Swados, Harvey-- "A Glance in the Mirror"

Taylor, Peter-- "Who Was Jesse's Friend and Protector?"

Young, Elisabeth Larsh-- "Counterclockwise"

The Best American Short Stories, 1961, and the Yearbook of the American Short Story, *edited by* **Martha Foley and David Burnett**

Baldwin, James-- "This Morning, This Evening, So Soon"

Berry, John-- "The Listener"

Chester, Alfred-- "Berceuse"

Gass, William H.-- "The Love and Sorrow of Henry Pimber"

Gold, Ivan-- "The Nickel Misery of George Washington Carver Brown"

Goyen, William-- "A Tale of Inheritance"

Harris, Mark-- "The Self-Made Brain Surgeon"

Hurlbut, Kaatje-- "The Vestibule"

Jacobs, Theodore-- "A Girl for Walter"

Lavin, Mary-- "The Yellow Beret"

Ludwig, Jack-- "Confusions"

Marsh, Willard-- "Mexican Hayride"

McKelway, St. Clair-- "First Marriage"

Olive, Jeannie-- "Society"

Olsen, Tillie-- "Tell Me a Riddle"

Peden, William-- "Night in Funland"

Pynchon, Thomas-- "Entropy"

Sandmel, Samuel-- "The Colleagues of Mr. Chips"

Taylor, Peter-- "Miss Leonora When Last Seen"

White, Ellington-- "The Perils of Flight"

The Best American Short Stories, 1962, and the Yearbook of the American Short Story, *edited by* **Martha Foley and David Burnett**

Arkin, Frieda-- "The Light of the Sea"

Choy, Wayson S.-- "The Sound of Waves"

Dahlberg, Edward-- "Because I Was Flesh"

Deal, Borden-- "Antaeus"

Elkin, Stanley-- "Criers and Kibbitzers, Kibbitzers and Criers"

Epstein, Seymour-- "Wheat Closed Higher, Cotton Was Mixed"

Garrett, George-- "The Old Army Game"

Gass, William H.-- "The Pedersen Kid"

Gilbert, Sister Mary-- "The Model Chapel"

Hall, Donald-- "A Day on Ragged"

Karmel-Wolfe, Henia-- "The Last Day"

Lavin, Mary-- "In the Middle of the Fields"

Leahy, Jack Thomas-- "Hanging Hair"

Maddow, Ben-- "'To Hell the Rabbis'"

McKenzie, Miriam-- "Déjà vu"

Miller, Arthur-- "The Prophecy"

Myers, E. Lucas-- "The Vindication of Dr. Nestor"

O'Connor, Flannery-- "Everything That Rises Must Converge"

Selz, Thalia-- "The Education of a Queen"

Shaw, Irwin-- "Love on a Dark Street"

Updike, John-- "Pigeon Feathers"

The Best American Short Stories, 1963, and the Yearbook of the American Short Story,
edited by **Martha Foley and David Burnett**

Andersen, U. S.-- "Turn Ever So Quickly"

Blattner, H. W.-- "Sound of a Drunken Drummer"

Carter, John Stewart-- "The Keyhole Eye"

Cheever, John-- "A Vision of the World"

Dawkins, Cecil-- "A Simple Case"

Dickerson, George-- "Chico"

Dikeman, May-- "The Sound of Young Laughter"

Elkin, Stanley-- "I Look out for Ed Wolfe"

Godfrey, Dave-- "Newfoundland Night"

Gordon, William J. J.-- "The Pures"

Hermann, John-- "Aunt Mary"

Loeser, Katinka-- "Beggarman, Rich Man, or Thief"

McKelway, St. Clair-- "The Fireflies"

Molinaro, Ursule-- "The Insufficient Rope"

Oates, Joyce Carol-- "The Fine White Mist of Winter"

Phelan, R. C.-- "Birds, Clouds, Frogs"

Richler, Mordecai-- "Some Grist for Mervyn's Mill"

Saroyan, William-- "What a World, Said the Bicycle Rider"

Sassoon, Babette-- "The Betrayal"

Shaw, Irwin-- "Noises in the City"

Taylor, Peter-- "At the Drugstore"

Tucci, Niccolò-- "The Desert in the Oasis"

West, Jessamyn-- "The Picnickers"

The Best American Short Stories, 1964, and the Yearbook of the American Short Story,
edited by **Martha Foley and David Burnett**

Arkin, Frieda-- "The Broomstick on the Porch"

Brown, Richard G.-- "Mr. Iscariot"

Carter, John Stewart-- "To a Tenor Dying Old"

Curley, Daniel-- "A Story of Love, Etc."

Dikeman, May-- "The Woman Across the Street"

Eastlake, William-- "A Long Day's Dying"

Goyen, William-- "Figure over the Town"

Horgan, Paul-- "Black Snowflakes"

Humphrey, William-- "The Pump"

Jackson, Shirley-- "Birthday Party"

Konecky, Edith-- "The Power"

Lolos, Kimon-- "Mule No. 095"

McCullers, Carson-- "Sucker"

Malamud, Bernard-- "The German Refugee"

Moriconi, Virginia-- "Simple Arithmetic"

Oates, Joyce Carol-- "Upon the Sweeping Flood"

Price, Reynolds-- "The Names and Faces of Heroes"

Randal, Vera-- "Waiting for Jim"

Swados, Harvey-- "A Story for Teddy"

Warren, Robert Penn-- "Have You Seen Sukie?"

The Best American Short Stories, 1965, and the Yearbook of the American Short Story,
edited by **Martha Foley**

Amster, L. J.-- "Center of Gravity"

De Paola, Daniel-- "The Returning"

Elkin, Stanley-- "The Transient"

Gilchrist, Jack-- "Opening Day"

Groshong, James W.-- "The Gesture"

Hamer, Martin J.-- "Sarah"

Howard, Maureen-- "Sherry"

Hutter, Donald-- "A Family Man"

Karmel-Wolfe, Henia-- "The Month of His Birthday"

Lavin, Mary-- "Heart of Gold"

Lynds, Dennis-- "A Blue Blonde in the Sky over Pennsylvania"

Morton, Frederic-- "The Guest"

Neugeboren, Jay-- "The Application"

Oates, Joyce Carol-- "First Views of the Enemy"

Robinson, Leonard Wallace-- "The Practice of an Art"

Singer, Isaac Bashevis-- "A Sacrifice"

Somerlott, Robert-- "Eskimo Pies"

Spencer, Elizabeth-- "The Visit"

Stafford, Jean-- "The Tea Time of Stouthearted Ladies"

Stein, Gerald-- "For I Have Wept"

Taylor, Peter-- "There"

Yu-Hwa, Lee-- "The Last Rite"

The Best American Short Stories, 1966, and the Yearbook of the American Short Story,
edited by **Martha Foley and David Burnett**

Cady, Jack-- "The Burning"

Dickerson, George-- "A Mussel Named Ecclesiastes"

Downey, Harris-- "The Vicar-General and the Wide Night"

Ely, David-- "The Academy"

Faulkner, William-- "Mr. Acarius"

Grau, Shirley Ann-- "The Beach Party"

Hedin, Mary-- "Places We Lost"

Hood, Hugh-- "Getting to Williamstown"

Jackson, Shirley-- "The Bus"

Jacobsen, Josephine-- "On the Island"

Kreisel, Henry-- "The Broken Globe"

Lavin, Mary-- "One Summer"

Leviant, Curt-- "Mourning Call"

Maxwell, William-- "Further Tales About Men and Women"

O'Connor, Flannery-- "Parker's Back"

Rothberg, Abraham-- "Pluto Is the Furthest Planet"

Terry, Walter S.-- "The Bottomless Well"

Wakefield, Dan-- "Autumn Full of Apples"

Whitehill, Joseph-- "One Night for Several Samurai"

Wilner, Herbert-- "Dovisch in the Wilderness"

The Best American Short Stories, 1967, and the Yearbook of the American Short Story,
edited by **Martha Foley and David Burnett**

Ayer, Ethan-- "The Promise of Heat"

Blake, George-- "A Place Not on the Map"

Boyle, Kay-- "The Wild Horses"

Carver, Raymond-- "Will You Please Be Quiet, Please?"

Francis, H. E.-- "One of the Boys"

Harris, MacDonald-- "Trepleff"

Hazel, Robert-- "White Anglo-Saxon Protestant"

Hunt, Hugh Allyn-- "Acme Rooms and Sweet Marjorie Russell"

Lee, Lawrence-- "The Heroic Journey"

Miller, Arthur-- "Search for a Future"

Moore, Brian-- "The Apartment Hunter"

Morgan, Berry-- "Andrew"

Oates, Joyce Carol-- "Where Are You Going, Where Have You Been?"

Radcliffe, Donald-- "Song of the Simidor"

Roth, Henry-- "The Surveyor"

Rubin, David-- "Longing for America"

Stuart, Jesse-- "The Accident"

Sturm, Carol-- "The Kid Who Fractioned"

Travers, Robert-- "The Big Brown Trout"

Wiser, William-- "House of the Blues"

The Best American Short Stories, 1968, and the Yearbook of the American Short Story,
edited by **Martha Foley and David Burnett**

Baldwin, James-- "Tell Me How Long the Train's Been Gone"

Bruce, Janet-- "Dried Rose Petals in a Silver Bowl"

Deck, John-- "Greased Samba"

Farrell, James T.-- "An American Student in Paris"

Freitag, George H.-- "An Old Man and His Hat"

Gardner, Herb-- "Who Is Harry Kellerman and Why Is He Saying Those Terrible Things About Me?"

Gass, William H.-- "In the Heart of the Heart of the Country"

Gavell, Mary Ladd-- "The Rotifer"

Gropman, Donald-- "The Heart of This or That Man"

Harrison, William-- "The Snooker Shark"
Higgins, Judith-- "The Only People"
Hudson, Helen-- "The Tenant"
Litwak, Leo E.-- "In Shock"
McKenna, Richard-- "The Sons of Martha"
Moseley, William-- "The Preacher and Margery Scott"

Ostrow, Joanna-- "Celtic Twilight"
Parker, Nancy Huddleston-- "Early Morning, Lonely Ride"
Phillips, John-- "Bleat Blodgette"
Spingarn, Lawrence P.-- "The Ambassador"
Weathers, Winston-- "The Games That We Played"

The Best American Short Stories, 1969, and the Yearbook of the American Short Story, *edited by* Martha Foley and David Burnett

Brennan, Maeve-- "The Eldest Child"
Cady, Jack-- "Play Like I'm Sherrif"
Costello, Mark-- "Murphy's Xmas"
Gerald, John Bart-- "Walking Wounded"
Hughes, Mary Gray-- "The Foreigner in the Blood"
Klein, Norma-- "The Boy in the Green Hat"
Lavin, Mary-- "Happiness"
McGregor, Matthew W.-- "Porkchops with Whiskey and Ice Cream"
MacLeod, Alistair-- "The Boat"
McPherson, James Alan-- "Gold Coast"

Madden, David-- "The Day the Flowers Came"
Malamud, Bernard-- "Pictures of Fidelman"
Milton, John R.-- "The Inheritance of Emmy One Horse"
Oates, Joyce Carol-- "By the River"
Pansing, Nancy Pelletier-- "The Visitation"
Plath, Sylvia-- "Johnny Panic and the Bible of Dreams"
Rugel, Miriam-- "Paper Poppy"
Shipley, Margaret-- "The Tea Bowl of Ninsei Nomura"
Singer, Isaac Bashevis-- "The Colony"
Winslow, Joyce Madelon-- "Benjamen Burning"

The Best American Short Stories, 1970, and the Yearbook of the American Short Story, *edited by* Martha Foley and David Burnett

Cady, Jack-- "With No Breeze"
Cleaver, Eldridge-- "The Flashlight"
Coover, Robert-- "The Magic Poker"
Davis, Olivia-- "The Other Child"
Dubus, Andre-- "If They Knew Yvonne"
Gerald, John Bart-- "Blood Letting"
Gillespie, Alfred-- "Tonight at Nine Thirty-six"
Leffland, Ella-- "The Forest"
Matthews, Jack-- "Another Story"
Maxwell, William-- "The Gardens of Mont-Saint-Michel"
Morris, Wright-- "Green Grass, Blue Sky, White House"

Oates, Joyce Carol-- "How I Contemplated the World from the Detroit House of Correction and Began My Life over Again"
Olsen, Paul-- "The Flag Is Down"
Ozick, Cynthia-- "Yiddish in America"
Siegel, Jules-- "In the Land of the Morning Calm, Deja Vu"
Singer, Isaac Bashevis-- "The Key"
Stone, Robert-- "Porque no tiene, porque le falta"
Taylor, Peter-- "Daphne's Lover"
Weisbrod, Rosine-- "The Ninth Cold Day"

The Best American Short Stories, 1971, and the Yearbook of the American Short Story, *edited by* Martha Foley and David Burnett

Banks, Russell-- "With Che in New Hampshire"
Bennett, Hal-- "Dotson Gerber Resurrected"
Blake, James-- "The Widow, Bereft"

Cady, Jack-- "I Take Care of Things"
Canzoneri, Robert-- "Barbed Wire"
Drake, Albert-- "The Chicken Which Became a Rat"

Eastlake, William-- "The Dancing Boy"
Harvor, Beth-- "Pain Was My Portion"
Madden, David-- "No Trace"
Mitchell, Don-- "Diesel"
Montgomery, Marion-- "The Decline and Fall of Officer Fergerson"
Morris, Wright-- "Magic"
O'Connor, Philip F.-- "The Gift Bearer"
Olsen, Tillie-- "Requa I"

Prashker, Ivan-- "Shirt Talk"
Rush, Norman-- "In Late Youth"
Santiago, Danny-- "The Somebody"
Strong, Jonathan-- "Xavier Fereira's Unfinished Book: Chapter One"
Tushnet, Leonard-- "The Klausners"
Valgardson, W. D.-- "Bloodflowers"
Woiwode, Larry-- "The Suitor"

The Best American Short Stories, 1972, and the Yearbook of the American Short Story, *edited by* **Martha Foley**

Beal, M. F.-- "Gold"
Brautigan, Richard-- "The World War I Los Angeles Airplane"
Cherry, Kelly-- "Convenant"
Gold, Herbert-- "A Death on the East Side"
Greenberg, Joanne-- "The Supremacy of the Hunza"
Heath, Mary-- "The Breadman"
Holmes, Edward M.-- "Drums Again"
Hughes, Mary Gray-- "The Judge"
Jones, Ann-- "In Black and White"
Just, Ward-- "Three Washington Stories"
Kalechofsky, Roberta-- "His Day Out"

Kavaler, Rebecca-- "The Further Adventures of Brunhild"
L'Heureux, John-- "Fox and Swan"
Malony, Ralph-- "Intimacy"
Mandell, Marvin-- "The Aesculapians"
Ozick, Cynthia-- "The Dock-Witch"
Porter, Joe Ashby-- "The Vacation"
Street, Penelope-- "The Magic Apple"
Warren, Robert Penn-- "Meet Me in the Green Glen"
Weesner, Theodore-- "Stealing Cars"
Yglesias, José-- "The Guns in the Closet"

The Best American Short Stories, 1973, the Yearbook of the American Short Story, *edited by* **Martha Foley**

Barthelme, Donald-- "A City of Churches"
Bromell, Henry-- "The Slightest Distance"
Cheever, John-- "The Jewels of the Cabots"
Clayton, John J.-- "Cambridge Is Sinking!"
Corrington, John William-- "Old Men Dream Dreams, Young Men See Visions"
Davenport, Guy-- "Robot"
Eastlake, William-- "The Death of Sun"
Greenberg, Alvin-- "The Real Meaning of the Faust Legend"
Hayden, Julie-- "In the Words Of"
Higgins, George V.-- "The Habits of Animals: The Progress of the Seasons"

Just, Ward-- "Burns"
Kenary, James S.-- "Going Home"
Knight, Wallace E.-- "The Way We Went"
Lardas, Konstantinos-- "The Broken Wings"
McPherson, James Alan-- "The Silver Bullet"
Malamud, Bernard-- "God's Wrath"
Oates, Joyce Carol-- "Silkie"
Plath, Sylvia-- "Mothers"
Sandberg-Diment, Erik-- "Come away, Oh Human Child"
Shetzline, David-- "Country of the Painted Freaks"
Williams, Tennessee-- "Happy August the Tenth"

The Best American Short Stories, 1974, and the Yearbook of the American Short Story,
edited by **Martha Foley**

Boyer, Agnes-- "The Deserter"

Bumpus, Jerry-- "Beginnings"

Clark, Eleanor-- "A Summer in Puerto Rico"

Esslinger-Carr, Pat M.-- "The Party"

Horne, Lewis B.-- "Mansion, Magic, and Miracle"

Ignatow, Rose Graubart-- "Down the American River"

Kumin, Maxine-- "Opening the Door on Sixty-second Street"

Lavin, Mary-- "Tom"

L'Heureux, John-- "A Family Affair"

Lopate, Phillip-- "The Chamber Music Evening"

Minot, Stephen-- "The Tide and Isaac Bates"

Mitchell, Beverly-- "Letter from Sakaye"

Rothschild, Michael-- "Dog in the Manger"

Sandberg, Peter L.-- "Calloway's Climb"

Saroyan, William-- "Isn't Today the Day?"

Schneider, Philip H.-- "The Gray"

Targan, Barry-- "Old Vemish"

Updike, John-- "Son"

Vivante, Arturo-- "Honeymoon"

Walker, Alice-- "The Revenge of Hannah Kemhuff"

The Best American Short Stories, 1975, and the Yearbook of the American Short Story,
edited by **Martha Foley**

Banks, Russell-- "The Lie"

Barthelme, Donald-- "The School"

Brown, Rosellen-- "How to Win"

Bumpus, Jerry-- "Desert Matinee"

Busch, Frederick-- "Bambi Meets the Furies"

Chaikin, Nancy G.-- "Waiting for Astronauts"

Clearman, Mary-- "Paths unto the Dead"

De Jenkins, Lyll Becerra-- "Tyranny"

Dubus, Andre-- "Cadence"

Ford, Jesse Hill-- "Big Boy"

Hoffman, William-- "The Spirit in Me"

Hunter, Evan-- "The Analyst"

Kaser, Paul-- "How Jerem Came Home"

MacLeod, Alistair-- "The Lost Salt Gift of Blood"

McNamara, Eugene-- "The Howard Parker Montcrief Hoax"

Matthews, Jack-- "The Burial"

Price, Reynolds-- "Night and Day at Panacea"

Rothberg, Abraham-- "Polonaise"

Silko, Leslie Marmon-- "Lullaby"

Targan, Barry-- "The Who Lived"

Yglesias, José-- "The American Sickness"

The Best American Short Stories, 1976, and the Yearbook of the American Short Story,
edited by **Martha Foley**

Adams, Alice-- "Roses, Rhododendron"

Battin, M. Pabst-- "Terminal Procedure"

Briskin, Mae Seidman-- "The Boy Who Was Astrid's Mother"

Chaikin, Nancy G.-- "Beautiful, Helpless Animals"

Corrington, John William-- "The Actes and Documents"

Francis, H. E.-- "A Chronicle of Love"

Hagge, John-- "Pontius Pilate"

Just, Ward-- "Dietz at War"

McCluskey, John-- "John Henry's Home"

Minot, Steven-- "Grubbing for Roots"

Nelson, Kent-- "Looking into Nothing"

Ozick, Cynthia-- "A Mercenary"

Price, Reynolds-- "Broad Day"

Rothschild, Michael-- "Wondermonger"

Targan, Barry-- "Surviving Adverse Seasons"

Taylor, Peter-- "The Hand of Emmagene"

Updike, John-- "The Man Who Loved Extinct Mammals"

The Best American Short Stories, 1977, and the Yearbook of the American Short Story,
edited by **Martha Foley**

Busch, Frederick-- "The Trouble with Being Food"

Caldwell, Price-- "Tarzan Meets the Department Head"

Cheever, John-- "Falconer"

Copeland, Ann-- "At Peace"

Corrington, John William-- "Pleadings"

Damon, Philip-- "Growing up in No Time"

Epstein, Leslie-- "The Steinway Quintet"

Garber, Eugene K.-- "The Lover"

Hampl, Patricia-- "Look at a Teacup"

Kerr, Baine-- "Rider"

Matthews, Jack-- "A Questionnaire for Rudolph Gordon"

Minot, Stephen-- "A Passion for History"

Newman, Charles-- "The Woman Who Thought like a Man"

Oates, Joyce Carol-- "Gay"

O'Brien, Tim-- "Going After Cacciato"

Robbins, Tom-- "The Chink and the Clock People"

Saroyan, William-- "A Fresno Fable"

Sayles, John-- "Breed"

Tyler, Anne-- "Your Place Is Empty"

Wilson, William S.-- "Anthropology: What Is Lost in Rotation"

The Best American Short Stories, 1978: Selected from U.S. and Canadian Magazines, including the Yearbook of the American Short Story,
edited by **Ted Solotaroff, with Shannon Ravenel**

Baumbach, Jonathan-- "The Return of Service"

Bowles, Jane-- "Two Scenes"

Brodkey, Harold-- "Verona: A Young Woman Speaks"

Cullinan, Elizabeth-- "A Good Loser"

Elkin, Stanley-- "The Conventional Wisdom"

Epstein, Leslie-- "Skaters on Wood"

Gardner, John-- "Redemption"

Helprin, Mark-- "The Schreuderspitze"

Kaplan, James-- "In Miami, Last Winter"

McCarthy, Tim-- "The Windmill Man"

McEwan, Ian-- "Psychopolis"

Marsh, Peter-- "By the Yellow Lake"

Oates, Joyce Carol-- "The Translation"

Petesch, Natalie L. M.-- "Main Street Morning"

Rishel, Mary Ann Malinchak-- "Staus"

Schott, Max-- "Murphy Jones: Pearblossom, California"

Schwartz, Lynne Sharon-- "Rough Strife"

Sintetos, L. Hluchan-- "Telling the Bees"

Sorrells, Robert T.-- "The Blacktop Champion of Ickey Honey"

Sorrentino, Gilbert-- "Decades"

Taylor, Peter-- "In the Miro District"

Williams, Joy-- "Bromeliads"

The Best American Short Stories, 1979: Selected from U.S. and Canadian Magazines,
edited by **Joyce Carol Oates, with Shannon Ravenel**

Barthelme, Donald-- "The New Music"

Bellow, Saul-- "A Silver Dish"

Bowles, Paul-- "The Eye"

Brown, Rosellen-- "The Wedding Week"

Coffin, Lyn-- "Falling off the Scaffold"

Hedin, Mary-- "The Middle Place"

Hurlbut, Kaatje-- "A Short Walk into Afternoon"

Kumin, Maxine-- "The Missing Person"

LaSalle, Peter-- "Some Manhattan in New England"

McLaughlin, Ruth-- "Seasons"

Malamud, Bernard-- "Home Is the Hero"

Munro, Alice-- "Spelling"

O'Connor, Flannery-- "An Exile in the East"

Phillips, Jayne Anne-- "Something That Happened"

Rubin, Louis D., Jr.-- "Finisterre"

Sanford, Annette-- "Trip in a Summer Dress"

Schwartz, Lynne Sharon-- "Plaisir D'amour"

Singer, Isaac Bashevis-- "A Party in Miami Beach"

Styron, William-- "Shadrach"

Tennenbaum, Silvia-- "A Lingering Death"

Thompson, Jean-- "Paper Covers Rock"
Virgo, Sean-- "Home and Native Land"
Wilner, Herbert-- "The Quarterback Speaks to His
    God"

Wilson, Robley, Jr.-- "Living Alone"
Yngve, Rolf-- "The Quail"

The Best American Short Stories, 1980: Selected from U.S. and Canadian Magazines, *edited by* **Stanley Elkin, with Shannon Ravenel**

Barthelme, Donald-- "The Emerald"
Busch, Frederick-- "Long Calls"
Evanier, David-- "The One-Star Jew"
Gallant, Mavis-- "The Remission; Speck's Idea"
Gass, William H.-- "The Old Folks"
Gertler, T.-- "In Case of Survival"
Hardwick, Elizabeth-- "The Faithful"
Heinemann, Larry-- "The First Clean Fact"
Henderson, Robert-- "Into the Wind"
Johnson, Curt-- "Lemon Tree"
Paley, Grace-- "Friends"

Robison, James-- "Home"
Rooke, Leon-- "Mama Tuddi Done Over"
Sayles, John-- "At the Anarchist's Convention"
Singer, Isaasc Bashevis-- "The Safe Deposit"
Stern, Richard-- "Dr. Cahn's Visit"
Targan, Barry-- "The Rags of Time"
Taylor, Peter-- "The Old Forest"
Updike, John-- "Gesturing"
Waksler, Norman-- "Markowitz and the Gypsies"
Weaver, Gordon-- "Hog's Heart"

The Best American Short Stories, 1981: Selected from U.S. and Canadian Magazines, *edited by* **Hortense Calisher, with Shannon Ravenel**

Abish, Walter-- "The Idea of Switzerland"
Apple, Max-- "Small Island Republics"
Beattie, Ann-- "Winter: 1978"
Coover, Robert-- "A Working Day"
Dethier, Vincent G.-- "The Moth and the Primrose"
Dubus, Andre-- "The Winter Father"
Gallant, Mavis-- "The Assembly"
Hardwick, Elizabeth-- "The Bookseller"
McElroy, Joseph-- "The Future"
McGrath, Elizabeth-- "Fogbound in Avalon"

Mason, Bobbie Ann-- "Shiloh"
Moseley, Amelia-- "The Mountains Where Cithaeron Is"
Munro, Alice-- "Wood"
Oates, Joyce Carol-- "Presque Isle"
Ozick, Cynthia-- "The Shawl"
Rubin, Louis D., Jr.-- "The St. Anthony Chorale"
Stern, Richard-- "Wissler Remembers"
Tallent, Elizabeth-- "Ice"
Updike, John-- "Still of Some Use"
Woiwode, Larry-- "Change"

The Best American Short Stories, 1982: Selected from U.S. and Canadian Magazines, *edited by* **John Gardner, with Shannon Ravenel**

Baker, Nicholson-- "K. 590"
Baxter, Charles-- "Harmony of the World"
Carver, Raymond-- "Cathedral"
Coggeshall, Rosanne-- "Lamb Says"
Ferry, James-- "Dancing Ducks and Talking Anus"
Freeman, Anne Hobson-- "The Girl Who Was No Kin
    to the Marshalls"

Greenberg, Alvin-- "The Power of Language Is Such
    That Even a Single Word Taken Truly to Heart Can
    Change Everything"
Gupta, Roberta-- "The Cafe de Paris"
Hauptmann, William-- "Good Rockin' Tonight"
Higgins, Joanna-- "The Courtship of Widow Sobcek"
Johnson, Charles-- "Exchange Value"

Licht, Fred--"Shelter the Pilgrim"
McLaughlin, Lissa--"The Continental Heart"
MacMillan, Ian--"Proud Monster: Sketches"
Milton, Edith--"Coming Over"
Oates, Joyce Carol--"Theft"

Renwick, Joyce--"The Dolphin Story"
Robison, Mary--"Coach"
Rosner, Anne F.--"Prize Tomatoes"
Smith, R. E.--"The Gift Horse's Mouth"

The Best American Short Stories, 1983: Selected from U.S. and Canadian Magazines, *edited by* Anne Tyler, with Shannon Ravenel

Barich, Bill--"Hard to be Good"
Bly, Carol--"The Dignity of Life"
Bond, James--"A Change of Season"
Carver, Raymond--"Where I'm Calling From"
Chute, Carolyn--"'Ollie, Oh . . .'"
Colwin, Laurie--"My Mistress"
Epstein, Joseph--"The Count and the Princess"
Erdrich, Louise--"Scales"
Le Guin, Ursula K.--"The Professor's Houses; Sur"
Mason, Bobbie Ann--"Graveyard Day"

Morris, Wright--"Victrola"
Schumacher, Julie--"Reunion"
Stark, Sharon Sheehe--"Best Quality Glass Company, New York"
Taylor, Robert--"Colorado"
Thurm, Marian--"Starlight"
Updike, John--"Deaths of Distant Friends"
Vanderhaeghe, Guy--"Reunion"
Vreuls, Diane--"Beebee"
Woiwode, Larry--"Firstborn"

The Best American Short Stories, 1984: Selected from U.S. and Canadian Magazines, *edited by* John Updike, with Shannon Ravenel (partial contents)

Abbott, Lee K.--"The Final Proof of Fate and Circumstance"
Bell, Madison Smartt--"The Naked Lady"
Benedict, Dianne--"Unknown Feathers"
Bowles, Paul--"In the Red Room"
Brown, Mary Ward--"The Cure"
DeMarinis, Rick--"Gent"
Dubus, Andre--"A Father's Story"
Gallant, Mavis--"Lena"
Hood, Mary--"Inexorable Progress"
Justice, Donald--"The Artificial Moonlight"

Kirk, Stephen--"Morrison's Reaction"
Minot, Susan--"Thorofare"
Morris, Wright--"Glimpse into Another Country"
Oates, Joyce Carol--"Nairobi"
Ozick, Cynthia--"Rosa"
Pei, Lowry--"The Cold Room"
Penner, Jonathan--"Things to be Thrown Away"
Rush, Norman--"Bruns"
Salter, James--"Foreign Shores"
Schinto, Jeanne--"Caddie's Day"

The Best American Short Stories, 1985: Selected from U.S. and Canadian Magazines, *edited by* Gail Godwin, with Shannon Ravenel

Banks, Russell--"Sarah Cole: A Type of Love Story"
Bishop, Michael--"Dogs' Lives"
Canin, Ethan--"Emperor of the Air"
Doctorow, E. L. --"The Leather Man"
Edwards, Margaret--"Roses"
Flythe, Starkey--"Walking, Walking"
Francis, H. E.--"The Sudden Trees"
Jafek, Bev--"You've Come a Long Way, Mickey Mouse"

L'Heureux, John--"Clothing"
Meinke, Peter--"The Piano Tuner"
Morris, Wright--"Fellow-Creatures"
Mukherjee, Bharati--"Angela"
Nugent, Beth--"City of Boys"
Oates, Joyce Carol--"Raven's Wing"
Rush, Norman--"Instruments of Seduction"

Sandor, Marjorie-- "The Gittel"
Seabrooke, Deborah-- "Secrets"
Smiley, Jane-- "Lily"

Stark, Sharon Sheehe-- "The Johnstown Polka"
Williams, Joy-- "The Skater"

The Best American Short Stories, 1986: Selected from U.S. and Canadian Magazines, *edited by* **Raymond Carver, with Shannon Ravenel**

Barthelme, Donald-- "Basil from Her Garden"
Baxter, Charles-- "Gryphon"
Beattie, Ann-- "Janus"
Burke, James Lee-- "The Convict"
Canin, Ethan-- "Star Food"
Conroy, Frank-- "Gossip"
Ford, Richard-- "Communist"
Gallagher, Tess-- "Bad Company"
Hempel, Amy-- "Today Will Be a Quiet Day"
Kaplan, David Michael-- "Doe Season"

Lipsky, David-- "Three Thousand Dollars"
McGuane, Thomas-- "Sportsmen"
McIlroy, Christopher-- "All My Relations"
Munro, Alice-- "Monsieur Les Deux Chapeaux"
Neely, Jessica-- "Skin Angels"
Nelson, Kent-- "Invisible Life"
Paley, Grace-- "Telling"
Simpson, Mona-- "Lawns"
Williams, Joy-- "Health"
Wolff, Tobias-- "The Rich Brother"

The Best American Short Stories, 1987: Selected from U.S. and Canadian Magazines, *edited by* **Ann Beattie, with Shannon Ravenel**

Abbott, Lee K.-- "Dreams of Distant Lives"
Baxter, Charles-- "How I Found My Brother"
Bell, Madison Smartt-- "Lie Detector"
Carlson, Ron-- "Milk"
Carver, Raymond-- "Boxes"
Gallant, Mavis-- "Kingdom Come"
Haruf, Kent-- "Private Debts/Public Holdings"
Lombreglia, Ralph-- "Men Under Water"
Miller, Sue-- "Lover of Women"
Mukherjee, Bharati-- "Tenant"
Munro, Alice-- "Circle of Prayer"

Nova, Craig-- "Prince"
O'Brien, Tim-- "Things They Carried"
Sontag, Susan-- "Way We Live Now"
Stern, Daniel-- "Interpretation of Dreams by Sigmund Freud: A Story"
Tallent, Elizabeth-- "Favor"
Taylor, Robert-- "Lady of Spain"
Updike, John-- "Afterlife"
Williams, Joy-- "Blue Men"
Wolff, Tobias-- "Other Miller"

The Best American Short Stories, 1988: Selected from U.S. and Canadian Magazines, *edited by* **Mark Helprin, with Shannon Ravenel**

Bass, Rick-- "Cats and Students, Bubbles and Abysses"
Bausch, Richard-- "Police Dreams"
Blythe, Will-- "Taming Power of the Small"
Carver, Raymond-- "Errand"
Currey, Richard-- "Waiting for Trains"
Erdrich, Louise-- "Snares"
Gallant, Mavis-- "Dede"
Godshalk, C. S.-- "Wonderland"
Goldman, E. S.-- "Way to the Dump"
Honig, Lucy-- "No Friends, All Strangers"

Jen, Gish-- "Water-Faucet Vision"
Johnson, Hilding-- "Victoria"
Kiteley, Brian-- "Still Life with Insects"
Lacy, Robert-- "Natural Father"
Lombreglia, Ralph-- "Inn Essence"
Milton, Edith-- "Entrechat"
Sandor, Marjorie-- "Still Life"
Stone, Robert-- "Helping"
Taylor-Hall, Mary Ann-- "Banana Boats"
Wolff, Tobias-- "Smorgasbord"

The Best American Short Stories, 1989: Selected from U.S. and Canadian Magazines,
edited by **Margaret Atwood, with Shannon Ravenel**

Baxter, Charles-- "Fenstad's Mother"

Bell, Madison Smartt-- "Customs of the Country"

Boswell, Robert-- "Living to Be a Hundred"

Boyd, Blanche McCrary-- "The Black Hand Girl"

Brown, Larry-- "Kubuku Riders (This Is It)"

Busch, Frederick-- "Ralph the Duck"

Cunningham, Michael-- "White Angel"

DeMarinis, Rick-- "The Flowers of Boredom"

Doerr, Harriet-- "Edie: A Life"

Gallant, Mavis-- "The Concert Party"

Glover, Douglas-- "Why I Decided to Kill Myself and Other Jokes"

Gowdy, Barbara-- "Disneyland"

Hogan, Linda-- "Aunt Moon's Young Man"

Louie, David Wong-- "Displacement"

Mukherjee, Bharati-- "The Management of Grief"

Munro, Alice-- "Meneseteung"

Phillips, Dale Ray-- "What Men Love For"

Richard, Mark-- "Strays"

Robinson, Arthur-- "The Boy on the Train"

Sharif, M. T.-- "The Letter Writer"

The Best American Short Stories, 1990: Selected from U.S. and Canadian Magazines,
edited by **Richard Ford, with Shannon Ravenel**

Allen, Edward-- "River of Toys"

Bausch, Richard-- "The Fireman's Wife"

Bausch, Richard-- "A Kind of Simple, Happy Grace"

Bell, Madison Smartt-- "Finding Natasha"

Godshalk, C. S.-- "The Wizard"

Henley, Patricia-- "The Secret of Cartwheels"

Houston, Pam-- "How to Talk to a Hunter"

Hustvedt, Siri-- "Mr. Morning"

Johnson, Denis-- "Car-Crash While Hitchhiking"

McFarland, Dennis-- "Nothing to Ask For"

Millhauser, Steven-- "Eisenheim the Illusionist"

Moore, Lorrie-- "You're Ugly, Too"

Munro, Alice-- "Differently"

Munro, Alice-- "Wigtime"

Powell, Padgett-- "Typical"

Segal, Lore—The Reverse Bug"

Tallent, Elizabeth-- "Prowler"

Tilghman, Christopher-- "In a Father's Place"

Wickersham, Joan-- "Commuter Marriage"

Williams, Joy-- "The Little Winter"

The Best American Short Stories, 1991: Selected from U.S. and Canadian Magazines,
edited by **Alice Adams, with Katrina Kenison**

Bass, Rick-- "Legend of Pig-Eye"

Baxter, Charles-- "The Disappeared"

Bloom, Amy-- "Love Is Not a Pie"

Braverman, Kate-- "Tall Tales from the Mekong Delta"

Butler, Robert Olen-- "The Trip Back"

D'Ambrosio, Charles, Jr.-- "The Point"

Dillon, Millicent-- "Oil and Water"

Doerr, Harriet-- "Another Short Day in La Luz"

Eisenberg, Deborah-- "The Custodian"

Gordon, Mary-- "Separation"

Graver, Elizabeth-- "The Body Shop"

Hustvedt, Siri-- "Houdini"

Iossel, Mikhail-- "Bologoye"

Jauss, David-- "Glossolalia"

Michaels, Leonard-- "Viva la Tropicana"

Moore, Lorrie-- "Willing"

Munro, Alice-- "Friend of My Youth"

Oates, Joyce Carol-- "American, Abroad"

Prose, Francine-- "Dog Stories"

Updike, John-- "A Sandstone Farmhouse"

The Best American Short Stories, 1992: Selected from U.S. and Canadian Magazines,
edited by **Alice Adams, with Katrina Kenison**

Adams, Alice-- "The Last Lovely City"

Bass, Rick-- "Days of Heaven"

Beller, Thomas-- "A Different Kind of Imperfection"

Bloom, Amy-- "Silver Water"

Butler, Robert Olen-- "A Good Scent from a Strange Mountain"

Gallant, Mavis-- "Across the Bridge"

Gautreaux, Tim-- "Same Place, Same Things"

Johnson, Denis-- "Emergency"

Jones, Thom-- "The Pugilist at Rest"

Klimasewiski, Marshall N.-- "JunHee"

Moore, Lorrie-- "Community Life"

Munro, Alice-- "Carried Away"

Oates, Joyce Carol-- "Is Laughter Contagious?"

Price, Reynolds-- "The Fare to the Moon"

Smith, Annick-- "It's Come to This"

Tilghman, Christopher-- "The Way People Run"

Wallace, David Foster-- "Forever Overhead"

Wheeler, Kate-- "Under the Roof"

Winthrop, Elizabeth-- "The Golden Darters"

Wolff, Tobias-- "Firelight"

The Best American Short Stories, 1993: Selected from U.S. and Canadian Magazines,
edited by **Louise Erdrich, with Katrina Kenison**

Berry, Wendell-- "Pray Without Ceasing"

Dixon, Stephen-- "Man, Woman, and Boy"

Earley, Tony-- "Charlotte"

Edwards, Kim-- "Gold"

Ellison, Harlan-- "The Man Who Rowed Christopher Columbus Ashore"

Fulton, Alice-- "Queen Wintergreen"

Gaitskill, Mary-- "The Girl on the Plane"

Gordon, Mary-- "The Important Houses"

Johnson, Diane-- "Great Barrier Reef"

Jones, Thom-- "I Want to Live!"

Lee, Andrea-- "Winter Barley"

Moore, Lorrie-- "Terrific Mother"

Munro, Alice-- "A Real Life"

Nelson, Antonya-- "Naked Ladies"

Peery, Janet-- "What the Thunder Said"

Power, Susan-- "Red Moccasins"

Scott, Joanna-- "Concerning Mold upon the Skin, Etc."

Shapiro, Jane-- "Poltergeists"

Updike, John-- "Playing with Dynamite"

Woiwode, Larry-- "Silent Passengers"

The Best American Short Stories, 1994: Selected from U.S. and Canadian Magazines,
edited by **Tobias Wolff, with Katrina Kenison**

Alexie, Sherman-- "This Is What It Means to Say Phoenix, Arizona"

Anshaw, Carol-- "Hammam"

Butler, Robert Olen-- "Salem"

Chang, Lan Samantha-- "Pipa's Story"

Cummins, Ann-- "Where I Work"

Dark, Alice Elliott-- "In the Gloaming"

Dybek, Stuart-- "We Didn't"

Earley, Tony-- "The Prophet from Jupiter"

Ferrell, Carolyn-- "Proper Library"

Gardiner, John Rolfe-- "The Voyage Out"

Gates, David-- "The Mail Lady"

Hannah, Barry-- "Nicodemus Bluff"

Jones, Thom-- "Cold Snap"

Keeble, John-- "The Chasm"

Krusoe, Nancy-- "Landscape and Dream"

Louis, Laura Glen-- "Fur"

Offutt, Chris-- "Melungeons"

Robinson, Roxana-- "Mr. Sumarsono"

Shepard, Jim-- "Batting Against Castro"

Tilghman, Christopher-- "Things Left Undone"

Wilson, Jonathan-- "From Shanghai"

The Best American Short Stories, 1995: Selected from U.S. and Canadian Magazines,
edited by **Jane Smiley, with Katrina Kenison**

Barrett, Andrea-- "The Behavior of the Hawkweeds"

Braverman, Kate-- "Pagan Night"

Cornell, Jennifer C.-- "Undertow"

Cozine, Andrew-- "Hand Jive"

Davies, Peter Ho-- "The Ugliest House in the World"

Delaney, Edward J.-- "The Drownings"

DeLillo, Don-- "The Angel Esmeralda"

Doybyns, Stephen-- "So I Guess You Know What I Told Him"

Falco, Edward-- "The Artist"

Garland, Max-- "Chiromancy "

Gilchrist, Ellen-- "The Stucco House"

Gordon, Jaimy-- "A Night's Work"

Jen, Gish-- "Birthmates"

Jones, Thom-- "Way Down Deep in the Jungle"

Kincaid, Jamaica-- "Xuela"

Mandelman, Avner-- "Pity"

Orozco, Daniel-- "Orientation"

Polansky, Steven-- "Leg"

Thon, Melanie Rae-- "First, Body"

Williams, Joy-- "Honored Guest"

The Best American Short Stories, 1996: Selected from U.S. and Canadian Magazines,
edited by **John Edgar Wideman, with Katrina Kenison**

Adams, Alice-- "Complicities"

Bass, Rick-- "Fires"

Brown, Jason-- "Driving the Heart"

Butler, Robert Olen-- "Jealous Husband Returns in Form of Parrot"

Chang, Lan Samantha-- "The Eve of the Spirit Festival"

Chaon, Dan-- "Fitting Ends"

Davies, Peter Ho-- "The Silver Screen"

Díaz, Junot-- "Ysrael"

Dixon, Stephen-- "Sleep"

Dybek, Stuart-- "Paper Lantern"

Galyan, Deborah-- "The Incredible Appearing Man"

Gordon, Mary-- "Intertextuality"

Huddle, David-- "Past My Future"

Keesey, Anna-- "Bright Winter"

Kincaid, Jamaica-- "In Roseau"

Lewis, William Henry-- "Shades"

Lychack, William—A Stand of Fables"

Oates, Joyce Carol-- "Ghost Girls"

Patrinos, Angela-- "Sculpture I"

Perabo, Susan-- "Some Say the World"

Schwartz, Lynne Sharon-- "The Trip to Halawa Valley"

Sharma, Akhil-- "If You Sing Like That for Me"

Thompson, Jean-- "All Shall Love Me and Despair"

Thon, Melanie Rae-- "Xmas, Jamaica Plain"

The Best American Short Stories, 1997: Selected from U.S. and Canadian Magazines,
edited by **E. Annie Proulx, with Katrina Kenison**

Bausch, Richard-- "Nobody in Hollywood"

Bender, Karen E.-- "Eternal Love"

Boyle, T. Coraghessan-- "Killing Babies"

Byers, Michael-- "Rites of Passage: Shipmates Down Under"

Cliff, Michelle-- "Identifying the Stranger: Transactions"

Cooke, Carolyn-- "Bob Darling"

Davis, Lydia-- "St. Martin"

Díaz, Junot-- "Perceived Social Values: Fiesta, 1980"

Durban, Pam-- "Soon"

Edgerton, Clyde-- "Send Me to the Electric Chair"

Eugenides, Jeffrey-- "Air Mail"

Franzen, Jonathan-- "Chez Lambert"

Gautreaux, Tim-- "Little Frogs in a Ditch"

Hagy, Alyson-- "Search Bay"

Hall, Donald-- "From Willow Temple"

Jin, Ha-- "Manners and Right Behavior: Saboteur"

Michaels, Leonard-- "A Girl with a Monkey"

Ozick, Cynthia-- "Save My Child!"

Spence, June-- "Missing Women"

Stone, Robert-- "Under the Pitons"

Wolff, Tobias-- "Powder"

The Best American Short Stories, 1998: Selected from U.S. and Canadian Magazines,
edited by **Garrison Keillor, with Katrina Kenison**

Adrian, Chris-- "Every Night for a Thousand Years"
Anshaw, Carol-- "Elvis Has Left the Building"
Ballantine, Poe-- "The Blue Devils of Blue River Avenue"
Broyard, Bliss-- "Mr. Sweetly Indecent"
Carter, Emily-- "Glory Goes and Gets Some"
Chetkovich, Kathryn-- "Appetites"
Crain, Matthew-- "Penance"
Gautreaux, Tim-- "Welding with Children"
Kaplan, Hester-- "Would You Know It Wasn't Love"
Larson, Doran-- "Morphine"

Moore, Lorrie-- "People Like That Are the Only People Here"
Nelson, Antonya-- "Unified Front"
Pearlman, Edith-- "Chance"
Powell, Padgett-- "Wayne in Love"
Proulx, E. Annie-- "The Half-Skinned Steer"
Schoemperlen, Diane-- "Body Language"
Sharma, Akhil-- "Cosmopolitain"
Swann, Maxine-- "Flower Children"
Updike, John-- "My Father on the Verge"
Wolitzer, Meg-- "Tea at the House"

The Best American Short Stories, 1999: Selected from U.S. and Canadian Magazines,
edited by **Amy Tan, with Katrina Kenison**

Bass, Rick-- "The Hermit's Story"
Díaz, Junot-- "The Sun, the Moon, the Stars"
Divakaruni, Chitra-- "Mrs. Dutta Writes a Letter"
Dobyns, Stephen-- "Kansas"
Englander, Nathan-- "The Tumblers"
Gautreaux, Tim-- "The Piano Tuner"
Hardy, Melissa-- "The Uncharted Heart"
Harrar, George-- "The Five Twenty-two"
Hemon, Aleksandar-- "Islands"
Houston, Pam-- "The Best Girlfriend You Never Had"
Jin, Ha-- "In the Kindergarten"

Julavits, Heidi-- "Marry the One Who Gets There First"
Kaplan, Hester-- "Live Life King-sized"
Kohler, Sheilia-- "Africans"
Lahiri, Jhumpa-- "Interpreter of Maladies"
Moore, Lorrie-- "Real Estate"
Munro, Alice-- "Save the Reaper"
Proulx, E. Annie-- "The Bunchgrass Edge of the World"
Spencer, James-- "The Robbers of Karnataka"
Upadhyay, Samrat-- "The Good Shopkeeper"
Yarbrough, Steve-- "The Rest of Her Life"

The Best American Short Stories of the Century,
edited by **John Updike**

To compile this volume, Updike selected the best stories that appeared in The Best American Short Stories series from 1915 through 1999; the stories are listed in chronological order of their publication in the series.

Rosenblatt, Benjamin-- "Zelig" (1915)
Lerner, Mary-- "Little Selves" (1916)
Glaspell, Susan-- "A Jury of Her Peers" (1917)
Anderson, Sherwood-- "The Other Woman" (1920)
Lardner, Ring-- "The Golden Honeymoon" (1922)
Toomer, Jean-- "Blood-Burning Moon" (1923)
Hemingway, Ernest-- "The Killers" (1927)
Cather, Willa-- "Double Birthday" (1929)
Coates, Grace Stone-- "Wild Plums" (1929)
Porter, Katherine Anne-- "Theft" (1930)

Faulkner, William-- "That Evening Sun Go Down" (1931)
Parker, Dorothy-- "Here We Are" (1931)
Fitzgerald, F. Scott-- "Crazy Sunday" (1933)
Godin, Alexander-- "My Dead Brother Comes to America" (1934)
Saroyan, William-- "Resurrection of a Life" (1935)
Warren, Robert Penn-- "Christmas Gift" (1938)
Wright, Richard-- "Bright and Morning Star" (1939)
Welty, Eudora-- "The Hitch-Hikers" (1940)

Horgan, Paul-- "The Peach Stone" (1943)

Nabokov, Vladimir-- "'That in Aleppo Once . . .'" (1944)

Stafford, Jean-- "The Interior Castle" (1947)

Gellhorn, Martha-- "Miami-New York" (1948)

White, E. B.-- "The Second Tree from the Corner" (1948)

Bishop, Elizabeth-- "The Farmer's Children" (1949)

Powers, J. F.-- "Death of a Favorite" (1951)

Williams, Tennessee-- "The Resemblance Between a Violin Case and a Coffin" (1951)

Cheever, John-- "The Country Husband" (1955)

O'Connor, Flannery-- "Greenleaf" (1957)

Hall, Lawrence Sargent-- "The Ledge" (1960)

Roth, Philip-- "Defender of the Faith" (1960)

Elkin, Stanley-- "Criers and Kibitzers, Kibitzers and Criers" (1962)

Malamud, Bernard-- "The German Refugee" (1964)

Oates, Joyce Carol-- "Where Are You Going, Where Have You Been?" (1967)

Gavell, Mary Ladd -- "The Rotifer" (1968)

McPherson, James Alan-- "Gold Coast" (1969)

Singer, Isaac Bashevis-- "The Key" (1970)

Barthelme, Donald-- "A City of Churches" (1973)

Brown, Rosellen-- "How to Win" (1975)

Adams, Alice-- "Roses, Rhododendron" (1976)

Brodkey, Harold-- "Verona: A Young Woman Speaks" (1978)

Bellow, Saul-- "A Silver Dish" (1979)

Updike, John-- "Gesturing" (1980)

Ozick, Cynthia-- "The Shawl" (1981)

Carver, Raymond-- "Where I'm Calling From" (1983)

Beattie, Ann-- "Janus" (1986)

Sontag, Susan-- "The Way We Live Now" (1987)

O'Brien, Tim-- "The Things They Carried" (1987)

Munro, Alice-- "Meneseteung" (1989)

Moore, Lorrie-- "You're Ugly, Too" (1990)

Jones, Thom-- "I Want to Live!" (1993)

Dark, Alice Elliott-- "In the Gloaming" (1994)

Ferrell, Carolyn-- "Proper Library" (1994)

Jen, Gish-- "Birthmates" (1995)

Durban, Pam-- "Soon" (1997)

Proulx, E. Annie-- "The Half-Skinned Steer" (1998)

Houston, Pam-- "The Best Girlfriend You Never Had" (1999)

The Best American Short Stories, 2000: Selected from U.S. and Canadian Magazines,
edited by **E.L. Doctorow, with Katrina Kenison.**

Becker, Geoffrey-- "Black Elvis"

Bloom, Amy-- "The Story"

Byers, Michael-- "The Beautiful Days"

Carlson, Ron-- "The Ordinary Son"

Carver, Raymond-- "Call If You Need Me"

Davenport, Kiana-- "Bones of the Inner Ear"

Díaz, Junot-- "Nilda"

Englander, Nathan-- "The Gilgul of Park Avenue"

Everett, Percival-- "The Fix"

Gautreaux, Tim-- "Good for the Soul"

Gurganus, Allan-- "He's at the Office"

Hemon, Aleksandar-- "Blind Jozef Pronek"

Hill, Kathleen-- "The Anointed"

Jin, Ha-- "The Bridegroom"

Krysl, Marilyn-- "The Thing Around Them"

Lahiri, Jhumpa-- "The Third and Final Continent"

Mosley, Walter-- "Pet Fly"

Packer, ZZ-- "Brownies"

Pearlman, Edith-- "Allog"

Proulx, E. Annie-- "People in Hell Just Want a Drink of Water"

Sherwood, Frances-- "Basil the Dog"

The Best American Short Stories, 2001: Selected from U.S. and Canadian Magazines,
edited by **Barbara Kingsolver, with Katrina Kenison**

Barrett, Andrea-- "Servants of the Map"

Bass, Rick-- "The Fireman"

Davies, Peter Ho-- "Think of England"

Davis, Claire-- "Labors of the Heart"

Graver, Elizabeth-- "The Mourning Door

Jin, Ha-- "After Cowboy Chicken Came to Town"

Lee, Andrea-- "Brothers and Sisters Around the World"

Moody, Rick-- "Boys"

Moss, Barbara Klein-- "Rug Weaver"

Munro, Alice-- "Post and Beam"

Orner, Peter-- "The Raft"

Parvin, Roy-- "Betty Hutton"

Reisman, Nancy-- "Illumination"

Row, Jess—The Secrets of Bats"

Sanford, Annette-- "Nobody Listens When I Talk"

Shonk, Katherine-- "My Mother's Garden"

Silver, Marisa-- "What I Saw from Where I Stood"

Trevanian-- "The Apple Tree"

Updike, John-- "Personal Archeology"

West, Dorothy-- "My Baby . . ."

The Best American Short Stories, 2002: Selected from U.S. and Canadian Magazines,
edited by **Sue Miller, with Katrina Kenison**

Chabon, Michael-- "Along the Frontage Road"

Cooke, Carolyn-- "The Sugar-Tit"

Cummins, Ann-- "The Red Ant House"

Danticat, Edwidge-- "Seven"

Doctorow, E. L.-- "A House on the Plains"

Ford, Richard-- "Puppy"

Hardy, Melissa-- "The Heifer"

Iagnemma, Karl-- "Zilkowski's Theorem"

Lahiri, Jhumpa-- "Nobody's Business"

Lordan, Beth-- "Digging"

McCorkle, Jill-- "Billy Goats"

McNeal, Tom-- "Watermelon Days"

Mattison, Alice-- "In Case We're Separated"

Michaels, Leonard-- "Nachman from Los Angeles"

Miller, Arthur-- "Bulldog"

Mullins, Meg-- "The Rug"

Munro, Alice-- "Family Furnishings"

Sharma, Akhil-- "Surrounded by Sleep"

Shepard, Jim-- "Love and Hydrogen"

Waters, Mary Yukari-- "Aftermath"

The Best American Short Stories, 2003: Selected from U.S. and Canadian Magazines,
edited by **Walter Mosley, with Katrina Kenison ;**

Allison, Dorothy-- "Compassion"

Brockmeier, Kevin-- "Space"

Chaon, Dan-- "The Bees"

Cooper, Rand Richards-- "Johnny Hamburger"

Danticat, Edwidge-- "Night Talkers"

Doctorow, E. L.-- "Baby Wilson"

Doerr, Anthony-- "The Shell Collector"

Erdich, Louise-- "Shamengwa"

Harty, Ryan-- "Why the Sky Turns Red When the Sun Goes Down"

Haslett, Adam-- "Devotion"

Krauss, Nicole-- "Future Emergencies"

Packer, ZZ-- "Every Tongue Shall Confess"

Paschal, Dean-- "Moriya"

Phipps, Marilene-- "Marie-Ange's Ginen"

Pomerantz, Sharon-- "Ghost Knife"

Raboteau, Emily Ishem-- "Kavita Through Glass"

Row, Jess-- "Heaven Lake"

Simpson, Mona-- "Coins"

Straight, Susan-- "Mines

Waters, Mary Yukari-- "Rationing"

The Best American Short Stories, 2004: Selected from U.S. and Canadian Magazines,
edited by **Lorrie Moore, with Katrina Kenison**

Alexie, Sherman-- "What You Pawn I Will Redeem"

Boyle, T. Coraghessan-- "Tooth and Claw"

Brady, Catherine-- "Written in Stone"

Bynum, Sarah Shun-lien-- "Accomplice"

D'Ambrosio, Charles-- "Screenwriter"

Dybek, Stuart-- "Breasts"

Eisenberg, Deborah-- "Some Other, Better Otto"

Fox, Paula-- "Grace"

Freudenberger, Nell-- "The Tutor"

Jones, Edward P.-- "A Rich Man"

Lewis, Trudy-- "Limestone Diner"

McCorkle, Jill-- "Intervention"

McGuane, Thomas-- "Gallatin Canyon"

Munro, Alice-- "Runaway"

Pneuman, Angela-- "All Saints Day"

Proulx, E. Annie-- "What Kind of Furniture Would Jesus Pick"

Smith, R. T.-- "Docent"

Updike, John-- "The Walk with Elizanne"

Waters, Mary Yukari-- "Mirror Studies"

Wideman, John Edgar-- "What We Cannot Speak About We Must Pass over in Silence"

The Best American Short Stories, 2005: Selected from U.S. and Canadian Magazines,
edited by **Michael Chabon, with Katrina Kenison**

Bellows, Nathaniel-- "First Four Measures"

Bezmozgis, David-- "Natasha"

Bissell, Tom-- "Death Defier"

D'Ambrosio, Charles-- "The Scheme of Things"

Doctorow, Cory-- "Anda's Game"

Jones, Edward P.-- "Old Boys, Old Girls"

Lehane, Dennis-- "Until Gwen"

Lennon, J. Robert-- "Eight Pieces for the Left Hand"

Link, Kelly-- "Stone Animals"

McGuane, Thomas-- "Old Friends"

Means, David-- "The Secret Goldfish"

Munro, Alice-- "Silence"

Oates, Joyce Carol-- "The Cousins"

Ohlin, Alix-- "Simple Exercises for the Beginning Student"

Perotta, Tom-- "The Smile on Happy Chang's Face"

Pratt, Tom-- "Heart and Boot"

Reddi, Rishi-- "Justice Shiva Ram Murthy"

Saunders, George-- "Bohemians"

Schwartz, Lynn Sharon -- "A Taste of Dust"

Williams, Joy-- "The Girls"

The Best American Short Stories, 2006: Selected from U.S. and Canadian Magazines,
edited by **Ann Patchett, with Katrina Kenison**

Beattie, Ann, with Harry Matthews-- "Mr. Nobody at All"

Bell, Katherine-- "The Casual Car Pool"

Bezmozgis, David-- "A New Gravestone for an Old Grave"

Coover, Robert-- "Grandmother's Nose"

Englander, Nathan-- "How We Avenged the Bums"

Gaitskill, Mary-- "Today I'm Yours"

Hemon, Aleksandar-- "The Conductor"

Li, Yiyun-- "After a Life"

Livings, Jack-- "The Dog"

McGuane, Thomas-- "Cowboy"

Moffett, Kevin-- "Tattooizm"

Munro, Alice-- "The View from Castle Rock"

Pearlman, Edith-- "Self-Reliance"

Percy, Benjamin-- "Refresh, Refresh"

Ryan, Patrick-- "So Much for Artemis"

Slouka, Mark-- "Dominion"

Swann, Maxine-- "Secret"

Tartt, Donna-- "The Ambush"

Woolf, Tobias-- "Awaiting Orders"

Yoon, Paul-- "Once the Shore"

The Best American Short Stories, 2007: Selected from U.S. and Canadian Magazines,
edited by **Stephen King, with Heidi Pitlor**

Auchincloss, Louis-- "Pa's Darling"

Barth, John-- "Toga Party"

Beattie, Ann-- "Solid Wood"

Boyle, T. Coraghessan-- "Balto"

DeVita, Randy-- "Riding the Doghouse"

Epstein, Joseph-- "My Brother Eli"

Gay, William-- "Where Will You Go When Your Skin Cannot Contain You?"

Gordon, Mary-- "Eleanor's Music"

Groff, Lauren-- "L. DeBard and Aliette, a Love Story"

Jensen, Beverly-- "Wake"

Kesey, Roy-- "Wait"

Kim, Stellar-- "Findings and Impressions"

Kyle, Aryn-- "Allegiance"

McAllister, Bruce-- "Boy in Zaquitos"

Munro, Alice-- "Dimension"

Pollack, Eileen-- "Bris"

Russell, Karen-- "St. Lucy's Home for Girls Raised by Wolves"

Russo, Richard-- "Horseman"

Shepard, Jim-- "Sans Farine"

Walbert, Kate-- "Do Something"

The Best American Short Stories, 2008: Selected from U.S. and Canadian Magazines,
edited by **Salman Rushdie, with Heidi Pitlor**

Boyle, T. Coraghessan-- "Admiral"

Brockmeier, Kevin-- "The Year of Silence"

Brown, Karen-- "Galatea"

Chase, Katie-- "Man and Wife"

Evans, Danielle-- "Virgins"

Goodman, Allegra-- "Closely Held"

Homes, A. M.-- "May We Be Forgotten"

Krauss, Nicole-- "From the Desk of Daniel Varsky"

Lethem, Jonathan-- "The King of Sentences"

Makkai, Rebecca-- "The Worst You Ever Feel"

Millhauser, Steven-- "The Wizard of West Orange"

Mueenuddin, Daniyal-- "Nawabdin Electrician"

Munro, Alice-- "Child's Play"

Penkov, Miroslav-- "Buying Lenin"

Russell, Karen-- "Vampires in the Lemon Grove"

Saunders, George-- "Puppy"

Sneed, Christine-- "Quality of Life"

Tice, Bradford-- "Missionaries"

Wisniewski, Mark-- "Straightaway"

Wolff, Tobias-- "Bible"

The Best American Short Stories, 2009: Selected from U.S. and Canadian Magazines,
edited by **Alice Sebold, with Heidi Pitlor**

Alarcón, Daniel-- "The Idiot President"

Bynum, Sarah Shun-lien-- "Yurt"

De Jarnatt, Steve-- "Rubiaux Rising"

Epstein, Joseph-- "Beyond the Pale"

Fulton, Alice-- "A Shadow Table"

Greenfeld, Karl Taro-- "NowTrends"

Henderson, Eleanor-- "The Farms"

Hrbek, Greg-- "Sagittarius"

Johnson, Adam-- "Hurricanes Anonymous"

Lancelotta, Victoria-- "The Anniversary Trip"

Li, Yiyun-- "A Man Like Him"

McCorkle, Jill-- "Magic Words"

Makkai, Rebecca-- "The Briefcase"

Moffett, Kevin-- "One Dog Year"

Powers, Richard-- "Modulation"

Proulx, E. Annie-- "Them Old Cowboy Songs"

Rash, Ron-- "Into the Gorge"

Rose, Alex-- "Ostracon"

Rutherford, Ethan-- "The Peripatetic Coffin"

Serpell, Namwali-- "Muzungu"

The Best American Short Stories, 2100: Selected from U.S. and Canadian Magazines,
edited by **Richard Russo, with Heidi Pitlor**

Almond, Steve--"Donkey Greedy, Donkey Gets Punched"

Barton, Marlin--"Into Silence"

Baxter, Charles--"The Cousins"

Egan, Jennifer--"Safari"

Evans, Danielle--"Someone Ought to Tell Her There's No Place to Go"

Ferris, Joshua--"The Valetudinarian"

Groff, Lauren--"Delicate Edible Birds"

Harrison, Wayne--"Least Resistance"

Lasdun, James--"The Hollow"

McCorkle, Jill--"P. S."

Makkai, Rebecca--"Painted Ship, Painted Ocean"

Matthews, Brendan--"My Last Attempt to Explain What Happened to the Lion Tamer"

Moffett, Kevin--"Further Interpretations of Real Life Events"

Obreht, Téa--"The Laugh"

Ostlund, Lori--"All Boy"

Rash, Ron--"The Ascent"

Russell, Karen--"The Seagull Army Descends on Strong Beach"

Shepard, Jim--"The Netherlands Lives with Water"

Shipstead, Maggie--"Cowboy Tango"

Tower, Wells--"Raw Water"

FLANNERY O'CONNOR AWARD FOR SHORT FICTION

Established in 1983, the University of Georgia Press presents this award to writers for an outstanding collection of short stories or novellas. The prize is named for the esteemed short-story writer and novelist Flannery O'Connor.

1983: David Walton--*Evening Out* and Leigh Allison Wilson--*From the Bottom Up*

1984: François Camoin--*Why Men Are Afraid of Women*, Mary Hood--*How Far She Went*, Susan Neville--*The Invention of Flight*, and Sandra Thompson--*Close-Ups*

1985: David Curley--*Living with Snakes* and Molly Giles--*Rough Translations*

1986: Tony Ardizzone--*The Evening News* and Peter Meinke--*The Piano Tuner*

1987: Salvatore La Puma--*The Boys of Bensonhurst* and Melissa Pritchard--*Spirit Seizures*

1988: Gail Galloway Adams--*The Purchase of Order* and Philip F. Deaver--*Silent Retreats*

1989: Carole L. Glickfeld--*Useful Gifts* and Antonya Nelson--*The Expendables*

1990: Debra Monroe--*The Source of Trouble* and Nancy Zafris--*The People I Know*

1991: Robert Abel--*Ghosts Traps* and T. M. McNally--*Low Flying Aircraft*

1992: Alfred DePew--*The Melancholy of Departure* and Dennis Hathaway--*The Consequences of Desire*

1993: Rita Ciresi-*Mother Rocket* and Dianne Nelson--*A Brief History of Male Nudes in America*

1994: Christopher McIlroy--*All My Relations* and Alyce Miller--*The Nature of Longing*

1995: Carol Lee Lorenzo--*Nervous Dancer* and C. M. Mayo--*Sky over El Nido*

1996: Wendy Brenner--*Large Animals in Everyday Life* and Paul Rawlins--*No Lie Like Love*

1997: Harvey Grossinger--*The Quarry,* Ha Jin--*Under the Red Flag,* and Andy Plattner--*Winter Money*

1998: Frank Soos--*Unified Field Theory*

1999: Mary Clyde--*Survival Rates* and Hester Kaplan--*The Edge of Marriage*

2000: Robert Anderson--*Ice Age* and Darrel Spencer--*Caution, Men in Trees*

2001: Dana Johnson--*Break Any Woman Down* and Bill Roorbach--*Big Bend*

2002: Gina Ochsner--*The Necessary Grace to Fall* and Kellie Wells--*Compression Scars*

2003: Ed Allen--*Ate It Anyway*, Catherine Brady--*Curled in the Bed of Love*, and Eric Shade--*Eyesores*

2004: Gary Fincke--*Sorry I Worried You* and Barbara Sutton--*The Send-Away Girl*

2005: David Crouse--*Copy Cats*
2006: Greg Downs--*Spit Baths* and Randy F. Nelson--*The Imaginary Lives of Mechanical Men*
2007: Peter LaSalle--*Tell Borges If You See Him: Tales of Contemporary Somnambulism*, Anne Panning--*Super America*, and Margot Singer--*The Pale of Settlement*

2008: Andrew Porter--*The Theory of Light and Matter* and Peter Selgin--*Drowning Lessons*
2009: Geoffrey Becker--*Black Elvis* and Lori Ostlund--*The Bigness of the World*
2010: Linda LeGarde Grover--*The Dance Boots* and Jessica Treadway--*Please Come Back To Me*

GRACE PALEY PRIZE FOR SHORT FICTION

The Association of Writers and Writing Programs annually presents this award for book-length works of short fiction. It is named for American short-story writer Grace Paley.

1978: Rebecca Kavaler--*The Further Adventure of Brunhild*
1979: Ian MacMillan--*Light and Power*
1980: Eugene Garber--*Metaphysical Tales*
1981: François Camoin--*The End of the World Is Los Angeles*
1982: Alvin Greenberg--*Delta q*
1983: Charles Baxter--*Harmony of the World*
1984: Rod Kessier--*Off in Zimbabwe*
1985: No winner
1986: Jesse Lee Kercheval--*The Dogeater: Stories*
1987: Anne Finge--*Basic Skills*
1988: Roland Sodowsky--*Things We Lose*
1989: Susan Hubbard--*Walking on Ice*
1990: Karen Brennan--*Wild Desire*
1991: Jack Driscoll--*Wanting Only to be Heard*
1992: Daniel Lyons--*The First Snow*
1993: E. Bumas--*Significance*
1994: A. Manette Ansay--*Read This and Tell Me What It Says*

1995: David Jauss--*Black Maps*
1996: Charlotte Bacon--*A Private State*
1997: Toni Graham--*The Daiquiri Girls*
1998: Bonnie Jo Campbell--*Women and Other Animals*
1999: C. J. Hribal--*The Clouds in Memphis*
2000: Michelle Richmond--*The Girl in the Fall-Away Dress*
2001: Christie Hodgen--*A Jeweler's Eye for Flaw*
2002: Joan Connor--*History Lessons*
2003: Doreen Baingana--*Tropical Fish*
2004: No winner
2005: Nona Caspers--*Heavier than Air*
2006: Karen Brown--*Pins and Needles*
2007: David Vann--*Legend of a Suicide*
2008: Ramola D--*Temporary Lives, and Other Stories*
2009: Christine Sneed--*Portraits of a Few of the People I've Made Cry*
2010: Douglas Light--*Girls in Trouble*

NATIONAL BOOK AWARD

Awarded annually since 1950 to books by U.S. citizens "that have contributed most significantly to human awareness, to the vitality of our national culture and to the spirit of excellence." This listing includes only authors who have won this award for works of short fiction.

1951: William Faulkner--*Collected Stories*
1959: Bernard Malamud--*The Magic Barrel*
1960: Philip Roth--*Goodbye, Columbus, and Five Short Stories*
1966: Katherine Anne Porter--*The Collected Stories of Katherine Anne Porter*

1972: Flannery O'Connor--*Flannery O'Connor: The Complete Stories*
1984: Ellen Gilchrist--*Victory over Japan: A Book of Stories*
1996: Andrea Barrett--*Ship Fever, and Other Stories*

PEN/Faulkner Award for Fiction

Awarded annually since 1981 to the most distinguished work of fiction by an American writer. This listing includes only authors who have won this award for works of short fiction.

1986: Peter Taylor--*The Old Forest, and Other Stories*

1989: James Salter--*Dusk, and Other Stories*

1997: Gina Berriault--*Women in Their Beds: New and Selected Stories*

2004: John Updike--*The Early Stories, 1953-1975*

2010: Sherman Alexie--*War Dances*

PEN/Malamud Award

The PEN/Malamud Award and Memorial Reading, awarded annually by the PEN/Faulkner Foundation, recognizes excellence in "the art of the short story."

1988: John Updike

1989: Saul Bellow

1990: George Garrett

1991: Frederick Busch and Andre Dubus

1992: Eudora Welty

1993: Peter Taylor

1994: Grace Paley

1995: Stuart Dybek and William Maxwell

1996: Joyce Carol Oates

1997: Alice Munro

1998: John Barth

1999: T. Coraghessan Boyle

2000: Ann Beattie and Nathan Englander

2001: Sherman Alexie and Richard Ford

2002: Junot Díaz and Ursula K. Le Guin

2003: Barry Hannah and Maile Meloy

2004: Richard Bausch and Nell Freudenberger

2005: Lorrie Moore

2006: Adam Haslett and Tobias Wolff

2007: Elizabeth Spencer

2008: Cynthia Ozick and Peter Ho Davies

2009: Alistair MacLeod and Amy Hempel

2010: Edward P. Jones and Nam Le

PEN/O. Henry Award

The O. Henry Awards, published each year in a volume entitled *Prize Stories*, were established in 1919; in 2009, prize officials partnered with the PEN American Center and the prize was renamed the PEN/O. Henry Award. The annual volume of prize-winners features stories written in English that were published- in American and Canadian magazines.

1919

First Prize

Montague, Margaret Prescott-- "England to America"

Second Prize

Steele, Wilbur Daniel-- "For They Know Not What They Do"

Other Selected Stories

Alsop, Guglielma-- "The Kitchen Gods"

Cabell, James Branch-- "Porcelain Cups"

Derieux, Samuel A.-- "The Trial in Tom Belcher's Store"

Ferber, Edna-- "April Twenty-fifth as Usual"

Hurst, Fannie-- "Humoresque"

Marshall, Edison-- "The Elephant Remembers"

Post, Melville D.-- "Five Thousand Dollars Reward"

Ravenel, Beatrice-- "The High Cost of Conscience"

Rice, Louise-- "The Lubbeny Kiss"

Springer, Thomas Grant-- "The Blood of the Dragon"

Terhune, Albert Payson-- "On Strike"

Williams, Ben Ames--"They Grind Exceedingly Small"

Wood, Frances Gilchrist-- "Turkey Red"

1920

First Prize

Burt, Maxwell Struthers-- "Each in His Generation"

Second Prize

Hart, Frances Noyes-- "Contact!"

Other Selected Stories

Fitzgerald, F. Scott-- "The Camel's Back"

Forbes, Esther-- "Break-Neck Hill"

Gilpatric, Guy-- "Black Art and Ambrose"

Hartman, Lee Foster-- "The Judgement of Vulcan"

Hull, Alexander-- "The Argosies"

Lewis, O. F.-- "Alma Mater"

Miller, Alice Duer-- "Slow Poison"

Pelley, William Dudley-- "The Face in the Window"

Perry, Lawrence-- "A Matter of Loyalty"

Robbins, L. H.-- "Professor Todd's Used Car"

Rutledge, Maurice-- "The Thing They Loved"

Sidney, Rose-- "Butterflies"

Smith, Gordon Arthur-- "No Flowers"

Steele, Wilbur Daniel-- "Footfalls"

Whitman, Stephen French-- "The Last Room of All"

1921

First Prize

Marshall, Edison-- "The Heart of Little Shikara"

Second Prize

Jackson, Charles Tenney-- "The Man Who Cursed the Lillies"

Other Selected Stories

Allen, Maryland-- "The Urge"

Beer, Thomas-- "Mummery"

Chittenden, Gerald-- "The Victim of His Vision"

Cooper, Courtney Ryley, and Lee F. Creagan-- "Martin Gerrity Gets Even"

Cram, Mildred-- "Stranger Things"

Derieux, Samuel A.-- "Comet"

Heerman, Elizabeth Alexander-- "Fifty-two Weeks for Florette"

Kerr, Sophie-- "Wild Earth"

Kniffin, Harry Anable-- "The Tribute"

Lewis, O. F.-- "The Get-Away"

Mumford, Ethel Watts-- "Aurore"

Robbins, L. H.-- "Mr. Downey Sits Down"

Steele, Wilbur Daniel-- "The Marriage in Kairwan"

Tupper, Tristram-- "Grit"

1922

First Prize

Cobb, Irvin S.-- "Snake Doctor"

Second Prize

Lane, Rose Wilder-- "Innocence"

Best Short Short

Buckley, F. R.-- "Gold-Mounted Guns"

Other Selected Stories

Alexander, Charles-- "As a Dog Should"

Barrett, Richmond Brooks-- "Art for Art's Sake"

Beer, Thomas-- "Tact"

Bennett, James W.-- "The Kiss of the Accolade"

Derieux, Samuel A.-- "The Sixth Shot"

Horn, R. de S.-- "The Jinx of the Shandon Belle"

Hull, Helen R.-- "His Sacred Family"

Jackson, Charles Tenney-- "The Horse of Hurricane Reef"

Lewis, O. F.-- "Old Peter Takes an Afternoon Off"

Morris, Gouverneur-- "Ig's Amock"

Steele, Wilbur Daniel-- "The Anglo-Saxon"

Terhune, Albert Payson-- "The Writer-Upward"

Vorse, Mary Heaton-- "Twilight of the God"

1923

First Prize

Smith, Edgar Valentine-- "Prelude"

Second Prize

Connell, Richard-- "A Friend of Napoleon"

Best Short Short

Folsom, Elizabeth Irons-- "Towers of Fame"

Other Selected Stories

Dell, Floyd-- "Phantom Adventure"

Farogoh, Francis Edwards-- "The Distant Street"

Glenn, Isa Urquhart-- "The Wager"

Hopper, James-- "Célestine"

Larsson, Genevieve-- "Witch Mary"

Lemmon, Robert S.-- "The Bamboo Trap"

Mahoney, James-- "The Hat of Eight Reflections"

Mason, Grace Sartwell-- "Home Brew"

Morris, Gouverneur-- "Derrick's Return"

Synon, Mary-- "Shadowed"

Tarkington, Booth-- "The One Hundred Dollar Bill"

Watts, Mary S.-- "Nice Neighbors"

Williams, Jesse Lynch-- "Not Wanted"

1924

First Place

Irwin, Inez Haynes-- "The Spring Flight"

Second Place

Crowell, Chester T.-- "Margaret Blake"

Best Short Short

Newman, Frances-- "Rachel and Her Children"

Other Selected Stories

Benét, Stephen Vincent-- "Uriah's Son"

Connell, Richard-- "The Most Dangerous Game"

Dobie, Charles Caldwell-- "Horse and Horse"

Mirrielees, Edith R.-- "Professor Boynton Rereads History"

Mosley, Jefferson-- "The Secret at the Crossroads"

Pattullo, George-- "The Tie That Binds"

Singmaster, Elsie-- "The Courier of the Czar"

Smith, Edgar Valentine-- "'Lijah"

Spears, Raymond S.-- "A River Combine-Professional"

Steele, Wilbur Daniel-- "What Do You Mean—Americans?"

Stone, Elinore Cowan-- "One Uses the Handkerchief"

Welles, Harriet-- "Progress"

1925

First Prize

Street, Julian-- "Mr. Bisbee's Princess"

Second Prize

Williams, Wythe-- "Splendid with Swords"

Best Short Short

Austin, Mary-- "Papago Wedding"

Other Selected Stories

Anderson, Sherwood-- "The Return"

Babcock, Edwina Stanton-- "Dunelight"

Brady, Mariel-- "Peter Projects"

Brecht, Harold W.-- "Two Heroes"

Carver, Ada Jack-- "Redbone"

Eliot, Ethel Cook-- "Maternal"

Hackett, Francis-- "Unshapely Things"

Heyward, DuBose-- "Crown's Bess"

Peterkin, Julia-- "Maum Lou"

Steele, Wilbur Daniel-- "The Man Who Saw Through Heaven"-- "Cornelia's Mountain"

Whitlock, Brand-- "The Sofa"

1926

First Prize

Steele, Wilbur Daniel-- "Bubbles"

Second Prize

Anderson, Sherwood-- "Death in the Woods"

Best Short Short

Wetjen, Albert Richard-- "Command"

Other Selected Stories

Carver, Ada Jack-- "Threeshy"

Detzer, Karl W.-- "The Wreck Job"

Dobie, Charles Caldwell-- "The Thrice Bereft Widow of Hung Gow"-- "Symphonesque"

Goodloe, Abbie Carter-- "Claustrophobia"

Graeve, Oscar-- "A Death on Eighth Avenue"

Jacobs, Marguerite-- "Singing Eagles"

Kelly, Eleanor Mercein-- "Basquerie"

Saxon, Lyle-- "Cane River"

Skinner, Constance Lindsay-- "The Dew on the Fleece"

Tarkington, Booth-- "Stella Crozier"

Vorse, Mary Heaton-- "The Madelaine"

Williams, Ben Ames-- "The Nurse"

1927

First Prize

Bradford, Roark-- "Child of God"

Second Prize

Hemingway, Ernest-- "The Killers"

Best Short Short

Bromfield, Louis-- "The Scarlet"

Other Selected Stories

Adams, Bill-- "Jukes"

Bellah, James Warner-- "Fear"

Brush, Katherine-- "Night Club"

Carver, Ada Jack-- "Singing Woman"

Chapman, Elizabeth Cobb-- "With Glory and Honor"

Daniels, Roger-- "Bulldog"

Douglas, Marjory Stoneman-- "He Man"

Ellerbe, Alma, and Paul Ellerbe-- "Don Got Over"

Kelly, Eleanor Mercein-- "Monkey Motions"

Sawyer, Ruth-- "Four Dreams of Gram Perkins"

Suckow, Ruth-- "The Little Girl from Town"

Taylor, Ellen Dupois-- "Shades of George Sand"

1928

First Prize

Duranty, Walter-- "The Parrot"

Second Prize

Douglas, Marjory Stoneman-- "The Peculiar Treasure of Kings"

Best Short Short

Gale, Zona-- "Bridal Pond"

Other Selected Stories

Adams, Bill-- "Home Is the Sailor"

Aldrich, Bess Streeter-- "The Man Who Caught the Weather"

Avery, Stephen Morehouse-- "Never in This World"

Blackman, M. C.-- "Hot Copy"

Bradford, Roark-- "River Witch"

Brown, Cambray-- "Episode in a Machine Age"

Cobb, Irvin S.-- "An Episode at Pintail Lake"

Connell, Richard-- "The Law Beaters"

Hartman, Lee Foster-- "Mr. Smith" (or "Two Minutes to Live")

Johnson, Nunnally-- "The Actor"

Marquis, Don-- "O'Meara, the Mayflower--and Mrs. MacLirr"-- "Lightning"

Tarleton, Fiswoode-- "Curtains" (or "Bloody Ground")

Wescott, Glenway-- "Prohibition"

1929

First Prize

Parker, Dorothy-- "Big Blonde"

Second Prize

Howard, Sidney-- "The Homesick Ladies"

Best Short Short

Brush, Katherine-- "Him and Her"

Other Selected Stories

Anderson, Sherwood-- "Alice"

Benét, Stephen Vincent-- "The King of the Cats"

Bromfield, Louis-- "The Skeleton at the Feast"

Brush, Katherine-- "Speakeasy"

Chapman, Maristan-- "Treat You Clever"

Johnston, Mary-- "Elephants Through the Country"

Leech, Margaret-- "Manicure"

Marquis, Don-- "The Red-Haired Woman"

Norris, Kathleen-- "Sinners"

Patterson, Pernet-- "Buttin' Blood"

Rushfeldt, Elise-- "A Coffin for Anna"

Sanborn, Ruth Burr-- "Professional Pride"

Slade, Caroline-- "Mrs. Sabin"

Steele, Wilbur Daniel-- "The Silver Sword"

1930

First Prize

Burnett, W. R.-- "Dressing-Up"

John, William H.-- "Neither Jew Nor Greek"

Second Prize

Roberts, Elizabeth Madox-- "The Sacrifice of the Maidens"

Best Short Short

Connelly, Marc-- "Coroner's Inquest"

Other Selected Stories

Bradford, Roark-- "Careless Love"

Burt, Katherine Newlin-- "Herself"

Clements, Colin-- "Lobster John's Annie"

Cobb, Irvin S.-- "Faith, Hope and Charity"

Cooper, Courtney Ryley-- "The Elephant Forgets"

DeFord, Miriam Allen-- "The Silver Knight"

Hallet, Richard Matthews-- "Misfortune's Isle"

Held, John, Jr.-- "A Man of the World"

Johnson, Nunnally-- "Mlle. Irene the Great"

March, William-- "The Little Wife"

Overbeck, Alicia O'Reardon-- "Encarnatión"

Pelley, William Dudley-- "The Continental Angle"

Peterkin, Julia-- "The Diamond Ring"

Ryerson, Florence-- "Lobster John's Annie"

Steele, Wilbur Daniel-- "Conjuh"

Street, Julian-- "A Matter of Standards"

Thomason, Capt. John W., Jr.-- "Born on an Iceberg"

1931

First Prize

Steele, Wilbur Daniel-- "Can't Cross Jordan by Myself"

Second Prize

Swain, John D.-- "One Head Well Done"

Third Prize

Bradley, Mary Hastings-- "The Five-Minute Girl"

Best Short Short

La Farge, Oliver-- "Haunted Ground"

Other Selected Stories

Beems, Griffith-- "Leaf Unfolding"

Brush, Katharine-- "Good Wednesday"
Chase, Mary Ellen-- "Salesmanship"
Ryerson, Florence, and Colin Clements-- "Useless"
Dobie, Charles Caldwell-- "The False Talisman"
Faulkner, William-- "Thrift"
Hume, Cyril-- "Forrester"
Loomis, Alfred F.-- "Professional Aid"
Luhrs, Marie-- "Mrs. Schwellenbach's Receptions"
March, William-- "Fifteen from Company K"
Rice, Laverne-- "Wings for Janie"
Smith, Edgar Valentine-- "Cock-a-Doodle-Done!"
Tarkington, Booth-- "Cider of Normandy"
Thorne, Crichton Alston-- "Chimney City"

1932
First Prize
Benét, Stephen Vincent-- "An End to Dreams"
Second Prize
Cozzens, James Gould-- "Farewell to Cuba"
Best Short Short
Granberry, Edwin-- "A Trip to Czardis"
Other Selected Stories
Boone, Jack H.-- "Big Singing"
Boyle, Kay-- "The First Lover"
Brush, Katherine-- "Football Girl"
Canfield, Dorothy-- "Ancestral Home"
Cobb, Irvin S.-- "A Colonel of Kentucky"
Constiner, Merle-- "Big Singing"
Coombes, Evan-- "Kittens Have Fathers"
Edmonds, Walter D.-- "The Cruise of the Cashalot"
Faulkner, William-- "Turn About"
Marquand, J. P.-- "Deep Water"
Tarkington, Booth-- "She Was Right Once"

1933
First Prize
Rawlings, Marjorie Kinnan-- "Gal Young Un"
Second Prize
Buck, Pearl S.-- "The Frill"
Best Short Short
Hale, Nancy-- "To the Invader"
Other Selected Stories
Adams, Bill-- "The Lubber"
Aiken, Conrad-- "The Impulse"
Arnold, Len-- "Portrait of a Woman"
Caldwell, Erskine-- "Country Full of Swedes"

Fitzgerald, F. Scott-- "Family in the Wind"
Frost, Francis M.-- "The Heart Being Perished"
Haardt, Sarah-- "Absolutely Perfect"
Lane, Rose Wilder-- "Old Maid"
Robinson, Selma-- "The Departure"
Smith, Robert-- "Love Story"
Thomas, Dorothy-- "The Consecrated Coal Scuttle"
Wilde, Hagar-- "Little Brat"

1934
First Prize
Paul, Louis-- "No More Trouble for Jedwick"
Second Prize
Gordon, Caroline-- "Old Red"
Third Prize
Saroyan, William-- "The Daring Young Man on the
    Flying Trapeze"
Other Selected Stories
Appel, Benjamin-- "Pigeon Flight"
Buck, Pearl S.-- "Shanghai Scene"
Caldwell, Erskine-- "Maud Island"
Cole, Madelene-- "Bus to Biarritz"
DeFord, Miriam Allen-- "Pride"
Edmonds, Walter D.-- "Honor of the County"
Faulkner, William-- "Wash"
Fisher, Vardis-- "The Scarecrow"
Johnson, Josephine W.-- "Dark"
Sherman, Richard-- "First Flight"
Steinbeck, John-- "The Murder"
Stribling, T. S.-- "Guileford"
Sylvester, Harry-- "A Boxer: Old"
Wexley, John-- "Southern Highway Fifty-one"
Wolfe, Thomas-- "Boom Town"
Zugsmith, Leane-- "King Lear in Evansville"

1935
First Prize
Boyle, Kay-- "The White Horses of Vienna"
Second Prize
Thomas, Dorothy-- "The Home Place"
Third Prize
Johnson, Josephine W.-- "John the Six"
Other Selected Stories
Algren, Nelson-- "The Brother's House"
Benét, Stephen Vincent-- "The Professor's Punch"

Hamill, Katherine--"Leora's Father"
Kantor, MacKinlay--"Silent Grow the Guns"
Mamet, Louis--"A Writer Interviews a Banker"
Marquis, Don--"Country Doctor"
McCleary, Dorothy--"Little Elise"
O'Donnell, E. P.--"Jesus Knew"
Paul, Louis--"Lay Me Low!"
Santee, Ross--"Water"
Saroyan, William--"Five Ripe Pears"
Shenton, Edward--"When Spring Brings Back. . ."
Sherman, Richard--"First Day"
Terrell, Upton--"Long Distance"
Weidman, Jerome--"My Father Sits in the Dark"
Wolfe, Thomas--"Only the Dead Know Brooklyn"

1936

First Prize

Cozzens, James Gould--"Total Stranger"

Second Prize

Benson, Sally--"Suite Twenty Forty-nine"

Best Short Short

March, William--"A Sum in Addition"

Other Selected Stories

Bessie, Alvah C.--"A Personal Issue"
Bird, Virginia--"Havoc Is Circle"
Brace, Ernest--"Silent Whistle"
Cain, James M.--"Dead Man"
Coatsworth, Elizabeth--"The Visit"
Colby, Nathalie--"Glass Houses"
Driftmier, Lucille--"For My Sister"
Edmonds, Walter D.--"Escape from the Mine"
Faulkner, William--"Lion"
Gale, Zona--"Crisis"
Godchaux, Elma--"Chains"
Heth, Edward Harris--"Big Days Beginning"
Horgan, Paul--"The Trunk"
Katterjohn, Elsie--"Teachers"
Knight, Eric--"The Marne"
Owen, Janet Curren--"Afternoon of a Young Girl"

1937

First Prize

Benét, Stephen Vincent--"The Devil and Daniel
    Webster"

Second Prize

Moll, Elick--"To Those Who Wait"

Third Prize

Coates, Robert M.--"The Fury"

Other Selected Stories

Appel, Benjamin--"Awroopdedoop!"
Bird, Virginia--"For Nancy's Sake"
DeJong, David Cornel--"The Chicory Neighbors"
Hale, Nancy--"To the North"
Hilton, Charles--"Gods of Darkness"
Hunt, Hamlen--"The Saluting Doll"
March, William--"The Last Meeting"
Martin, Charles--"Hobogenesis"
McKeon, J. M.--"The Gladiator"
O'Hara, John--"My Girls"
Patten, Katherine--"Man Among Men"
Pereda, Prudencio de--"The Spaniard"
Seager, Allan--"Pro Arte"
Still, James--"Job's Tears"
Stuart, Jesse--"Whip-Poor-Willie"
Thibault, David--"A Woman Like Dilsie"
Warren, Robert Penn--"Christmas Gift"
Weidman, Jerome--"Thomas Hardy's Meat"

1938

First Prize

Maltz, Albert--"The Happiest Man on Earth"

Second Prize

Wright, Richard--"Fire and Cloud"

Third Prize

Steinbeck, John--"The Promise"

Other Selected Stories

Benét, Stephen Vincent--"Johnny Pye and the
    Fool-Killer"
Caldwell, Erskine--"Man and Woman"
Daly, Maureen--"Sixteen"
Fuchs, Daniel--"The Amazing Mystery at Storick,
    Dorschi, Pflaumer, Inc."
Hale, Nancy--"Always Afternoon"
Bradley, Mary Hastings--"The Life of the Party"
Hunt, Hamlen--"Only by Chance Are Pioneers Made"
Moll, Elick--"Memoir of Spring"
Saroyan, William--"The Summer of the Beautiful
    White Horse"
Still, James--"So Large a Thing as Seven"
Whitehand, Robert--"The Fragile Bud"

1939

First Prize

Faulkner, William-- "Barn Burning"

Second Prize

Still, James-- "Bat Flight"

Third Prize

DeJong, David Cornel-- "Calves"

Other Selected Stories

Baker, Dorothy-- "Keeley Street Blues"

Boyle, Kay-- "Anschluss"

Brand, Millen-- "The Pump"

Burt, Maxwell Struthers-- "The Fawn"

Caldwell, Erskine-- "The People V. Abe Lathan, Colored"

Cooke, Charles-- "Nothing Can Change It"

Foster, Joseph O'Kane-- "Gideon"

Gordon, Caroline-- "Frankie and Thomas and Bud Asbury"

Shaw, Irwin-- "God on a Friday Night"

St. Joseph, Ellis-- "A Knocking at the Gate"

Thielen, Benedict-- "Silver Virgin"

Welty, Eudora-- "Petrified Man"

1940

First Prize

Benét, Stephen Vincent-- "Freedom's a Hard-Bought Thing"

Second Prize

Lull, Roderick-- "Don't Get Me Wrong"

Third Prize

Havill, Edward-- "The Kill"

Other Selected Stories

Boyle, Kay-- "Poor Monsieur Panalitus"

Brooks, Roy Patchen-- "Without Hal"

Coates, Robert M.-- "Let's Not Talk About It Now"

Faulkner, William-- "Hand upon the Waters"

Hale, Nancy-- "That Woman"

King, Mary-- "Chicken on the Wind"

Lumpkin, Grace-- "The Treasure"

McCleary, Dorothy-- "Mother's Helper"

Porter, Katherine Anne-- "The Downward Path to Wisdom"

Rawlings, Marjorie Kinnan-- "The Pelican's Shadow"

Robinson, Mabel L.-- "Called For"

Saroyan, William-- "The Three Swimmers and the Educated Grocer"

Tracy, Tom-- "Homecoming"

Wright, Richard-- "Almos' a Man"

1941

First Prize

Boyle, Kay-- "Defeat"

Second Prize

Welty, Eudora-- "A Worn Path"

Third Prize

Abbett, Hallie Southgate-- "Eighteenth Summer"

Best First-Published Story

Logan, Andy-- "The Visit"

Other Selected Stories

Aiken, Conrad-- "Hello, Tib"

Algren, Nelson-- "A Bottle of Milk for Mother (Biceps)"

Benson, Sally-- "Retreat"

Cheever, John-- "I'm Going to Asia"

Clark, Walter Van Tilburg-- "Hook"

DeJong, David Cornel-- "Seven Boys Take a Hill"

Faulkner, William-- "The Old People"

Gallico, Paul-- "The Snow Goose"

Hale, Nancy-- "Those Are as Brothers"

Kunasz, Paul-- "I'd Give It All up for Tahiti"

Maltz, Albert-- "Afternoon in the Jungle"

Morris, Edita-- "Caput Mortum"

O'Hara, Mary-- "My Friend Flicka"

Sheean, Vincent-- "The Conqueror"

Still, James-- "The Proud Walkers"

Thomas, Dorothy-- "My Pigeon Pair"

1942

First Prize

Welty, Eudora-- "The Wide Net"

Second Prize

Stegner, Wallace-- "Two Rivers"

Third Prize

Schramm, Wilbur L.-- "Windwagon Smith"

Best First-Published Story

Wylie, Jeanne E.-- "A Long Way to Go"

Other Selected Stories

Boyle, Kay-- "Their Name Is Macaroni"

Clark, Walter Van Tilburg-- "The Portable
    Phonograph"
Davis, Robert Gorham-- "An Interval Like This"
DeJong, David Cornel-- "Snow-on-the-Mountain"
Faulkner, William-- "Two Soldiers"
Green, Eleanor-- "The Dear Little Doves"
Hale, Nancy-- "Sunday-1913"
Jaynes, Clare-- "The Coming of Age"
Johnson, Josephine W.-- "Alexander to the Park"
Laing, Alexander-- "The Workmanship Has to be
    Wasted"
McCullers, Carson-- "The Jockey"
Shuman, John Rogers-- "Yankee Odyssey"
Steinbeck, John-- "How Edith McGillcuddy Met R. L.
    Stevenson"
Stuart, Alison-- "The Yodeler"
Sullivan, Richard-- "Feathers"
Weidman, Jerome-- "Basket Carry"
Worthington, Marjorie-- "Hunger"

1943

First Prize

Welty, Eudora-- "Livvie Is Back"

Second Prize

Canfield, Dorothy-- "The Knot Hole"

Third Prize

Fifield, William-- "The Fisherman of Patzcuaro"

Best First-Published Story

Laidlaw, Clara-- "The Little Black Boys"

Other Selected Stories

Boyle, Kay-- "The Canals of Mars"
Breuer, Bessie-- "Pigeons en Casserole"
Buck, Pearl S.-- "The Enemy"
Clark, Walter Van Tilburg-- "The Ascent of Ariel
    Goodbody"
Cook, Whitfield-- "The Unfaithful"
Grinnell, Sarah-- "Standby"
Grossberg, Elmer-- "Black Boy's Good Time"
Hale, Nancy-- "Who Lived and Died Believing"
Johnson, Josephine W.-- "The Glass Pigeon"
Lampman, Ben Hur-- "Blinker was a Good Dog"
McCullers, Carson-- "A Tree. A Rock. A Cloud"
Saroyan, William-- "Knife-like, Flower-like, Like
    Nothing at All in the World"

Smith, Margarita G.-- "White for the Living"
Strong, Austin-- "She Shall Have Music"
Stuart, Alison-- "Death and My Uncle Felix"
Thurber, James-- "The Cane in the Corridor"
Von der Goltz, Peggy-- "The Old She 'Gator"
White, William C.-- "Pecos Bill and the Willful
    Coyote"

1944

First Prize

Shaw, Irwin-- "Walking Wounded"

Second Prize

Breuer, Bessie-- "Home Is a Place"

Third Prize

Beems, Griffith-- "The Stagecoach"

Best First-Published Story

Yerby, Frank G.-- "Health Card"

Other Selected Stories

Clark, Walter Van Tilburg-- "The Buck in the Hills"
Eastman, Elizabeth-- "Like a Field Mouse over the
    Heart"
Fineman, Morton-- "Soldier of the Republic"
Fleming, Berry-- "Strike up a Stirring Music"
Hope, Marjorie-- "That's My Brother"
Johnson, Josephine W.-- "Night Flight"
Knight, Ruth Adams-- "What a Darling Little Boy"
Loveridge, George-- "The Fur Coat"
Osborne, Margaret-- "Maine"
Powers, J. F.-- "Lions, Harts, Leaping Does"
Roane, Marianne-- "Quitter"
Schmitt, Gladys-- "All Souls'"
Schorer, Mark-- "Blockbuster"
Stuart, Alison-- "Sunday Liberty"
Weston, Christine-- "Raziya"
Wilcox, Wendall-- "The Pleasures of Travel"
Young, Marguerite-- "Old James"

1945

First Prize

Clark, Walter Van Tilburg-- "The Wind and the Snow
    of Winter"

Second Prize

Shaw, Irwin-- "Gunner's Passage"

Third Prize

Lampman, Ben Hur-- "Old Bill Bent to Drink"

Other Selected Stories

Breuer, Bessie-- "Bury Your Own Dead"

Critchell, Laurence-- "Flesh and Blood"

Deasy, Mary-- "Long Shadow on the Lawn"

Fenton, Edward-- "Burial in the Desert"

Gerry, Bill-- "Understand What I Mean"

Gordon, Ethel Edison-- "War Front: Louisiana"

Hardwick, Elizabeth-- "The People on the Roller Coaster"

Heyert, Murray-- "The New Kid"

Hubbell, Catherine-- "Monday at Six"

Lavin, Mary-- "The Sand Castle"

Martin, Hansford-- "The Thousand-Yard Stare"

Patton, Frances Gray-- "A Piece of Bread"

Portugal, Ruth-- "Call a Solemn Assembly"

Powers, J. F.-- "The Trouble"

Seager, Allan-- "The Conqueror"

Shattuck, Katharine-- "Subway System"

Smith, Louise Reinhardt-- "The Hour of Knowing"

West, Jessamyn-- "Lead Her Like a Pigeon"

Wilson, Michael-- "Come Away Home"

1946

First Prize

Goss, John Mayo-- "Bird Song"

Second Prize

Shedd, Margaret-- "The Innocent Bystander"

Third Prize

Ullman, Victor-- "Sometimes You Break Even"

Best First-Published Story

Meyer, Cord, Jr.-- "Waves of Darkness"

Other Selected Stories

Berryman, John-- "The Imaginary Jew"

Boyle, Kay-- "Winter Night"

Brookhouser, Frank-- "Request for Sherwood Anderson"

Canfield, Dorothy-- "Sex Education"

Capote, Truman-- "Miriam"

Enright, Elizabeth-- "I Forgot Where I Was"

Hardwick, Elizabeth-- "What We Have Missed"

Highsmith, Patricia-- "The Heroine"

Hutchins, M. P.-- "Innocents"

Le Sueur, Meridel-- "Breathe Upon These Slain"

Lytle, Andrew-- "The Guide"

McCleary, Dorothy-- "Not Very Close"

Rawlings, Marjorie Kinnan-- "Black Secret"

Savler, David S.-- "The Beggar"

Shaw, Irwin-- "Act of Faith"

Thielen, Benedict-- "The Empty Sky"

Welty, Eudora-- "A Sketching Trip"

West, Jessamyn-- "The Blackboard"

1947

First Prize

Clayton, John Bell-- "The White Circle"

Second Prize

Burdick, Eugene L.-- "Rest Camp on Maui"

Third Prize

Parsons, Elizabeth-- "The Nightingales Sing"

Best First-Published Story

Lewis, Robert-- "Little Victor"

Other Selected Stories

Bowles, Paul-- "The Echo"

Bradbury, Ray-- "Homecoming"

Breuer, Bessie-- "The Skeleton and the Easter Lily"

Cobb, Jane-- "The Hot Day"

Deasy, Mary-- "The Holiday"

DeJong, David Cornel-- "The Record"

Elder, Walter-- "You Can Wreck It"

Eustis, Helen-- "An American Home"

Govan, Christine Noble-- "Miss Winters and the Wind"

Kuehn, Susan-- "The Rosebush"

Lynch, John A.-- "The Burden"

Powers, J. F.-- "The Valiant Woman"

Shedd, Margaret-- "The Great Fire of 1945"

Shorer, Mark-- "What We Don't Know Hurts Us"

Smith, John Caswell, Jr.-- "Fighter"

Stafford, Jean-- "The Hope Chest"

Thielen, Benedict-- "Old Boy--New Boy"

Welty, Eudora-- "The Whole World Knows"

West, Jessamyn-- "Horace Chooney, M.D."

1948

First Prize

Capote, Truman-- "Shut a Final Door"

Second Prize

Stegner, Wallace-- "Beyond the Glass Mountain"

Third Prize

Bradbury, Ray-- "Powerhouse"

Best First-Published Story

Grennard, Elliot-- "Sparrow's Last Jump"

Other Selected Stories
Brookhouser, Frank-- "She Did Not Cry at All"
Gidney, James B.-- "The Muse and Mr. Parkinson"
Gordon, Caroline-- "The Petrified Woman"
Greene, Mary Frances-- "The Silent Day"
Hartley, Lodwick-- "Mr. Henig's Wall"
Hauser, Marianne-- "The Other Side of the River"
Ingles, James Wesley-- "The Wind Is Blind"
Janeway, Elizabeth-- "Child of God"
La Farge, Christopher-- "The Three Aspects"
Malkin, Richard-- "Pico Never Forgets"
Morse, Robert-- "The Professor and the Puli"
Parsons, Elizabeth-- "Welcome Home"
Shattuck, Katharine-- "The Answer"
Shelton, William R.-- "The Snow Girl"
Sorenson, Virginia-- "The Talking Stick"
Sulkin, Sidney-- "The Plan"
Terrett, Courtenay-- "The Saddle"
Watson, John-- "The Gun on the Table"
West, Ray B., Jr.-- "The Ascent"

1949
First Prize
Faulkner, William-- "A Courtship"
Second Prize
Van Doren, Mark-- "The Watchman"
Third Prize
Dorrance, Ward-- "The White Hound"
Other Selected Stories
Ashworth, John-- "High Diver"
Bowles, Paul-- "Pastor Dowe at Tacate"
Calisher, Hortense-- "The Middle Drawer"
Coatsworth, Elizabeth-- "Bremen's"
Connell, Evan S., Jr.-- "I'll Take You to Tennessee"
Conrad, Barnaby-- "Cayetano the Perfect"
Cramer, Alice Carver-- "The Boy Next Door"
Downey, Harris-- "The Mulhausen Girls"
Enright, Elizabeth-- "The Trumpeter Swan"
Goss, John Mayo-- "Evening and Morning Prayer"
Jackson, Shirley-- "The Lottery"
Lavin, Mary-- "Single Lady"
Pierce, Phoebe-- "The Season of Miss Maggie Reginald"
Plagemann, Bentz-- "The Best Bread"
Rice, John Andrew-- "You Can Get Just So Much Justice"

Salinger, J. D.-- "Just Before the War with the Eskimos"
Stafford, Jean-- "A Summer Day"
Weaver, John D.-- "Meeting Time"
West, Jessamyn-- "Public Address System"
Wilson, Leon-- "Six Months Is No Long Time"

1950
First Prize
Stegner, Wallace-- "The Blue-Winged Teal"
Second Prize
Leiper, Gudger Bart-- "The Magnolias"
Third Prize
Lowry, Robert-- "Be Nice to Mr. Campbell"
Other Selected Stories
Algren, Nelson-- "The Captain Is Impaled"
Bennett, Peggy-- "Death Under the Hawthorns"
Berry, John-- "New Shoes"
Boyle, Kay-- "Summer Evening"
Cheever, John-- "Vega"
Chidester, Ann-- "Mrs. Ketting and Clark Gable"
Enright, Elizabeth-- "The Sardillion"
Humphrey, William-- "The Hardy's"
Justice, Donald-- "The Lady"
Kuehn, Susan-- "The Hunt"
Lamkin, Speed-- "Comes a Day"
Newhouse, Edward-- "Seventy Thousand Dollars"
Parsons, Elizabeth-- "Not a Soul Will Come Along"
Putman, Clay-- "The Wounded"
Robinson, Leonard Wallace-- "The Ruin of Soul"
Salinger, J. D.-- "For Esmé--With Love and Squalor"
Switzer, Robert-- "Death of a Prize Fighter"
Taylor, Peter-- "Their Losses"
Van Ness, Lilian-- "Give My Love to Maggie"
Winslow, Anne Goodwin-- "Seasmiles"

1951
First Prize
Downey, Harris-- "The Hunters"
Second Prize
Welty, Eudora-- "The Burning"
Third Prize
Capote, Truman-- "The House of Flowers"
Other Selected Stories
Casper, Leonard-- "Sense of Direction"

Cheever, John-- "The Pot of Gold"

Connell, Evan S., Jr.-- "I Came from Yonder Mountain"

Culver, Monty-- "Black Water Blues"

Faulkner, William-- "A Name for the City"

Hall, James B.-- "In the Time of Demonstrations"

Hersey, John-- "Peggety's Parcel of Shortcomings"

Kensinger, Faye Riter-- "A Sense of Destination"

La Farge, Oliver-- "Old Century's River"

Love, Peggy Harding-- "The Jersey Heifer"

Macauley, Robie-- "The Invaders"

McCullers, Carson-- "The Sojourner"

Miller, Arthur-- "Monte Saint Angelo"

Patt, Esther-- "The Butcherbirds"

Patterson, Elizabeth Gregg-- "Homecoming"

Phillips, Thomas Hal-- "The Shadow of an Arm"

Rooney, Frank-- "Cyclists' Raid"

Shirley, Sylvia-- "Slow Journey"

Smith, John Campbell-- "Who Too Was a Soldier"

Stafford, Jean-- "A Country Love Story"

Thompson, R. E.-- "It's a Nice Day--Sunday"

1954

First Prize

Mabry, Thomas-- "The Indian Feather"

Second Prize

Putman, Clay-- "The News from Troy"

Third Prize

Wilbur, Richard-- "A Game of Catch"

Other Selected Stories

Cassill, R. V.-- "The War in the Air"

Clay, Richard-- "Very Sharp for Jagging"

Elliott, George P.-- "A Family Matter"

Gold, Herbert-- "The Witch"

Hall, James B.-- "Estate and Trespass: A Gothic Story"

Harnden, Ruth-- "Rebellion"

Justice, Donald-- "Vineland's Burning"

Lowrey, P. H.-- "Too Young to Have a Gun"

Maxwell, James A.-- "Fighter"

O'Connor, Flannery-- "The Life You Save May Be Your Own"

Rugel, Miriam-- "The Flower"

Stafford, Jean-- "The Shorn Lamb"

Stern, Richard G.-- "The Sorrows of Captain Schreiber"

Walker, Augusta-- "The Day of the Cipher"

Wallace, Robert-- "The Secret Weapon of Joe Smith"

West, Jessamyn-- "Breach of Promise"

Whitmore, Stanford-- "Lost Soldier"

Whittemore, Reed-- "The Stutz and the Tub"

Wilner, Herbert-- "Whistle and the Heroes"

Worthington, Rex-- "A Kind of Scandal"

1955

First Prize

Stafford, Jean-- "In the Zoo"

Second Prize

O'Connor, Flannery-- "A Circle in the Fire"

Third Prize

Buechner, Frederick-- "The Tiger"

Other Selected Stories

Bingham, Robert-- "The Unpopular Passenger"

Calisher, Hortense-- "A Christmas Carillon"

Cassill, R. V.-- "The Inland Years"

Cheever, John-- "The Five-forty-eight"

Elliott, George P.-- "Miss Cudahy of Stowes Landing"

Enright, Elizabeth-- "The Operator"

Fowler, Mary Dewees-- "Man of Distinction"

Fuchs, Daniel-- "Twilight in Southern California"

Grau, Shirley Ann-- "Joshua"

Graves, John-- "The Green Fly"

Powers, J. F.-- "The Presence of Grace"

Shultz, William Henry-- "The Shirts off Their Backs"

Steele, Max-- "The Wanton Troopers"

Stegner, Wallace-- "The City of the Living"

Wolfert, Ira-- "The Indomitable Blue"

1956

First Prize

Cheever, John-- "The Country Husband"

Second Prize

Buechler, James-- "Pepicelli"

Third Prize

Cassill, R. V.-- "The Prize"

Other Selected Stories

Bellow, Saul-- "The Gonzaga Manuscripts"

Calisher, Hortense-- "The Night Club in the Woods"

Carr, Archie-- "The Black Beach"

Coates, Robert M.-- "In a Foreign City"

Faulkner, William-- "Race at Morning"

Gold, Herbert-- "A Celebration for Joe"

Macauley, Robie-- "The Chevigny Man"
Nemerov, Howard-- "Tradition"
Stafford, Jean-- "Beatrice Trueblood's Story"
Steinbeck, John-- "The Affair at Seven, Rue de M---"
Whitehill, Joseph-- "Able Baker"
Yates, Richard-- "The Best of Everything"

1957
First Prize
O'Connor, Flannery-- "Greenleaf"
Second Prize
Gold, Herbert-- "Encounter in Haiti"
Third Prize
Elliott, George P.-- "Miracle Play"
Other Selected Stories
Blassingame, Wyatt-- "Man's Courage"
Cassill, R. V.-- "When Old Age Shall This
    Generation Waste"
Cheever, John-- "The Journal of an Old Gent"
Faulkner, William-- "By the People"
Granit, Arthur-- "Free the Canaries from Their Cages!"
Langdon, John-- "The Blue Serge Suit"
Liberman, M. M.-- "Big Buick to the Pyramids"
Marsh, Willard-- "Last Tag"
McCarthy, Mary-- "Yellowstone Park"
Miller, Nolan-- "A New Life"
Rich, Cynthia Marshall-- "My Sister's Marriage"
Settle, Mary Lee-- "The Old Wives' Tale"
Shaw, Irwin-- "Then We Were Three"
Stafford, Jean-- "The Warlock"
Sunwall, Betty-- "Things Changed"
Thurman, Richard Young-- "The Credit Line"
Walter, Eugene-- "I Love You Batty Sisters"

1958
First Prize
Gellhorn, Martha-- "In Sickness as in Health"
Second Prize
Calisher, Hortense-- "What a Thing, to Keep a Wolf
    in a Cage!"
Third Prize
Steiner, George-- "The Deeps of the Sea"
Other Selected Stories
Berriault, Gina-- "The Stone Boy"
Blanton, Lowell D.-- "The Long Night"
Brown, T. K., III-- "A Drink of Water"

Clemons, Walter-- "A Summer Shower"
Enright, Elizabeth-- "The Eclipse"
Granat, Robert-- "My Apples"
Hale, Nancy-- "A Slow Boat to China"
Litwak, Leo-- "The Making of a Clock"
Matthiessen, Peter-- "Travelin Man"
Newhouse, Edward-- "The Ambassador"
Shore, Wilma-- "A Cow on the Roof"
Stafford, Jean-- "My Blithe, Sad Bird"
White, Robin-- "First Voice"
Wilner, Herbert-- "The Passion for Silver's Arm"

1959
First Prize
Taylor, Peter-- "Venus, Cupid, Folly, and Time"
Second Prize
Elliott, George P.-- "Among the Dangs"
Third Prize
Turner, Thomas C.-- "Something to Explain"
Other Selected Stories
Baldwin, James-- "Come Out of the Wilderness"
Buchwald, Emilie Bix-- "The Present"
Cheever, John-- "The Trouble of Marcie Flint"
Currie, Ellen-- "Tib's Eve"
Eastlake, William-- "Flight of the Circle Heart"
Filer, Tom-- "The Last Voyage"
Harris, MacDonald-- "Second Circle"
O'Connor, Flannery-- "A View of the Woods"
Sandburg, Helga-- "Witch Chicken"
Stafford, Jean-- "A Reasonable Facsimile"
Stone, Alma-- "The Bible Salesman"
Williams, Thomas-- "Goose Pond"

1960
First Prize
Hall, Lawrence Sargent-- "The Ledge"
Second Prize
Roth, Philip-- "Defender of the Faith"
Third Prize
White, Robin-- "Shower of Ashes"
Other Selected Stories
Berkman, Sylvia-- "Ellen Craig"
Berriault, Gina-- "Sublime Child"
Enright, Elizabeth-- "A Gift of Light"
Fowler, Janet-- "A Day for Fishing"
Gold, Herbert-- "Love and Like"

Granat, Robert-- "To Endure"
Henderson, Robert-- "Immortality"
Kentfield, Calvin-- "In the Cauldron"
Ogden, Maurice-- "Freeway to Wherever"
Purdy, James-- "Encore"
Spencer, Elizabeth-- "First Dark"
Swarthout, Glendon-- "A Glass of Blessings"
Ziller, Eugene-- "Sparrows"

1961
First Prize
Olson, Tillie-- "Tell Me a Riddle"
Second Prize
Gold, Ivan-- "The Nickel Misery of George Washington Carver Brown"
Third Prize
Price, Reynolds-- "One Sunday in Late July"
Other Selected Stories
Burgess, Jackson-- "The Magician"
Currie, Ellen-- "O Lovely Appearance of Death"
Ford, Jesse Hill-- "How the Mountains Are Made"
Krause, Ervin D.-- "The Quick and the Dead"
Ludwig, Jack-- "Thoreau in California"
Miller, Arthur-- "I Don't Need You Any More"
Shaber, David-- "A Nous La Liberté"
Taylor, Peter-- "Heads of Houses"
Updike, John-- "Wife-Wooing"

1962
First Prize
Porter, Katherine Anne-- "Holiday"
Second Prize
Pynchon, Thomas-- "Under the Rose"
Third Prize
Cole, Tom-- "Familiar Usage in Leningrad"
Other Selected Stories
Adams, Thomas E.-- "Sled"
Deasy, Mary-- "The People with the Charm"
Grau, Shirley Ann-- "Eight O'Clock One Morning"
Graves, John-- "The Aztec Dog"
Howard, Maureen-- "Bridgeport Bus"
Jackson, David-- "The English Gardens"
McKenzie, Miriam-- "Deja Vu"
Price, Reynolds-- "The Warrior Princess Ozimba"
Schoonover, Shirley W.-- "The Star Blanket"
Shaber, David-- "Professorio Collegio"

Updike, John-- "The Doctor's Wife"
Whitbread, Thomas-- "The Rememberer"

1963
First Prize
O'Connor, Flannery-- "Everything That Rises Must Converge"
Second Prize
Krause, Ervin D.-- "The Snake"
Third Prize
Selz, Thalia-- "The Education of a Queen"
Other Selected Stories
Ansell, Helen Essary-- "The Threesome"
Berkman, Sylvia-- "Pontifex"
Cox, James Trammell-- "That Golden Crane"
Douglas, Ellen-- "On the Lake"
Klein, Norma-- "The Burglar"
Maddow, Ben-- "In a Cold Hotel"
McClure, J. G.-- "The Rise of the Proletariat"
Oates, Joyce Carol-- "The Fine White Mist of Winter"
Saroyan, William-- "Gaston"
Southern, Terry-- "The Road Out of Axotle"
West, Jessamyn-- "The Picknickers"

1964
First Prize
Cheever, John-- "The Embarkment for Cythera"
Second Prize
Oates, Joyce Carol-- "Stigmata"
Third Prize
Shedd, Margaret-- "The Everlasting Witness"
Other Selected Stories
Bingham, Sallie-- "The Banks of the Ohio"
Calisher, Hortense-- "The Scream on Fifty-seventh Street"
Lanning, George-- "Something Just for Me"
Malamud, Bernard-- "The Jewbird"
Ross, Lillian-- "Night and Day, Day and Night"
Roth, Philip-- "Novotnoy's Pain"
Sara-- "So I'm Not Lady Chatterly, So Better I Should Know It Now"
Schoonover, Shirley W.-- "Old and Country Tale"
Shaw, Irwin-- "The Inhabitants of Venus"
Stacton, David-- "The Metamorphosis of Kenko"
Stegner, Wallace-- "Carrion Spring"
Zorn, George A.-- "Thompson"

1965
First Prize
O'Connor, Flannery-- "Revelation"
Second Prize
Friedman, Sanford-- "Ocean"
Third Prize
Humphrey, William-- "The Ballad of Jesse Neighbours"
Other Selected Stories
Barthelme, Donald-- "Margins"
Beagle, Peter S.-- "Come Lady Death"
Cavanaugh, Arthur-- "What I Wish (Oh, I Wish) I Had Said"
Curley, Daniel-- "Love in the Winter"
Ludwig, Jack-- "A Woman of Her Age"
Manoff, Eva-- "Mama and the Spy"
Mayer, Tom-- "Homecoming"
McCarthy, Mary-- "The Hounds of Summer"
McCullers, Carson-- "Sucker"
Miller, Warren-- "Chaos, Disorder, and the Late Show"
Oates, Joyce Carol-- "First Views of the Enemy"
Potter, Nancy A. J.-- "Sunday's Children"
Rooke, Leon-- "If Lost Return to the Swiss Arms"
Taylor, Peter-- "There"
Wolf, Leonard-- "Fifty-Fifty"

1966
First Prize
Updike, John-- "The Bulgarian Poetess"
Second Prize
Howard, Maureen-- "Sherry"
Third Prize
Cole, Tom-- "On the Edge of Arcadia"
Other Selected Stories
Berriault, Gina-- "The Birthday Party"
Bingham, Sallie-- "Bare Bones"
Davis, Christopher-- "A Man of Affairs"
Ford, Jesse Hill-- "To the Open Water"
Greene, Philip L.-- "One of You Must Be Wendell Corey"
Hale, Nancy-- "Sunday Lunch"
McKinley, Georgia-- "The Mighty Distance"
Michaels, Leonard-- "Sticks and Stones"
Petrakis, Harry Mark-- "The Prison"
Randall, Vera-- "Alice Blaine"

Spencer, Elizabeth-- "Ship Island"
Williams, Joy-- "The Roomer"
Zorn, George A.-- "Mr. and Mrs. McGill"

1967
First Prize
Oates, Joyce Carol-- "In the Region of Ice"
Second Prize
Barthelme, Donald-- "See the Moon?"
Third Prize
Strong, Jonathan-- "Supperburger"
Other Selected Stories
Buechler, James-- "The Second Best Girl"
Finney, Ernest J.-- "The Investigator"
Ford, Jesse Hill-- "The Bitter Bread"
Jacobsen, Josephine-- "On the Island"
Knickerbocker, Conrad-- "Diseases of the Heart"
Kurtz, M. R.-- "Waxing Wroth"
Macauley, Robie-- "Dressed in Shade"
Mudrick, Marvin-- "Cleopatra"
Oliver, Diane-- "Neighbors"
Updike, John-- "Marching Through Boston"
Wheelis, Allen-- "Sea-Girls"
Yates, Richard-- "A Good and Gallant Woman"

1968
First Prize
Welty, Eudora-- "The Demonstrators"
Second Prize
Broner, E. M.-- "The New Nobility"
Third Prize
Katz, Shlomo-- "My Redeemer Cometh . . ."
Other Selected Stories
Branda, Eldon-- "The Dark Days of Christmas"
Brower, Brock-- "Storm Still"
Franklin, F. K.-- "Nigger Horse"
Gration, Gwen-- "Teacher"
Hale, Nancy-- "The Most Elegant Drawing Room in Europe"
Hall, James B.-- "A Kind of Savage"
Harris, Marilyn-- "Icarus Again"
Kentfield, Calvin-- "Near the Line"
Klein, Norma-- "Magic"
Neugeboren, Jay-- "Ebbets Field"
Oates, Joyce Carol-- "Where Are You Going, Where Have You Been?"

Stacton, David-- "Little Brother Nun"
Tyner, Paul-- "How You Play the Game"
Updike, John-- "Your Lover Just Called"

1969
First Prize
Malamud, Bernard-- "Man in the Drawer"
Second Prize
Oates, Joyce Carol-- "Accomplished Desires"
Third Prize
Barth, John-- "Lost in the Funhouse"
Other Selected Stories
Corfman, Eunice Luccock-- "To Be an Athlete"
Engberg, Susan-- "Lambs of God"
Litwak, Leo-- "In Shock"
Maddow, Ben-- "You, Johann Sebastian Bach"
Michaels, Leonard-- "Manikin"
Mountzoures, H. L.-- "The Empire of Things"
Packer, Nancy Huddleston-- "Early Morning, Lonely Ride"
Paley, Grace-- "Distance"
Rubin, Michael-- "Service"
Shefner, Evelyn-- "The Invitations"
Steele, Max-- "Color the Daydream Yellow"
Sterling, Thomas-- "Bedlam's Rent"
Taylor, Peter-- "First Heat"
Tyler, Anne-- "The Common Courtesies"

1970
First Prize
Hemenway, Robert-- "The Girl Who Sang with the Beatles"
Second Prize
Eastlake, William-- "The Biggest Thing Since Custer"
Third Prize
Rindfleisch, Norval-- "A Cliff of Fall"
Special Award for Continuing Achievement
Oates, Joyce Carol-- "How I Contemplated the World from the Detroit House of Correction and Began My Life Over Again"
Other Selected Stories-- "Unmailed, Unwritten Letters"
Blake, George-- "A Modern Development"
Buchan, Perdita-- "It's Cold out There"
Cole, Tom-- "Saint John of the Hershey Kisses: 1964"
Donahue, H. E. F.-- "Joe College"

Griffith, Patricia Browning-- "Nights at O'Rear's"
Grinstead, David-- "A Day in Operations"
Malamud, Bernard-- "My Son the Murderer"
McPherson, James Alan-- "Of Cabbages and Kings"
Salter, James-- "Am Strande Von Tanger"
Strong, Jonathan-- "Patients"
Updike, John-- "Bech Takes Pot Luck"
Willard, Nancy-- "Theo's Girl"

1971
First Prize
Hecht, Florence M.-- "Twin Bed Bridge"
Second Prize
Cardwell, Guy A.-- "Did You Once See Shelley?"
Third Prize
Adams, Alice-- "Gift of Grass"
Other Selected Stories
Cleaver, Eldridge-- "The Flashlight"
Greene, Philip L.-- "The Dichotomy"
Harter, Evelyn-- "The Stone Lovers"
Hoagland, Edward-- "The Final Fate of the Alligators"
Inman, Robert-- "I'll Call You"
Jacobsen, Josephine-- "The Jungle of Lord Lion"
Larson, Charles R.-- "Up From Slavery"
Mazor, Julian-- "The Skylark"
Michaels, Leonard-- "Robinson Crusoe Liebowitz"
Minot, Stephen-- "Mars Revisited"
Oates, Joyce Carol-- "The Children"
Parker, Thomas-- "Troop Withdrawal--The Initial Step"
Price, Reynolds-- "Waiting at Dachau"
Taylor, Eleanor Ross-- "Jujitsu"

1972
First Prize
Batki, John-- "Strange-Dreaming Charlie, Cow-Eyed Charlie"
Second Prize
Oates, Joyce Carol-- "Saul Bird Says: Relate! Communicate! Liberate!"
Third Prize
Rascoe, Judith-- "Small Sounds and Tilting Shadows"
Other Selected Stories
Adams, Alice-- "Ripped Off"
Barthelme, Donald-- "Subpoena"
Brown, Rosellen-- "A Letter to Ismael in the Grave"

Brown, Margery Finn-- "In the Forests of the Riga the
  Beasts Are Very Wild Indeed"
Eaton, Charles Edward-- "The Case of the Missing
  Photographs"
Flythe, Starkey, Jr.-- "Point of Conversion"
Gill, Brendan-- "Fat Girl"
Gold, Herbert-- "A Death on the East Side"
Gottlieb, Elaine-- "The Lizard"
Matthews, Jack-- "On the Shore of Chad Creek"
McClatchy, J. D.-- "Allonym"
Salter, James-- "The Destruction of the Goetheanum"
Tyler, Anne-- "With All Flags Flying"
Zelver, Patricia-- "On the Desert"

1973
First Prize
Oates, Joyce Carol-- "The Dead"
Second Prize
Malamud, Bernard-- "Talking Horse"
Third Prize
Brown, Rosellen-- "Mainlanders"
Other Selected Stories
Adams, Alice-- "The Swastika on Our Door"
Bromell, Henry-- "Photographs"
Carver, Raymond-- "What Is It?"
Cheever, John-- "The Jewels of the Cabots"
Jacobsen, Josephine-- "A Walk with Raschid"
Johnson, Diane-- "An Apple, An Orange"
Johnson, Curt-- "Trespasser"
Malone, John-- "The Fugitives"
Mayhall, Jane-- "The Enemy"
McPherson, James Alan-- "The Silver Bullet"
Rascoe, Judith-- "A Line of Order"
Reid, Randall-- "Detritus"
Shaber, David-- "Scotch Sour"
Sikes, Shirley-- "The Death of Cousin Stanley"
Zelver, Patricia-- "The Flood"

1974
First Prize
Adler, Renata-- "Brownstone"
Second Prize
Henson, Robert-- "Lizzie Borden in the P.M."
Third Prize
Adams, Alice-- "Alternatives"

Other Selected Stories
Busch, Frederick-- "Is Anyone Left This Time of
  Year?"
Carver, Raymond-- "Put Yourself in My Shoes"
Clayton, John J.-- "Cambridge Is Sinking!"
Davenport, Guy-- "Robot"
Eastlake, William-- "The Death of Sun"
Fuller, Blair-- "Bakti's Hand"
Gardner, John-- "The Things"
Hemenway, Robert-- "Troy Street"
Hill, Richard-- "Out in the Garage"
Hochstein, Rolaine-- "What Kind of a Man Cuts His
  Finger Off"
Klein, Norma-- "The Wrong Man"
Leach, Peter-- "The Fish Trap"
McPherson, James Alan-- "The Faithful"
Salter, James-- "Via Negativa"

1975
First Prize
Brodkey, Harold-- "A Story in an Almost Classical
  Mode"
Ozick, Cynthia-- "Usurpation (Other People's Stories)"
Other Selected Stories
Arensberg, Ann-- "Art History"
Arking, Linda-- "Certain Hard Places"
Banks, Russell-- "With Che at Kitty Hawk"
Bayer, Ann-- "Department Store"
Carver, Raymond-- "Are You a Doctor?"
Disch, Thomas M.-- "Getting into Death"
Doctorow, E. L.-- "Ragtime"
Kotzwinkle, William-- "Swimmer in the Secret Sea"
Maxwell, William-- "Over by the River"
McCorkle, Susannah-- "Ramona by the Sea"
McPherson, James Alan-- "The Story of a Scar"
Schell, Jessie-- "Alvira, Lettie, and Pip"
Shelnutt, Eve-- "Angel"
Updike, John-- "Nakedness"
Zelver, Patricia-- "Norwegians"

1976
First Prize
Brodkey, Harold-- "His Son in His Arms, in Light,
  Aloft"

Second Prize

Sayles, John-- "I-80 Nebraska, M. 490-M. 205"

Third Prize

Adams, Alice-- "Roses, Rhododendrons"

Special Award for Continuing Achievement

Updike, John-- "Separating"

Other Selected Stories

Berryman, John-- "Wash Far Away"

Brown, Rosellen-- "Why I Quit the Gowanus Liberation Front"

Bumpus, Jerry-- "The Idols of Afternoon"

Corrington, John William-- "The Actes and Monuments"

Davenport, Guy-- "The Richard Nixon Freischutz Rag"

Francis, H. E.-- "A Chronicle of Love"

Goyen, William-- "Bridge of Music, River of Sand"

Griffith, Patricia Browning-- "Dust"

Halley, Anne-- "The Sisterhood"

Helprin, Mark-- "Leaving the Church"

Hudson, Helen-- "The Theft"

Jacobsen, Josephine-- "Nel Bagno"

O'Brien, Tim-- "Night March"

Oates, Joyce Carol-- "Blood-Swollen Landscape"

Sadoff, Ira-- "An Enemy of the People"

Shreve, Anita-- "Past the Island, Drifting"

1977

First Prize

Hazzard, Shirley-- "A Long Story Short"

Leffland, Ella-- "Last Courtesies"

Other Selected Stories

Adams, Alice-- "Flights"

Ballantyne, Sheila-- "Perpetual Care"

Cheever, John-- "The President of the Argentine"

Colwin, Laurie-- "The Lone Pilgrim"

Dixon, Stephen-- "Mac in Love"

Engberg, Susan-- "A Stay by the River"

Fetler, Andrew-- "Shadows on the Water"

Hedin, Mary-- "Ladybug, Fly Away Home"

McCully, Emily Arnold-- "How's Your Vacuum Cleaner Working?"

Minot, Stephen-- "A Passion for History"

Russ, Joanna-- "Autobiography of My Mother"

Sayles, John-- "Breed"

Simmons, Charles-- "Certain Changes"

Summers, Hollis-- "A Hundred Paths"

Theroux, Paul-- "The Autumn Dog"

Zelver, Patricia-- "The Little Pub"

1978

First Prize

Allen, Woody-- "The Kugelmass Episode"

Second Prize

Schorer, Mark-- "A Lamp"

Third Prize

Henson, Robert-- "The Upper and the Lower Millstone"

Other Selected Stories

Adams, Alice-- "Beautiful Girl"

Apple, Max-- "Paddycake, Paddycake . . . A Memoir"

Brodkey, Harold-- "Verona: A Young Woman Speaks"

Clayton, John J.-- "Bodies Like Mouths"

Engberg, Susan-- "Pastorale"

Fuller, Blair-- "All Right"

Helprin, Mark-- "The Schreuerspitze"

Jacobsen, Josephine-- "Jack Frost"

Leviant, Curt-- "Ladies and Gentlemen, The Original Music of the Hebrew Alphabet"

O'Brien, Tim-- "Speaking of Courage"

Oates, Joyce Carol-- "The Tattoo"

Pearlman, Edith-- "Hanging Fire"

Schaeffer, Susan Fromberg-- "The Exact Nature of Plot"

Schell, Jessie-- "Undeveloped Photographs"

Schevill, James-- "A Hero in the Highway"

1979

First Prize

Weaver, Gordon-- "Getting Serious"

Second Prize

Bromell, Henry-- "Travel Stories"

Third Prize

Hecht, Julie-- "I Want You, I Need You, I Love You"

Other Selected Stories

Adams, Alice-- "The Girl Across the Room"

Baumbach, Jonathan-- "Passion?"

Caputi, Anthony-- "The Derby Hopeful"

Disch, Thomas M.-- "Xmas"

Gold, Herbert-- "The Smallest Part"

Goldberg, Lester-- "Shy Bearers"

Heller, Steve-- "The Summer Game"

Leaton, Anne-- "The Passion of Marco Z---"

Molyneux, Thomas W.-- "Visiting the Point"

Oates, Joyce Carol-- "In the Autumn of the Year"

Peterson, Mary-- "Travelling"

Pfeil, Fred-- "The Quality of Light in Maine"

Schwartz, Lynne Sharon-- "Rough Strife"

Smith, Lee-- "Mrs. Darcy Meets the Blue-eyed Stranger at the Beach"

Thomas, Annabel-- "Coon Hunt"

Van Dyke, Henry-- "Du Cote de Chez Britz"

Yates, Richard-- "Oh, Joseph, I'm So Tired"

Zelver, Patricia-- "My Father's Jokes"

1980

First Prize

Bellow, Saul-- "A Silver Dish"

Second Prize

Hallinan, Nancy-- "Woman in a Roman Courtyard"

Third Prize

Michaels, Leonard-- "The Men's Club"

Other Selected Stories

Adams, Alice-- "Truth or Consequences"

Arensberg, Ann-- "Group Sex"

Beattie, Ann-- "The Cinderella Waltz"

Chasin, Helen-- "Fatal"

Dillon, Millicent-- "All the Pelageyas"

Dubus, Andre-- "The Pitcher"

Dunn, Robert-- "Hopeless Acts Performed Properly, with Grace"

Gertler, T.-- "In Case of Survival"

Godwin, Gail-- "Amanuensis: A Tale of the Creative Life"

Krysl, Marilyn-- "Looking for Mother"

L'Heureux, John-- "The Priest's Wife"

Phillips, Jayne Anne-- "Snow"

Rose, Daniel Asa-- "The Goodbye Present"

Stafford, Jean-- "An Influx of Poets"

Sullivan, Walter-- "Elizabeth"

Taggart, Shirley Ann-- "Ghosts Like Them"

Targan, Barry-- "Old Light"

Taylor, Peter-- "The Old Forest"

Vaughn, Stephanie-- "Sweet Talk"

1981

First Prize

Ozick, Cynthia

Other Selected Stories-- "The Shawl"

Adams, Alice-- "Snow"

Boyle, Kay-- "St. Stephen's Green"

Flowers, Sandra Hollin-- "Hope of Zion"

Goodman, Ivy-- "Baby"

Irving, John-- "Interior Space"

L'Heureux, John-- "Brief Lives in California"

Matthews, Jack-- "The Last Abandonment"

Novick, Marian-- "Advent"

Oates, Joyce Carol-- "Mutilated Woman"

Packer, Nancy Huddleston-- "The Women Who Walk"

Reid, Barbara-- "The Waltz Dream"

Rottenberg, Annette T.-- "The Separation"

Smith, Lee-- "Between the Lines"

Stern, Steve-- "Isaac and the Undertaker's Daughter"

Tabor, James-- "The Runner"

Theroux, Paul-- "World's Fair"

Thomas, Annabel-- "The Photographic Woman"

Walker, Alice-- "The Abortion"

Wetherell, W. D.-- "The Man Who Loved Levittown"

Wolff, Tobias-- "In the Garden of North American Martyrs"

1982

First Prize

Kenney, Susan-- "Facing Front"

Second Prize

McElroy, Joseph-- "The Future"

Third Prize

Brooks, Ben-- "A Postal Creed"

Special Award for Continuing Achievement

Adams, Alice-- "Greyhound People"-- "To See You Again"

Other Selected Stories

Carkeet, David-- "The Greatest Slump of All Time"

Dixon, Stephen-- "Layaways"

Gewertz, Kenneth-- "I Thought of Chatterton, The Marvelous Boy"

Goodman, Ivy-- "White Boy"

Holt, T. E.-- "Charybdis"

Johnson, Nora-- "The Jungle of Injustice"

Malone, Michael-- "Fast Love"
O'Brien, Tim-- "The Ghost Soldiers"
Oates, Joyce Carol-- "The Man Whom Women Adored"
Smiley, Jane-- "The Pleasure of Her Company"
Taylor, Peter-- "The Gift of the Prodigal"
Trefethen, Florence-- "Infidelities"
Wheeler, Kate-- "La Victoire"
Wolff, Tobias-- "Next Door"

1983
First Prize
Carver, Raymond-- "A Small, Good Thing"
Second Prize
Oates, Joyce Carol-- "My Warsawa"
Third Prize
Morris, Wright-- "Victrola"
Other Selected Stories
Benedict, Elizabeth-- "Feasting"
Bienen, Leigh Buchanan-- "My Life as a West African
    Gray Parrot"
Faust, Irvin-- "Melanie and the Purple People Eaters"
Gordon, Mary-- "The Only Son of a Doctor"
Jauss, David-- "Shards"
Klass, Perri-- "The Secret Lives of Dieters"
Lloyd, Lynda-- "Poor Boy"
Meinke, Peter-- "The Ponoes"
Norris, Gloria-- "When the Lord Calls"
Plante, David-- "Work"
Schwartz, Steven-- "Slow-Motion"
Spencer, Elizabeth-- "Jeanne-Pierre"
Svendsen, Linda-- "Heartbeat'
Updike, John-- "The City"
Van Wert, William F.-- "Putting & Gardening"
Wetherell, W. D.-- "If a Woodchuck Could
    Chuck Wood"
Whelan, Gloria-- "The Dogs in Renoir's Garden"

1984
First Prize
Ozick, Cynthia-- "Rosa"
Other Selected Stories
Abbott, Lee K.-- "Living Alone in Iota"
Adams, Alice-- "Alaska"
Baumbach, Jonathan-- "The Life and Times of Major
    Fiction"

Dickinson, Charles-- "Risk"
Fetler, Andrew-- "The Third Count"
Johnson, Willis-- "Prayer for the Dying"
Justice, Donald-- "The Artificial Moonlight"
Klass, Perri-- "Not a Good Girl"
Leavitt, David-- "Counting Months"
Lish, Gordon-- "For Jerome--with Love and Kisses"
Malamud, Bernard-- "The Model"
Menaker, Daniel-- "The Old Left"
Norris, Helen-- "The Love Child"
Norris, Gloria-- "Revive Us Again"
Paley, Grace-- "The Story Hearer"
Pearlman, Edith-- "Conveniences"
Pritchard, Melissa Brown-- "A Private Landscape"
Salter, James-- "Lost Sons"
Tallent, Elizabeth-- "The Evolution of Birds
    of Paradise"

1985
First Prize
Dybek, Stuart-- "Hot Ice"
Smiley, Jane-- "Lily"
Other Selected Stories
Beattie, Ann-- "In the White Night"
Cameron, Peter-- "Homework"
Erdrich, Louise-- "Saint Marie"
Hamilton, R. C.-- "Da Vinci Is Dead"
Heller, Steve-- "The Crow Woman"
Hochstein, Rolaine-- "She Should Have Died
    Hereafter"
Jacobsen, Josephine-- "The Mango Community"
Just, Ward-- "About Boston"
Koch, Claude-- "Bread and Butter Questions"
McElroy, Joseph-- "Daughter of the Revolution"
Minot, Susan-- "Lust"
Morris, Wright-- "Glimpse into Another Country"
Norris, Helen-- "The Quarry"
Oates, Joyce Carol-- "The Seasons"
Raymond, Ilene-- "Taking a Chance on Jack"
Updike, John-- "The Other"
Wilson, Eric-- "The Axe, the Axe, the Axe"
Wolff, Tobias-- "Sister"

1986
First Prize
Walker, Alice-- "Kindred Spirits"
Special Award for Continuing Achievement
Oates, Joyce Carol-- "Master Race"
Other Selected Stories
Adams, Alice-- "Molly's Dog"
Cameron, Peter-- "Excerpts from Swan Lake"
DiFranco, Anthony-- "The Garden of Redemption"
Dybek, Stuart-- "Pet Milk"
Eisenberg, Deborah-- "Transactions in a Foreign Currency"
Faust, Irvin-- "The Year of the Hot Jock"
Gerber, Merrill Joan-- "I Don't Believe This"
Johnson, Greg-- "Crazy Ladies"
Just, Ward-- "The Costa Brava, 1959"
Kornblatt, Joyce R.-- "Offerings"
L'Heureux, John-- "The Comedian"
Lish, Gordon-- "Resurrection"
Mason, Bobbie Ann-- "Big Bertha Stories"
Meinke, Peter-- "Uncle George and Uncle Stefan"
Norris, Gloria-- "Holding On"
Spencer, Elizabeth-- "The Cousins"
Vaughn, Stephanie-- "Kid MacArthur"
Wilmot, Jeanne-- "Dirt Angel"

1987
First Prize
Erdrich, Louise-- "Fleur"
Johnson, Joyce-- "The Children's Wing"
Other Selected Stories
Adams, Alice-- "Tide Pools"
Barthelme, Donald-- "Basil from Her Garden"
Bausch, Richard-- "What Feels Like the World"
Berriault, Gina-- "The Island of Ven"
Boswell, Robert-- "The Darkness of Love"
Dillon, Millicent-- "Monitor"
Dybek, Stuart-- "Blight"
Home, Lewis-- "Taking Care"
Lavers, Norman-- "Big Dog"
Lott, James-- "The Janeites"
Norris, Helen-- "The Singing Well"
Oates, Joyce Carol-- "Ancient Airs, Voices"
Paley, Grace-- "Midrash on Happiness"
Pitzen, Jim-- "The Village"

Robison, Mary-- "I Get By"
Stern, Daniel-- "The Interpretation of Dreams by Sigmund Freud: A Story"
Taylor, Robert, Jr.-- "Lady of Spain"
Wallace, Warren-- "Up Home"

1988
First Prize
Carver, Raymond-- "Errand"
Other Selected Stories
Adams, Alice-- "Ocrakoke Island"
Baumbach, Jonathan-- "The Dinner Party"
Beattie, Ann-- "Honey"
Currey, Richard-- "The Wars of Heaven"
Deaver, Philip F.-- "Arcola Girls"
Dubus, Andre-- "Blessings"
Hazzard, Shirley-- "The Place to Be"
Kohler, Sheila-- "The Mountain"
La Puma, Salvatore-- "The Gangster's Ghost"
LaSalle, Peter-- "Dolphin Dreaming"
Mason, Bobbie Ann-- "Bumblebees"
Neugeboren, Jay-- "Don't Worry About the Kids"
Oates, Joyce Carol-- "Yarrow"
Plant, Richard-- "Cecil Grounded"
Sayles, John-- "The Halfway Diner"
Smiley, Jane-- "Long Distance"
Spencer, Elizabeth-- "The Business Venture"
Updike, John-- "Leaf Season"
Williams, Joy-- "Rot"

1989
First Prize
Finney, Ernest J.-- "Peacocks"
Second Prize
Oates, Joyce Carol-- "House Hunting"
Third Prize
Doerr, Harriet-- "Edie: A Life"
Other Selected Stories
Adams, Alice-- "After You're Gone"
Bass, Rick-- "The Watch"
Boyle, T. Coraghessan-- "Sinking House"
Casey, John-- "Avid"
Dickinson, Charles-- "Child in the Leaves"
Dillon, Millicent-- "Wrong Stories"
Harrison, Barbara Grizzuti-- "To Be"
Herman, Ellen-- "Unstable Ground"

Lary, Banning K.-- "Death of a Duke"

Minot, Susan-- "Île Séche"

Petroski, Catherine-- "The Hit"

Ross, Jean-- "The Sky Fading Upward to Yellow: A Footnote to Literary History"

Salter, James-- "American Express"

Sherwook, Frances-- "History"

Simmons, Charles-- "Clandestine Acts"

Starkey, Flythe, Jr.-- "CV Ten"

Wallace, David Foster-- "Here and There"

1990
First Prize
Litwak, Leo-- "The Eleventh Edition"
Second Prize
Matthiessen, Peter-- "Lumumba Lives"
Third Prize
Segal, Lore-- "The Reverse Bug"
Other Selected Stories
Ackerman, Felicia-- "The Forecasting Game: A Story"

Adams, Alice-- "1940: Fall"

Blaylock, James P.-- "Unidentified Objects"

Boyle, T. Coraghessan-- "The Ape Lady in Retirement"

Brinson, Claudia Smith-- "Einstein's Daughter"

Eidus, Janice-- "Vito Loves Geraldine"

Fleming, Bruce-- "The Autobiography of Gertrude Stein"

Gillette, Jane Brown-- "Sins Against Animals"

Greenberg, Joanne-- "Elizabeth Baird"

Jersild, Devon-- "In Which John Imagines His Mind as a Pond"

Kaplan, David Michael-- "Stand"

McKnight, Reginald-- "The Kind of Light That Shines on Texas"

Oates, Joyce Carol-- "Heat"

Osborn, Carolyn-- "The Grands"

Schumacher, Julie-- "The Private Life of Robert Shumann"

Sides, Marilyn-- "The Island of the Mapmaker's Wife"

Steinbach, Meredith-- "In Recent History"

1991
Selected Stories
Adams, Alice-- "Earthquake Damage"

Averill, Thomas Fox-- "During the Twelfth Summer of Elmer D. Peterson"

Baxter, Charles-- "Saul and Patsy Are Pregnant"

Broughton, T. Alan-- "Ashes"

Dillon, Millicent-- "Oil and Water"

Hall, Martha Lacy-- "The Apple-Green Triumph"

Johnson, Wayne-- "Hippies, Indians, Buffalo"

Klass, Perri-- "For Women Everywhere"

Le Guin, Ursula K.-- "Hand, Cup, Shell"

Lear, Patricia-- "Powwow"

Levenberg, Diane-- "The Ilui"

McFarland, Dennis-- "Nothing to Ask For"

Norris, Helen-- "Raisin Faces"

Oates, Joyce Carol-- "The Swimmers"

Stark, Sharon Sheehe-- "Overland"

Sukenick, Ronald-- "Ecco"

Swick, Marly-- "Moscow Nights"

Updike, John-- "A Sandstone Farmhouse"

Walker, Charlotte Zoe-- "The Very Pineapple"

Watanabe, Sylvia A.-- "Talking to the Dead"

1992
First Prize
Ozick, Cynthia-- "Puttermesser Paired"

Updike, John-- "A Sandstone Farmhouse"
Other Selected Stories
Adams, Alice-- "The Last Lovely City"

Barnes, Yolanda-- "Red Lipstick"

Braverman, Kate-- "Tall Tales from the Mekong Delta"

Chowder, Ken-- "With Seth in Tana Toraja"

Dillon, Millicent-- "Lost in L.A."

Doerr, Harriet-- "Way Stations"

Herrick, Amy-- "Pinocchio's Nose"

Honig, Lucy-- "English as a Second Language"

Klass, Perri-- "Dedication"

Long, David-- "Blue Spruce"

McNeal, Tom-- "What Happened to Tully"

Meltzer, Daniel-- "People"

Myers, Les-- "The Kite"

Nelson, Kent-- "The Mine from Nicaragua"

Nelson, Antonya-- "The Control Group"

Oates, Joyce Carol-- "Why Don't You Come Live With Me It's Time"

Packer, Ann-- "Babies"

Pomerance, Murray-- "Decor"

Sherwood, Frances-- "Demiurges"

Wagner, Mary Michael-- "Acts of Kindness"

1993

First Prize

Jones, Thom-- "The Pugilist at Rest"

Second Prize

Lee, Andrea-- "Winter Barley"

Third Prize

Van Wert, William F.-- "Shaking"

Other Selected Stories

Adams, Alice-- "The Islands"

Askew, Rilla-- "The Killing Blanket"

Dixon, Stephen-- "The Rare Muscovite"

Eastman, Charles-- "Yellow Flags"

Egan, Jennifer-- "Puerto Vallerta"

Jacobsen, Josephine-- "The Pier-Glass"

Johnson, Charles-- "Kwoon"

Levenberg, Diane-- "A Modern Love Story"

Moore, Lorrie-- "Charades"

Nelson, Antonya-- "Dirty Words"

Nixon, Cornelia-- "Risk"

Oates, Joyce Carol-- "Goose-Girl"

Poverman, C. E.-- "The Man Who Died"

Richardson, John H.-- "The Pink House"

Schwartz, Steven-- "Madagascar"

Stern, Daniel-- "A Hunger Artist by Franz Kafka: A Story"

Svendsen, Linda-- "The Edger Man"

Van Kirk, John-- "Newark Job"

Weltner, Peter-- "The Greek Head"

Wheeler, Kate-- "Improving My Average"

1994

First Prize

Baker, Alison-- "Better Be Ready 'Bout Half Past Eight"

Second Prize

Gardiner, John Rolfe-- "The Voyage Out"

Third Place

Moore, Lorrie-- "Terrific Mother"

Other Selected Stories

Bain, Terry-- "Games"

Barton, Marlin-- "Jeremiah's Road"

Bloom, Amy-- "Semper Fidelis"

Cherry, Kelly-- "Not the Phil Donahue Show"

Cox, Elizabeth-- "The Third of July"

Dybek, Stuart-- "We Didn't"

Eidus, Janice-- "Pandora's Box"

Fox, Michael-- "Rise and Shine"

Fremont, Helen-- "Where She Was"

Graver, Elizabeth-- "The Boy Who Fell Forty Feet"

Hester, Katherine L.-- "Labor"

Kennedy, Thomas E.-- "Landing Zone X-Ray"

McLean, David-- "Marine Corps Issue"

Oness, Elizabeth-- "The Oracle"

Ortiz Cofer, Judith-- "Nada"

Richards, Susan Starr-- "The Hanging in the Foaling Barn"

Tannen, Mary-- "Elaine's House"

Trudell, Dennis-- "Gook"

1995

First Prize

Nixon, Cornelia-- "The Women Come and Go"

Second Prize

Clayton, John J.-- "Talking to Charlie"

Other Selected Stories

Adams, Alice-- "The Haunted Beach"

Baker, Alison-- "Loving Wanda Beaver"

Baxter, Charles-- "Kiss Away"

Bradford, Robin-- "If This Letter Were a Beaded Object"

Byers, Michael-- "Settled on the Cranberry Coast"

Cameron, Peter-- "Departing"

Cooper, Bernard-- "Truth Serum"

Delaney, Edward J.-- "The Drowning"

Eisenberg, Deborah-- "Across the Lake"

Gates, David-- "The Intruder"

Gilchrist, Ellen-- "The Stucco House"

Goodman, Allegra-- "Sarah"

Hardwick, Elizabeth-- "Shot: A New York Story"

Klass, Perri-- "City Sidewalks"

Krieger, Elliot-- "Cantor Pepper"

Oates, Joyce Carol-- "You Petted Me and I Followed You Home"

Pierce, Anne Whitney-- "Star Box"

Powell, Padgett-- "Trick or Treat"

Updike, John-- "The Black Room"

1996

First Prize

King, Stephen-- "The Man in the Black Suit"

Second Prize

Sharma, Akhil-- "If You Sing Like That for Me"

Other Selected Stories

Adams, Alice-- "His Women"

Baker, Alison-- "Convocation"

Dillen, Frederick G.-- "Alice"

Douglas, Ellen-- "Grant"

Graver, Elizabeth-- "Between"

Hagenston, Becky-- "'Til Death Do Us Part"

Hoffman, William-- "Stones"

Honig, Lucy-- "Citizens Review"

Kriegel, Leonard-- "Players"

Lombreglia, Ralph-- "Somebody Up There Likes Me"

McNally, T. M.-- "Skin Deep"

Menaker, Daniel-- "Influenza"

Mosley, Walter-- "The Thief"

Oates, Joyce Carol-- "Mark of Satan"

Paine, Tom-- "Will You Say Something Monsieur Eliot"

Schumacher, Julie-- "Dummies"

Smiley, Jane-- "The Life of the Body"

Wiegand, David-- "Buffalo Safety"

1997

First Prize

Gordon, Mary-- "City Life"

Second Prize

Saunders, George-- "The Falls"

Third Prize

Abbott, Lee K.-- "The Talk Talked Between Worms"

Other Selected Stories

Barth, John-- "On with the Story"

Bradford, Arthur-- "Catface"

Cooke, Carolyn-- "The TWA Corbies"

Davenport, Kiana-- "The Lipstick Tree"

Dubus, Andre-- "Dancing After Hours"

Eisenberg, Deborah-- "Mermaids"

Gaitskill, Mary-- "Comfort"

Glave, Thomas-- "The Final Inning"

Klam, Matthew-- "The Royal Palms"

MacMillan, Ian-- "The Red House"

Moody, Rick-- "Demonology"

Morgan, Robert-- "The Balm of Gilead Tree"

Munro, Alice-- "The Love of a Good Woman"

Ruff, Patricia Elam-- "The Taxi Ride"

Schaeffer, Susan Fromberg-- "The Old Farmhouse and the Dog-Wife"

Schutt, Christine-- "His Chorus"

Shields, Carol-- "Mirrors"

1998

First Prize

Moore, Lorrie-- "People Like That Are the Only People Here"

Second Prize

Millhauser, Steven-- "The Knife Thrower"

Third Prize

Munro, Alice-- "The Children Stay"

Other Selected Stories

Bass, Rick-- "The Myths of Bears"

Cooke, Carolyn-- "Eating Dirt"

Davies, Peter Ho-- "Relief"

Erdrich, Louise-- "Satan: Hijacker of a Planet"

Evenson, Brian-- "Two Brothers"

Heuler, Karen-- "Me and My Enemy"

Jones, Thom-- "Tarantula"

MacDonald, D. R.-- "Ashes"

McKnight, Reginald-- "Boot"

Mehta, Suketu-- "Gare du Nord"

Novakovich, Josip-- "Crimson"

Proulx, E. Annie-- "Brokeback Mountain"

Saunders, George-- "Winky"

Sharma, Akhil-- "Cosmopolitan"

Swann, Maxine-- "Flower Children"

Weltner, Peter-- "Movietone: Detour"

Zancanella, Don-- "The Chimpanzees of Wyoming Territory"

1999

First Prize

Baida, Peter-- "A Nurse's Story"

Second Prize

Holladay, Cary-- "Merry-Go-Sorry"

Third Prize

Munro, Alice-- "Save the Reaper"

Other Selected Stories

Benedict, Pinckney-- "Miracle Boy"

Boyle, T. Coraghessan-- "The Underground Gardens"

Chabon, Michael--"Son of the Wolfman"
Cunningham, Michael--"Mister Brother"
Davenport, Kiana--"Fork Used in Eating Reverend Baker"
Forbes, Charlotte--"Sign"
Houston, Pam--"Cataract"
Lahiri, Jhumpa--"Interpreter of Maladies"
Potok, Chaim--"Moon"
Proulx, E. Annie--"The Mud Below"
Reilly, Gerald--"Nixon Under the Bodhi Tree"
Saunders, George--"Sea Oak"
Schirmer, Robert--"Burning"
Schwartz, Sheila--"Afterbirth"
Wallace, David Foster--"The Depressed Person"
Wetherell, W. D.--"Watching Girls Play"
Whitty, Julia--"A Tortoise for the Queen of Tonga"

2000
First Prize
Wideman, John Edgar--"Weight"
Second Prize
Lordan, Beth--"The Man with the Lapdog"
Third Prize
Gordon, Mary--"The Deacon"
Other Selected Stories
Banks, Russell--"Plains of Abraham"
Banner, Keith--"The Smallest People Alive"
Barrett, Andrea--"Theories of Rain"
Bertles, Jeannette--"Whileaway"
Biguenet, John--"Rose"
Budnitz, Judy--"Flush"
Brockmeier, Kevin--"These Hands"
Byers, Michael--"The Beautiful Days"
Carver, Raymond--"Kindling"
Dark, Alice Elliott--"Watch the Animals"
Davenport, Kiana--"Bones of the Inner Ear"
Englander, Nathan--"The Gilgul of Park Avenue"
Gautreux, Tim--"Easy Pickings"
Gurganus, Allan--"He's at the Office"
Lennon, J. Robert--"The Fool's Proxy"
Pritchard, Melissa--"Salve Regina"
Walbert, Kate--"The Gardens of Kyoto"

2001
First Prize
Swan, Mary--"The Deep"

Second Prize
Chaon, Dan--"Big Me"
Third Prize
Munro, Alice--"Floating Bridge"
Other Selected Stories
Barrett, Andrea--"Servants of Map"
Benedict, Pinckney--"Zog 19: A Scientific Romance"
Boyle, T. Coraghessan--"The Love of My Life"
Carlson, Ron--"At the Jim Bridger"
Erdrich, Louise--"Revival Road"
Gay, William--"The Paperhanger"
Graver, Elizabeth--"The Mourning Door"
Kalam, Murad--"Bow Down"
Leebron, Fred G.--"That Winter"
Nelson, Antonya--"Female Trouble"
Oates, Joyce Carol--"The Girl with the Blackened Eye"
Peck, Dale--"Bliss"
Saunders, George--"Pastoralia"
Schickler, David--"The Smoker"

2002
First Prize
Brockmeier, Kevin--"The Ceiling"
Second Prize
Lewis, Mark Ray--"Scordatura"
Third Prize
Erdrich, Louise--"The Butcher's Wife"
Other Selected Stories
Beattie, Ann--"The Last Odd Day in L.A."
Danticat, Edwidge--"Seven"
Divakaruni, Chitra Banerjee--"The Lives of Strangers"
Doerr, Anthony--"The Hunter's Wife"
Eisenberg, Deborah--"Like It or Not"
Ford, Richard--"Charity"
Gates, David--"George Lassos Moon"
Homes, A. M.--"Do Not Disturb"
Leavitt, David--"Speonk"
Lee, Andrea--"Anthropology"
Lee, Don--"The Possible Husband"
Munro, Alice--"Family Furnishings"
Nolan, Jonathan--"Memento Mori"
Roorbach, Bill--"Big Bend"
Schmidt, Heidi Jon--"Blood Poison"
Wallace, David Foster--"Good Old Neon"

Waters, Mary Yukari-- "Egg-Face"

2003
Juror Favorites
Byatt, A. S-- "The Thing in the Forest"

Johnson, Denis-- "Train Dreams"

Other Selected Stories
Adichie, Chimamanda Ngozi-- "The American Embassy"

Boyle, T. Coraghessan-- "Swept Away"

Connell, Evan S., Jr.-- "Election Eve"

Desnoyers, Adam-- "Bleed Blue in Indonesia"

Doerr, Anthony-- "The Shell Collector"

Giles, Molly-- "Two Words"

Harleman, Ann-- "Meanwhile"

Johnston, Tim-- "Irish Girl"

Kemper, Marjorie-- "God's Goodness"

Kittredge, William-- "Kissing"

Leff, Robyn Jay-- "Burn Your Maps"

Light, Douglas-- "Three Days. A Month. More"

Morrow, Bradford-- "Lush"

Munro, Alice-- "Fathers"

O'Brien, Tim-- "What Went Wrong"

Pearlman, Edith-- "The Story"

Silber, Joan-- "The High Road"

Trevor, William--Sacred Statues"

2004 (No prizes awarded)
2005
Juror Favorites
Alexie, Sherman-- "What You Pawn I Will Redeem"

Jhabvala, Ruth Prawer-- "Refuge in London"

Stuckey-French, French-- "Mudlavia"

Other Selected Stories
Berry, Wendell-- "The Hurt Man"

Brockmeier, Kevin-- "The Brief History of the Dead"

Crouse, Timothy-- "Sphinxes"

D'Ambrosio, Charles-- "The High Divide"

Fountain, Ben-- "Fantasy for Eleven Fingers:

Fox, Paula-- "Grace"

Freudenberg, Nell-- "The Tutor"

Hadley, Tessa-- "The Card Trick"

Jones, Edward P.-- "A Rich Man"

Jones, Gail-- "Desolation"

Macy, Caitlin-- "Christie"

Parker, Michael-- "The Golden Era of Heartbreak'

Peck, Dale-- "Dues"

Peebles, Frances de Pontes-- "The Drowned Woman"

Rash, Ron-- "Speckle Trout"

Reisman, Nancy-- "Tea"

Ward, Liza-- "Snowbound"

2006
Juror Favorites
Eisenberg, Deborah-- "Window"

Jones, Edward P.-- "Old Boys, Old Girls"

Munro, Alice-- "Passion"

Other Selected Stories
Brown, Karen-- "Unction"

Clark, George Makana-- "The Center of the World"

Erdrich, Louise-- "The Plague of Doves"

Fox, Paula-- "The Broad Estates of Death"

Kay, Jackie-- "You Go When You Can No Longer Stay"

Means, David-- "Sault Ste. Marie

Morse, David Lawrence-- "Conceived"

Peelle, Lydia-- "Mule Killers"

Reents, Stephanie-- "Disquisition on Tears"

Schaeffer, Susan Fromberg-- "Wolves"

Svoboda, Terese-- "'80's Lilies"

Thon, Melanie Rae-- "Letters in the Snow . . . "

Trevor, Douglas-- "Girls I Know"

Trevor, William--The Dressmaker's Child"

Vapnyar, Lara-- "Puffed Rice and Meatballs"

Vaswani, Neela-- "The Pelvis Series"

Xu Xi-- "Famine"

2007
Juror Favorites
Chuculate, Eddie-- "Galveston Bay, 1826"

Trevor, William--The Room"

Other Selected Stories
Altschul, Andrew Foster-- "A New Kind of Gravity"

Anapol, Bay-- "A Stone House"

Curtis, Rebecca-- "Summer, with Twins"

Dorfman, Ariel-- "Gringos"

D'Souza, Tony-- "Djamilla"

Dymond, Justine-- "Cherubs"

Ellison, Jan-- "The Company of Men"

Evenson, Brian-- "Mudder Tongue"

Haslett, Adam-- "City Visit"

Kraskikov, Sana-- "Companion"

Lambert, Charles-- "The Scent of Cinnamon"

McCann, Richard-- "The Diarist"
Munro, Alice-- "The View from Castle Rock"
Murphy, Yannick-- "In a Bear's Eye"
Schutt, Christine-- "The Duchess of Albany"
Silbert, Joan-- "War Buddies
Straight, Susan-- "El Ojo de Agua"
Tran, Vu-- "The Gift of Years"

2008
Juror Favorites
Munro, Alice-- "What Do You Want to Know For?"
Trevor, William--Folie à Deux"
Zentner, Alexi-- "Touch"
Other Selected Stories
Cain, Shannon-- "The Necessity of Certain Behaviors"
Doerr, Anthony-- "Village 113"
Faber, Michel-- "Bye-Bye Natalia"
Gaitskill, Mary-- "The Little Boy"
Gass, William H.-- "A Little History of Modern Music"
Jin, Ha-- "A Composer and His Parakeets"
Jones, Edward P.-- "Bad Neighbors"
Kohler, Sheila-- "The Transitional Object"
Li, Yiyun-- "Prison"
McDonald, Roger-- "The Bullock Run"
Malouf, David-- "Every Move You Make"
Millhauser, Steven-- "A Change in Fashion"
Olafsson, Olaf-- "On the Lake"
Segal, Lore-- "Other People's Deaths"
Sonnenberg, Brittani-- "Taiping"
Tremain, Rose-- "A Game of Cards"
Tulathimutte, Tony-- "Scenes from the Life of the Only
  Girl in Water Shield, Alaska"

2009
Juror Favorites
Díaz, Junot-- "Wildwood"
Graham, Joyce-- "An Ordinary Soldier of the Queen"
Other Selected Stories
Brown, Karen-- "Isabel's Daughter"
Burnside, John-- "The Bell Ringer"
Dien, Viet-- "Substitutes"
Godimer, Nadine-- "A Beneficiary"
Greer, Andrew Sean-- "Darkness"

Horrocks, Caitlin-- "This Is Not Your City"
Jin, Ha-- "The House Behind a Weeping Cherry"
Lunstrum, Kristen Sundberg-- "The Nursery"
Miller, L. E.-- "Kind"
Morgan, Alistair-- "Icebergs"
Muñoz, Manuel-- "Tell Him About Brother John"
Nash, Roger-- "The Camera and the Cobra"
Sikka, Mohan-- "Uncle Musto Takes a Mistress"
Silver, Marisa-- "The Visitor"
Slate, E. V.-- "Purple Bamboo Park"
Theroux, Paul-- "Twenty-Two Stories"
Troy, Judy-- "The Order of Things"
Yoon, Paul-- "And We Will Be Here"

2010
Juror Awards
Lasdun, John-- "On Death"
Mueenuddi, Daniyal-- "A Spoiled Man"
Trevor, William--The Woman of the House
Other Selected Stories
Adichie, Chimamanda Ngozi-- "Stand by Me"
Alarcón, Daniel-- "The Bridge"
Allio, Kirstin-- "Clothed, Female Figure
Bakopoulos, Natalie-- "Fresco, Byzantine"
Berry, Wendell-- "Sheep May Safely Graze"
Bradley, George-- "An East Egg Update"
Cameron, Peter-- "The End of My Life in New York"
Galgut, Damon-- "The Lover"
Munro, Alice-- "Some Women"
Proulx, E. Annie-- "Them Old Cowboy Songs"
Rash, Ron-- "Into the Gorge"
Row, Jess-- "Sheep May Safely Graze"
Samarasan, Pretta-- "Birth Memorial"
Sanders, Ted-- "Obit"
Segal, Lore-- "Making Good"
Watson, Brad-- "Visitation"
Wideman, John Edgar-- "Microstories"

PULITZER PRIZE IN LETTERS

Awarded annually since 1917, this award was given for novels only until 1948, but is now given for any work of fiction. This listing includes only authors who have received this award for works of short fiction.

1966: Katherine Ann Porter--*The Collected Stories of Katherine Ann Porter*

1970: Jean Stafford--*The Collected Stories of Jean Stafford*

1978: James Alan McPherson--*Elbow Room*

1979: John Cheever--*The Stories of John Cheever*

1993: Robert Olen Butler--*A Good Scent from a Strange Mountain: Stories*

2000: Jhumpa Lahiri--*Interpreter of Maladies: Stories*

REA AWARD

Awarded annually since 1986 to living American writers who have made a significant contribution to the short-story form.

1986: Cynthia Ozick

1987: Robert Coover

1988: Donald Barthelme

1989: Tobias Wolff

1990: Joyce Carol Oates

1991: Paul Bowles

1992: Eudora Welty

1993: Grace Paley

1994: Tillie Olsen

1995: Richard Ford

1996: Andre Dubus

1997: Gina Berriault

1998: John Edgar Wideman

1999: Joy Williams

2000: Deborah Eisenberg

2001: Alice Munro

2002: Mavis Gallant

2003: Antonya Nelson

2004: Lorrie Moore

2005: Ann Beattie

2006: John Updike

2007: Stuart Dybek

2008: Amy Hempel

2009: Mary Robison

STORY PRIZE

Established in 2004, the Story Prize award honors the author of an outstanding collection of short fiction that is written in English and initially published in the United States.

2004: Edwidge Danticat--*The Dew Breaker*

2005: Patrick O'Keefe--*The Hill Road*

2006: Mary Gordon--*The Stories of Mary Gordon*

2007: Jim Shepard--*Like You'd Understand, Anyway*

2008: Tobias Wolff--*Our Story Begins*

2009: Daniyal Mueenuddin--*In Other Rooms, Other Wonders*

CANADIAN AWARDS

DANUTA GLEED LITERARY AWARD

The Writers' Union of Canada presents this $10,000 prize annually to a Canadian author who has written the best first collection of short fiction in the English language.

1998: Curtis Gillespie--*The Progress of an Object in Motion*
1999: Mike Barnes--*Aquarium*
2000: Ivan E. Coyote--*Close to Spiderman*
2001: Barbara Lamber--*The Allegra Series*
2002: Gloria Sawai--*A Song for Nettie Johnson*
2003: Lee Henderson--*The Broken Record Technique*
2004: Jacqueline Baker--*A Hard Witching, and Other Stories*

2005: David Bezmozgis--*Natasha, and Other Stories*
2006: Charlotte Gill--*Ladykiller*
2007: Nathan Sellyn--*Indigenous Beasts*
2008: Andrew Hood--*Pardon Our Monsters*
2009: Pasha Malla--*The Withdrawal Method*
2010: Sarah Roberts--*Wax Boats*

WRITERS' TRUST OF CANADA/McCLELLAND AND STEWART JOURNEY PRIZE

The Journey Prize is awarded annually to an emerging writer for the best short story published in a Canadian literary publication. The award is endowed with the Canadian royalties that James A. Michener earned from his novel *Journey*, which was published in 1988 by McClelland and Stewart. This company also publishes an annual anthology of the year's nominated short stories.

1989: Holley Rubinsky-- "Rapid Transits"
1990: Cynthia Flood-- "My Father Took a Cake to France"
1991: Yann Martel-- "The Facts Behind the Helsinki Roccamatios"
1992: Rozena Maart-- "No Rosa No District Six"
1993: Gayla Reid-- "Sister Doyle's Men"
1994: Melissa Hardy-- "Long Man the River"
1995: Kathryn Woodward-- "Of Marranos and Gilded Angels"
1996: Elyse Gasco-- "Can You Wave Bye Bye Baby?"
1997: Gabriella Goliger-- "Maladies of the Inner Ear" and Anne Simpson-- "Dreaming Snow" (tie)

1998: John Brooke-- "The Finer Points of Apples"
1999: Alissa York-- "The Back of the Bear's Mouth"
2000: Timothy Taylor-- "Doves of Townsend"
2001: Kevin Armstrong-- "The Cane Field"
2002: Jocelyn Brown-- "Miss Canada"
2003: Jessica Grant-- "My Husband's Jump"
2004: Devin Krukoff-- "The Last Spark"
2005: Matt Shaw-- "Matchbook for a Mother's Hair"
2006: Heather Birrell-- "BriannaSusannaAlana"
2007: Craig Boyko-- "Ozy"
2008: Saleema Nawaz-- "My Three Girls"
2009: Yasuko Thanh-- "Floating like the Dead"
2010: Devon Code-- "Uncle Oscar

COMMONWEALTH AWARDS

COMMONWEALTH SHORT STORY COMPETITION

The Commonwealth Short Story Competition aims to promote new writing for radio. The prize has been awarded since 2008 and is funded and administered by the Commonwealth Foundation and the Commonwealth Broadcasting Association. Competition for the prize is open to all citizens of the Commonwealth countries.

2008:
Overall Winner: Julie Curwin--"World Backwards"--Canada

Regional Winner, Africa: Taddeo Bwambale Nyonda--"Die, Dear Tofa"--Uganda

Regional Winner, Asia: Salil Chaturvedi--"The Bombay Run"--India

Regional Winner, Europe: Tania Hershman--"Straight Up"--England

Regional Winner, Pacific: Jennifer Mills--"Jack's Red Hat"--Australia

2009:
Overall Winner: Jennifer Moore--"Table Talk"--England

Regional Winner, Africa: Kachi A. Ozumba--"The One-Armed Thief"--Nigeria

Regional Winner, Asia: Manasi Subramaniam--"Debbie's Call--India

Regional Winner Caribbean Alake Pilgrim--"Shades"--Trinidad and Tobago

Regional Winner, Pacific: Terri-Anne Green--"The Colour of Rain"--Australia

2010:
Overall Winner: Shachi Kaul--"Retirement"—India

Regional Winner, Africa: Karen Jennings--"From Dark"--South Africa

Regional Winner,Canada and Europe: Melissa Madore--"Swallow Dive"--Canada

Regional Winner, Caribbean: Barbara Jenkins--"Something from Nothing"--Trinidad and Tobago

Regional Winner, Pacific: Jena Woodhouse--"Praise Be"--Australia

Special Prize, Science, Technology and Society: Anuradha Kumar--"The First Hello"--India

Special Prize, Story for Children: Iona Massey--"Grandma Makes Meatballs"--Australia

Anietie Isong Special Prize for a Story from Nigeria: Shola Olowu-Asante--"Dinner for Three"--Nigeria

COMMONWEALTH WRITERS' PRIZE

Established in 1987, this prize recognizes the best works of fiction written by an established writer from the Commonwealth countries. Only one work of short fiction has received the prize:

1987: Olive Senior--*Summer Lightning, and Other Stories*--Jamaica

GEORG BÜCHNER PRIZE

The Georg Büchner Prize (Georg-Büchner-Preis) is the most important literary prize of Germany. The award was created in 1923 in memory of writer Georg Büchner and initially was only given to artists, poets, actors and singers who came from or were connected to Büchner's home of Hesse. In 1951, the prize changed to a general literary prize, and it is presented annually by the Deutsche Akademie für Sprache und Dichtung to authors who write in the German language. This listing cites only the prize-winning authors whose works include short fiction.

1924: Alfred Bock
1927: Kasimir Edschmid
1930: Nikolaux Schwarzkopf
1932: Albert H. Rausch
1947: Anna Seghers
1950: Elisabeth Langgässer
1953: Ernst Kreuder
1954: Martin Kessel
1955: Marie Luise Kaschnitz
1957: Erich Kästner
1958: Max Frisch
1961: Hans Erich Nossack
1964: Ingeborg Bachmann
1966: Wolfgang Hildesheimer
1967: Heinrich Boll
1970: Thomas Bernhard
1971: Uwe Johnson

1973: Peter Handke
1974: Hermann Kesten
1976: Heinz Piontek
1977: Hermann Lenz
1980: Christa Wolf
1981: Martin Walser
1983: Wolfdietrich Schnurre
1985: Heiner Müller
1986: Friedrich Dürrenmatt
1993: Peter Rühmkorf
1997: H. C. Artmann
2000: Volker Braun
2003: Alexander Kluge
2005: Brigette Kronauer
2007: Martin Mosebach
2009: Walter Kappacher
2010: Reinhard Jirgl

PRIX GONCOURT DE LA NOUVELLE

The Prix Goncourt de la Nouvelle is a French literary award for a work of short fiction. It is jointly presented by the Académie Goncourt and the city of Strasbourg.

1999: Elvire de Brissac--Les Anges d'en bas
2000: Catherine Paysan--Les Désarmés
2001: Stéphane Denis--Elle a maigri pour le festival
2002: Sébastien Lapaque--Mythologie Française
2003: Philippe Claudel--Les Petites Mécaniques
2004: Olivier Adam--Passer l'hiver
2005: Georges-Olivier Chateaureynaud--Singe savant tabassé par deux clowns

2006: Franz Bartelt--Le Bar des habitudes
2007: Brigitte Giraud--L'Amour est très surestimé
2008: Jean-Yves Masson--Ultimes vérités sur la mort du nageur
2009: Sylvain Tesson--Une vie à coucher dehors
2010: Éric-Emmanuel Schmitt--Concerto à la mémoire d'un ange

Strega Prize

The Strega Prize (Premio Strega) is the most prestigious Italian literary award. Since 1947, it has been awarded annually for the best work of prose fiction by an Italian author. This listing includes only authors who received the award for works of short fiction.

1952: Alberto Moravia--*I racconti, 1927-1951*

1955: Giovanni Comisso--*Un gatto attraversa la strada: Racconti*

1956:Giorgio Bassani--*Cinque storie ferraresi*

1958: Dino Buzzati--*Sessanta racconti*

1975: Tommaso Landolfi--*A caso*

1999: Dacia Maraini--*Buio*

Indian Awards

Jnanpith Award

Any Indian citizen who writes in any of the official languages of India is eligible for the Jnanpith Award. Before 1982, the awards were given for a single work by a writer; since 1982, the prize has been presented for a lifetime contribution to Indian literature. This listing cites only the prize-winning authors whose works include short fiction.

1966: Tarashankar Bandopadhyaya

1967: Kuppali V. Puttappa

1970: Viswanatha Satyanarayana

1973: Gopinath Mohanty

1974: Vishnu Sakharam Khandekar

1975: P. V. Akilan

1976: Ashapurna Devi

1977: K. Shivaram Karanth

1978: Sachchidananda Hirananda Vatsyayan (pseudonym Ajneya)

1979: Birendra Kumar Bhattacharya

1980: S. K. Pottekkatt

1981: Amrita Pritam

1983: Masti Venkatesha Iyengar

1984: Thakazhi Sivasankara Pillai

1985: Pannalal Patel

1986: Sachidananda Roautroy

1987: Vishnu Vāman Shirwādkar (pseudonym Kusumāgraj)

1989: Qurratulain Hyder

1994: U. R. Aranthamurthy

1995: M. T. Vasudevan Nair

1996: Mahasweta Devi

1999: Nirmal Verma and S. Gurdial Singh

2000: Indira Goswami

2002: D. Jayakanthan

2005: Kunwar Narayan

International Awards

Frank O'Connor International Short Story Award

Named in honor of Irish writer Frank O'Connor, this award is presented annually for a collection of short stories. The award was inaugurated in 2005.

2005: Yiyun Li--*A Thousand Years of Good Prayers*--China/United States

2006: Haruki Murakami--*Blind Willow, Sleeping Woman*--Japan

2007: Miranda July--*No One Belongs Here More than You*--United States

2008: Jhumpa Lahiri--*Unaccustomed Earth*--United States

2009: Simon Van Booy--*Love Begins in Winter*--England

2010: Ron Rash--*Burning Bright*--United States

FRANZ KAFKA PRIZE

This international prize honors writer Franz Kafka by presenting an award to a writer for his or her lifetime achievement. First presented in 2001, the prize is cosponsored by the Franz Kafka Society and the city of Prague, Czech Republic. This listing cites only the prize-winning authors whose works include short fiction.

2001: Philip Roth--United States
2002: Ivan Klíma--Czech Republic
2003: Péter Nádas--Hungary

2006: Haruki Murakami--Japan
2008: Arnošt Lustig--Czech Republic
2009: Peter Handke--Austria

JERUSALEM PRIZE FOR THE FREEDOM OF THE INDIVIDUAL IN SOCIETY

The Jerusalem Prize is a biennial literary award presented to writers whose works have dealt with themes of human freedom in society. This listing cites only the prize-winning authors whose works include short fiction.

1965: Max Frisch--Switzerland
1969: Ignazio Silone--Italy
1971: Jorge Luis Borges--Argentina
1973: Eugene Ionesco--Romania/France
1975: Simone de Beauvoir--France
1981: Graham Green--England
1983: V. S. Naipaul--Trinidad and Tobago/England

1985: Milan Kundera--Czech Republic/France
1993: Stefan Heym--Germany
1995: Mario Vargas Llosa--Peru
1999: Don DeLillo--United States
2001: Susan Sontag--United States
2003: Arthur Miller--United States
2009: Haruki Murakami--Japan

MAN BOOKER INTERNATIONAL PRIZE

Established in 2005, this award is presented biennially to a living author of any nationality for fiction published in English or generally available in English translation. The first four winners have all written short fiction.

2005: Ismail Kadaré--Albania
2007: Chinua Achebe--Nigeria

2009: Alice Munro--Canada
2011: Philip Roth--United States

NEUSTADT INTERNATIONAL PRIZE FOR LITERATURE

Awarded biennially since 1970, this award, sponsored by the University of Oklahoma, honors writers for a body of work. This listing cites only the prize-winning authors whose works include short fiction.

1970: Giuseppe Ungaretti--Italy
1972: Gabriel García Márquez--Colombia
1976: Elizabeth Bishop--United States
1980: Josef Škvorecký--Czechoslovakia/Canada
1984: Paavo Haavikko--Finland
1986: Max Frisch--Switzerland

1988: Raja Rao--India/United States
1998: Nuruddin Farah--Somalia
2000: David Malouf--Australia
2002: Álvaro Mutis--Colombia
2006: Claribel Alegría--Nicaragua/El Salvador
2008: Patricia Grace--New Zealand

NOBEL PRIZE IN LITERATURE

Awarded annually since 1901, this award is generally regarded as the highest honor that can be bestowed upon an author for his or her total body of literary work. This listing of winners includes only authors whose works include short fiction.

1904: José Echegaray y Eizaguirre--Spain

1905: Henryk Sienkiewicz--Poland

1907: Rudyard Kipling--England

1909: Selma Lagerlöf--Sweden

1910: Paul Heyse--Germany

1912: Gerhart Hauptmann--Germany

1913: Rabindranath Tagore--India

1916: Verner von Heidenstam--Sweden

1917: Henrik Pontoppidan--Denmark

1920: Knut Hamsun--Norway

1921: Anatole France--France

1922: Jacinto Benavente--Spain

1923: William B. Yeats--Ireland

1924: Władysław Reymont--Poland

1925: George Bernard Shaw--Ireland

1926: Grazia Deledda--Italy

1928: Sigrid Undset--Norway

1929: Thomas Mann--Germany

1930: Sinclair Lewis--United States

1932: John Galsworthy--England

1933: Ivan Bunin--Russia

1934: Luigi Pirandello--Italy

1938: Pearl S. Buck--United States

1939: Frans Eemil Sillanpää--Finland

1944: Johannes V. Jensen--Denmark

1946: Hermann Hesse--Switzerland

1947: André Gide--France

1949: William Faulkner--United States

1951: Pär Lagerkvist--Sweden

1954: Ernest Hemingway--United States

1955: Halldór Laxness--Iceland

1957: Albert Camus--France

1958: Boris Pasternak (declined)--Russia

1961: Ivo Andrić--Yugoslavia

1962: John Steinbeck--United States

1964: Jean-Paul Sartre (declined)--France

1965: Mikhail Sholokhov--Russia

1966: Shmuel Yosef Agnon--Israel; Nelly Sachs--Sweden

1967: Miguel Angel Asturias--Guatemala

1968: Yasunari Kawabata--Japan

1969: Samuel Beckett--Ireland

1970: Aleksandr Solzhenitsyn--Russia

1972: Heinrich Böll--Germany

1973: Patrick White--Australia

1974: Eyvind Johnson--Sweden

1976: Saul Bellow--United States

1978: Isaac Bashevis Singer--United States

1982: Gabriel García Márquez--Colombia

1983: William Golding--England

1988: Naguib Mahfouz--Egypt

1989: Camilo José Cela--Spain

1991: Nadine Gordimer--South Africa

1994: Kenzaburō Ōe--Japan

1998: José Saramago--Portugal

2000: Gao Xingjian--China

2001: V. S. Naipaul--Trinidad and Tobago/England

2007: Doris Lessing--England

2008: J. M. G. Le Clézio--France/Mauritias

2009: Herta Müller--Germany

2010: Mario Vargas Llosa--Peru

JAPANESE AWARD

AKUTAGAWA PRIZE

The Akutagawa Prize is a Japanese literary award presented twice a year, once in January and again in July. The prize, established in memory of the writer Ryūnosuke Akutagawa, has been awarded since 1935 to the best serious literary story published in a newspaper or magazine by a new or rising author. This list only includes those authors covered in *Critical Survey of Short Fiction*.

January 1958: Kenzaburō Ōe-- "Shiiku" ("The Catch")

LATIN AMERICAN/SPANISH LANGUAGE AWARDS

JUAN RULFO PRIZE FOR LATIN AMERICAN AND CARIBBEAN LITERATURE

The Guadalajara International Book Fair presents its annual literary award to a writer from the Americas who writes in Spanish, Portuguese, French, or English. Award organizers include Mexico's National Council for Culture and Arts and the University of Guadalajara. This listing cites only the prize-winning authors whose works include short fiction.

1992: Juan José Arreola--Mexico

1994: Julio Ramón Ribeyro--Peru

1996: Augusto Monterroso--Guatemala

1997: Juan Marsé--Spain

1999: Sergio Pitol--Mexico

2001: Juan García Ponce--Mexico

2002: Cintio Vitier--Cuba

2003: Rubem Fonseca--Brazil

2004: Juan Goytisolo--Spain

2010: Margo Glantz--Mexico

MIGUEL DE CERVANTES PRIZE

The Miguel de Cervantes Prize, or Premio Miguel de Cervantes, established in 1976, is awarded annually to honor the lifetime achievement of an outstanding writer in the Spanish language from any Spanish-speaking nation. This listing cites only the prize-winning authors whose works include short fiction.

1977: Alejo Carpentier--Cuba

1979: Jorge Luis Borges--Argentina

1980: Juan Carlos Onetti--Uruguay

1987: Carlos Fuentes--Mexico

1989: Augusto Roa Bastos--Paraguay

1990: Adolfo Bioy Casares--Argentina

1991: Francisco Ayala--Spain

1993: Miguel Delibes--Spain

1994: Mario Vargas Llosa--Peru

1995: Camilio José Cela--Spain

1997: Guillermo Cabrera Infante--Cuba

1999: Jorge Edwards--Chile

2000: Francisco Umbral--Spain

2005: Sergio Pitol--Mexico

2006: Antonio Gamoneda--Spain

2009: José Emilio Pacheco--Mexico

2010: Ana María Matute--Spain

RUSSIAN AWARD

RUSSIAN LITTLE BOOKER PRIZE

Established in 1992, the Russian Little Booker Prize is an annual award for a nominated genre of writing. As of 2011, only one prize had been awarded for short fiction.

1993: Victor Pelevin--*Shii fonor* (*The Blue Lantern, and Other Stories*)

CHRONOLOGICAL LIST OF WRITERS

This chronology lists authors covered in all subsets of this edition of the *Critical Survey of Short Fiction* in order of their dates of birth. This arrangement serves as a supplemental time line for those interested in the development of short fiction over time.

BORN UP TO 1700

Homer (c. early eighth century B.C.E.)
Vergil (October 15, 70 B.C.E.)
Ovid (March 20, 43 B.C.E.)
Petronius (c. 20 C.E.)
Chrétien de Troyes (c. 1150)
Marie de France (c. 1150)
Dante (May or June, 1265)
Boccaccio, Giovanni (June or July, 1313)
Chaucer, Geoffrey (c. 1343)
Malory, Sir Thomas (early fifteenth century)
Cervantes, Miguel de (September 29, 1547)
Greene, Robert (c. July, 1558)
Pu Songling (June 5, 1640)
Ihara Saikaku (1642)
Congreve, William (January 24, 1670)
Steele, Sir Richard (March 12, 1672 baptized)
Addison, Joseph (May 1, 1672)
Voltaire (November 21, 1694)

BORN 1701-1800

Franklin, Benjamin (January 17, 1706)
Johnson, Samuel (September 18, 1709)
Diderot, Denis (October 5, 1713)
Hawkesworth, John (1715?)
Goldsmith, Oliver (November 10, 1728 or 1730)
Goethe, Johann Wolfgang von (August 28, 1749)
Edgeworth, Maria (January 1, 1768)
Scott, Sir Walter (August 15, 1771)
Nahman of Bratslav, Rabbi (April 4, 1772)
Austen, Jane (December 16, 1775)
Hoffmann, E. T. A. (January 24, 1776)
Kleist, Heinrich von (October 18, 1777)
Irving, Washington (April 3, 1783)

Grimm, Jacob (January 4, 1785)
Grimm, Wilhelm (February 24, 1786)
Longstreet, Augustus Baldwin (September 22, 1790)
Carleton, William (March 4, 1794)
Balzac, Honoré de (May 20, 1799)
Pushkin, Alexander (June 6, 1799)

BORN 1801-1825

Mérimée, Prosper (September 28, 1803)
Hawthorne, Nathaniel (July 4, 1804)
Andersen, Hans Christian (April 2, 1805)
Simms, William Gilmore (April 17, 1806)
Nerval, Gérard de (May 22, 1808)
Poe, Edgar Allan (January 19, 1809)
Gogol, Nikolai (March 31, 1809)
Thackeray, William Makepeace (July 18, 1811)
Gautier, Théophile (August 30, 1811)
Dickens, Charles (February 7, 1812)
Le Fanu, Joseph Sheridan (August 28, 1814)
Turgenev, Ivan (November 9, 1818)
Melville, Herman (August 1, 1819)
Eliot, George (November 22, 1819)
Dostoevski, Fyodor (November 11, 1821)
Flaubert, Gustave (December 12, 1821)

BORN 1826-1850

O'Brien, Fitz-James (c. 1828)
Tolstoy, Leo (September 9, 1828)
Leskov, Nikolai (February 16, 1831)
Alarcón, Pedro Antonio de (March 10, 1833)
Stockton, Frank R. (April 5, 1834)
Twain, Mark (November 30, 1835)

Harte, Bret (August 25, 1836)
Aldrich, Thomas Bailey (November 11, 1836)
Howells, William Dean (March 1, 1837)
Machado de Assis, Joaquim Maria (June 21, 1839)
Zola, Émile (April 2, 1840)
Daudet, Alphonse (May 13, 1840)
Hardy, Thomas (June 2, 1840)
Verga, Giovanni (September 2, 1840)
Bierce, Ambrose (June 24, 1842)
James, Henry (April 15, 1843)
France, Anatole (April 16, 1844)
Cable, George Washington (October 12, 1844)
Harris, Joel Chandler (December 9, 1848)
Jewett, Sarah Orne (September 3, 1849)
Hearn, Lafcadio (June 27, 1850)
Maupassant, Guy de (August 5, 1850)
Stevenson, Robert Louis (November 13, 1850)

BORN 1851-1870

Chopin, Kate (February 8, 1851)
Pardo Bazán, Emilia (September 16, 1851)
Moore, George (February 24, 1852)
Peretz, Isaac Leib (May 18, 1852)
Freeman, Mary E. Wilkins (October 31, 1852)
Conrad, Joseph (December 3, 1857)
Chesnutt, Charles Waddell (June 20, 1858)
Aleichem, Sholom (March 2, 1859)
Doyle, Sir Arthur Conan (May 22, 1859)
Chekhov, Anton (January 29, 1860)
Gilman, Charlotte Perkins (July 3, 1860)
Garland, Hamlin (September 14, 1860)
Svevo, Italo (December 19, 1861)
Wharton, Edith (January 24, 1862)
James, M. R. (August 1, 1862)
Henry, O. (September 11, 1862)
Machen, Arthur (March 3, 1863)
Jacobs, W. W. (September 8, 1863)
Unamuno y Jugo, Miguel de (September 29, 1864)
Yeats, William Butler (June 13, 1865)
Kipling, Rudyard (December 30, 1865)
Wells, H. G. (September 21, 1866)
Lawson, Henry (June 17, 1867)
Pirandello, Luigi (June 28, 1867)
Galsworthy, John (August 14, 1867)
Gorky, Maxim (March 28, 1868)

Blackwood, Algernon (March 14, 1869)
Norris, Frank (March 5, 1870)
Bunin, Ivan (October 22, 1870)
Saki (December 18, 1870)

BORN 1871-1880

Dreiser, Theodore (August 27, 1871)
Crane, Stephen (November 1, 1871)
Dunbar, Paul Laurence (June 27, 1872)
Beerbohm, Max (August 24, 1872)
Colette (January 28, 1873)
Glasgow, Ellen (April 22, 1873)
de la Mare, Walter (April 25, 1873)
Cather, Willa (December 7, 1873)
Maugham, W. Somerset (January 25, 1874)
Stein, Gertrude (February 3, 1874)
Chesterton, G. K. (May 29, 1874)
Mann, Thomas (June 6, 1875)
London, Jack (January 12, 1876)
Anderson, Sherwood (September 13, 1876)
Hesse, Hermann (July 2, 1877)
Coppard, A. E. (January 4, 1878)
Walser, Robert (April 15, 1878)
Dunsany, Lord (July 24, 1878)
Quiroga, Horacio (December 31, 1878)
Forster, E. M. (January 1, 1879)

BORN 1881-1890

Lu Xun (September 25, 1881)
Roberts, Elizabeth Madox (October 30, 1881)
Woolf, Virginia (January 25, 1882)
Joyce, James (February 2, 1882)
Lewis, Wyndham (November 18, 1882)
Kafka, Franz (July 3, 1883)
Williams, William Carlos (September 17, 1883)
Zamyatin, Yevgeny (January 20, 1884)
Lardner, Ring (March 6, 1885)
Dinesen, Isak (April 17, 1885)
Lawrence, D. H. (September 11, 1885)
Steele, Wilbur Daniel (March 17, 1886)
Tanizaki, Jun'ichirō (July 24, 1886)
Agnon, Shmuel Yosef (July 17, 1888)
Chandler, Raymond (July 23, 1888)
Mansfield, Katherine (October 14, 1888)
Aiken, Conrad (August 5, 1889)

Karel Čapek (January 9, 1890)
Pasternak, Boris (February 10, 1890)
Porter, Katherine Anne (May 15, 1890)
Lovecraft, H. P. (August 20, 1890)
Christie, Agatha (September 15, 1890)

BORN 1891-1900
Hurston, Zora Neale (January 7, 1891)
Lagerkvist, Pär (May 23, 1891)
Akutagawa, Ryūnosuke (March 1, 1892)
Buck, Pearl S. (June 26, 1892)
Cain, James M. (July 1, 1892)
Schulz, Bruno (July 12, 1892)
Parker, Dorothy (August 22, 1893)
Warner, Sylvia Townsend (December 6, 1893)
Hammett, Dashiell (May 27, 1894)
Babel, Isaac (July 13, 1894)
Huxley, Aldous (July 26, 1894)
Rhys, Jean (August 24, 1894)
Thurber, James (December 8, 1894)
Toomer, Jean (December 26, 1894)
Zoshchenko, Mikhail (August 10, 1895)
Gordon, Caroline (October 6, 1895)
O'Flaherty, Liam (August 28, 1896)
Fitzgerald, F. Scott (September 24, 1896)
Faulkner, William (September 25, 1897)
Brecht, Bertolt (February 10, 1898)
Benét, Stephen Vincent (July 22, 1898)
Nabokov, Vladimir (April 23, 1899)
Bowen, Elizabeth (June 7, 1899)
Kawabata, Yasunari (June 11, 1899)
White, E. B. (July 11, 1899)
Hemingway, Ernest (July 21, 1899)
Borges, Jorge Luis (August 24, 1899)
Asturias, Miguel Ángel (October 19, 1899)
O'Faoláin, Seán (February 22, 1900)
Wolfe, Thomas (October 3, 1900)
Pritchett, V. S. (December 16, 1900)

BORN 1901-1905
Kavan, Anna (April 10, 1901)
Wescott, Glenway (April 11, 1901)
Collier, John (May 3, 1901)
Davies, Rhys (November 9, 1901 or 1903)
Hughes, Langston (February 1, 1902)

Boyle, Kay (February 19, 1902)
Steinbeck, John (February 27, 1902)
West, Jessamyn (July 18, 1902)
Bontemps, Arna (October 13, 1902)
O'Connor, Frank (1903)
Nin, Anaïs (February 21, 1903)
Callaghan, Morley (February 22, 1903)
Cozzens, James Gould (August 19, 1903)
Plomer, William (December 10, 1903)
Caldwell, Erskine (December 17, 1903)
Perelman, S. J. (February 1, 1904)
Farrell, James T. (February 27, 1904)
Singer, Isaac Bashevis (July 14 or November 21, 1904)
Greene, Graham (October 2, 1904)
Carpentier, Alejo (December 26, 1904)
Boyle, Patrick (1905)
Lee, Manfred B. (January 11, 1905)
O'Hara, John (January 31, 1905)
Warren, Robert Penn (April 24, 1905)
Bates, H. E. (May 16, 1905)
Sartre, Jean-Paul (June 21, 1905)
Dannay, Frederic (October 20, 1905)

BORN 1906-1910
Beckett, Samuel (April 13, 1906)
Still, James (July 16, 1906)
Narayan, R. K. (October 10, 1906)
Buzzati, Dino (October 16, 1906)
Carr, John Dickson (November 30, 1906)
Shalamov, Varlam (July 1, 1907)
Heinlein, Robert A. (July 7, 1907)
Stuart, Jesse (August 8, 1907)
Moravia, Alberto (November 28, 1907)
Hale, Nancy (May 6, 1908)
Guimarães Rosa, João (June 27, 1908)
Landolfi, Tommaso (August 9, 1908)
Saroyan, William (August 31, 1908)
Wright, Richard (September 4, 1908)
Pavese, Cesare (September 9, 1908)
Petry, Ann (October 12, 1908)
Stegner, Wallace (February 18, 1909)
Derleth, August (February 24, 1909)
Algren, Nelson (March 28, 1909)
Welty, Eudora (April 13, 1909)

Dazai, Osamu (June 19, 1909)
Onetti, Juan Carlos (July 1, 1909)
Himes, Chester (July 29, 1909)
Clark, Walter Van Tilburg (August 3, 1909)
Agee, James (November 27, 1909)
Morris, Wright (January 6, 1910)
Doerr, Harriet (April 8, 1910)
Bombal, María Luisa (June 8, 1910)
Bowles, Paul (December 30, 1910)

BORN 1911-1915
Williams, Tennessee (March 26, 1911)
Mahfouz, Naguib (December 11, 1911)
Calisher, Hortense (December 20, 1911)
Olsen, Tillie (January 14, 1912)
Sansom, William (January 18, 1912)
Cheever, John (May 27, 1912)
Lavin, Mary (June 11, 1912)
McCarthy, Mary (June 21, 1912)
Taylor, Elizabeth (July 3, 1912)
Shaw, Irwin (February 27, 1913)
Weidman, Jerome (April 4, 1913)
Wilson, Angus (August 11, 1913)
Camus, Albert (November 7, 1913)
Schwartz, Delmore (December 8, 1913)
Ellison, Ralph (March 1, 1914)
Malamud, Bernard (April 26, 1914)
Purdy, James (July 17, 1914)
Cortázar, Julio (August 26, 1914)
Thomas, Dylan (October 27, 1914)
Welch, Denton (March 29, 1915)
Hall, Lawrence Sargent (April 23, 1915)
Goyen, William (April 24, 1915)
Bellow, Saul (June 10, 1915)
Stafford, Jean (July 1, 1915)

BORN 1916-1920
Dahl, Roald (September 13, 1916)
Hildesheimer, Wolfgang (December 9, 1916)
Jackson, Shirley (December 14, 1916)
Fitzgerald, Penelope (December 17, 1916)
Taylor, Peter (January 8, 1917)
McCullers, Carson (February 19, 1917)
Bowles, Jane (February 22, 1917)
Powers, J. F. (July 8, 1917)

Auchincloss, Louis (September 27, 1917)
Clarke, Arthur C. (December 16, 1917)
Böll, Heinrich (December 21, 1917)
Spark, Muriel (February 1, 1918)
Sturgeon, Theodore (February 26, 1918)
Rulfo, Juan (May 16, 1918)
Elliott, George P. (June 16, 1918)
Arreola, Juan José (September 21, 1918)
Solzhenitsyn, Aleksandr (December 11, 1918)
Salinger, J. D. (January 1, 1919)
Cassill, R. V. (May 17, 1919)
Kiely, Benedict (August 15, 1919)
Lessing, Doris (October 22, 1919)
Mphahlele, Ezekiel (December 17, 1919)
Asimov, Isaac (January 2, 1920)
Bradbury, Ray (August 22, 1920)

BORN 1921-1925
Highsmith, Patricia (January 19, 1921)
Douglas, Ellen (July 12, 1921)
Spencer, Elizabeth (July 19, 1921)
Lem, Stanisław (September 12, 1921)
Aichinger, Ilse (November 1, 1921)
Gallant, Mavis (August 11, 1922)
Robbe-Grillet, Alain (August 18, 1922)
Vonnegut, Kurt (November 11, 1922)
Borowski, Tadeusz (November 12, 1922)
Paley, Grace (December 11, 1922)
Endō, Shūsaku (March 27, 1923)
Fox, Paula (April 22, 1923)
Hall, Martha Lacy (August 19, 1923)
Calvino, Italo (October 15, 1923)
Gordimer, Nadine (November 20, 1923)
Gold, Herbert (March 9, 1924)
Humphrey, William (June 18, 1924)
Gass, William H. (July 30, 1924)
Baldwin, James (August 2, 1924)
Connell, Evan S. (August 17, 1924)
Capote, Truman (September 30, 1924)
Donoso, José (October 5, 1924)
Mishima, Yukio (January 14, 1925)
Wain, John (March 14, 1925)
O'Connor, Flannery (March 25, 1925)
Tuohy, Frank (May 2, 1925)
Salter, James (June 10, 1925)

Sinyavsky, Andrei (October 8, 1925)

Lispector, Clarice (December 10, 1925)

BORN 1926-1930

Berriault, Gina (January 1, 1926)

Fowles, John (March 31, 1926)

Laurence, Margaret (July 18, 1926)

Adams, Alice (August 14, 1926)

Knowles, John (September 16, 1926)

Lind, Jacov (February 10, 1927)

Higgins, Aidan (March 3, 1927)

García Márquez, Gabriel (March 6, 1927)

Jhabvala, Ruth Prawer (May 7, 1927)

Davenport, Guy (November 23, 1927)

Stern, Richard G. (February 25, 1928)

Sillitoe, Alan (March 4, 1928)

Angelou, Maya (April 4, 1928)

Ozick, Cynthia (April 17, 1928)

Trevor, William (May 24, 1928)

Fuentes, Carlos (November 11, 1928)

Dick, Philip K. (December 16, 1928)

Friel, Brian (January 9, 1929)

Wolf, Christa (March 18, 1929)

Kundera, Milan (April 1, 1929)

Marshall, Paule (April 9, 1929)

Garrett, George (June 11, 1929)

Grau, Shirley Ann (July 8, 1929)

Le Guin, Ursula K. (October 21, 1929)

Hoch, Edward D. (February 22, 1930)

Friedman, Bruce Jay (April 26, 1930)

Elkin, Stanley (May 11, 1930)

Barth, John (May 27, 1930)

Brodkey, Harold (October 25, 1930)

Ballard, J. G. (November 15, 1930)

Achebe, Chinua (November 16, 1930)

O'Brien, Edna (December 15, 1930)

BORN 1931-1935

Doctorow, E. L. (January 6, 1931)

Richler, Mordecai (January 27, 1931)

Barthelme, Donald (April 7, 1931)

Munro, Alice (July 10, 1931)

Weldon, Fay (September 22, 1931)

Coover, Robert (February 4, 1932)

Updike, John (March 18, 1932)

Gilliatt, Penelope (March 25, 1932)

Betts, Doris (June 4, 1932)

Naipaul, V. S. (August 17, 1932)

Greenberg, Joanne (September 24, 1932)

Plath, Sylvia (October 27, 1932)

Targan, Barry (November 30, 1932)

Michaels, Leonard (January 2, 1933)

Gaines, Ernest J. (January 15, 1933)

Sontag, Susan (January 16, 1933)

Price, Reynolds (February 1, 1933)

Roth, Philip (March 19, 1933)

Gardner, John (July 21, 1933)

Malouf, David (March 20, 1934)

Ellison, Harlan (May 27, 1934)

Berry, Wendell (August 5, 1934)

Rooke, Leon (September 11, 1934)

Baraka, Amiri (October 7, 1934)

Vizenor, Gerald (October 22, 1934)

L'Heureux, John (October 26, 1934)

McGahern, John (November 12, 1934)

Brautigan, Richard (January 30, 1935)

Ōe, Kenzaburō (January 31, 1935)

Gilchrist, Ellen (February 20, 1935)

Kiš, Danilo (February 22, 1935)

Kinsella, W. P. (May 25, 1935)

Shields, Carol (June 2, 1935)

Meckel, Christoph (June 12, 1935)

Proulx, E. Annie (August 22, 1935)

Allen, Woody (December 1, 1935)

Rivera, Tomás (December 22, 1935)

BORN 1936-1940

Conroy, Frank (January 15, 1936)

Vargas Llosa, Mario (March 28, 1936)

Chappell, Fred (May 28, 1936)

Dixon, Stephen (June 6, 1936)

Pearlman, Edith (June 26, 1936)

MacLeod, Alistair (July 20, 1936)

Dubus, Andre (August 11, 1936)

Byatt, A. S. (August 24, 1936)

Burke, James Lee (December 5, 1936)

Major, Clarence (December 31, 1936)

Rasputin, Valentin (March 15, 1937)

Zhang Jie (April 27, 1937)

Pynchon, Thomas (May 8, 1937)

Godwin, Gail (June 18, 1937)
Desai, Anita (June 24, 1937)
Callaghan, Barry (July 5, 1937)
Head, Bessie (July 6, 1937)
Norman, Gurney (July 22, 1937)
Stone, Robert (August 21, 1937)
Harrison, Jim (December 11, 1937)
Ngugi wa Thiong'o (January 5, 1938)
Carver, Raymond (May 25, 1938)
Oates, Joyce Carol (June 16, 1938)
Valenzuela, Luisa (November 26, 1938)
Schwartz, Lynne Sharon (March 19, 1939)
Bambara, Toni Cade (March 25, 1939)
Oz, Amos (May 4, 1939)
Atwood, Margaret (November 18, 1939)
McGuane, Thomas(December 11, 1939)
Disch, Thomas M. (February 2, 1940)
Banks, Russell (March 28, 1940)
Le Clézio, J. M. G. (April 13, 1940)
Mason, Bobbie Ann (May 1, 1940)
Carter, Angela (May 7, 1940)
Mukherjee, Bharati (July 27, 1940)
Kingston, Maxine Hong (October 27, 1940)
Cherry, Kelly (December 21, 1940)

BORN 1941-1945
Wideman, John Edgar (June 14, 1941)
Busch, Frederick (August 1, 1941)
Marshall, Owen (August 17, 1941)
Dovlatov, Sergei (September 3, 1941)
Apple, Max (October 22, 1941)
Tyler, Anne (October 25, 1941)
Woiwode, Larry (October 30, 1941)
Senior, Olive (December 23, 1941)
Aidoo, Ama Ata (March 23, 1942)
Delany, Samuel R. (April 1, 1942)
Dybek, Stuart (April 10, 1942)
Hannah, Barry (April 23, 1942)
Allende, Isabel (August 2, 1942)
Keillor, Garrison (August 7, 1942)
MacLaverty, Bernard (September 14, 1942)
Hospital, Janette Turner (November 12, 1942)
Gay, William (1943)
Ducornet, Rikki (April 19, 1943)
Carey, Peter (May 7, 1943)

Tremain, Rose (August 2, 1943)
Millhauser, Steven (August 3, 1943)
McPherson, James Alan (September 16, 1943)
Tabucchi, Antonio (September 24, 1943)
Barthelme, Frederick (October 10, 1943)
Shepard, Sam (November 5, 1943)
Miller, Sue (November 29, 1943)
Walker, Alice (February 9, 1944)
Williams, Joy (February 11, 1944)
Ford, Richard (February 16, 1944)
Smith, Lee (November 1, 1944)
Lopez, Barry (January 6, 1945)
Butler, Robert Olen (January 20, 1945)
Jones, Thom (January 26, 1945)
Dorris, Michael (January 30, 1945)
Bausch, Richard (April 18, 1945)
Wolff, Tobias (June 19, 1945)
Eisenberg, Deborah (November 20, 1945)

BORN 1946-1950
Barnes, Julian (January 19, 1946)
Kaplan, David Michael (April 9, 1946)
Tilghman, Christopher (September 5, 1946)
O'Brien, Tim (October 1, 1946)
Cliff, Michelle (November 2, 1946)
Robinson, Roxana (November 30, 1946)
Davis, Lydia (1947)
Gates, David (January 8, 1947)
Prose, Francine (April 1, 1947)
Baxter, Charles (May 13, 1947)
Gurganus, Allan (June 11, 1947)
Rushdie, Salman (June 19, 1947)
Helprin, Mark (June 28, 1947)
Beattie, Ann (September 8, 1947)
Carlson, Ron (September 15, 1947)
King, Stephen (September 21, 1947)
Abbott, Lee K. (October 17, 1947)
Gautreaux, Tim (October 19, 1947)
Wiggins, Marianne (November 8, 1947)
Hansen, Ron (December 8, 1947)
Silko, Leslie Marmon (March 5, 1948)
Boylan, Clare (April 21, 1948)
Johnson, Charles (April 23, 1948)
McEwan, Ian (June 21, 1948)
Wicomb, Zoë (November 23, 1948)

Lordan, Beth (December 1, 1948)
Boyle, T. Coraghessan (December 2, 1948)
Murakami, Haruki (January 12, 1949)
Robison, Mary (January 14, 1949)
Allison, Dorothy (April 11, 1949)
Swift, Graham (May 4, 1949)
Kincaid, Jamaica (May 25, 1949)
Johnson, Denis (July 1, 1949)
Russo, Richard (July 15, 1949)
Smiley, Jane (September 26, 1949)
Amis, Martin (August 25, 1949)
Gordon, Mary (December 8, 1949)
Thompson, Jean (January 3, 1950)
Braverman, Kate (February 5, 1950)
Jordan, Neil (February 25, 1950)
Leegant, Joan (May 1, 1950)
Sayles, John (September 28, 1950)
Jones, Edward P. (October 5, 1950)
Hogan, Desmond (December 10, 1950)

Born 1951-1955
Vanderhaeghe, Guy (April 5, 1951)
Tolstaya, Tatyana (May 3, 1951)
Harjo, Joy (May 9, 1951)
Brown, Larry (July 9, 1951)
Card, Orson Scott (August 24, 1951)
Shacochis, Bob (September 9, 1951)
Hempel, Amy (December 14, 1951)
Mosley, Walter (January 12, 1952)
Tan, Amy (February 19, 1952)
Ortiz Cofer, Judith (February 24, 1952)
Powell, Padgett (April 25, 1952)
Pancake, Breece D'J (June 29, 1952)
Mistry, Rohinton (July 3, 1952)
Phillips, Jayne Anne (July 19, 1952)
Crone, Moira (August 10, 1952)
Lee, Andrea (January 1, 1953)
Bloom, Amy (June 18, 1953)
Rash, Ron (September 25, 1953)
Boswell, Robert (December 8, 1953)
Nugent, Beth (1954)
Xu Xi (1954)
Viramontes, Helena María (February 26, 1954)
Wang Anyi (March 6, 1954)
Erdrich, Louise (June 7, 1954)

Tallent, Elizabeth (August 8, 1954)
Mars-Jones, Adam (October 26, 1954)
Ishiguro, Kazuo (November 8, 1954)
Gaitskill, Mary (November 11, 1954)
Kureishi, Hanif (December 5, 1954)
Cisneros, Sandra (December 20, 1954)
Pollock, Donald Ray (December 23, 1954)
Brady, Catherine (January 1, 1955)
Grisham, John (February 8, 1955)
Kingsolver, Barbara (April 8, 1955)
Bissoondath, Neil (April 19, 1955)
Tóibín, Colm (May 30, 1955)
Barrett, Andrea (July 17, 1955)
Richard, Mark (November 9, 1955)

Born 1956-1960
Strout, Elizabeth (January 6, 1956)
Jin, Ha (February 21, 1956)
McKnight, Reginald (February 26, 1956)
Divakaruni, Chitra Banerjee (July 29, 1956)
Galloway, Janice (December 2, 1956)
Minot, Susan (December 7, 1956)
Everett, Percival (December 22, 1956)
Moore, Lorrie (January 13, 1957)
Simpson, Helen (March 2, 1957)
Simpson, Mona (June 14, 1957)
Bell, Madison Smartt (August 1, 1957)
D'Ambrosio, Charles (1958)
Bass, Rick (March 7, 1958)
Lasdun, James (June 8, 1958)
McCorkle, Jill (July 7, 1958)
Offutt, Chris (August 24, 1958)
Lott, Bret (October 8, 1958)
Saunders, George (December 2, 1958)
Donovan, Gerard (1959)
Okri, Ben (March 15, 1959)
Slavin, Julia (1960)
Silver, Marisa (April 23, 1960)
Canin, Ethan (July 19, 1960)
Hagy, Alyson (August 1, 1960)
Winton, Tim (August 4, 1960)
Bank, Melissa (October 11, 1960)
Straight, Susan (October 19, 1960)

BORN 1961-1965

Means, David (1961)
Nelson, Antonya (January 6, 1961)
Earley, Tony (June 15, 1961)
Leavitt, David (June 23, 1961)
Chandra, Vikram (July 23, 1961)
Walbert, Kate (August 13, 1961)
Moody, Rick (October 18, 1961)
Homes, A. M. (December 18, 1961)
Paine, Tom (c. 1962)
Houston, Pam (1962)
Wallace, David Foster (February 21, 1962)
Enright, Anne (October 11, 1962)
Mueenuddin, Daniyal (April, 1963)
Chabon, Michael (May 24, 1963)
Lethem, Jonathan (February 19, 1964)
Benedict, Pinckney (April 12, 1964)
Chaon, Dan (June 11, 1964)
Hemon, Aleksandar (September 9, 1964)
Chang, Lan Samantha (1965)
Waters, Mary Yukari (January 1, 1965)
McCann, Colum (February 28, 1965)
Banner Keith (April 18, 1965)
Kennedy, A. L. (October 22, 1965)

BORN 1966-1970

Reid, Elwood (1966)
Barker, Nicola (March 30, 1966)
Kelman, James (June 9, 1966)
Evenson, Brian (August 12, 1966)
Davies, Peter Ho (August 30, 1966)
Broyard, Bliss (September 5, 1966)
Alexie, Sherman (October 7, 1966)
Almond, Steve (October 27, 1966)

Lahiri, Jhumpa (July 11, 1967)
Johnson, Adam (July 12, 1967)
Peck, Dale (July 13, 1967)
Keegan, Claire (September 2, 1968)
Díaz, Junot (December 31, 1968)
Perabo, Susan (January 6, 1969)
Danticat, Edwidge (January 19, 1969)
Brown, Jason (May 30, 1969)
Bender, Aimee (June 28, 1969)
Englander, Nathan (1970)
Lennon, J. Robert (January 1, 1970)
Haslett, Adam (December 24, 1970)

BORN 1971 AND LATER

Byers, Michael (1971)
Seiffert, Rachel (January, 1971)
Johnston, Bret Anthony (December 23, 1971)
Meloy, Maile (January 1, 1972)
Bynum, Sarah Shun-Lien (February 14, 1972)
Li, Yiyun (November 4, 1972)
Brockmeier, Kevin (December 6, 1972)
Packer, ZZ (January 12, 1973)
Tower, Wells (April 14, 1973)
Bezmogis, David (June 2, 1973)
Orringer, Julie (June 12, 1973)
Doerr, Anthony (October 27, 1973)
Freudenberger, Nell (April 21, 1975)
Alarcón, Daniel (1977)
Adichie, Chimamanda Ngozi (September 15, 1977)
Henríquez, Cristina (1978)
Le, Nam (October 15, 1978)
Yoon, Paul (1980)

INDEXES

CATEGORICAL INDEX

In Critical Survey of Short Fiction, Fourth Revised Edition's *categorical index, the* **boldface** *letter preceding numbers in this index indicate the set in which the entry can be found*: **AF**= American Fiction, **BF**= British, Irish, and Commonweath Ficition, **EF**= European Fiction, **WF**= World Ficition, and **TE**= Topical Essays.

ABSURDISM

Aichinger, Ilse, **EF**: 1
Barth, John, **AF**: 110
Barthelme, Donald, **AF**: 118
Beckett, Samuel, **EF**: 21
Boyle, T. Coraghessan, **AF**: 227
Camus, Albert, **EF**: 64
Caponegro, Mary, **AF**: 333
Coover, Robert, **AF**: 450
Disch, Thomas M., **AF**: 522
Friedman, Bruce Jay, **AF**: 675
L'Heureux, John, **AF**: 1073
Lind, Jakov, **EF**: 231
Powell, Padget, **AF**: 1367
Sartre, Jean-Paul, **EF**: 328
Tower, Wells, **AF**: 1652
Wallace, David Foster, **AF**: 1711

ADVENTURE

Bates, H. E., **BF**: 41
Bellow, Saul, **AF**: 157
Boyle, T. Coraghessan, **AF**: 227
Conrad, Joseph, **BF**: 152
Crane, Stephen, **AF**: 462
Doyle, Sir Arthur Conan, **BF**: 194
Greene, Robert, **BF**: 282
Harrison, Jim, **AF**: 826
Harte, Bret, **AF**: 833
Homer, **EF**: 176
Houston, Pam, **AF**: 912
Johnson, Samuel, **BF**: 336
LeGuin, Ursula K., **AF**: 1057
Petronius, **EF**: 311
Stevenson, Robert Louis, **BF**: 636
Vargas Llosa, Mario, **WF**: 404
Wells, H. G., **BF**: 711
Winton, Tim, **BF**: 721

AFRICAN AMERICAN CULTURE

Angelou, Maya, **AF**: 52
Baldwin, James, **AF**: 77
Bambara, Toni Cade, **AF**: 83
Baraka, Amiri, **AF**: 101
Bontemps, Arna, **AF**: 200
Chesnutt, Charles Waddell, **AF**: 416
Cliff, Michelle, **WF**: 95
Delany, Samuel R., **AF**: 501
Dunbar, Paul Laurence, **AF**: 569
Ellison, Ralph, **AF**: 604
Everett, Percival, **AF**: 621
Gaines, Ernest J., **AF**: 681
Harris, Joel Chandler, **AF**: 820
Himes, Chester, **AF**: 894
Hughes, **AF**: 920
Hurston, Zora Neale, **AF**: 932
Johnson, Charles, **AF**: 971
Jones, Edward P., **AF**: 985
Kincaid, Jamaica, **AF**: 1003
Lee, Andrea, **AF**: 1049
Machado, Joaquim Maria, **WF**: 229
Major, Clarence, **AF**: 1109
Marshall, Paule, **AF**: 1121
McKnight, Reginald, **AF**: 1155
McPherson, James Alan, **AF**: 1159
Mosley, Walter, **AF**: 1209
Packer, ZZ, **AF**: 1294
Petry, Ann, **AF**: 1331
Straight, Susan, **AF**: 1597
Toomer, Jean, **AF**: 1646
Walker, Alice, **AF**: 1701
Wideman, John Edgar, **AF**: 1759
Wright, Richard, **AF**: 1805

AFRICAN CULTURE

Adichie, Chimamanda Ngozi, **WF**: 6
Aidoo, Ama Ata, **WF**: 16
Head, Bessie, **WF**: 178

Dostoevski, Fyodor, **WF:** 118
Erdrich, Louise, **AF:** 612
Fox, Paula, **AF:** 654
Hemon, Aleksandar, **EF:** 154
Henríquez, Cristina, **AF:** 879
Hesse, Hermann, **EF:** 158
Higgins, Aidan, **BF:** 298
Hogan, Desmond, **BF:** 303
Houston, Pam, **AF:** 912
Jhabvala, Ruth Prawer, **BF:** 332
Johnson, Charles, **AF:** 971
Jones, Thom, **AF:** 989
Jordan, Neil, **BF:** 342
Laurence, Margaret, **BF:** 403
Lavin, Mary, **BF:** 408
Lawrence, D. H., **BF:** 415
Lee, Andrea, **AF:** 1049
Michaels, Leonard, **AF:** 1179
Moravia, **EF:** 267
Naipaul, V. S., **WF:** 272
Nerval, Gerard de, **EF:** 276
Ngugi wa Thiongo, **WF:** 282
O'Faoláin, Seán, **BF:** 552
Ortiz Cofer, Judith, **AF:** 1283
Plomer, William, **BF:** 565
Richler, Mordecai, **BF:** 583
Salter, James, **AF:** 1462
Saroyan, William, **AF:** 1466
Sayles, John, **AF:** 1475
Schwartz, Delmore, **AF:** 1479
Shalamov, Varlam, **WF:** 354
Sontag, Susan, **AF:** 1541
Stafford, Jean, **AF:** 1551
Thurber, James, **AF:** 1637
Weidman, Jerome, **AF:** 1725
Wiggins, Marianne, **AF:** 1767
Williams, Tennessee, **AF:** 1776
Williams, William Carlos, **AF:** 1783
Woiwode, Larry, **AF:** 1788
Wolf, Christa, **EF:** 389
Wolff, Tobias, **AF:** 1799

BLACK HUMOR

Atwood, Margaret, **BF:** 11
Bierce, Ambrose, **AF:** 190
Bradbury, Ray, **AF:** 235
Caponegro, Mary, **AF:** 333
Collier, John, **BF:** 143

Dick, Philip K., **AF:** 516
Disch, Thomas M., **AF:** 522
Elkin, Stanley, **AF:** 586
Friedman, Bruce Jay, **AF:** 675
Gurganus, Allan, **AF:** 782
Highsmith, Patricia, **AF:** 887
Homes, A. M., **AF:** 908
Okri, Ben, **WF:** 295
Perelman, S. J., **AF:** 1326
Pynchon, Thomas, **AF:** 1400
Richler, Mordecai, **BF:** 583
Stuart, Jesse, **AF:** 1606
Thurber, James, **AF:** 1637
Vonnegut, Kurt, **AF:** 1688
Weldon, Fay, **BF:** 705
Wilson, Angus, **BF:** 717

BRITISH CULTURE

Amis, Martin, **BF:** 6
Bowen, Elizabeth, **BF:** 64
Carter, Angela, **BF:** 104
Coppard, A. E., **BF:** 162
Dahl, Roald, **BF:** 168
Davies, Rhys, **BF:** 174
Delamare, Walter, **BF:** 179
Dickens, Charles, **BF:** 184
Doyle, Sir Arthur Conan, **BF:** 194
Eliot, George, **BF:** 218
Fitzgerald, Penelope, **BF:** 227
Forster, E. M., **BF:** 231
Fowles, John, **BF:** 237
Galsworthy, John, **BF:** 258
Garrett, George, **AF:** 704
Greene, Graham, **BF:** 275
Greene, Robert, **BF:** 282
Hardy, Thomas, **BF:** 288
Kelman, James, **BF:** 364
Kipling, Rudyard, **BF:** 385
Kureishi, Hanif, **BF:** 394
Lawrence, D. H., **BF:** 415
Malory, Sir Thomas, **BF:** 469
McEwan, Ian, **BF:** 505
Pritchett, V. S., **BF:** 569
Saki, **BF:** 595
Sillitoe, Alan, **BF:** 620
Simpson, Helen, **AF:** 1517
Spark, Muriel, **BF:** 625
Taylor, Elizabeth, **BF:** 646

EASTERN UNITED STATES

EGYPTIAN CULTURE

EPIC

EPIPHANY

EXPRESSIONISM

Joyce, James, **BF:** 346
Kafka, Franz, **EF:** 182
Lu Xun, **WF:** 219
Schulz, Bruno, **EF:** 335
Williams, Tennessee, **AF:** 1776
Zamyatin, Yevgeny, **WF:** 424

FABLE

Agee, James, **AF:** 10
Akutagawa, Ryunosuke, **WF:** 20
Anderson, Hans Christian, **EF:** 9
Arreola, Juan Jose, **WF:** 39
Barth, John, **AF:** 110
Barthelme, Donald, **AF:** 118
Baxter, Charles, **AF:** 140
Beckett, Samuel, **EF:** 21
Bender, Aimee, **AF:** 164
Benet, Stephen Vincent, **AF:** 171
Boccaccio, Giovanni, **EF:** 28
Boll, Heinrich, **EF:** 34
Borges, Jorge Luis, **WF:** 62
Bowles, Paul, **AF:** 212
Callaghan, Barry, **BF:** 83
Calvino, Italo, **EF:** 58
Camus, Albert, **EF:** 64
Cervantes, Miguel de, **EF:** 74
Chaucer, Geoffrey, **BF:** 108
Cheever, John, **AF:** 403
Chekhov, Anton, **WF:** 86
Clark, Walter Van Tilburg, **AF:** 435
Delamare, Walter, **BF:** 179
Dinesen, Isak, **EF:** 114
Dostoevski, Fyodor, **WF:** 118
Ducornet, Rikki, **AF:** 565
Fitzgerald, F. Scott, **AF:** 640
Fox, Paula, **AF:** 654
Garcia Marquez, Gabriel, **WF:** 145
Gardner, John, **AF:** 691
Godwin, Gail, **AF:** 745
Goethe, Johann, **EF:** 141
Grimm, Brothers, **EF:** 147
Harris, Joel Chandler, **AF:** 820
Hawkesworth, John, **BF:** 294
Hawthorne, Nathaniel, **AF:** 843
Hearn, Lafcadio, **WF:** 182
Helprin, Mark, **AF:** 858
Johnson, Charles, **AF:** 971

Kinsella, W. P., **BF:** 379
Kipling, Rudyard, **BF:** 385
Malamud, Bernard, **AF:** 1113
Marie de France, **EF:** 244
Melville, Herman, **AF:** 1172
Poe, Edgar Allan, **AF:** 1346
Pu Songling, **WF:** 316
Pynchon, Thomas, **AF:** 1400
Quiroga, Horacio, **WF:** 330
Stockton, Frank R., **AF:** 1589
Thurber, James, **AF:** 1637
Vonnegut, Kurt, **AF:** 1688
Zhang Jie, **WF:** 430

FAIRY TALE

Anderson, Hans Christian, **EF:** 9
Brockmeier, Kevin, **AF:** 261
Busch, Frederick, **AF:** 291
Byatt, A. S., **BF:** 78
Bynum, Sarah Shun-Lien, **AF:** 303
Carter, Angela, **BF:** 104
Delamare, Walter, **BF:** 179
Douglas, Ellen, **AF:** 550
Dunsany, Lord, **BF:** 203
Goethe, Johann, **EF:** 141
Grimm, Brothers, **EF:** 147
Hesse, Hermann, **EF:** 158
Hoffmann, E. T. A., **EF:** 170
Lind, Jakov, **EF:** 231
Rooke, Leon, **BF:** 589
Stockton, Frank R., **AF:** 1589
Thurber, James, **AF:** 1637
Warner, Sylvia Townsend, **BF:** 692
Yeats, William Butler, **BF:** 732

FANTASY

Aiken, Conrad, **AF:** 14
Alarcón, Pedro Antonio de, **EF:** 4
Allende, Isabel, **WF:** 35
Amis, Martin, **BF:** 6
Beerbohm, Max, **BF:** 47
Bell, Madison Smartt, **AF:** 153
Bombal, Maria Luisa, **WF:** 58
Borges, Jorge Luis, **WF:** 62
Boyle, T. Coraghessan, **AF:** 227
Bradbury, Ray, **AF:** 235
Brockmeier, Kevin, **AF:** 261
Buzzati, Dino, **EF:** 52

LOCAL COLOR

Cable, George Washington, **AF:** 308
Caldwell, Erskine, **AF:** 318
Crone, Moira, **AF:** 471
Grau, Shirley Ann, **AF:** 767
Hall, Martha Lacy, **AF:** 799
Harte, Bret, **AF:** 833
Henry, O., **AF:** 882
Humphrey, William, **AF:** 926
Jewett, Sarah Orne, **AF:** 961
Keillor, Garrison, **AF:** 996
Mérimée, Prosper, **EF:** 263
Offutt, Chris, **AF:** 1264
Shacochis, Bob, **AF:** 1488
Simms, William Gilmore, **AF:** 1510
Still, James, **AF:** 1585
Straight, Susan, **AF:** 1597
Strout, Elizabeth, **AF:** 1602
Stuart, Jesse, **AF:** 1606
Tabucchi, Antonio, **EF:** 355
Thompson, Jean, **AF:** 1635
Twain, Mark, **AF:** 1656
Tóibín, Colm, **BF:** 662
Vargas Llosa, Mario, **WF:** 404
Wallace, David Foster, **AF:** 1711
Waters, Mary Yukari, **AF:** 1721
Welty, Eudora, **AF:** 1729
Winton, Tim, **BF:** 721

LYRICAL SHORT STORIES

Abbott, Lee K., **AF:** 1
Agnon, Shmuel Yosef, **WF:** 10
Aiken, Conrad, **AF:** 14
Anderson, Sherwood, **AF:** 45
Bates, H. E., **BF:** 41
Cheever, John, **AF:** 403
Chekhov, Anton, **WF:** 86
D'Ambrosio, Charles, **AF:** 475
Dostoevski, Fyodor, **WF:** 118
Gautreaux, Tim, **AF:** 719
Hogan, Desmond, **BF:** 303
Kawabata, Yasunari, **WF:** 201
Kincaid, Jamaica, **AF:** 1003
Lawrence, D. H., **BF:** 415
Lispector, Clarice, **WF:** 213
Major, Clarence, **AF:** 1109
Mansfield, Katherine, **BF:** 477

McGahern, John, **BF:** 510
Ozick, Cynthia, **AF:** 1287
Paine, Tom, **AF:** 1298
Paley, Grace, **AF:** 1301
Pasternak, Boris, **WF:** 310
Phillips, Jayne Anne, **AF:** 1338
Richard, Mark, **AF:** 1422
Roberts, Elizabeth, **AF:** 1430
Salter, James, **AF:** 1462
Steinbeck, John, **AF:** 1573
Thomas, Dylan, **BF:** 656
Turgenev, Ivan, **WF:** 391
Updike, John, **AF:** 1668
Wang Anyi, **WF:** 409
Welty, Eudora, **AF:** 1729
Wolff, Tobias, **AF:** 1799
Woolf, Virginia, **BF:** 725
Yoon, Paul, **AF:** 1811
Zola, Emile, **EF:** 395

MAGICAL REALISM

Allende, Isabel, **WF:** 35
Bass, Rick, **AF:** 130
Bombal, Maria Luisa, **WF:** 58
Borges, Jorge Luis, **WF:** 62
Calvino, Italo, **EF:** 58
Carpentier, Alejo, **WF:** 78
Cortazar, Julio, **WF:** 99
Dybek, Stuart, **AF:** 573
Fuentes, Carlos, **WF:** 138
Garcia Marquez, Gabriel, **WF:** 145
Guimaraes Rosa, Joao, **WF:** 173
Harjo, Joy, **AF:** 816
Kincaid, Jamaica, **AF:** 1003
L'Heureux, John, **AF:** 1073
Lordan, Beth, **AF:** 1095
Lott, Brett, **AF:** 1099
Slavin, Julia, **AF:** 1525
Valenzuela, Luisa, **WF:** 400
Vizenor, Gerald R., **AF:** 1683

MANNERS, FICTION OF

Auchincloss, Louis, **AF:** 67
Cheever, John, **AF:** 403
Hale, Nancy, **AF:** 791
Saki, **BF:** 595
Wilson, Angus, **BF:** 717

O'Hara, John, **AF:** 1268
Perabo, Susan, **AF:** 1323
Poe, Edgar Allan, **AF:** 1346
Porter, Katherine Anne, **AF:** 1359
Powers, J. F., **AF:** 1371
Pritchett, V. S., **BF:** 569
Sansom, William, **BF:** 599
Saroyan, William, **AF:** 1466
Schulz, Bruno, **EF:** 335
Scott, Sir Walter, **BF:** 606
Steele, Wilbur Daniel, **AF:** 1556
Stevenson, Robert Louis, **BF:** 636
Taylor, Peter, **AF:** 1629
Updike, John, **AF:** 1668
Verga, Giovanni, **EF:** 365
Welty, Eudora, **AF:** 1729
White, E. B., **AF:** 1755
Wolff, Tobias, **AF:** 1799

MODERNISM

Anderson, Sherwood, **AF:** 45
Bates, H. E., **BF:** 41
Bell, Madison Smartt, **AF:** 153
Callaghan, Morley, **BF:** 87
Cheever, John, **AF:** 403
Chekhov, Anton, **WF:** 86
Davenport, Guy, **AF:** 483
Elliott, George P., **AF:** 591
Hemingway, Ernest, **AF:** 866
Henry, O., **AF:** 882
Houston, Pam, **AF:** 912
James, Henry, **AF:** 952
Joyce, James, **BF:** 346
Lewis, Wyndham, **BF:** 447
Malamud, Bernard, **AF:** 1113
Mansfield, Katherine, **BF:** 477
Salter, James, **AF:** 1462
Schulz, Bruno, **EF:** 335
Smiley, Jane, **AF:** 1528
Svevo, Italo, **EF:** 351
Updike, John, **AF:** 1668
Walser, Robert, **EF:** 383
Wharton, Edith, **AF:** 1748
Williams, William Carlos, **AF:** 1783
Wright, Richard, **AF:** 1805

MORAL STORIES

Aidoo, Ama Ata, **WF:** 16
Austen, Jane, **BF:** 20
Berry, Wendell, **AF:** 180
Boccaccio, Giovanni, **EF:** 28
Carver, Raymond, **AF:** 358
Dickens, Charles, **BF:** 184
Douglas, Ellen, **AF:** 550
Edgeworth, Maria, **BF:** 209
Eliot, George, **BF:** 218
Flaubert, Gustave, **EF:** 122
Fox, Paula, **AF:** 654
Franklin, Benjamin, **AF:** 658
Gautreaux, Tim, **AF:** 719
Gay, William, **AF:** 723
Hansen, Ron, **AF:** 812
Hawkesworth, John, **BF:** 294
Hawthorne, Nathaniel, **AF:** 843
Helprin, Mark, **AF:** 858
Homes, A. M., **AF:** 908
Joyce, James, **BF:** 346
Lardner, Ring, **AF:** 1037
Leskov, Nikolai, **WF:** 207
Lopez, Barry, **AF:** 1091
Malamud, Bernard, **AF:** 1113
Moravia, Alberto, **EF:** 267
Mosley, Walter, **AF:** 1209
Parker, Dorothy, **AF:** 1311
Pasternak, Boris, **WF:** 310
Porter, Katherine Anne, **AF:** 1359
Powers, J. F., **AF:** 1371
Pu Songling, **WF:** 316
Quiroga, Horacio, **WF:** 330
Simms, William Gilmore, **AF:** 1510
Spencer, Elizabeth, **AF:** 1545
Stevenson, Robert Louis, **BF:** 636
Sturgeon, Theodore, **AF:** 1612
Tilghman, Christopher, **AF:** 1642
Tolstoy, Leo, **WF:** 382
Twain, Mark, **AF:** 1656
Unamuno y Jugo, Miguel de, **EF:** 360
Wain, John, **BF:** 688

MYTHIC STORIES

Borges, Jorge Luis, **WF:** 62
Cheever, John, **AF:** 403
Davenport, Guy, **AF:** 483
Derleth, August, **AF:** 507

PAKISTANI CULTURE

Kureishi, Hanif, **BF:** 394
Mueenuddin, Daniyal, **WF:** 249

PARABLE

Callaghan, Barry, **BF:** 83
Erdrich, Louise, **AF:** 612
Gold, Herbert, **AF:** 749
Hawthorne, Nathaniel, **AF:** 843

PARODY

Alexie, Sherman, **AF:** 23
Allen, Woody, **AF:** 31
Austen, Jane, **BF:** 20
Barthelme, Donald, **AF:** 118
Beerbohm, Max, **BF:** 47
Borges, Jorge Luis, **WF:** 62
Boyle, T. Coraghessan, **AF:** 227
Chekhov, Anton, **WF:** 86
Coover, Robert, **AF:** 450
Crane, Stephen, **AF:** 462
Dostoevski, Fyodor, **WF:** 118
Dunsany, Lord, **BF:** 203
Elkin, Stanley, **AF:** 586
Elliott, George P., **AF:** 591
Evenson, Brian, **AF:** 617
Fitzgerald, F. Scott, **AF:** 640
Nabokov, Vladimir, **AF:** 1214
Perelman, S. J., **AF:** 1326
Poe, Edgar Allan, **AF:** 1346
Pynchon, Thomas, **AF:** 1400
Rooke, Leon, **BF:** 589
Saki, **BF:** 595
Thurber, James, **AF:** 1637
Twain, Mark, **AF:** 1656
White, E. B., **AF:** 1755
Zoshchenko, Mikhail, **WF:** 436

PHILOSOPHICAL STORIES

Akutagawa, Ryunosuke, **WF:** 20
Amis, Martin, **BF:** 6
Barth, John, **AF:** 110
Beckett, Samuel, **EF:** 21
Bellow, Saul, **AF:** 157
Boccaccio, Giovanni, **EF:** 28
Borges, Jorge Luis, **WF:** 62
Buzzati, Dino, **EF:** 52

Callaghan, Morley, **BF:** 87
Camus, Albert, **EF:** 64
Dostoevski, Fyodor, **WF:** 118
Faulkner, William, **AF:** 632
Gass, William H., **AF:** 710
Goldsmith, Oliver, **BF:** 269
Hesse, Hermann, **EF:** 158
Hospital, Janette Turner, **BF:** 308
Johnson, Charles, **AF:** 971
Johnson, Samuel, **BF:** 336
Jones, Thom, **AF:** 989
Kundera, Milan, **EF:** 200
LeGuin, Ursula K., **AF:** 1057
Mann, Thomas, **EF:** 235
Maupassant, Guy de, **EF:** 250
Moody, Rick, **AF:** 1195
Naipaul, V. S., **WF:** 272
O'Connor, Flannery, **AF:** 1255
Pavese, Cesare, **EF:** 301
Pirandello, Luigi, **EF:** 317
Sartre, Jean-Paul, **EF:** 328
Unamuno y Jugo, Miguel de, **EF:** 360
Valenzuela, Luisa, **WF:** 400
Vanderhaeghe, Guy, **BF:** 684
Vargas Llosa, Mario, **WF:** 404
Voltaire, **EF:** 376
Wallace, David Foster, **AF:** 1711

POETIC SHORT STORIES

Braverman, Kate, **AF:** 257
Chaucer, Geoffrey, **BF:** 108
Cliff, Michelle, **WF:** 95
Dante, **EF:** 96
Davis, Lydia, **AF:** 497
Homer, **EF:** 176
Kawabata, Yasunari, **WF:** 201
Marie de France, **EF:** 244
Means, David, **AF:** 1164
Michaels, Leonard, **AF:** 1179
Ovid, **EF:** 286
Roberts, Elizabeth, **AF:** 1430
Vergil, **EF:** 370
Yeats, William Butler, **BF:** 732
Zola, Emile, **EF:** 395

POSTMODERNISM

Alexie, Sherman, **AF:** 23
Amis, Martin, **BF:** 6

Evenson, Brian, **AF**: 617
Farrell, James T., **AF**: 626
Faulkner, William, **AF**: 632
Fitzgerald, F. Scott, **AF**: 640
Flaubert, Gustave, **EF**: 122
Forster, E. M., **BF**: 231
Gaines, Ernest J., **AF**: 681
Gaitskill, Mary, **AF**: 687
Gallant, Mavis, **BF**: 248
Gardner, John, **AF**: 691
Gay, William, **AF**: 723
Gilman, Charlotte Perkins, **AF**: 735
Glasgow, Ellen, **AF**: 739
Godwin, Gail, **AF**: 745
Gordimer, Nadine, **WF**: 159
Gordon, Caroline, **AF**: 753
Greenberg, Joanne, **AF**: 773
Greene, Graham, **BF**: 275
Hansen, Ron, **AF**: 812
Harjo, Joy, **AF**: 816
Haslett, Adam, **AF**: 840
Hawthorne, Nathaniel, **AF**: 843
Hempel, Amy, **AF**: 875
Himes, Chester, **AF**: 894
Homes, A. M., **AF**: 908
Hospital, Janette Turner, **BF**: 308
Ishiguro, Kazuo, **BF**: 318
James, Henry, **AF**: 952
Johnson, Charles, **AF**: 971
King, Stephen, **AF**: 1009
Kundera, Milan, **EF**: 200
Lawson, Henry, **BF**: 424
Leavitt, David, **AF**: 1041
Lessing, Doris, **BF**: 439
Lispector, Clarice, **WF**: 213
Marshall, Paule, **AF**: 1121
Mishima, Yukio, **WF**: 239
Mukherjee, Bharati, **WF**: 253
Munro, Alice, **BF**: 523
Oates, Joyce Carol, **AF**: 1240
O'Brien, Edna, **BF**: 534
O'Brien, Tim, **AF**: 1251
Offutt, Chris, **AF**: 1264
Ozick, Cynthia, **AF**: 1287
Paley, Grace, **AF**: 1301
Peretz, Isaac Leib, **EF**: 306
Petry, Ann, **AF**: 1331
Pirandello, Luigi, **EF**: 317

Plath, Sylvia, **AF**: 1342
Poe, Edgar Allan, **AF**: 1346
Porter, Katherine Anne, **AF**: 1359
Price, Reynolds, **AF**: 1375
Purdy, James, **AF**: 1392
Schwartz, Lynne, Sharon, **AF**: 1484
Seiffert, Rachel, **BF**: 611
Shepard, Sam, **AF**: 1495
Shields, Carol, **BF**: 615
Silver, Marisa, **AF**: 1507
Simpson, Helen, **AF**: 1517
Still, James, **AF**: 1585
Straight, Susan, **AF**: 1597
Tabucchi, Antonio, **EF**: 355
Thompson, Jean, **AF**: 1635
Tolstoy, Leo, **WF**: 382
Tower, Wells, **AF**: 1652
Tóibín, Colm, **BF**: 662
Walbert, Kate, **AF**: 1697
Wang Anyi, **WF**: 409
Waters, Mary Yukari, **AF**: 1721
Wicomb, Zoë, **WF**: 415
Winton, Tim, **BF**: 721
Wolf, Christa, **EF**: 389

PSYCHOLOGICAL STORIES

Aiken, Conrad, **AF**: 14
Almond, Steve, **AF**: 41
Bloom, Amy, **AF**: 196
Boswell, Robert, **AF**: 204
Chaucer, Geoffrey, **BF**: 108
Conrad, Joseph, **BF**: 152
D'Ambrosio, Charles, **AF**: 475
Dinesen, Isak, **EF**: 114
Evenson, Brian, **AF**: 617
Galloway, Janice, **BF**: 254
Goethe, Johann, **EF**: 141
Goyen, William, **AF**: 763
Hardy, Thomas, **BF**: 288
Haslett, Adam, **AF**: 840
Higgins, Aidan, **BF**: 298
Highsmith, Patricia, **AF**: 887
Kavan, Anna, **BF**: 355
LeClezio, J. M. G., **EF**: 220
LeFanu, Joseph Sheridan, **BF**: 432
L'Heureux, John, **AF**: 1073
Maupassant, Guy de, **EF**: 250
Means, David, **AF**: 1164

REGIONAL STORIES

RUSSIAN CULTURE

SATIRE

SCIENCE FICTION

SCIENCE FICTION *(continued)*

Clarke, Arthur C., **BF:** 136
Delany, Samuel R., **AF:** 501
Dick, Philip K., **AF:** 516
Disch, Thomas M., **AF:** 522
Doyle, Sir Arthur Conan, **BF:** 194
Ducornet, Rikki, **AF:** 565
Ellison, Harlan, **AF:** 597
Forster, E. M., **BF:** 231
Heinlein, Robert A., **AF:** 852
Huxley, Aldous, **BF:** 312
Johnson, Adam, **AF:** 967
Kavan, Anna, **BF:** 355
LeGuin, Ursula K., **AF:** 1057
O'Brien, Fitz-James, **BF:** 541
Poe, Edgar Allan, **AF:** 1346
Stockton, Frank R., **AF:** 1589
Sturgeon, Theodore, **AF:** 1612
Twain, Mark, **AF:** 1656
Vonnegut, Kurt, **AF:** 1688
Wells, H. G., **BF:** 711

SHORT SHORT STORY

Almond, Steve, **AF:** 41
Davis, Lydia, **AF:** 497
Highsmith, Patricia, **AF:** 887
Kawabata, Yasunari, **WF:** 201
McCorkle, Jill, **AF:** 1140

SKETCHES

Addison, Joseph, **BF:** 1
Alarcón, Pedro Antonio de, **EF:** 4
Berry, Wendell, **AF:** 180
Bierce, Ambrose, **AF:** 190
Borowski, Tadeusz, **EF:** 40
Bunin, Ivan, **WF:** 72
Callaghan, Morley, **BF:** 87
Chekhov, Anton, **WF:** 86
Cisneros, Sandra, **AF:** 428
Crane, Stephen, **AF:** 462
Dickens, Charles, **BF:** 184
Doerr, Harriet, **AF:** 541
Dovlatov, Sergei, **WF:** 124
Dunbar, Paul Laurence, **AF:** 569
Erdrich, Louise, **AF:** 612
Franklin, Benjamin, **AF:** 658
Garrett, George, **AF:** 704
Gilliatt, Penelope, **BF:** 263

Goldsmith, Oliver, **BF:** 269
Gordon, Caroline, **AF:** 753
Grimm, Brothers, **EF:** 147
Huxley, Aldous, **BF:** 312
Irving, Washington, **AF:** 939
James, Henry, **AF:** 952
Jhabvala, Ruth Prawer, **BF:** 332
Kincaid, Jamaica, **AF:** 1003
Lagerkvist, Par, **EF:** 209
Lessing, Doris, **BF:** 439
Longstreet, Augustus Baldwin, **AF:** 1086
Mansfield, Katherine, **BF:** 477
Narayan, R. K., **WF:** 276
Oates, Joyce Carol, **AF:** 1240
Pardo Bazán, Emilia, **EF:** 295
Price, Reynolds, **AF:** 1375
Steele, Sir Richard, **BF:** 631
Thackeray, William Makepeace, **BF:** 650
Thurber, James, **AF:** 1637
Toomer, Jean, **AF:** 1646
Twain, Mark, **AF:** 1656
Zoshchenko, Mikhail, **WF:** 436

SOCIAL CRITICISM

Adichie, Chimamanda Ngozi, **WF:** 6
Baldwin, James, **AF:** 77
Bambara, Toni Cade, **AF:** 83
Banks, Russell, **AF:** 91
Brecht, Bertolt, **EF:** 45
Bunin, Ivan, **WF:** 72
Burke, James Lee, **AF:** 287
Caldwell, Erskine, **AF:** 318
Cliff, Michelle, **WF:** 95
Dovlatov, Sergei, **WF:** 124
Dunbar, Paul Laurence, **AF:** 569
Eisenberg, Deborah, **AF:** 582
France, Anatole, **EF:** 130
Galsworthy, John, **BF:** 258
Gogol, Nikolai, **WF:** 151
Gordimer, Nadine, **WF:** 159
Grisham, John, **AF:** 778
Kingston, Maxine Hong, **AF:** 1022
Kureishi, Hanif, **BF:** 394
Maupassant, Guy de, **EF:** 250
Mosley, Walter, **AF:** 1209
Mueenuddin, Daniyal, **WF:** 249
Narayan, R. K., **WF:** 276
Ngugi wa Thiongo, **WF:** 282

Paine, Tom, **AF:** 1298
Pynchon, Thomas, **AF:** 1400
Robison, Mary, **AF:** 1437
Saunders, George, **AF:** 1471
Senior, Olive, **WF:** 350
Shacochis, Bob, **AF:** 1488
Taylor, Elizabeth, **BF:** 646
Verga, Giovanni, **EF:** 365
Viramontes Helena Maria, **AF:** 1680
Voltaire, **EF:** 376
Wain, John, **BF:** 688
Walker, Alice, **AF:** 1701
Zamyatin, Yevgeny, **WF:** 424

SOCIAL REALISM

Achebe, Chinua, **WF:** 1
Aiken, Conrad, **AF:** 14
Alarcón, Daniel, **WF:** 25
Alexie, Sherman, **AF:** 23
Allende, Isabel, **WF:** 35
Allison, Dorothy, **AF:** 37
Angelou, Maya, **AF:** 52
Atwood, Margaret, **BF:** 11
Auchincloss, Louis, **AF:** 67
Baldwin, James, **AF:** 77
Balzac, Honoré de, **EF:** 16
Bambara, Toni Cade, **AF:** 83
Barthelme, Frederick, **AF:** 126
Bass, Rick, **AF:** 130
Boll, Heinrich, **EF:** 34
Borowski, Tadeusz, **EF:** 40
Bowen, Elizabeth, **BF:** 64
Bowles, Jane, **AF:** 206
Boyle, Kay, **AF:** 219
Burke, James Lee, **AF:** 287
Calisher, Hortense, **AF:** 323
Camus, Albert, **EF:** 64
Carleton, William, **BF:** 98
Cather, Willa, **AF:** 371
Chabon, Michael, **AF:** 377
Chappell, Fred, **AF:** 398
Cheever, John, **AF:** 403
Chekhov, Anton, **WF:** 86
Chesnutt, Charles Waddell, **AF:** 416
Chopin, Kate, **AF:** 423
Cisneros, Sandra, **AF:** 428
Cliff, Michelle, **WF:** 95
Colette, **EF:** 87

Cozzens, James Gould, **AF:** 457
Daudet, Alphonse, **EF:** 102
Dybek, Stuart, **AF:** 573
Earley, Tony, **AF:** 578
Ellison, Ralph, **AF:** 604
Fitzgerald, F. Scott, **AF:** 640
Ford, Richard, **AF:** 648
France, Anatole, **EF:** 130
Freeman, Mary E. Wilkins, **AF:** 664
Gaines, Ernest J., **AF:** 681
Gallant, Mavis, **BF:** 248
Gardner, John, **AF:** 691
Gordimer, Nadine, **WF:** 159
Gordon, Caroline, **AF:** 753
Gorky, Maxim, **WF:** 168
Hannah, Barry, **AF:** 807
Head, Bessie, **WF:** 178
Howells, William Dean, **AF:** 915
Huxley, Aldous, **BF:** 312
Jones, Edward P., **AF:** 985
Kelman, James, **BF:** 364
Kingsolver, Barbara, **AF:** 1018
Kundera, Milan, **EF:** 200
Lagerkvist, Par, **EF:** 209
Lavin, Mary, **BF:** 408
Lott, Brett, **AF:** 1099
Lu Xun, **WF:** 219
MacLaverty, Bernard, **BF:** 461
Mason, Bobbie Ann, **AF:** 1127
McGuane, Thomas, **AF:** 1151
McPherson, James Alan, **AF:** 1159
Minot, Susan, **AF:** 1191
Moore, George, **BF:** 518
Moore, Lorrie, **AF:** 1199
Mueenuddin, Daniyal, **WF:** 249
Mukherjee, Bharati, **WF:** 253
Ngugi wa Thiongo, **WF:** 282
Oates, Joyce Carol, **AF:** 1240
Ozick, Cynthia, **AF:** 1287
Packer, ZZ, **AF:** 1294
Parker, Dorothy, **AF:** 1311
Petry, Ann, **AF:** 1331
Pollock, Donald Ray, **AF:** 1355
Porter, Katherine Anne, **AF:** 1359
Price, Reynolds, **AF:** 1375
Purdy, James, **AF:** 1392
Rash, Ron, **AF:** 1415
Rasputin, Valentin, **WF:** 337

SPANISH CULTURE

SUPERNATURAL STORIES

SURREALISM

SUBJECT INDEX

All personages whose names appear in **boldface** *type in this index are the subjects of articles in* Critical Survey of Short Fiction, Fourth Revised Edition. *The* **boldface** *letter preceding numbers in this index indicate the set in which the entry can be found:* **AF**= American Fiction, **BF**= British, Irish, and Commonweath Fiction, **EF**= European Fiction, **WF**= World Fiction, and **TE**= Topical Essays.

A

"A & P" (Updike), **AF:** 1671, **TE:** 278

"A la deriva." *See* "Drifting"

A legião estrangeira. See *Foreign Legion, The*

"A. V. Laider" (Beerbohm), **TE:** 248

Aarne, Antti, **TE:** 49

Aarne-Thompson Index, **TE:** 49

Abad, Mercedes, **TE:** 525

"Abattoir" (Nugent), **AF:** 1237

"Abbé Aubain, The", **TE:** 221

Abbott, Lee K., **AF:** 1-4, **TE:** 285

'Abdallah, Yahya Taher, **TE:** 473

Abd al Qadir, Abdullah, **TE:** 474

Abel Sánchez (Unamuno y Jugo), **EF:** 361

Aboulela, Leila, **TE:** 312

"About Loving Women" (Douglas), **AF:** 551

"Abrazo de Vergara, El." *See* "Embrace at Vergara, The"

"Abroad" (Gordimer), **WF:** 162

"Absence of Mercy" (Stone), **AF:** 1595

Absurd literature, **EF:** 21

Accident: A Day's News (Wolf), **EF:** 392

"Accompanist, The" (Desai), **WF:** 112

"Accompanist, The" (Pritchett), **BF:** 575

"Accomplice" (Bynum), **AF:** 304

"Accounting" (Leegant), **AF:** 1055

Achebe, Chinua, **WF:** 1-6, **TE:** 307

Acquainted with the Night, and Other Stories (Schwartz, L. S.), **AF:** 1485

Acres and Pains (Perelman), **AF:** 1327

"Across the Bridge" (Gallant), **BF:** 252

"Across the Lake" (Eisenberg), **AF:** 584

Actual, The (Bellow), **AF:** 161

"Adam, One Afternoon" (Calvino), **EF:** 60

Adams, Alice, **AF:** 5-9

Addison, Joseph, **BF:** 1-6, **TE:** 179, **TE:** 189, **TE:** 190

Adichie, Chimamanda Ngozi, **WF:** 6-10

"Admiral and the Nuns, The" (Tuohy), **BF:** 680

"Admiralty Spire, The" (Nabokov), **AF:** 1218

"Adoration of the Magi, The" (Yeats), **BF:** 735

"Adore Her" (Robison), **AF:** 1442

"Adrianna Takes a Trip" (Pirandello), **EF:** 320

"Adulterous Woman, The" (Camus, A.), **EF:** 65

"Adultery" (Dubus), **AF:** 562

"Advanced Beginners" (Bank), **AF:** 89

"Advancing Luna" (Walker), **TE:** 326

"Adventure of a Bather, The" (Calvino), **EF:** 61

"Adventure of the Camberwell Beauty, The" (Derleth), **AF:** 510

"Adventure of the Dancing Men, The" (Doyle), **BF:** 199

"Adventure of the Empty House, The" (Doyle), **BF:** 199

"Adventure of the Remarkable Worm, The" (Derleth), **AF:** 509

"Adventure of the Rudberg Numbers, The" (Derleth), **AF:** 509

Adventures of Ellery Queen, The (Queen), **TE:** 22

Aeneid (Vergil), **EF:** 371, **TE:** 115, **TE:** 117

"Aeroplanes at Brescia, The" (Davenport), **AF:** 485

Aesop (Caxton), **TE:** 34, **TE:** 37, **TE:** 113

Aestheticism, **EF:** 403

Aesthetic movement, **BF:** 48

Afolabi, Segun, **TE:** 312

Africa, **TE:** 301

African American culture, **TE:** 315-331; African American short fiction, **TE:** 315

African culture, **TE:** 301-314; African short fiction, **TE:** 301

"After Holbein" (Wharton), **AF:** 1751

After Leston (Lott), **AF:** 1101

Afterlife, and Other Stories, The (Updike), **AF:** 1676, **TE:** 278

"After Long Absence" (Hospital), **BF:** 309

"Aftermath" (Waters), **AF:** 1723

K

Salinger, J. D., **AF**: 1455-1462
Salkey, Andrew, **TE**: 456
"Sally's Story" (Malouf), **BF**: 475
Salter, James, **AF**: 1462-1466
"Samaia liubimaia." *See* "Most Beloved"
Same Door, The (Updike), **AF**: 1670
"Same Place, Same Things" (Gautreaux), **AF**: 719
Samizdat, **TE**: 390, **TE**: 501
Samuel Johnson Is Indignant (Davis), **AF**: 499
San Manuel Bueno, mártir. See Saint Manuel Bueno, Martyr
Sanatorium pod klepsydrą. See Sanatorium Under the Sign of the Hourglass
Sanatorium Under the Sign of the Hourglass (Schulz), **EF**: 339
Sansei, **TE**: 339
Sansom, William, **BF**: 599-605
Santos, Bienvenido, **TE**: 343
Saragossa Manuscript, The (Potocki), **TE**: 96
"Sarah" (Lavin), **TE**: 420
"Sarah Gwynn" (Moore, G.), **BF**: 519
Sarah Phillips (Lee, A.), **AF**: 1051
Sargeson, Frank, **TE**: 357
Sari, Fereshteh, **TE**: 475
Sarmiento, Domingo Faustino, **TE**: 450
Saroyan, William, **AF**: 1466-1471
Sartre, Jean-Paul, **EF**: 328-335, **TE**: 269
"Sarzan" (Diop), **TE**: 305
Sasaki, R. A., **TE**: 342
Satire, **EF**: 414, **TE**: 84, **TE**: 116
Satires (Horace), **TE**: 35
"Saturday Afternoon" (Caldwell), **AF**: 320
"Saturn Street" (Leavitt), **AF**: 1046
Satyricon, The (Petronius), **TE**: 116, **EF**: 312
"Saucer of Larks, The" (Friel), **BF**: 245
Saudi Arabian writers, **TE**: 474
Saunders, George, **AF**: 1471-1475, **TE**: 296
Save Every Lamb (Stuart), **AF**: 1610
"Sawdust" (Offutt), **AF**: 1265
"Say Could That Lad Be I" (Lavin), **BF**: 411
"Say Yes" (Wolff), **TE**: 282
Sayers, Dorothy L., **TE**: 20
Sayles, John, **AF**: 1475-1479
"Scala Scare, The" (Buzzati), **EF**: 54
"Scandal in Bohemia, A" (Doyle), **BF**: 196
"Scandalous Woman, A" (O'Brien, E.), **BF**: 536
"Scarecrow, The" (Roberts), **AF**: 1432
"Scar" (Lu Xinhua), **TE**: 383

"Scat" (Major), **AF**: 1111
Scenes of Childhood (Warner), **BF**: 697
"Schalken the Painter" (Le Fanu), **BF**: 433
"Schiffman's Ape" (Sayles), **AF**: 1476
Schlegel, Friedrich, **TE**: 1
"Schloimele" (Singer), **EF**: 348
"Schläferung." *See* "Sleep"
Schmitz, Ettore. *See* Svevo, Italo
"Schocken, Salman", **WF**: 11
Schorer, Mark, **TE**: 206
"Schott's Bridge" (Pollock), **AF**: 1357
Schulz Bruno, **EF**: 335-342, **TE**: 494
Schwartz, Delmore, **AF**: 1479-1483
Schwartz, Lynne Sharon, **AF**: 1484-1487
Science fiction, **TE**: 79-90; avant-garde, **TE**: 86; contemporary, **TE**: 87; eighteenth century, **TE**: 79; Europe, **TE**: 80; Great Britain, **TE**: 85; pulp, **TE**: 81; science-fiction story, the, **TE**: 79; United States, **TE**: 79
Scientific romance, **TE**: 80
Scission (Winton), **BF**: 722
"Scissors, Paper, Rock" (Brady), **AF**: 248
Scotland, **TE**: 503-507; Scottish short fiction, **TE**: 503
Scott, Duncan Campbell, **TE**: 366
Scott, Sir Walter, **BF**: 606-611, **TE**: 197, **TE**: 504
"Scoundrel, The" (Nabokov), **AF**: 1217
"Scream, The" (Mistry), **BF**: 517
"Scream, The" (Oates), **AF**: 1245
"Screamers, The" (Baraka), **AF**: 103
"Sculptor's Funeral, The" (Cather), **AF**: 372
"Sealed Angel, The" (Leskov), **WF**: 210
Searching for Survivors (Banks), **AF**: 93
"Sebastian" (Caponegro), **AF**: 335
Sebastopol (Tolstoy), **WF**: 385
"Second Bakery Attack, The" (Murakami), **WF**: 265
Second Birth (Pasternak), **WF**: 313
Second Chance (Auchincloss), **AF**: 72
"Second Tree from the Corner, The" (White), **AF**: 1756
"Second Variety" (Dick), **AF**: 519
"Secret Garden, The" (Chesterton), **BF**: 125
Secret Goldfish, The (Means), **AF**: 1165, **TE**: 298
"Secret Integration, The" (Pynchon), **AF**: 1403
"Secret Life of Walter Mitty, The" (Thurber), **AF**: 1638
"Secret of Father Brown, The" (Chesterton), **BF**: 124
"Secret Room, The" (Robbe-Grillet), **EF**: 326

"Short Happy Life of Francis Macomber, The"
    (Hemingway), **AF:** 871
Short novel, **TE:** 254
Short Sentimental Journey, and Other Stories
    (Svevo), **EF:** 353
Short story, **EF:** 414
"Short-Shift Saturday" (Casey), **TE:** 353
Short Story in English, The (Canby), **TE:** 2
Short Story Theories (May), **TE:** 9
Short Story Theory at a Crossroads (Lohafer and
    Clarey), **TE:** 10
"Shortcut" (Lennon), **AF:** 1066
"Shot, The" (Pushkin), **WF:** 323
"Shower of Gold, A" (Barthelme, D.), **AF:** 120
"Shunkinshō." *See* "Portrait of Shunkin, A"
"Shut-In Number, The" (Rooke), **BF:** 591
Shwe U-Daung, **TE:** 516
"Sicily Burns's Wedding" (Harris, G. W.), **TE:** 230
"Sick Call, A" (Callaghan, M.), **BF:** 91
"Sick Child, The" (Colette), **EF:** 93
Sidney, Sir Philip, **TE:** 161, **TE:** 165
"Siege, The" (Lasdun), **BF:** 400
Siemienowicz, Miranda, **TE:** 107
Sienkiewicz, Henryk, **TE:** 493
"Signalman, The", **TE:** 222, **TE:** 393
"Significant Moments in the Life of My Mother"
    (Atwood), **BF:** 15
Signified, **EF:** 414
Signifier, **EF:** 414
"Signing, The" (Dixon), **AF:** 532
"Signora Frola and Her Son-in-Law, Signor Ponza"
    (Pirandello), **EF:** 320
"Signora Frola e il signor Ponza, suo genero, La." *See*
    "Signora Frola and Her Son-in-Law, Signor
    Ponza"
"Signs and Symbols" (Nabokov), **AF:** 1219, **TE:** 271
"Silence, The" (Barnes), **BF:** 39
"Silence Dogood Essays" (Franklin), **TE:** 182
Silence of the Llano, The (Anaya), **TE:** 464
Silent Passengers (Woiwode), **AF:** 1791
"Silent Snow, Secret Snow" (Aiken), **AF:** 14
Silent Spring (Masumoto), **TE:** 342
Silko, Leslie Marmon, AF: 1499-1506, **TE:** 476,
    TE: 477, **TE:** 486
Sillitoe, Alan, BF: 620-625
Silver, Marisa, AF: 1507-1510
"Silver Dish, A" (Bellow), **TE:** 56
Silverberg, Robert, **TE:** 87

Šimáček, M. A., **TE:** 388
Simak, Clifford, **TE:** 83
"Simetrías." *See* "Symmetries"
Simile, **EF:** 414
Simms, William Gilmore, AF: 1510-1516
"Simple Heart, A" (Flaubert), **EF:** 123, **TE:** 234
"Simple Susan" (Edgeworth), **BF:** 211
Simpson, Helen, AF: 1517-1520
Simpson, Mona, AF: 1521-1524
"Sin Dolor" (Boyle, T. C.), **AF:** 233
Singapore, **TE:** 519
Singer, Isaac Bashevis, EF: 342-351, **TE:** 54, **TE:**
    55, **TE:** 268
"Singing Bone, The" (Grimm), **EF:** 152
"Singular Event, A" (Machado de Assis), **WF:** 230
"Singular occurrência." *See* "Singular Event, A"
"Sins of the Third Age" (Gordimer), **WF:** 164
Sinuhe, **TE:** 109
Sinyavsky, Andrei, WF: 359-365, **TE:** 501
"Sisters" (McCann), **BF:** 502
Six Easy Pieces (Mosley), **AF:** 1212
"Six Feet of the Country" (Gordimer), **WF:** 162
"Six Soldiers of Fortune" (Grimm), **EF:** 149
Six Stories Written in the First Person Singular
    (Maugham), **BF:** 498
Sixteenth century, TE: 160-177
Sixty-Three Dream Palace (Purdy), **AF:** 1396
Skallagrimsson, Egill, **TE:** 123
"Skandál a žurnalistika." *See* "Scandal and the Press,
    Scandal"
Skating in the Dark (Kaplan), **AF:** 995
Skaz, **EF:** 414
"Skeleton, The" (Pritchett), **BF:** 573
Sketch, TE: 91-95, **TE:** 189, **TE:** 190, **TE:** 191,
    TE: 196, **TE:** 498, **TE:** 499, **EF:** 414
Sketch Book of Geoffrey Crayon, Gent., The
    (Irving), **TE:** 97
Sketches by Boz (Dickens), **TE:** 197
"Skinless" (Bender), **AF:** 165
Sklepy cynamonowe. See Cinnamon Shops
"Skripka Rotshil'da." *See* "Rothschild's Fiddle"
"Skuchnaia istoriia." *See* "Boring Story, A"
"Sky Is Gray, The" (Gaines), **AF:** 683
"Sky Writing" (Peck), **AF:** 1321
Slap in the Face Et Cetera, A (Walser), **EF:** 387
Slavin, Julia, AF: 1525-1528
"Sleep" (Hildesheimer), **EF:** 168
Sleep It Off, Lady (Rhys), **BF:** 580